Russian Statecraft

Iurii Krizhanich. A sculpture by Vanja Radaus. Reproduced from Zivot I. Djelo, *Jurja* Križanića, (Zagreb, 1974).

Russian Statecraft

The *Politika* of Iurii Krizhanich

JOHN M. LETICHE AND BASIL DMYTRYSHYN

An analysis and translation of
Iurii Krizhanich's *Politika*

Basil Blackwell

Introduction, editing and English translation © John M. Letiche and
Basil Dmytryshyn 1985

Iurii Krizhanich's *Politika* (1663) was edited by M. N. Tikhomirov, translated into
modern Russian by A.D. Goldberg, prepared for the press by V.V. Zelenin and
published by the Academy of Sciences of the USSR, Moscow, 1965

English translation first published 1985

Basil Blackwell Publisher
108 Cowley Road, Oxford OX4 1JF, UK

Basil Blackwell Inc.
432 Park Avenue South, Suite 1505,
New York, NY 10016, USA

British Library Cataloguing in Publication Data

Krizhanich, Iurii
Russian statecraft: the Politika of Iurii Krizhanich: an analysis and
translation of Iurii Krizhanich's Politika.
1. Soviet Union—History—Epoch of confusion, 1605–1613
2. Soviet Union—History—1613–1689   3. Soviet Union—Politics
and government—1613–1689
I. Title   II. Letiche, John M.   III. Dmytryshyn, Basil
IV. Politika. *English*
947'.047   DK114
ISBN 0–631–13809–9

Library of Congress Cataloging in Publication Data

Krizanić, Juraj, 1618–1683.
Russian statecraft.
Translation of: Politika.
1. Political science—Soviet Union—History—17th century.
2. Soviet Union—Social conditions—to 1801.   3. Soviet Union—
Politics and government.   4. Soviet Union—Foreign opinion.
I. Letiche, John M, 1918–   .   II. Dmytryshyn, Basil, 1925–
III. Title.
JA84.S65K7513   1985   947'.048   84–20472
ISBN 0–631–13809–9

Typeset by Freeman Graphic, Tonbridge, Kent
Printed in Great Britain by Bell and Bain Ltd, Glasgow

Contents

TABLES

FIGURES

Preface

Although all books have a way of acquiring a life of their own, Krizhanich's classic—*Politika*—has demonstrated particular and lasting relevance, especially during eras of antagonism between Russia and the West. It has enlightened and fascinated millions of Slavic readers. Surprisingly, it has never before been translated into English.

Our objective has been to provide an accurate rendering of Krizhanich's thoughts and nuances. We have endeavored to recreate a basic work of reference on the social, political, and economic history of Russia in the seventeenth century and a vivid account of the life and character, the behavior and actions, of the Russian people. Krizhanich's chapters, however, vary greatly in length and quality of exposition. Some are brilliant, revealing careful scholarship; others are skeletal, reflecting no more than an outline. Many of the books Krizhanich cited were presumably not available to him in Siberian exile, where he wrote *Politika*. The quotations are therefore often imprecise. With a few exceptions, we have let his renditions stand, but it should be borne in mind that they have a tendency to diverge, sometimes almost wilfully, from the originals. Certain sections abound in repetitious, illustrative material that contributes nothing to the substance or development of the argument. Furthermore, on controversial issues Krizhanich all too often took cover behind biblical citations and classical writings. We have deleted many such passages. Krizhanich's cumbersome numbering of paragraphs has also been abandoned, and on occasion paragraphs have been rearranged with a view to clarity and continuity.

Krizhanich resorted to the rhetoric of extremes. So as not to prejudge his case, we have retained samples of his spectacular tirades against foreigners, and against Germans in particular. Primarily, however, our aim has been to achieve a satisfactory edited version—in the spirit of the original—rather than a strictly literal translation. For this reason, we have made every effort to employ a straightforward unembellished style.

Krizhanich had entitled his book *Discourses on Government* (Besedy o pravlenii), but it has become widely known by its synonym. Our own translation is based on the excellent publication *Politika* edited, with a

Preface, by M. N. Tikhomirov; translated into modern Russian, with commentaries, by A. D. Goldberg; prepared for the press by V. V. Zelenin, and published under the auspices of the Academy of Sciences of the USSR in Moscow in 1965. This work is commendable for including Krizhanich's original version in "Common Slavonic", which we often had occasion to compare with the Russian translation. Although this edition does not contain Krizhanich's entire bulky manuscript, which is available in Soviet archives, the editors made a good selection, since much of the remaining unpublished material is either repetitive or deals with less interesting issues.

As regards transliteration from Cyrillic to Roman characters, we have adhered, with minor exceptions, to the Library of Congress system, and have omitted all diacritical marks. Russian terms not readily translatable have been defined in order of appearance. We have anglicized plurals of words that defy English translation. An index (not present in the original or in the modern Russian printing) has been supplied.

It is a pleasure to acknowledge the assistance of the numerous scholars and librarians of many nations who have provided archival materials and information that would otherwise have been unavailable to us. In order to absolve them of any blame for our own imperfections, it seems prudent that many remain anonymous. We would be remiss, however, if we did not express our gratitude to the following: Mr Denis Reidy, for providing rare materials from the British Museum Library; Bishop Metzler, OMI, Sister Sophia Senyk, and Professor Donald A. Riley, for obtaining documents from the Vatican Library; Professor N. A. Tsagolov, and Professor Andrei Anikin, for reproductions from the Moscow Historical Library; Assistant Curator Carol Urness, for primary sources from the James Ford Bell Library, University of Minnesota; and Mr Frank T. Brechka, for exceptional assistance at the Library of the University of California, Berkeley. We are indebted to Mr René Olivieri of Basil Blackwell for thoughtful counsel on the architectural structure of the book. Our warmest thanks are due to Professor Howard S. Ellis, Mr Peter Dreyer, and Dr John A. Taylor for providing superb editorial advice and suggestions. Professor Nicholas V. Riasanovsky gave us the benefit of highly valued, expert comments. Dr Henri Vandendriessche read the page proofs meticulously and made improvements. To Barbara Priest, Betty Kendall, Louise Sullivan, and Lenora Warkentin we express sincere appreciation for their technical competence and personal interest in preparing the typescript.

We dedicate this book to Emily Kuyper Letiche and Virginia Roehl Dmytryshyn, our beloved wives and steadfast literary critics. They celebrate with us a twenty-five year anniversary since we began work on this project and we greatly hope that the reader will have occasion to share in our satisfaction at its completion.

Coinage and units of measure in Krizhanich's Russia referred to in the text

COINS

2 dengi	=	1 kopeck (*kopeika*)
4 dengi	=	1 grosh (Polish *grosz,* German *Groschen*)
6 dengi	=	1 altyn (from the Tartar word for "six")
20 dengi	=	1 grivna (plural *grivny*)
100 dengi	=	1 poltina, or half a ruble
200 dengi	=	1 ruble
50 kopeika	=	1 efimok (plural *efimki**), or Bohemian Joachimsthaler

*In the mid-seventeenth century the tsar's treasury accepted efimki at the value of one efimok equals 50 kopeika, and issued efimki bearing the Russian state emblem at the value of one efimok equals 64 kopeika.

MEASURES OF WEIGHT

1 zolotnik	=	4.718 grams
1 grivna	=	410 grams
1 pud	=	16.38 kg, or 36.11 pounds

LAND MEASURES

1 verst (*versta*) = 0.663 miles, or 1.067 km

Map 1 Europe circa 1650

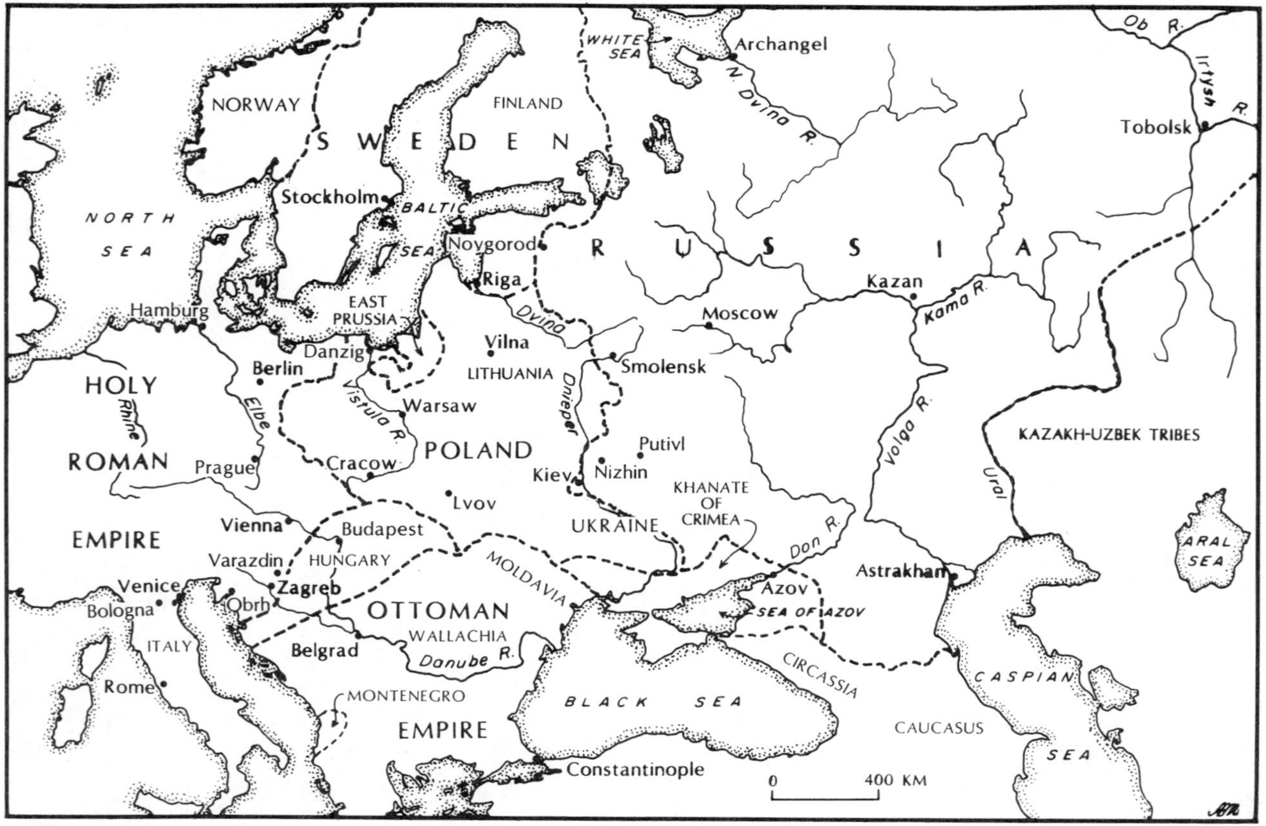

An Introductory Analysis of the *Politika*

1

The historical background of the *Politika*

Iurii Krizhanich, originally named Juraj Križanić, was of Croatian origin, born into a merchant family in the township of Obrh in 1618. He died mysteriously while accompanying the Polish army of King Jan Sobieski that relieved Vienna during the second Ottoman siege of the city in 1683.[1] Scholar, linguist, diplomat, philosopher, priest, adventurer, and sufferer, Krizhanich took as his vocation no less a task than the reconciliation of Eastern Orthodoxy with Roman Catholicism and a concomitant unification of the Slavic peoples under the hegemony of Muscovy. At the age of forty, he set out for Moscow. Not long after his arrival, in 1659, he was suspected of subversion, arrested, and banished to Tobolsk in Siberia. There, adhering to the tsar's decree, he made himself useful to the local administration and, more significantly, collected a great deal of material on the country, especially its economic life. He composed the greater part of the work known as the *Politika* in Tobolsk between 1663 and 1666. Young Tsar Feodor Alexeevich pardoned Krizhanich in 1676, but the administrative authorities refused to give him permission to leave the country. The Danish ambassador, Frederick von Gabel, prompted by his secretary Hildenbrand von Horn, whom Krizhanich had befriended, interceded to secure his release, and on November 9, 1677 Krizhanich finally departed from Moscow.[2]

[1] An extensive literature on the life of Krizhanich is now available, although most of it is not in English. For an encyclopedic collection of essays in English, French, and German on Krizhanich and his times, ranging from his relation to predecessors and contemporaries to his views on Siberia and China, see Thomas Eekman and Ante Kadić, eds, *Juraj Križanić (1618–1683). Russophile and Ecumenic Visionary: A Symposium* (The Hague, 1976), hereafter cited as Eekman and Kadić. Except for a few additional special studies to which reference is made at appropriate points, no other secondary works in English were of much help to us. For the most part, therefore, our formulation is based on the *Politika* and on the best available primary and secondary sources in foreign languages. See Selected Bibliography, 259–70.

[2] Krizhanich expressed appreciation to von Horn in his Preface to *Historia de Sibiria* (1680); see A.A. Titov, ed., *Sibir v XVII veke. Sbornik starinnykh russkikh statei o Sibiri i prilezhashchikh k nei zemliakh* (Moscow, 1890), 162–3.

Proficient in French, Dutch, German, Italian, Latin, Greek, Croatian, Polish, Ukrainian, and Russian, Krizhanich wrote many other books, but the *Politika* is his principal work. It is to this book – a fundamental source on Russian history as well as on European economic, political, cultural, and military thought of the seventeenth century – that he owes his primary interest to us today. One of its express purposes was to reflect on what might be called statecraft: how a good ruler rules, with particular application to Russia. Krizhanich was deeply interested in trade, agriculture, and manufacturing, as well as in what modern economists call human capital. He was profoundly aware of Russia's need to import knowledge, training, and technology, but he was deeply worried about foreign exploitation of the Slavic people. He perceived that the gap between potential and actual development was larger in Russia than in virtually any other country. In his view, Russia had immense potentialities for greatness—if only its human and physical resources were used wisely, with moderation.

Although we have searched in the voluminous primary and secondary sources for evidence that Krizhanich had an impact on Russia's rulers, whether direct or indirect, no conclusive proof could be found. Judging by what he wrote of his aims, his tenacious pursuit of these ends, and his demonstrable adherence to plan, however, it is practically inconceivable that Krizhanich did not request that a copy of his book be brought to the attention of Tsar Alexei Mikhailovich, who ruled from 1645 to 1676. The doubt, often expressed in the literature, as to whether high government officials at the time were cognizant of Krizhanich's *Politika* is entirely unwarranted: he personally requested Archbishop Semeon of Tobolsk to give a copy of his manuscript to the Metropolitan Paul of Moscow. After Paul died in September 1675, the manuscript was found in his library and, together with Paul's other books, deposited in the Moscow Synod Printing Office. Moreover, Tsar Alexei ordered that a copy be bound and deposited in his personal library.[3] Apparently the Moscow Printing Office made a number of copies, for the book has also been discovered in the libraries of several key Russian figures of the time. Both Sylvester Medvedev, erstwhile advisor to Princess Sophia, and Prince Vasilii V. Golitsyn, advisor to Tsar Fedor II and de facto ruler of Russia from 1682

---

[3] Alexander Brückner, "Iu. Krizhanich," *Russkii vestnik* (July 1887), 31–2. The presence of a book in a person's library is no warrant, of course, that it has been read. But on the basis of available evidence, it seems reasonable to believe that Tsar Alexei was acquainted with the *Politika*.

[4] Ibid., N.N. Danilov, "Vasilij Vasilevič Golicyn (1682–1714)," *Jahrbücher für Geschichte Osteuropas*, vol. 2 (1937), 557–8, 577; S.P. Luppov, *Kniga v Rossii v XVII veke* (Leningrad, 1970), 110.

to 1689, possessed copies.[4] Furthermore, a good many of the measures Krizhanich recommended were actually undertaken by Peter the Great, though we have been unable to discover evidence of direct influence.

Through his own observation of the more developed countries of Europe, Peter might, of course, have reached conclusions similar to those of Krizhanich without having any acquaintance with the *Politika*. Other commentators in Peter's time, or before, may also, whether consciously or not, have served as transmitters. A. L. Ordin-Nashchokin, a contemporary of Krizhanich's, may well have served in that role; Feodor Saltykov, a contemporary of Peter's, provided him independently with many proposals similar to those of Krizhanich. Nikolaas Corneliszoon Witsen, a noted Dutch traveler and geographer, made reference to Krizhanich in his massive work *Noord en oost Tartaryen*,[5] and it has been claimed, although without the presentation of evidence, that when Peter was in Holland he was so impressed by Witsen's reports on Krizhanich that, upon returning to Russia, he gave instructions for the publication of Krizhanich's works. This was not done, allegedly due to the chaotic state of Russian printing.[6]

Incontrovertibly, Witsen traveled to Moscow in 1664 as a member of a Dutch delegation headed by I. Boreel. During the next three years, encompassing the very period when Krizhanich was writing the *Politika*, Witsen traveled to the Caspian Sea and to the outskirts of Siberia. He befriended a number of high-ranking Russian officials, including Izbrandes, Dolgorukii, Ukraintsev, and Vinius. In 1689, he published and dedicated to the then young Peter and his half-brother Ivan V a map of the eastern and southern parts of Europe and Asia, incorporating Krizhanich's knowledge of the existence of a water route from Russia's North Siberian possessions to China and India. Peter granted Witsen the exclusive right to sell the map in Russia, and during Peter's subsequent visit to Holland in 1697, Witsen served as his official guide, introducing him to distinguished scholars and technicians. They became good friends, and Peter invited Witsen to serve as his diplomatic emissary, with particular emphasis on helping him secure Dutch craftsmen for Russia's iron smelting and other industries. Numerous scholars, past and present,

[5] Nikolaas Corneliszoon Witsen, *Noord en oost Tartaryen* (Amsterdam, 1785 [1st ed., 1692]), vol. 2, 735; see also the discussion in his *Moscovische Reyse, 1664–1665* (The Hague, 1967), vol. 68, part 3, 448–9, and fn 2.

[6] See S. A. Belokurov, "Iurii Krizhanich v Rossii," *Prilozheniia,* in *Chteniia v imperatorskom obshchestvie istorii i drevnostei rossiiskikh* (1903), vol. 206, book 3, 26–7. For brief accounts of Krizhanich's influence on Witsen (and Spathary)—and hence, indirectly, on Alexei and Peter—see John F. Baddeley, *Russia, Mongolia, China* (London, 1919), vol. 2, esp. 212–13; and Albert Parry, "Juraj Križanić's Views on Siberia and China of the Seventeenth Century," in Eekman and Kadić, esp. 252–7.

have made unsubstantiated claims on the intermediation of Witsen in the connection between Peter I and Krizhanich. Witsen indeed wrote that in 1680 "Fredericus Krizanicz, Polish monk [sic!], who for many years has been living in *Tobol*"[7] had suggested to the Polish king Jan Sobieski that the Stroganov family be called "vassals" rather than slaves, in recognition of their contributions to the "Victory over Siberien," and Witsen several times appears to have drawn on Krizhanich's *Historia de Siberia* (1680). Witsen may well have called Krizhanich's work to Peter's attention, although unsubstantiated and seemingly exaggerated claims abound in the literature.[8]

After Krizhanich's death, his great work lay virtually unnoticed until Russian scholars rediscovered and published it in 1859.[9] Ever since, it has been an object of widespread interest to historians, political scientists, economists, theologians, linguists, and literary scholars. Written in a curious "pan-Slavic" language invented by Krizhanich himself, it is a patchwork of various Slavic languages—Russian, Polish, Serbo-Croatian, Ukrainian, and Old Church Slavonic. Krizhanich was very much a pan-Slav *avant la lettre,* and this language was supposed to symbolize, and even promote, Slavic unity.

The book is a mine of information about economic conditions, political institutions, and customs in seventeenth-century Russia. It provides not

[7] Witsen, *Noord en oost Tartaryen,* 735.

[8] For a good, early discussion on this issue, see I. Tyzhnov, "Obzor inostrannykh izvestii o Sibiri s 2-i poloviny XVI [XVII]," *Sibirskii Sbornik,* appendix to *Vostochnoe Obozrenie,* ed. N.M. Iadrintsev (St Petersburg, 1887), 101–47. Evidence on the Witsen–Peter I connection is provided in Friedrich v. Adelung, *Kritisch-Literarische Ubersicht der Reisenden bis 1700 . . .* (St Petersburg, 1846), vol. 2, 338–44; and Jacobus Scheltema, *Rusland en de Nederlanden* (Amsterdam, 1818), vol. 2, 66–77, 181–6, 331–4; vol. 3, 130–39. However, two sets of basic documentary collections on Peter's reign, *Pisma: i bumagi Imperatora Petra Velikogo* (Moscow, 1887–1979), 16 vols; and *Deianiia Petra Velikogo,* I.I. Golikov, ed. (Moscow, 1838), 15 vols, contain no reference to Krizhanich.

[9] Cf. P.A. Bezsonov, who after the passive discovery by the Polish professor A.G. Bielewski, rediscovered the existence of the *Politika* in the library of the Moscow Synod Printing Office, and successfully—but unsatisfactorily—published part of the work in six installments under the title "Russkoe gosudarstvo v polovine XVII veka. Rukopis vremen tsaria Alekseia Mikhailovicha," in *Russkaia Beseda* (1859). Subsequently, Bezsonov published this material, under the same title, in two volumes (Moscow, 1859–60). See also Belokurov, "Iurii Krizhanich v Rossii," 208–9; A.G. Brückner, "Iu. Krizhanich," in *Russkii Vestnik* (July 1887), 28–9; and Aleksandr L. Goldberg, "Juraj Križanić in Russian Historiography," translated by Leslie Bailey, in Eekman and Kadić, 53–8. In the middle of the 1880s, Bezsonov attempted to publish "a complete edition of Križanić's writings," but only the proofs of two volumes appeared—including Krizhanich's biography and the first part of "Russkoe gosudarstvo." See Belokurov, "Iurii Krizhanich v Rossii," 37–41. These proofs of the two volumes were not published, although statements to the contrary have appeared in the literature.

only vivid, first-hand testimony about virtually all facets of Russian life, but insight into the historical foundations and continuity of Russian characteristics, thought, and action. With appropriate qualification for time and place, Krizhanich was a highly civilized, humane, apostolic, and illuminating "modernizer". A penetrating observer, he was even prophetic of the emerging Russian scene. Krizhanich wrote a remarkable book, only to be matched by the remarkable man himself. It is a fascinating text: quaint yet perceptive, bombastic but thoughtful.

THE HISTORICAL BACKGROUND

About a century before Krizhanich's arrival in Moscow, Russia began to pursue war and commerce as simultaneous but not, as in England for example, coterminous objectives of political power and economic plenty. In England, that is, writers on political-economic thought generally believed that more economic plenty would bring about more political power, and vice versa. Practically never was the view expressed that some economic plenty might have to be sacrificed for more political power. In Russia, however, writers did not maintain a similar degree of confidence in the interdependence between economic plenty and political power. The obligation of citizens was to enhance the wealth of the tsar, and regarding the government's objectives, primacy was placed on military security. Several Western European countries became increasingly interested in expanding their commerce with Russia. In an interrelated attempt to reduce Russia's dependence on her immediate western neighbors, and establish direct diplomatic and commercial ties with European maritime powers, Moscow sought a "window to the West." Efforts to create a unified state brought about the need for the beginnings of modern bureaucracy, and for a strong military establishment. Administrative departments of the central government were instituted (the so-called *Prikaz* system) and the highly diverse fiscal and judicial appointees were replaced by its agents. A network of local administrative officials was installed to man the autocracy and provide continuity in local government. Moreover, the management of financial and economic affairs came to be entrusted substantially to skilled foreign agents, who also provided information on such matters as European politics, security, discoveries, and economic conditions. These agents were reinforced by a select group of merchants who joined other government officials in assisting as commercial agents and overseers of law, order, and internal security.

Internal security was given attention not only to obtain strict political control over the populace, but also as a requisite for the growth of markets and commerce. The largest markets in Russia developed in the city of Moscow, where the key Russian exportables attracted domestic as well as European merchants. Lithuanian, Polish, and German traders, in particular, brought large quantities of their wares, and purchased Russian goods in return. Similarly, Dutch and English merchants brought the products not only of their own countries but also those of Central Europe, the Mediterranean, and the East Indies—significantly reorienting Russia's foreign trade toward the commercial markets of England and the Low Countries as early as the second half of the sixteenth century. In effect, the foreign trade of Moscow and Archangel jointly brought about an overall export balance in Russia's foreign trade from the mid-sixteenth to the mid-seventeenth centuries; and this was especially so with England and Holland. It also included substantial entrepôt trade from Persia, with which Russia ordinarily had a trade deficit.[10]

Before foreigners could sell their wares they were required to pay the prevailing duties and grant the tsar's agents priority of selection. Otherwise, for the most part, they were able to conduct business in Moscow or Archangel at wholesale on a practically equal basis. On the Russian side, however, from the mid-sixteenth century on, a significant state monopoly existed in the sale of raw materials and a small number of crudely manufactured commodities. The export of bullion and precious metals was prohibited, and the machinery of the central government was extended to give the tsar practically unlimited political and economic control. Moreover, the keen interest of the tsars in promulgating commercial and security relations with Western European countries was more often referred to in terms of their "honor and profit" rather than the Russian nation's power and commercial development.[11]

[10] See Arthur Attman, "The Russian Market in World Trade, 1500–1860," *Scandanavian Economic History Review*, vol. 29, no. 3 (1981), 180–84, 202; and Paul Bushkovitch, *The Merchants of Moscow, 1580–1650* (New York, 1980), 25–42.

[11] For cogent material on this issue, see V.O. Kliuchevskii, *A Course in Russian History: The Seventeenth Century*, Natalie Duddington, trans. (Chicago, 1968), 113–29; and Jacob Viner, "Power versus Plenty as Objectives of Foreign Policy in the Seventeenth and Eighteenth Centuries," *World Politics*, vol. 1 (1948), 1–29. Cf. also N.I. Kostomarov, "Ocherki torgovli Moskovskogo gosudarstva v XVI i XVII stoletiiakh," *Sobranie Sochinenii* (St Petersburg, 1905, vol. 20, book 8), 233–422; K.V. Bazilevich, "Kollektivnye chelobitiia torgovykh liudei i borba za russkii rynok v pervoi polovine XVII veka," *Izvestiia Akademii Nauk SSSR. Otdelenie obshchestvennykh nauk*, no. 2 (1932), 91–123; Peter I. Lyashchenko, *History of the National Economy of Russia*, L.M. Herman, trans. (New York, 1949), 217–47; Walther Kirchner, *Commercial Relations Between Russia and Europe 1400–1800: Collected Essays* (Bloomington, 1966), 26–45; and Richard Hakluyt, *Principal Navigations, Voyages, Traffiques, and Discoveries of the English Nation* (Glasgow, 1903), vol. 2, 225–36, 297–303.

Russian rulers were scornful of the important role of the bourgeoisie in England's and Holland's determination of commercial and diplomatic policies. By inference, this scorn underlines the comparative insignificance of the bourgeoisie in Russia and their unquestioned concurrent need for the tsar and his officialdom to adopt measures from above to help overcome Russia's backward economic condition. Because Russia suffered from illiteracy and related backwardness at all socioeconomic levels, indigenous sources of significant private entrepreneurial activity were in extraordinarily scarce supply. A desperate dependency on foreigners infected the nation with an extreme form of xenophobia that was only to be matched by a parallel xenomania. Krizhanich devotes two chapters of *Politika* to these phenomena, to which he was not immune.[12]

Following the death of Ivan IV (the Terrible) in 1584, a period of turmoil befell the country, whose stamp the Russia Krizhanich studied still bore. Ivan had arbitrarily designated part of the realm as his private appanage land, leaving the remainder to be ruled in the traditional manner by the Boyar Duma. This caused a retrogressive disruption that was long costly to the agricultural sector of the economy. More profoundly, Ivan left the national treasury the same fiscal entity it had been when he acquired it. Vast masses of gold, silver, and gems were intended for display, not for commerce—intended, that is, to be hung on the Kremlin walls, and not to be used for economic development. Travelers to Russia before and during Krizhanich's time remarked on this barbaric splendor.[13] Krizhanich called attention to this problem, and recommended thoroughgoing reform of the fiscal system.

Ivan the Terrible's rule was followed by the brief reign of his feeble-minded son, Feodor. The shrewd Boris Godunov then assumed the throne. Russian writers have called his reign (1598–1605) and the eight years that followed the "Time of Troubles" (1598–1613). To check the flight of tenant farmers from the fields of brutal landlords, Godunov invoked ever more restrictive decrees. This helped win support from the increasingly important small landholders, but it fueled the ground-fires that were already creeping toward Moscow and other centers. Not born to the crown, Godunov soon suffered from the subversion that had stalked even more legitimate rulers of the Kremlin. To hold the throne, he resorted to deportation of notable families, fraternal espionage, barbaric

---

[12] *Politika,* infra, esp. 128–9 and 228–33.

[13] For a pictorial presentation of this treasury, see David Douglas Duncan, *Great Treasures of the Kremlin* (New York, 1979), 79–100, with a resource supplement, 160–71. Cf. also Paul of Aleppo, *The Travels of Macarius: Extracts from the Diary of the Travels of Macarius, Patriarch of Antioch,* written by his son, Paul, Archdeacon of Aleppo, 1652–1660, F.C. Balfour, trans. (London, 1936), 30–33; and *Politika,* infra, 194, 211.

executions, and torture. A serious food shortage in 1601 turned into famine, with practically nothing edible entering Moscow for three years. Godunov's day was done; he died in 1605, and his son was assassinated after ruling as tsar for only six weeks.

Godunov's son was followed by the False Dmitri, to whom Krizhanich has occasion to allude. An impostor who had served for a brief time in the Kremlin, Dmitri had fled to Poland, where he had the backing of exiled Russians, and in October 1604—after many battles and with support from the rich agricultural area of the Seversk and Polish towns—he led an army into the Kremlin and was crowned tsar.[14]

Less than a year thereafter, Dmitri and a multitude of his Polish and Russian supporters were murdered in the courtyard of the Kremlin. Vasilii Shuiskii overthrew him, seized the throne, and when new followers rallied to the banner of a second False Dmitri, Polish, Swedish, and Cossack armies took advantage of the turmoil and pillaged the countryside. Tsar Shuiskii was overthrown, captured by the Poles, and taken to Warsaw, where he was dragged through the streets. Krizhanich vividly relates how Polish troops then captured the Kremlin and placed upon the throne a boy named Wladislaw, the son of their own King Sigismund.[15] The youth and his troops were soon annihilated by the first spontaneous national army raised in Russia. Initially this army had to fight both the Poles and the Cossacks, who ravaged the land no less than did the invaders. Meanwhile, the Swedes had occupied the city of Novgorod, and soon afterwards fresh Polish columns invaded Russia to relieve a starving garrison trapped in the Kremlin. At that point, however, the newly formed Russian army, sympathizing cossacks and others, joined forces to face the common foe. They repulsed the Polish invasion, ripped the Polish flag from the Kremlin, and liberated a young nobleman, Mikhail Feodorovich Romanov, from a monastery outside Moscow. Mikhail was crowned tsar, bringing the most chaotic period of the Time of Troubles to a close. The events of this period were a national humiliation that left the Russian people with a serious neurosis, combining fanatical allegiance to Mother Russia with obsessive fear for the security of her frontiers against potential enemies, foreign and domestic.

---

[14] A comprehensive analysis of the Time of Troubles is provided by S.F. Platonov, *The Time of Troubles*, J.T. Alexander, trans. (Lawrence, 1970). Cf. also V.O. Kliuchevskii, *A Course in Russian History: The Seventeenth Century*, Natalie Duddington, trans. (Chicago, 1968), 3–58; A.N. Nasonov et al., eds, *Ocherki istorii SSSR. Period feodalizma. Konets XV v. – nachalo XVII v.* (Moscow, 1955), 444–623; and G. Vernadsky, *The Tsardom of Moscow 1547–1682* (New Haven, 1969), Part 1, 223–91; *Politika*, infra, 130, 202, 210.
[15] *Politika*, infra, 134–5; see also 130, 233.

Recovery under the first two Romanovs, Mikhail Feodorovich (1613–45) and Alexei Mikhailovich (1645–76), was painful and prolonged. The landed assembly, or Zemskii Sobor, which, after the Time of Troubles, was dominated by the so-called service nobility, endeavored to meet the needs of the government by imposing greater demands on the already impoverished masses. Local government was in the hands of military governors. Military matters were, in fact, in many respects the main concern of government, and the *streltsy*, or musketeers, who had been powerful under Ivan the Terrible, re-emerged as a standing army, financed by the tsar's treasury. Without transforming its primitive agriculture, however, the Russian economy could not sustain yet larger military expenditures without further undermining its social structure.

Krizhanich's "democratic" ideas on the problems of political succession drew on the experience of the Time of Troubles and its aftermath. Crowned when he was sixteen years of age, Mikhail Feodorovich was devoid of ambition, nearly illiterate, and flaccid. He was the choice of the campaigning members of the first unmanipulated landed assembly. Since the service nobility planned to dominate him, his inadequacies were the necessary condition for his election.

During the first six years of Mikhail's reign (1613–19), his avaricious mother loomed behind the throne. Thereafter, his father—an intriguer who knew little of the church—was installed as Patriarch Philaret of Russia. Since Mikhail was neither interested in ruling nor competent to do so, Philaret wielded the power of both church and state from 1619 to 1633. He brought a semblance of unity and stability to the nation. A restorer rather than a reformer, he skillfully signed peace treaties with Poland and Sweden, and, to a limited degree, opened Russia's borders to merchants and scientists. In 1632, however, he imprudently plunged Russia into an abortive military campaign against Poland. Peace was restored in 1634, shortly after he died. Tsar Mikhail survived without distinction until 1645, when he too died a natural death. Tsar Alexei was then crowned peacefully and jubilantly, an event that signified not only that the Romanov Dynasty had become an established fact of Russian history but that a significant socioeconomic transition was in process. This transition was practically imperceptible at the time. Understandably, insufficient attention has been accorded to it. [16]

---

[16] A definitive work in English on the political structure of seventeenth-century Russia still awaits its historian. In Russian, prerevolutionary classic works include: M.F. Vladimirskii-Budanov, *Obzor istorii russkogo prava*, 6th ed. (St Petersburg-Kiev, 1909),

Tsar Alexei's reign (1645–76) encompassed Krizhanich's fifteen years of incarceration in Tobolsk. The quarter of a century before Alexei's reign had witnessed in important respects the beginning of the transition frᵒm primitive, medieval conditions to more modern, secular ones. But it was during his reign that a revolution in military technology combined with other underlying factors to accelerate this transition. In the earlier period, postwar reconstruction enhanced national consciousness: the Kremlin was in need of much repair; palaces and churches were dilapidated; and many buildings–in fact, entire towns–had to be rebuilt. Most directly in the arts, a movement developed away from the more traditional, canonical forms and toward more lifelike, naturalistic ones. In architecture, much of the work done revealed confidence, vigor, a sense of beauty, and a search for perfection. Perhaps with excessive zeal, a distinguished Russian art historian has gone so far as to characterize the work of this period (particularly 1625–30) as a "joyous assertion of human values."[17] In most other spheres, however, the transitionary changes came later and markedly so in Alexei's reign.

Russian priests, though fanatically pious, were still almost universally illiterate. Interest in secular education was slowly spreading, however, especially among the nobles and townspeople. The change taking place in cultural life was exemplified in the moderating influence of Tsarina Natalia on Alexei. Natalia's foster mother was Mary Hamilton, the Scottish wife of Alexei's principal advisor and intimate friend, Artamon S. Matveev. Though still only to a small degree, the influence of Western culture, science, commerce, and industry was becoming ever more manifest. Russian writing showed an increasing interest in secular themes, partially shedding its predominantly theological character. Literary language became more colorful and observations more acute. These trends away from rigid symbolism and toward common sense and naturalism give the entire period of transition its distinctive character.

---

148 ff; M. Diakonov, *Ocherki obshchestvennogo i gosudarstvennogo stroia drevnei Rusi,* 2nd ed. (St. Petersburg, 1908), 434 ff; and V.O. Kliuchevskii, *Boiarskaia duma drevnei Rusi,* 4th ed. (Moscow, 1909), 388 ff. For a standard Soviet treatment, see A.A. Novoselskii and N.V. Ustiugov, eds., *Ocherki istorii SSSR: Period feodalizma XVII v* (Moscow, 1955), 344 ff. Insights on the political structure, with substantial information on administrative procedures, are also to be found in Benjamin Phillip Uroff, "Grigorii Karpovich, Kotoshikin on Russia in the Reign of Alexis Mikhailovich" (Ph.D. dissertation, Columbia University, 1970), 673 pages; and J. Michael Hittle, *The City: State and Townsmen in Russia, 1600–1800* (Cambridge, Mass., 1979), 1–76.

[17] Abraam F. Kaganovich, *Arts of Russia: Seventeenth and Eighteenth Centuries,* James Hogarth, trans. (New York, 1968), 32.

Krizhanich's *Politika,* in fact, bespeaks this transition and is a manifestation of it. Understandably, fierce opposition to change was also a key element of the era.[18] Increasing secularization could not but conflict with the dogmatic ideology, influence, and power of the church, and the struggle was exacerbated by the dramatis personae of the conflict. In 1652, when Alexei was twenty-three years old, he begged the Metropolitan Nikon, who had distinguished himself in Novgorod, to accept the patriarchal throne. Once in power, Nikon and his intolerant followers intended to rid Russia of "sensuous sins and vices"; of pervasive corruption and drunkenness; and of malevolent foreigners and their heretical influence. Strong-willed and arrogant, Nikon further sought to establish church supremacy over the state and, thereafter, to assert the pre-eminence of the Moscow patriarchate over the entire orthodox world.

The country was propelled into one of its historic cataclysms, this time in the form of a religious convulsion designated by the term *raskol,* meaning split or schism. Actually, the schismatic crisis in the Russian Orthodox church had evolved gradually. Between 1654 and 1681, however, it had assumed a dual character: a schism within the church and a conflict between church and state.[19] A number of religious and political leaders had endeavored to reform the church in order to achieve a rapprochement between the Russian and other orthodox churches. This, they had hoped, would enhance Russia's power and prestige both at home and abroad. But many civil and religious leaders dissented from this comparatively moderate approach. Led by Nikon, they believed it was essential not only to correct the numerous errors in translations from the Greek (and other *errata*) that had penetrated Russian religious texts, but also to rid the rituals of all "un-Christian ceremonies and practices." These rituals had become sacrosanct to the predominantly illiterate clergy. To the "Old Believers," the Archpriest Avvakum and his fol-

---

[18] Reactionary policies were a distinct and integral part of the transition. For pertinent discussions on the historical evolution of this period, see J.L. Keep, "The Régime of Filaret, 1619–1633," *Slavonic and East European Review* 38 (London, June 1960), 334–60; V.O. Kliuchevskii, *Russian History,* 69 ff; G. Vernadsky, *The Tsardom of Moscow,* part 1, 292–431; and P.A. Khromov, *Ekonomicheskoe razvitie Rossii* (Moscow, 1967), 170 ff.

[19] The literature on the Russian religious schism in the seventeenth century is voluminous. Before leaving for Moscow in December 1658, Krizhanich himself had compiled an unfinished work, titled "Bibliotheca Schismaticorum Universa," which comprised a list of controversies with respect to the Orthodox Church comparable to Cardinal Bellarmine's work on controversies with respect to Protestantism (see Selected Bibliography). Krizhanich's "Bibliotheca" was not published; the manuscript is available, however, in the Bibliotheca Casanatense, Rome. On Krizhanich as theologian, see I. Golub, "Križanić théologien—sa conception ecclésiologique des événements et de l'histoire," in Eekman and Kadić, 165–79.

lowers, and, symbolically at least, to the vast mass of Russian peasants, Nikon seemed the Antichrist: an apostate in conflict with the piety of princes and tsars whose Orthodox faith had been "pure and undefiled."[20] Many of the Old Believers, a substantial number of whom were well-established peasants and traders, joined with still other groups protesting against the harsh and carnal religious and politico-economic injustices of the Muscovite regime.

In introducing changes in the liturgy and ritual by which all the Russian people worshipped, Nikon made fanatical enemies of Avvakum, his erstwhile friend, and many thousands of Old Believers. At first, Tsar Alexei gave Nikon unquestioned support. For six years Nikon acted as the virtual ruler of Russia. Alexei's ministers of state feared him more than the tsar himself. Nikon arrogantly assumed ever more power, and by 1658 Alexei had become aware that the patriarch was a political competitor. Tension developed between them, and Alexei publicly called Nikon a "stupid clown."[21] Dramatically, Nikon left Moscow, insisting that he would not return until the tsar had reaffirmed confidence in him. Their quarrel continued in the ecclesiastical courts and finally, in 1666, the Synod charged Nikon with, among other things, exalting the church above the state. Nikon responded dogmatically that the patriarchal office was superior to that of the temporal ruler. He proclaimed:

> Hast thou not learned . . . that the highest authority of the priesthood is not received from kings or emperors [lit. Tsars], but, contrariwise, it is by the priesthood that rulers are annointed to the empire? Therefore it is abundantly plain that priesthood is a very much greater thing than royalty.[22]

[20] See *The Life of the Archpriest Avvakum*, by himself, translated from the seventeenth-century Russian by Jane Harrison and Hope Mirrlees, with a preface by Prince D.S. Mirsky (Hamden, 1963): ". . . till the time of Nikon, the apostate, in our Russia under our pious princes and tsars the orthodox faith was pure and undefiled, in the Church was no sedition," 121. Cf. also 108 and 125.

[21] Paul of Aleppo, *Travels of Macarius*, 85.

[22] William Palmer, "The Replies of the Humble Nicon," *The Patriarch and the Tsar* (London, 1871), vol. 1, 189–90. For excellent discussions in English on the "great schism," cf. F.C. Conybear, *Russian Dissenters* (Cambridge, 1921); James H. Billington, *The Icon and the Axe: An Interpretive History of Russian Culture* (New York, 1966); George Vernadsky, *The Tsardom of Moscow, 1547–1682*, vol. 2, part 2 (New Haven, 1969), 557–608; Michael Cherniavsky, "The Old Believers and the New Religion," *Slavic Review* 25 (1966), 1–39; Robert O. Crummey, *The Old Believers in the World of Anti-Christ* (Madison, 1970); and Robert A. Massie, "The Great Schism," in *Peter the Great: His Life and World* (New York, 1981), 53–64. See also Pierre Pascal, *Avvakum et les débuts du raskol* (The Hague, 1963); and V.O. Kliuchevskii, "Zapadnoe vliianie i tserkovnyi raskol v Rossii XVII v.," *Ocherki i rechi* (Petrograd, 1918).

Though the Synod confirmed and sustained Nikon's changes in the Russian ritual and liturgy, it reasserted the traditional balance of power between church and state. The tsar, it ruled, was supreme over all subjects, including clergy and patriarch, except in matters of church doctrine. Nikon was condemned to exile. Although the great schism had complex and independent roots, it was both related to and aggravated the unrest and stress of the times. No reformation had taken place, however; no side stood for reform in the sense of adapting ecclesiastical institutions and views to new circumstances. The schism epitomized the transitional character of the second and third quarters of the century. This was the background from which Krizhanich's critical appraisal of Russian conditions and his agenda for reform emerged.

2

Krizhanich: the man and his life

During Krizhanich's formative years, his homeland was in a precarious condition. For two centuries, Croatia had been under recurring attack by the Turks. Its independence was in jeopardy.

> The Croatian poets, from Marko Marulić to Ivan Gundulić, from 1501 to 1638, addressed their prayers to the Almighty and sent incessant supplications to the popes and various princes, begging them to unite the divided Christendom in its last effort, before everything should be lost. . . . Italy [they believed] would long have been conquered if the Ottoman onslaught had not been dispersed at the Croatian shores. [1]

Moreover, the Germans were expanding southward, and most Slavic countries were in decline. Poland, then a major power, appeared unable to play a liberating role. The more desperate the situation became, the more Krizhanich's Croatian predecessors and contemporaries turned to Russia as the only Slavic country of the north capable of helping its Slavic brethren of the south to expel the Turkish aggressor. [2]

Although Krizhanich was a meticulous recorder of his times, the record of his own life contains many lacunae. He attended the Jesuit grammar school in Ljubljana and, from 1629 to 1635, the Jesuit *gymnasium* in Zagreb. At the time of graduation he was seventeen; this was also the approximate time of his father's death. Upon the death of his father, Krizhanich was aided financially by Burkhardt Hizing, a local nobleman,

[1] Ante Kadić, *From Croatian Renaissance to Yugoslav Socialism* (The Hague, 1969), 45.
[2] Cf. Jaroslav Šidak, "Juraj Križanić als Problem der kroatischen und der serbischen Literatur," in Eekman and Kadić, 3–49; and Ante Kadić, "Križanić and Possevino—Missionaries to Muscovy," in Eekman and Kadić, 86–88; and Ivan Golub, "Biografska Pozadina Križanićevih Djela," in *Život i djelo Jurja Križanića: Zbornik Radova* (Zagreb, 1974), 37.

and this enabled him to attend the Institut Ferdinandum in Graz. He graduated from this institute in August 1638 (sixth in a class of thirty), and presently enrolled at the University of Bologna to study theology.[3]

At Bologna, Krizhanich first decided to seek a career as a missionary working among his Orthodox Slavic compatriots. Accordingly, he initially expressed a wish to serve among Serb refugees who had fled to Croatia from Turkish domination. Then, to the surprise of his superior, he abruptly changed his mind and—notwithstanding their opposition—launched a plan for a one-man mission to Moscow. His declared goal was to bring about a union between the Roman Catholic and Russian Orthodox churches. This second objective became a lifelong obsession, with related goals that were neither simple nor singular.

To prepare for his mission, Krizhanich studied the history and culture of Greece. He learned Greek and Russian, perused the Greek classics, and developed an expertise in Orthodox liturgy, ceremonies, and literature, claiming to have read every available book on these subjects. In 1640 he was awarded a master's degree. Soon thereafter, he was admitted to the Greek College of St Athanasius, the principal center in Rome for the training of Catholic missionaries to work among Orthodox Christians.[4] Here, in early 1641, he composed a lengthy memorandum on his planned mission to Moscow and submitted it to the Congregation for the Propagation of the Faith (*Congregatio de propaganda fide*).

Krizhanich gave two reasons in applying for admission to St Athanasius, not usually granted a Latin cleric. First, it would facilitate his becoming proficient in Greek; second, this would enable him to read more widely in the literature on controversial theological issues, essential if he was to work at the court of Muscovy after graduation. His proposal was accepted provisionally by Francesco Ingoli, secretary of the Congregation for the Propagation of the Faith, who notified him that once ordained, he should proceed to Moscow to fulfill his duties as a missionary.[5]

The memorandum of 1641, which embraced his entire *modus operandi*, was divided into three parts.[6] The first furnished background information

---

[3] See Belokurov, "Iurii Krizhanich v Rossii," 54–5. It is noteworthy that the University of Bologna was renowned at the time for scholarship in the law and medicine rather than economics.

[4] V. Jagić, "Zur Biographie G. Križanić's," *Archiv für slavische Philologie*, VI (1882), 120.

[5] Belokurov, "Iurii Krizhanich v Rossii," 55.

[6] See "The Krizhanich Memorandum of 1641," Archives of the Sacred Congregation for the Evangelization of Peoples. Scritture riferite nelle Congregazioni Generali (SOCG) vol. 338, fol. 533^RV–542^RV. Belokurov claimed that the Krizhanich memorandum consisted of two parts. In 1896, Paul Pierling discovered it in the Congregation archives and, with

on the religion, government, geography, economy, people, and customs of Russia. It was based on two works written by distinguished Western European emissaries to Moscow: Sigismund von Herberstein, ambassador of the Holy Roman Empire, who had visited the Russian capital in 1517 and in 1526, and Antonio Possevino, a Jesuit papal legate who in 1582 had been invited by Ivan IV to visit Moscow and to arrange a truce between Russia and the Polish-Lithuanian Commonwealth.[7]

The second part contained the core of his argument. The Russians, Krizhanich maintained, were not heretics but misguided Christians. He would therefore endeavor to establish a dialogue with the object of exhorting them not only to piety and learning, but also to modernization. And for this, he emphasized, the establishment of basic crafts was a primary requisite. Whenever appropriate, Krizhanich said, he would explain the harmful effects of the past mistakes and contemporary vices of the Russians—consequences, he claimed, of fallacious Greek teachings. Krizhanich believed that by assisting in the correction of Russian theology without actually proselytizing, he would indirectly improve Russian behavior.

To achieve these objectives, it was imperative that he visit Moscow, and in the third part of his memorandum he suggested two possible ways of doing so. He could join a Russian diplomatic embassy or commercial legation traveling to Moscow; or, preferably, he could obtain an invitation from the tsar by offering to serve as an interpreter, ambassador, translator, or tutor to the tsar's children. He proposed to write a major work on general history, devoting particular attention to the circumstances under which "all our nations"—Poles, Bohemians, Muscovites, Bulgarians, Ukrainians, Croatians, Bosnians, and so forth—had received their Christian faith, and demonstrating their attendant progress or retrogression.[8] Once the book was finished, he would dedicate it to the tsar and

---

his approval, Belokurov published it in his "Iurii Krizhanich v Rossii," 87–106. This transcript was, however, based on a copy that contained many errors. Kadić discovered the original Latin-Italian version and republished it in that form: Ante Kadić, "Križanić's Memorandum," *Jahrbücher für Geschichte Osteuropas*, vol. 12, no. 3 (October 1964), 331–49. Cf. also his *From Croatian Renaissance to Yugoslav Socialism*, 74–92, and Križanić and Possevino," in Eekman and Kadić, 81–86. The original memorandum indeed consists of three parts.

[7] Von Herberstein wrote *Rerum Moscoviticarum Commentarii* (Vienna, 1549), and Possevino, *Commentarii de rebus Moscoviticus* (Vilna, 1586). See also Sigismund von Herberstein, *Notes upon Russia*, R.H. Major, trans., 2 vols., 1851 (reprinted New York, 1963). Possevino's book, which Krizhanich had read while at Bologna, played a role in inspiring him to explore the possibility of unifying the Slavs ecclesiastically.

[8] See "Memorandum," Punto 12.

personally present it to him. This, he conjectured, would assure his welcome in Moscow as an advisor on either foreign or domestic affairs. For shorter-range results, however, he would, on reaching Moscow, prepare several tracts praising Russian rulers and magnifying their achievements. This ploy, he thought, would do no harm in gaining the confidence of the tsar.

To avoid arousing suspicion or jealousy among the tsar's associates, Krizhanich proposed to accept no reward for his services. Once he had gained the confidence of the tsar, he would seek authorization to translate into Russian certain basic books, the originals of which were known to be available in Venice. With the tsar's permission, he would then proceed to Venice to obtain them. While he was in Venice, he continued, the papacy would have the opportunity of transmitting to Moscow—via his inter-mediation—the necessary proposals for the unification of the two churches. Since he thought it would take no longer than four or five years to execute these plans, he would concurrently make suggestions to the tsar aimed at enhancing the honor and glory of Russia. Finally, he would recommend a military campaign against the Ottoman Empire with the objective of liberating the tsar's co-religionists in the Balkans from the Turkish yoke, among them the Greeks, Bulgars, Serbs, Bosnians, and Romanians. Assuming a favorable hearing from the tsar, Krizhanich went on, he would point out that this plan could most successfully be implemented through the coordination of the Russian war effort with campaigns by the Holy Roman Empire and other Catholic states. To that end, he would volunteer to serve as the tsar's principal envoy to states that might be expected to participate. Krizhanich explained that since Russia was backward in weapons, the tsar would require the assistance of Western Catholic princes. They would refuse to cooperate, however, unless he agreed to church union. Such agreement, Krizhanich recognized, would be difficult to achieve and, not surprisingly, he closed his 1641 memorandum with the invocation: "Let our Lord accomplish this to His glory and honor."[9]

DISAPPOINTMENTS

Despite this memorandum, upon Krizhanich's receiving his doctorate in theology from the College of Athanasius in 1642, the Congregation for

---

[9] Ibid., sec. 7. Cf. also Belokurov, "Iurii Krizhanich v Rossii," 56–60; and for related documents, particularly his *Prilozheniia*, 87–106; see also Golub, "Biografska," 39–46.

the Propagation of the Faith appointed him missionary to Orthodox refugees who had arrived in Croatia. The reason given by the Congregation for the change in plans was that the experience would render Krizhanich better prepared for the Russian undertaking at a later time.[10] He had no choice but to accept the mission and return forthwith to Zagreb, where he was soon also appointed a teacher at the Zagreb Theological Seminary and was parish priest at the churches in neighboring Nedelišće (1643—4) and Varaždin (1645—6). But his aim constantly centered on Moscow, as witness a request to be tonsured some time before leaving Rome and the contacts he persistently maintained after reaching Zagreb. The records reveal that in 1643 Krizhanich held a meeting in Zagreb with Methodius Terletskii, Uniate Bishop of Kholm, who was an ardent advocate of union between the Catholic and Orthodox churches. Terletskii appears to have encouraged Krizhanich in his plans to reach Moscow, but the latter's persistent financial problems hindered his immediate pursuit of them. Instead, he kept in touch with Terletskii and simultaneously requested the Congregation to provide him with a letter of introduction to Polish Catholic prelates. After much delay, he was notified in mid-1646 that Peter Parczewski, Catholic Bishop of Smolensk, was coming to Rome and would endeavor to assist him in reaching Moscow. Krizhanich prepared to journey to Vienna in the hope of meeting the bishop. He was forewarned by the Congregation that if his Moscow plans fell through, he would nevertheless be obliged to serve for three years under Parczewski's jurisdiction. Krizhanich agreed. Further, in a letter to Secretary Ingoli, he requested permission to proceed from Vienna to Smolensk in case he arrived in Vienna too late to consult with the bishop. This was, indeed, what happened, and Krizhanich was instructed that en route from Warsaw to Smolensk he would be accompanied by a man named Leon Flegen. The itinerary, as depicted on our map of Krizhanich's journeys, entailed traveling from Vienna to Cracow, and thence to Warsaw, where Krizhanich arrived in November 1646. There he met Bishop Parczewski, Flegen, and numerous other Polish religious and civil dignitaries.[11]

Parczewski's deep skepticism about the possible success of Krizhanich's

---

[10] See Belokurov, *Prilozheniia,* 182; Kadić, "Križanić's Formative Years as a Pan-Slavist," *American Contributions to the Vth International Congress of Slavists* (The Hague, 1963), 18–19; and Golub, "Biografska," 48.

[11] Jagić correctly observes that the canons of Zagreb rescinded Krizhanich's canonicate simply because he was absent from his chapter—this being according to the rule of "absens carens." See Thomas Eekman, "Vatroslav Jagić on Križanić," in Eekman and Kadić, 322–3; and Belokurov, "Iurii Krizhanich v Rossii," 63–6.

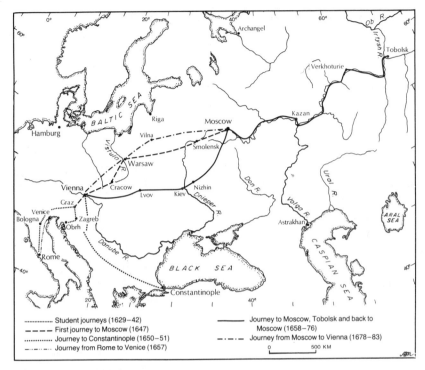

Map 2   Krizhanich's travels

mission to Moscow proved to be matched only by Flegen's indiscreet loquaciousness as a traveling companion. Flegen boasted in public that Krizhanich and he were on a mission to Moscow. Krizhanich, for his part, thought they should remain anonymous. He feared that once their mission became known, the Orthodox Christians living among the Catholic Poles would denounce them to the Russians as Italian missionaries. Though missionaries of other nationalities had failed in similar undertakings, Krizhanich believed that as a Slav he could succeed.[12] While in Warsaw, however, Krizhanich made the acquaintance of Gerasim S. Dokhturov, a Russian diplomatic courier who had come to notify the Polish authorities of Russian military successes against the Turks. At their meeting Krizhanich identified himself as a Croatian Roman Catholic priest, but was circumspect about his objectives. He made reference to his proficiency in various Slavic languages, said he was in Warsaw to concentrate on Polish and Russian studies, and extolled the

---

[12] See Belokurov, *Prilozheniia,* 166.

Russian Old Church Slavonic language as the key Slavic language, used to conduct not only all Russian governmental, but also church affairs.

Krizhanich made a formal appeal to Dokhturov, indicating ways in which he could be useful professionally to the tsar. Dokhturov gave him reason to believe that he was favorably impressed by his credentials, and Krizhanich implored him to intervene on his behalf for an appropriate appointment. His only conditional request was that no one in Moscow question or ridicule his religious beliefs. An assistant of Dokhturov's suggested that Krizhanich would have a better chance of obtaining an appointment if he embraced Orthodoxy—a suggestion he could not accept. Provisionally, however, he asked to join Dokhturov's embassy on its return trip to Moscow. Not only was this request denied, but upon returning to Moscow Dokhturov failed even to mention their encounter to his superiors.[13]

Disappointed, Krizhanich left Warsaw for Smolensk, which he found to be a frontier wasteland. No one understood or appreciated his undertaking. In a letter dated April 9, 1647, he wrote to Rome again, expressed his dissatisfaction, and asked for a three-year period of leave to study in Vilna, capital of Lithuania.[14] He proposed to work on mathematics and astronomy while continuing to master Russian, and to write the major work on Russian history and politics that he proposed to dedicate to the tsar. In return, he hoped that the tsar would open a school in Moscow and engage him as a teacher. Should that not occur, he noted, it would still be propitious for the Roman church to authorize his visiting Moscow to acquire firsthand knowledge and experience that he could put to use in converting Orthodox Slavs in the Balkans.

Krizhanich further reported to Rome that he had read every accessible book on Russia and studied public finance as well as other topics of major relevance to Russia's political economy, development, and way of life. Problems arising from the vast size of Russia called for particular attention, he wrote. He cautioned that because of Russian suspicion of all foreigners, he would need to make every effort to conceal the real purpose of his mission. He would tell Russian officials that he had come to

[13] An account of the incident is given in Belokurov, "Iurii Krizhanich v Rossii," 66–8. See also Kadić, "Križanić's Formative Years," 20–21; and Golub, "Biografska," 53.

[14] Krizhanich sent this letter care of his friend Rafael Levaković, Bishop of Ohrid. In effect, he was a disciple of the bishop, and requested that he use his discretion as to which passages should be transmitted to the cardinals. Archives of the Sacred Congregation, Fondo SOCG, vol. 338, fol. 546^{RV}–562^{RV}. Details of the letter are also published in Belokurov, "Iurii Krizhanich v Rossii," 161, 182–7. See also Kadić, *From Croatian Renaissance*, 62–3.

Moscow on his own initiative and for the sole purpose of studying their language and history. Moreover, he would affirm that although he was a Roman Catholic priest, he wished them no harm. To preserve the secrecy of his mission, he requested that the pope formally designated him as a missionary to Orthodox Christians in the Balkans. But no such authorization was granted. Krizhanich remained in Smolensk for about a year, until he finally somehow arranged to be included as an apostolic missionary in a seven-hundred-man Polish "diplomatic-commercial" mission en route to Moscow.[15] He was in the Russian capital from October 25 until December 19, 1647.

During this brief visit Krizhanich accomplished a great deal. He consulted with leading churchmen, gathered books and pamphlets on the religious schism, and met with political officials. In contacts with state and church authorities, he emphasized the need to correct and revise the Russian language. The high point of his stay in Moscow was an audience with Patriarch Joseph. Krizhanich was thus able to examine Russian conditions and the potential of a long-term mission for himself. In all these activities, he was a well-informed person benefiting from that unique experience of appraising for the first time the particular characteristics of an important capital.

Upon returning to Poland he immediately prepared a brief, emotional report on his impressions of Moscow, and forwarded it to the Congregation in Rome.[16] His views of Tsar Alexei and Patriarch Joseph were favorable, but he was extremely critical of a recently published work called *Cyril's Book* (*Kirillova Kniga*, Moscow, 1644). According to Krizhanich, this abounded in distorted views of the Catholic church, and it was of primary importance that the papacy prepare a response in Russian to these heresies, an endeavor in which he would be pleased to collaborate. The papacy did not reply to his communication, and in mid-June 1648, he repeated the main points in yet another letter.[17] It was not

---

[15] Krizhanich's companion during this mission was Alexander Kotowicz, who later succeeded Parczewski and, at the close of Krizhanich's life, paid homage to him. See Belokurov, *Prilozheniia*, 266–7.

[16] This report, probably written in December 1647, was not well prepared. It was published by S.A. Belokurov, "Iurii Krizhanich v Rossii," 237–42.

[17] Written to secretary Ingoli from Grodno (June 13, 1648), Krizhanich laments: "For the past two years, I have received not a single letter from your most serene and respected lordship." Archives of the Sacred Congregation, Fondo SOCG, vol. 338, fol. 567^{RV}–568^{RV}; and S.A. Belokurov, "Iurii Krizhanich v Rossii," *Prilozheniia*, 242–6. Krizhanich forwarded this letter via Louis Fantoni, "secretary to the Polish Royal Majesty, Guardian of Warsaw and Canon of Varmia, who currently resides in Warsaw," ibid., Archives.

until September 1648 that a papal message was sent to Krizhanich, instructing him to forward a report to Rome on his visit to Moscow.[18] Apparently the message did not reach Krizhanich, or he did not reply, for no record of his response exists in the papal archives. Indeed, there is no record whatsoever of Krizhanich's activities from mid-June 1648 until early March 1650, when he dispatched an urgent letter from Vienna to Dionisio Massari, the new secretary of the Congregation, inquiring as to how the papacy had viewed the substance of his two previous letters and reiterating the ambition of his life: to achieve union between the Roman Catholics and the misguided Orthodox Slavs.[19]

Awaiting a reply, and short of money, Krizhanich for some months lived in Vienna, gravely concerned about his finances. According to a document discovered in the Viennese archives, he notified Massari that if he were not invited to Rome, he would have to accept an appointment for financial reasons and proceed to Constantinople. Finally, at the end of October 1650, he seized an opportunity to join the legation of the imperial emissary to Turkey, Johann Rudolf Schmidt Freiherr von Schwarzenhorn, who was requested by the Greek Metropolitan in Constantinople to help in their fight against the Calvinists and Lutherans there. Schmidt advised them to anathematize these "heretics" and with Krizhanich's assistance verified that they had done so.[20] During his brief visit to Constantinople (January 15 to March 13, 1651), Krizhanich served as official chaplain to the embassy and as von Schwarzenhorn's secretary, an appointment that enabled him to exchange views with high officials of the Greek Orthodox church. In his meetings with distinguished Greek scholars—among them the eminent Mamonas-Panagiotes Nikousios—Krizhanich devoted particular attention to familiarizing himself with the basic problems facing the Ottoman Empire.[21]

In mid-March 1651 Krizhanich left Constantinople and returned to

---

[18] As Kadić states: "Krizhanich was requested to send his copy of *Cyril's Book*, but Ingoli did not hint that he himself should come to Rome" (*From Croatian Renaissance*, 64); see Belokurov, *Prilozheniia*, no. 21, letter dated September 1, 1648, 248.

[19] "I have no other ambition," Krizhanich wrote, "than to continue to serve the Sacred Congregation in behalf of the nation of my race [Slavs] that has been almost entirely infested by the Greek schism." Archives of the Sacred Congregation, Fondo SOCG, vol. 339, fol. 143^{RV}–144^{RV}; letter dated 9 March 1650. He explains that the cause for his prolonged silence was "a year-long illness and various misfortunes," ibid.

[20] See Golub, "Biografska," 55; and Belokurov, "Iurii Krizhanich v Rossii," 68–71.

[21] Krizhanich and Nikousios (1613–73) had high regard for one another: Krizhanich made reference to his conversations with Nikousios, and Nikousios wrote (1669–70) about Krizhanich with esteem, calling him "my friend." See Belokurov, "Iurii Krizhanich v Rossii," 69; and Golub, "Contributions a l'histoire," in Eekman and Kadić, 127–29. Further archival research on Krizhanich's trip to Constantinople may contribute to our

Vienna. From there he journeyed to Rome, where he spent the next five years working on the history of the church schism. At some time during this period, he presumably conveyed his impressions of conditions in Moscow and Constantinople to the appropriate papal authorities.[22] In early 1657 he traveled from Rome to Venice in order to meet a Russian legation headed by I. I. Chemodanov and A. Postnikov, an encounter that proved fruitless for all concerned. Later that year, when he learned that yet another Russian legation, headed by Ia. N. Likharev, would be visiting Vienna in early 1658, he made arrangements to meet this delegation as well.[23] During the interim, however, on October 1, 1657, the Office of the Congregation issued a decree granting Krizhanich permission to undertake a mission to Moscow.[24] But on January 26, 1658, Pope Alexander VII intervened, in effect vetoing that decision, and ordered Krizhanich to complete his work on the schismatics in Rome.[25]

---

understanding of his comparatively restrained view of the Turks as expressed in the *Politika*. Before visiting Constantinople Krizhanich had spoken contemptuously of the Turks. "Indeed," he wrote, "it was as difficult to discuss the problem of faith with the Muscovites as it was to talk with a Turk." Letter written to the Congregation (December 1647). Belokurov, "Iurii Krizhanich v Rossii," *Prilozheniia,* 242.

[22] According to records in the Vatican library, Krizhanich was at the Church of St Jerome on September 30, 1653, and October 7, 1653, but he did not reappear until March 30, 1655. On November 10, 1652, he was elected a canon of the Croatian (Illyrian) Confraternity of St Jerome, and on September 22, 1653, he was chosen chaplain. The latter appointment was set aside, however, by Secretary Massari, with whom Krizhanich was at loggerheads. Krizhanich became involved in a controversy as to whether he was entitled to membership in the St Jerome hospice, where only Illyrians who spoke the Illyrian language could reside. Massari had ruled against him, but powerful friends came to Krizhanich's defense. In effect, Athanasius Kircher, distinguished scholar (whose patron was the emperor of Austria), and Luc Holstenius, renowned geographer (and bibliographer of the Vatican library), rescinded Massari's decision and Krizhanich stayed at St Jerome at least until April 1656. See Vatican library Codex 1654–1659, volume 236, and as reported in Golub, "Contributions à l'histoire des relations de Križanić avec ses contemporains (1651–58)," in Eekman and Kadić, 94, 132–3.

[23] Pope Alexander VII, who was interested in entering and extending contacts with distant countries, knew of Krizhanich's activities. Perpetually impecunious, Krizhanich had apparently requested financial assistance from the Office of the Congregation to meet with the Russian legation in Venice (January 11–May 1, 1657), and it was Virgilio Spada, author of "Discorso di Monete" (1647), member of the Congregation and brother of Cardinal Bernardin Spada who had suggested to Luc Holstenius that Krizhanich be granted fifteen écus by the Office. See Jagic, *Život i rad,* 94–96. ("Discorso di Monete" was not published; a copy of the manuscript [No. 12, 489] is available in the Department of Manuscripts, British Library, London.)

[24] See Belokurov, "Iurii Krizhanich v Rossii," 72.

[25] Succeeding Massari, a new secretary of the Congregation, Mario Alberici, reported: "His Highness said that it would seem to him more opportune to help [Krizhanich] in his poverty with some stipend so that he could complete his work in Rome against the schismatics, work that he has already started." Our translation of the Latin as cited in: V.

Krizhanich disobeyed the papal order and clandestinely undertook his mission to Moscow. The papal records and Krizhanich's subsequent comments indicate that he departed from Vienna in December 1658, with Likharev's embassy. He had heard that a school of philosophy was about to be established in Moscow, and was eager not to miss the opportunity of a teaching appointment. Krizhanich later wrote that when he had learned about the opening of new humanistic schools in which Greek and Latin were being taught, he had suggested to Pope Alexander VII (probably through Virgilio Spada) that this opportunity should be exploited in order to refute *Cyril's Book* and quell Russian misgivings about Catholicism. At the time (1658), Russia and Poland were at war, and the pope suggested that Krizhanich wait for more peaceful times. This was not consistent with his temperament, however, and he also considered it demeaning to accept financial help attendant upon "his poverty" as though he were a beggar.[26]

Krizhanich did not travel all the way to Moscow with Likharev's embassy. They parted company just before reaching the Polish border. The embassy traveled on to Moscow via Silesia, Saxony, Hamburg, and Archangel, reaching Moscow in mid-September 1659, whereas Krizhanich took a more direct route, traveling via present-day Slovakia, Galicia, and the Ukraine. In April 1659 he reached Nizhin, an administrative center northeast of Kiev, near what was then the Ukrainian-Russian border.[27]

For five months Krizhanich remained in Nizhin, living in the house of a Ukrainian Orthodox priest. Relations between the Ukraine and Russia were badly strained. In June 1659, a battle broke out between Ukrainian cossacks and Russian forces at Konotop. Even though the Russians were

---

Jagic, "Zur biographie G. Križanić's," 120–21: ("Sanctissimus dixit ei opportunius videri aliquo stipendio ipsius paupertati succurere, ret possit hic Romae labores iam coeptos contra schismaticos perficere.") At the January 26, 1658 meeting with the Pope, Alberici presented him with a gift from Krizhanich—a copy of his *Asserta musicalia* (1656)—and he referred to Krizhanich's previous work in Russia, mentioning that his writings in defense of Catholicism were held in high regard both by Cardinal Francesco Brancaccio and by Luc Holstenius. Alberici added, however: "I do not believe that he had great success in those missions; nor does he seem to me qualified for a mission" ["Ma non credo che in quelle missioni facesse gran riuscita, ne veramente mi par soggetto da missione"] (Jagić, "Zur biographie," 120–21).

[26] See Belokurov, *Prilizheniia,* 279; and Golub, "Contributions à l'histoire," 137.

[27] Bezsonov's description of Krizhanich's trip from Vienna to Moscow, and especially his assertion that it was only on his way through Lvov that he bought and studied the Polish books he later used in the *Politika,* appear to be gross embellishments. See Jagić, *Život i rad,* 104; Eekman, "Vatroslav Jagić on Križhanić," in Eekman and Kadić, 324; and the detailed discussion of Krizhanich's travels as presented in Belokurov, "Iurii Krizhanich v Rossii," 71–75.

annihilated, disunity between pro- and anti-Russian cossacks prevailed. It is noteworthy that Krizhanich sided with the pro-Russian group. He wrote a tract, *Discourses for Ukrainians,* urging the Ukrainians to submit to Russian rule. The *Discourses* were read at public meetings in Nizhin, whose inhabitants were, in effect, the first Ukrainians to follow Krizhanich's counsel. His arguments were consistent with his pan-Slavic vision, but he also appears to have maintained a steadfastly pro-Russian stance in order to gain entry to Moscow. Indeed, on September 1, 1659, accompanied by a group of Nizhin delegates, Krizhanich left for Putivl, headquarters of the Russian armed forces, and the authorities there transferred the entire group to Moscow, where they arrived on September 17, 1659.[28]

Upon arrival, Krizhanich was immediately brought to the Chancellery of Foreign Affairs for intensive questioning about the purpose of his coming to Russia, a procedure rigorously followed with respect to all newly arrived foreigners. His answers show how fearfully he regarded the interrogation. Concealing his origin, he claimed to be Juraj Biliš Serbenin, a Serb (and hence Orthodox?) born in a town under Turkish domination. His father, he accurately said, had been a merchant; but he was careless with the truth in stating that his father had died when he was still a young lad. He also pretended to have been reared by an uncle who had financed his education in Padua, where for six years he had allegedly studied Italian, Latin, Greek, Slavonic, rhetoric, philosophy, grammar, mathematics, and music. As to his journey, he claimed to have left Serbia in February 1659 and to have traveled via Vienna, Slovakia, Galicia, and the Ukraine to Nizhin, where he had spent five months with the Orthodox priest before being transferred by the Russian military authorities to Moscow. His sole purpose in coming to Russia, he declared, was to offer his services to the tsar.

The interrogation completed, Krizhanich was, on the tsar's orders, given some English cloth, a kaftan, forty marten furs (widely used as currency), and a daily cash allowance for food and lodging. This generosity was not unusual, as virtually all foreigners who joined the tsar's service were similarly treated. Once settled in Moscow, Krizhanich submitted to the Chancellery of Foreign Affairs three memoranda that he had previously prepared in Nizhin: *Discourses for Ukrainians*; "An Account of a Journey from Lvov to Moscow"; and "A Serbian Letter."[29] The letter was

---

[28] Belokurov, "Iurii Krizhanich v Rossii," 75–80; and Golub, "Contributions à l'histoire," 65–66.

[29] Belokurov, "Iurii Krizhanich v Rossii," 75–80.

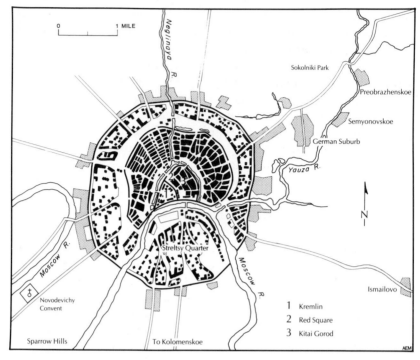

Map 3   Moscow circa *1680*

most significant. Addressed to Tsar Alexei, it called attention to the libels
against the Russian nation that had been spread abroad by Krizhanich's
bête noire, the renowned German traveler and writer Adam Olearius, who
had served as secretary to the Duke of Holstein.[30] Krizhanich emphasized
that Russia's enemies, the Poles and Ukrainians in particular, had to be

---

[30] It is generally agreed that Olearius was responsible for spreading the rumor that the
Muscovite court was about to establish the School of Philosophy, precipitating Krizhanich's
hurried departure for Moscow. In a new edition of a well-known work which Krizhanich
doubtless had read, Olearius wrote: "Very close to the Patriarch's palace they have already
built a Latin and Greek school that is under the supervision and direction of a Greek
named Arsenius." See the tome by Adam Olearius, *Vermehrte Newe Beschreibung Der
Muscowitischen und Persischen Reyse* (Schleswig, 1656 [Tubingen, 1971]) 280; cf. also
Samuel H. Baron, *The Travels of Olearius in Seventeenth Century Russia* (Stanford, 1967),
238; and his "Križanić and Olearius," in Eekman and Kadić, 183–208. According to
Belokurov, this school was established in 1652/3, and Arsenius was identified as one of the
Greek scholars who had come to Russia with Paisii, the Patriarch of Jerusalem (Belokurov,
"Iurii Krizhanich v Rossii," 73, 177). Soviet scholars claim to have identified Arsenius as a
Ukrainian teacher named Arsenius Satanovskii. See *Ocherki istorii SSSR. Period feodalizma,
XVII v.* (Moscow, 1955), 563.

warned about the dire consequences of their own internal anarchy.[31] It was important not only to publish an accurate history of Russia, but to glorify the superiority of Russia's political system over that of other nations and to prepare an authoritative Slavic grammar. These things Krizhanich volunteered to do. In return, he requested that the tsar appoint him as his official librarian with permission to translate selected books on government, politics, and economics for the tsar's personal use.

The tsar's father-in-law at the time, Boris I. Morozov, and two of the tsar's close associates, Feodor M. Rtishchev and Almaz Ivanov, encouraged Krizhanich to undertake the translations. But the tsar granted him permission to work only on the Slavic grammar and to translate some Latin and Greek documents. No information, official or otherwise, reveals any substantive discussions that Krizhanich may have had with other civil servants or religious officials. However, on January 8, 1661, his stay in Moscow came to an abrupt end. Acting on a complaint lodged by the Department of Baltic Affairs, which was in charge of Polish and Swedish matters, the tsar issued a decree banishing Krizhanich to the misery of Siberia.

The cause of his exile remains unknown. Some scholars believe that Krizhanich participated in the religious controversies that racked Russian society at the time and, as a Catholic priest, aroused hostile suspicion. Others have suggested that his criticism of the Greeks, with whom Patriarch Nikon was attempting reconciliation, joined with his criticisms of Russian society, may have been the cause. Still others have offered political reasons for his banishment, but with no evidence. Krizhanich himself thought he had been exiled because of "some foolish thing" he had said to someone, who had mentioned it to the authorities.[32] Whatever the reasons, Krizhanich was ordered to leave Moscow on January 20, 1661. He was transported along the main Siberian route via Verkhoturie and arrived in Tobolsk on March 8, 1661.

---

[31] Krizhanich, in the least, gave the impression of hating the Poles. Nonetheless, he also wrote that they were good neighbors (*Politika,* infra, 114). He loathed the Germans. Russia's enemies at the time were much more Poland-Lithuania, Sweden, and Ottoman Turkey than Germany or the Ukraine or Poland per se.

[32] The presumed causes of Krizhanich's exile, and his own conjectures, are extensively put forth in Jagić, "Biographie," and in Belokurov, "Iurii Krizhanich v Rossii," 84–96; cf. also Golub, "Contributions à l'histoire," 66–69; George Vernadsky, *History of Russia* (New Haven, 1969), vol. 5, part 2, 679; *Politika,* infra, 142.

3

Politics, economics and society

Regardless of the merits or eccentricities of Krizhanich's mission, the timing of his arrival in Moscow could hardly have been less propitious. The country, as we have seen, was in the midst of a religious convulsion. The so-called "great schism" revealed serious weaknesses in the apparently mighty Russian state and monolithic Muscovite church. When Krizhanich reached Tobolsk and began working on his *Politika,* Russia was in turmoil, born of desperation and compounded by oppressive social conditions. Savage repression was in the air.

Russia was indeed a society of extremes, undergoing extraordinary stress. Officially, the country was an Orthodox Slavic state ruled by an autocratic, hereditary tsar wielding unrestricted and, ordinarily, unchallenged power. Like his predecessors, he assumed divine right, was nominal head of the Orthodox Church, commander-in-chief, supreme judge and the wealthiest man in the realm. His peremptory power was incomparably greater than that of any other European monarch. He possessed inherent power to appoint and dismiss all notable civil and religious officials, to issue all major decrees, to interpret all laws, to confiscate property at will—in sum, to wield the power of life and death over all the subjects of his vast domain.

MUSCOVITE INSTITUTIONS

The tsar's power was vested in five principal institutions.

● The Boyar Duma. Historically one of the main political institutions of the Kieven state (*ca.* tenth and twelfth centuries), in the sixteenth and seventeenth centuries the Boyar Duma was a council of Muscovy's most elite subjects and advised the tsar on domestic and foreign affairs. Its membership represented notable families—including descendants of the former grand and appanage princes—who manned the highest political, military, and administrative posts in the land. Two quite distinct groups, however, comprised the Boyar Duma: the "aristocrats" and the "servitors."[1] These two groups, in turn, were assigned specific ranks. The aristocrats included boyars and *okolnichii* (who were just below boyar rank and usually served as military commanders, ambassadors, judges, and high administrators). The servitors included the *dumnye dvoriane* (who often served as royal advisors, or courtiers, and were obliged to perform military service throughout their careers) and the *dumnye diaki* (who were responsible for the preparation of reports on matters demanding the attention of the Duma, the recording and maintaining of its official records, and generally assuming the technical functions of state secretaries). All members of the Duma were appointed by the tsar. Not infrequently, boyars served as directors of the main chancelleries, and this linked the administrative offices with the Boyar Duma. However, the rights and functions of the Duma were never legally or systematically defined: it had no definite, legal limitation on the sovereign's power. Nonetheless, in the seventeenth century, it underwent gradual and complex changes in numbers, composition, and functions. Its size increased fourfold, ranging from 28–45 members during the period 1613–46 to 107–153 members during the period 1682–90. When Krizhanich wrote the *Politika,* the Boyar Duma was not only an important institution in its customary capacity, but also participated in the legislative, administrative, and judicial affairs of the state, as well as in diplomatic relations with other nations.[2]

● The Zemskii Sobor. Literally the "Assembly of the Land," it was composed of so-called "free subjects of the realm." In principle, the Zemskii Sobor was to serve as the medium of contact between the tsar and

[1] Recent research on the Boyar Duma has found this classification of terms useful, the precise meaning of which is explained in the text and in the Appendix infra. Strictly speaking, however, both groups were "servitors," and the term "service nobility" has usually been used to designate the social group here called "servitors." See Robert O. Crummey, *Aristocrats and Servitors* (Princeton, 1983), 12–64, Appendix A, 175–7, Appendix C, 215–20.

[2] For a discussion of the Boyar Duma from the Kievan period until its demise, see Nicholas V. Riasanovsky, *A History of Russia* (Oxford, 1984), 50–51, 160–92, and 214–30. The Russian classic on the subject is V.O. Kliuchevskii, *Boyarskaia duma drevnei Rusi,* 4th ed. (Moscow, 1909). In the sixteenth century, the second *Sudebnik* (1550 Code of Law in Moscow, article 98) considered the Boyar Duma's decisions a normal way of making new laws though this was not, of course, always observed. After overthrowing the regency government of Sophia and Prince V.V. Golitsyn (who had ruled Russia since 1682), Peter I virtually ceased to appoint new members to the Boyar Duma by 1693. He replaced it with the Senate in 1711. Cf. *Dictionary of Russian Historical Terms from the Eleventh Century to 1917,* compiled by Sergei G. Pushkarev, and edited by George Vernadsky and Ralph T. Fisher, Jr. (New Haven, 1970), 4–5, 14–15.

his subjects. Its form and composition underwent significant changes in the sixteenth and seventeenth centuries, however, with the consultative form giving way to an electoral form during several periods of national crisis. The first Zemskii Sobor is believed to have been convened by Ivan IV in 1549–50; in 1566, he consulted a second Sobor that voted for the continuation of the Livonian war with Poland and Lithuania. This Sobor was composed of members of the assembly of the Muscovite high church hierarchy; members of the Boyar Duma; office-holding military service men; and elected administrators of the Moscow townspeople. It has been referred to as a conference of the central government with its own local agents. At the end of the Riurik Dynasty (1598), and during the Time of Troubles (1598–1613), when there was no recognized tsar on the throne, the Zemskii Sobor emerged as the highest authority in the land. As we have seen, in 1612 the leaders of an auxiliary armed force summoned a Zemskii Sobor for the express purpose of assuming the functions of civil and military government. Indeed, after the national forces had retaken Moscow, which had been occupied by a Polish garrison, the elected representatives of fifty cities and their districts came to Moscow and, together with the boyars, the clergy, and leading Moscow citizens, held a convention in the form of a Zemskii Sobor that in February 1613 elected a new tsar—the young Mikhail Romanov. This was composed not only of nobles, clergy, merchants, and townspeople, but even of state peasants from the northern regions, and cossacks. From 1613–23, the Zemskii Sobor was in session almost every year, voting new taxes and helping mobilize armed forces to restore order. During the wars with Poland in 1632 and 1634 and at a time of potential conflict with Turkey and the Crimean Tartars in 1642, the government also convened sobory to obtain essential assistance and military counsel. The greatest contribution of the Zemskii Sobor was in the reign of Alexei Mikhailovich (1645–76), who convened the sobor of 1648–9 to help quell internal disorders. It participated actively in the preparation of one of the most important and comprehensive codes in Russian legal history: the *Sobornoe Ulozhenie* of 1649, which was discussed, approved, and signed by the sobor's members. In 1651 and 1653 the government summoned the Zemskii Sobor to discuss the requests of Ukrainian Hetman Bogdan Khmelnytskii that the Ukraine be taken under the tsar's protection; the tsar followed its predictable advice. In the second half of the seventeenth century, the authority of the Zemskii Sobor declined as the government generally gained stability and self-confidence. Thus the electoral sobory of 1598 and 1613 were temporary bearers of the supreme state power. Although exceptional, they signified the importance of the institution in times of political crisis. Customarily, however, the Zemskii Sobor performed only consultative functions as illustrated above. It had neither the power nor the inclination to limit the power of the tsar, but rather supported and aided his absolute authority.

● The administration. Consisting of myriad agencies and departments, each usually headed by an influential boyar, assisted by lesser nobles, secretaries, clerks, and poorly paid, overworked underlings, the administration was notorious for its abuse of authority, unscrupulous behavior, debauchery, and corruption.[3]

● The streltsy. The streltsy, a permanent but unkempt and unreliable group of pikemen and musketeers recruited from among the "commoners," were the core of the military establishment. They guarded the Kremlin and therefore wielded ultimate power at times of national crisis. European and Asian mercenaries also played significant roles, but they were expensive and their loyalty was often dubious. In addition, various units of cossacks operated in Siberia and on the southern frontiers of the country.

● The church. Lastly, although weakened by the outcome of the great schism, the hierarchy of the Russian Orthodox church constituted an important pillar of the tsar's power.

SOCIAL STRUCTURE

Though no significant society is entirely hierarchical in its socioeconomic structure, the Muscovite state of the mid-seventeenth century definitely

---

[3] There were, of course, some exceptional administrators of outstanding intellectual capacity and integrity, such as A.L. Ordin-Nashchokin (*ca.* 1620–80). Trained in mathematics, German, Polish, and Swedish, he combined distinguished qualities of diplomat, military leader, and administrator. While serving as military and administrative leader of Pskov he persuaded the officials under his jurisdiction and the decision makers of the area to adopt a charter of self-government—albeit, most of his administrative reforms were obstructed by influential members of the landed aristocracy. For an appraisal of his political thought in English, see C.B. O'Brien, "Early Political Consciousness in Muscovy: The Views of Juraj Križanić and Afanasij Ordin-Naščokin," in Eekman and Kadić, 209–22; for comprehensive discussions of his ideas and works in Russian, see V.S. Ikonnikov, "Blizhnii boiarin Afanasii Lavrentevich Ordyn-Nashchokin," in *Russkaia Starina*, XL (1883), 17–66 and 273–308; V.O. Kliuchevskii, *Kurs russkoi istorii* (Moscow, 1957), III, 334–51; and I. Galaktionov, *Ranniaia perepiska A.L. Ordina-Nashchokina* (Saratov, 1968).

approached that form. The society was based in principle on the obligations of its members to the tsar. Three groups can readily be identified. First, there was the landowning class, who, under the principle of the "servitor state," manned the military and the civil service; they were designated "service people" (*sluzhilye liudi*). This group included princes, boyars, petty nobles, and churchmen. In return for the landed estates and other rewards granted them, they were under obligation to perform lifelong service to the tsar in whatever capacity he deemed fit. The second group were designated taxpayers (*tiaglye liudi*), and included military men, merchants, craftsmen, workers, and peasants. They were obliged to work for the state, the servitors, or the church. The third group consisted of foreigners in Russian government service: Western Europeans hired on a contractual basis and conquered colonial natives of Siberia and northern Asia (*inorodtsy*), who were required to pay an annual tribute to the tsar. Much of this stratification was expressed in the Ulozhenie of 1649, which perpetuated the reigning political structure. It formally marked the decline of the ancient aristocracy, the continued and significant growth of the landed gentry, and the weak emergence of a commercial and industrial class.

The population of Russia was most probably about 10 million, of whom around 85 per cent were serfs (and state peasants). Actual slaves comprised the second largest social group—about 10 per cent of the population. Next came the townsmen (approximately 2 per cent) and the "service elite" (less than 2 per cent). In addition to farming, hunting was widespread in the northern parts of the country. Official classifications usually recorded the occupations of craftsmen—for example, bakers and distillers; artisans, such as furriers, tanners, and smiths; and miscellaneous industrial workers employed in metallurgical and armament enterprises, potash manufacture, mining, salt production, and so forth.

As compared with most Western European nations, to whose history Krizhanich illuminatingly refers, an extremely small proportion of the Russian population was engaged in manufacturing, commerce, and foreign trade. In the aforementioned nations, there had already been a more or less integrated expansion of agriculture, commerce, manufacturing, and banking institutions. This was Krizhanich's explicit economic objective for Russia.[4]

But Russia had hardly begun to integrate these economic sectors on any significant scale. It had not even commenced to experience the agrarian

---

[4] The interdependence is stressed in *Politika*, particularly in chapters 13, 31, and 43; infra, 91–4, 161–5, 212–27.

revolutions that, especially in England, had structurally and legally transformed medieval manors into grain, wool, and meat factories, and thus gradually destroyed the old repressive relationship of landlord and peasant. Because of their extremely slow development during the six-teenth and seventeenth centuries, capitalist institutions in agriculture, commerce, and industry had impinged only slightly on the continued rule of the landed military classes in Russia.

A primitive agriculture therefore remained at the base of the Russian socioeconomic pyramid, and Krizhanich ascribed major significance for Russia's economic development to its transformation. It was organized along the lines of peasant serfdom, but with uniquely Russian features. Contrary to the case in most Western European countries, serfdom in Russia had virtually nothing to do with feudalism.[5] From the mid-sixteenth to the mid-seventeenth century, the Muscovite state expanded enormously, accompanied not only by an extension of centralization and standardization, but by a *strengthening* of serfdom, particularly in the southern, southeastern, and, to a large extent, the western parts of the country. No law had ever been passed establishing serfdom; it simply grew by custom, with the peasants initially bound to the land, not to a lord. Unlike slaves, serfs owned their own means of production, such as tools, seed, and buildings, though not the land they tilled. Ordinarily, they paid taxes and, of course, rent in the form of money, produce, and assigned labor on the lord's estates. With the striking exception of Siberia and a few other areas, enserfment of the peasants had actually reached its completion before the mid-seventeenth century. The Ulozhenie of 1649 eliminated any statute of limitations for fugitive serfs, thereby granting the provincial nobility, in particular, what it wanted: the right to treat serfs practically as slaves. By that time, serfs comprised all tillers of the soil on private landholdings, and the existing hierarchy of social stratifi-cation had become virtually a caste system.

The landholding system comprised extensive hereditary estates, palace and state lands, church and monastery holdings, and communal and

---

[5] The first Russian census was taken during the period 1550–80, and it had the effect of strengthening serfdom, for it recorded peasant residences and listed children of serfs in the same category as their parents. The Russian *locus classicus* on these issues is V.O. Kliuchevskii, *Istoriia soslovii v Rossii*, 3rd edition (Petrograd, 1918). For comprehensive discussions in English, see Richard Hellie, *Enserfment and Military Change in Muscovy* (Chicago, 1971), and *Slavery in Russia, 1450–1725* (Chicago, 1982), esp. the discussion on "Slave Occupations," 460–502, and on "The Importance of Slavery in Russia," 679–720. See also his "Recent Soviet Historiography on Medieval and Early Modern Russian Slavery," *Russian Review* (January 1976); and Jerome Blum, *Lord and Peasant in Russia: From the Ninth to the Nineteenth Century* (Princeton, 1961), esp. 199–276.

peasant-held land. In all cases, however, the form of organization was abysmally backward, the methods of production primitive. The administration of large estates was centralized and unwieldy. Absentee landlords usually hired a chief steward—a bondslave of Russian or foreign origin—to run a central office in Moscow. Ordinarily, the lord also hired a local steward for each estate to carry out orders from the center. At the bottom of the command were peasant officials who, in conjunction with the local steward, collected some of the lord's revenue and produce.[6] For the most part, unauthorized movement of peasants and of nearly all other workers was prohibited by law. The underlying causes of the grinding poverty of the peasants, frequent famines, and widespread starvation lay in the incompetent, rapacious rulers and supervisory personnel whose regulations and practices thwarted and distorted economic incentives; in the harsh climatic conditions and poor soil; and in the illiteracy and apathy of the peasants. Low sun-spot activity, known as the "Maunder minimum," further reduced agricultural yields. In consequence, approximately 10 per cent of Russia's peasants, the "poorest of the poor," intermittently had no better alternative than to sell themselves into slavery: for neither the state, the church, nor the rich landlords undertook any responsibility for the destitute. Their position continued so to deteriorate that, by the time Krizhanich was writing his *Politika,* the buying, selling, and "willing" of serfs had become common practices.

The gentry and other slaveowners, whose services were increasingly demanded by the state, were in turn provided with an assured cheap labor supply. Unlike other societies based on slavery, however, most slaves in Russia were indigenous in origin. They were primarily household slaves, dependant on the wealth and income of their owners, and it is doubtful whether they contributed much to the net national output. The slaves held the lowest rank in Muscovite households, agriculture, and military activity. They were the sluggish substratum of an economically backward and apathetic peasantry, the two together forming the traditional agricultural base of the Russian political economy.

---

[6] The available evidence shows that agricultural productivity was extremely low; moreover, it appears to have been about the same in the beginning and end of the century. Even on the better managed estates, e.g., those of Boris I. Morozov, in 1661 the rye and oats crop, respectively, ranged between 2.5–5.2 and 2.1–5.4 times the amount of seed sown. See D.I. Petrikeev, *Krupnoe krepostnoe khoziaistvo XVII v.* (Leningrad, 1967), 95. The prices of rye and oats between 1627–8 and 1679–80, relative to indexes of available "overall" prices, do not appear to have significantly changed. See Iu. A. Tikhonov, *Pomeshch'ic krest'iane v Rossii* (Moscow, 1974), 105–16. During crisis prices fluctuated enormously. For pertinent background information, see R.E.F. Smith, *Peasant Farming in Muscovy* (Cambridge, 1977), 128–9, 141–57, 227–40.

The spread of serfdom and slavery substantially influenced the lifestyle of the slaveowners. Possession of slaves contributed to the prestige and support of both the rising gentry and the upper-middle service classes. Slavery as an institution reinforced the interdependence of power, fear, and hatred at all levels of the society and provided the upper service classes with some relief from the incessant financial and personal pressures emanating from the highest levels of tsarist officialdom.

As already noted, Siberia was an exception to the establishment of serfdom in the Muscovite state. The realities of geography, economics, and politics there favored the development of a social system different from that of the rest of Russia. The state treasury had a strong interest in the taxation of the Siberian fur trade, however, and the Siberian department in Moscow had charge of the area. It was nonetheless impossible to control the escape of fugitive serfs in that vast, glacial territory, and neither had the government any need of the gentry's administrative services in Siberia, nor the nobility any desire to serve there. As government officials and other European Russians arrived and assimilated with the natives—intermarriage was a commonplace—the region exhibited qualities of sturdiness and independence. Faced with these clear and formidable realities, the Russian state and church adapted shrewdly and flexibly. Although not without elements of brutality and harshness, Russia's expansion into and colonization of Siberia was comparatively "moderate"—a gigantic and successful imperial endeavor.[7]

Krizhanich recognized that the divergence between complex administrative needs and a rigid administration would generate further social and political stress. He provides ample and powerfully stated evidence for the probable legacy of a peasantry so browbeaten as to be benumbed and fatalistic. He forewarned that continued oppression of the peasants would ossify Russia's backwardness and induce rebellion. In effect, he was

---

[7] Classic works by Russian scholars on early Siberian colonization and administration include: S.V. Bakhrushin, *Ocherki po istorii kolonizatsii Sibiri v XVI i XVII vekakh* (Moscow, 1927); V.I. Ogorodnikov, *Ocherki istorii Sibiri do nachala XIX st.* (Vladivostok, 1924); and V.I. Shunkov, *Ocherki po istorii kolonizatsii Sibiri v XVII—nachale XVIII v* (Moscow, 1946); *Istoriia Sibiri*, 5 vols. (Leningrad, 1968), esp. vol. 2. Outstanding works in English on Siberia's early fur trade and administration are: Raymond H. Fisher, *The Russian Fur Trade, 1550–1700* (Berkeley, 1943), and George V. Lantzeff, *Siberia in the Seventeenth Century* (Berkeley, 1943). More recent works important to our analysis have drawn on illuminating information contained in the Siberian archives, superseding some of the earlier conclusions of both Russian and Western scholars; see footnote 26. For a brief analysis of the historical literature and recent source materials, see Basil Dmytryshyn, "Russian Expansion to the Pacific, 1580–1700: A Historiographical Review," *Slavic Studies* 25 (Hokkaido University, 1980), 1–25.

among the first of the Slavic "modernizers"—if not the first—who argued perceptively for transforming the role of the Russian peasantry toward a freer, more flexible agriculture. To his credit, he also was one of the first Russophiles to examine the implications of Siberian colonization and development in detail.

As the size of various units of the armed forces grew in conjunction with Russia's wars of conquest in Europe and Asia, the rigidly stratified civil bureaucracy was enlarged. This drain of ablebodied men further aggravated economic conditions and engendered social stress. Krizhanich had observed that these features of Russian society had made their appearance long before his time. But the magnitude of Russia's resumed territorial expansion in the three or four decades before his exile to Tobolsk was truly phenomenal. To be sure, as early as the beginning of the sixteenth century, Russia had already expanded from a landlocked state of some 90,000 square miles to a powerful empire extending from the Arctic Ocean to the 55th parallel and from the Gulf of Finland to the Ural Mountains. Moscow had terminated centuries-old Mongol domination, annexed several of the lesser principalities of "Rus," conquered the vast republic of Novgorod, and waged a series of comparatively successful wars against Sweden, Lithuania, and Livonia for free access to the Baltic. During the period 1580 to 1650, moreover, huge territorial gains had been made in Asia. By the mid-seventeenth century, the principality of Moscow had therefore emerged as the major power in Russia, and Russia had emerged as a potentially major military power both in Europe and in Asia.[8]

Krizhanich drew attention, however, to the strains caused in his own lifetime by Russia's wars with Poland, the Ukrainian Cossacks, and the Crimean Tartars. Although he sympathetically portrayed the indelible suffering and fear caused by foreign invasions, marauding, and brigandage, he nonetheless cautioned against Russia's own overextended use of military power. Indirectly, he even expressed concern about the developing conflict with China over Russian intrusion into areas claimed by the Chinese. He insisted that Russia should pursue peaceful international economic policies, particularly with neighboring countries, as well as with other nations of Europe and Asia: "It is better to have a loyal and willing neighbor than to annex him and become one nation," he wrote,

[8] During the sixteenth and seventeenth centuries, respectively, Russia nearly doubled and tripled its territory. It expanded from approximately 5,400,000 square kilometers in 1600 to 15,280,000 square kilometers in 1700, the latter size being 68.2 per cent of present-day territory of the Soviet Union.

"since such a firm neighborhood bond creates an area free of danger for the monarchy."[9]

INDUSTRY AND TRADE

From the 1620s to the 1660s, Russian commerce and industry—notably in the fields closely linked with military expansion and modernization—gradually underwent a limited degree of economic development. In these fields, on the surface at least, the environment appeared stable. But emerging conflicts of interest between classes, and among different groups within them, intensified national stress. The status of prominent merchants and various categories of the bureaucracy, in particular, was exceptionally fluid. The first edition of the Ulozhenie of 1649 placed the *diaki* (state secretaries who were at the apex of the professional bureaucracy) above the *gosti* (an eminent group of merchants). In a second printing of the Ulozhenie later that year, however, as they jostled for presumed power, this ranking was reversed and the *gosti* were placed above the *diaki*.[10] Actually, none of the occupational groups exerted any significant political or economic influence on the government independently or if at variance with overall policies of the state.

By the early 1660s, in a small number of significant cases, Russian large-scale industry (as distinguished from handicrafts and household small-scale industry) had developed to a moderate degree. Basically, it had evolved as manorial industry. Throughout the sixteenth and seventeenth centuries, large-scale projects in salt extraction and potash production were established by prominent Russian families, to whom Krizhanich had occasion to refer.[11] The early 1630s, however, marked a turning point: an epoch followed, including the period of Krizhanich's writing of the *Politika,* when Russia's new large-scale industries were established primarily by foreigners. Assisted by the state, they were organized by way of charters granted by the tsar. Often with the encouragement of their own governments and of Russian agents, selected foreign merchants migrated to Russia, where they became merchant-manufacturers. The skills and experience of European masters and tech-

---

[9] *Politika,* infra, 57.
[10] Richard Hellie, *Slavery in Russia, 1450–1725,* 12; Samuel H. Baron, "Who Were the Gosti?" *California Slavic Studies* 7 (1973), 1–40; N.I. Kostomarov, "Ocherki torgovli Moskovskogo gosudarstva v XVI i XVII stoletiiakh," *Sobranie Sochinenii* (St Petersburg, 1905), vol. 20, book 8, 319.
[11] *Politika,* infra, e.g., 21–2, 42–3, 53.

BARENTS SEA

Ust
Tsylma
Berezov
FURS
Surgut
Archangel
WHITE
SEA
TIMBER
BALTIC
SEA
Solvychegodsk
Tobolsk
Solikamsk
Pskov Novgorod
Irbit
Iaroslavl
FLAX Tver Nizhnii
Novgorod Kazan
RYE
Smolensk
Moscow
Temnikov
Tula POTASH
POLAND Briansk WHEAT
Kursk
Kiev OATS
Belgorod BARLEY CATTLE
UKRAINE HORSES
SHEEP
Azov ASTRAKHAN Astrakhan
KIRGHIZ STEPPE
ARAL
SEA
KHANATE
OF
CRIMEA
CASPIAN
SEA
BLACK SEA

▲ Iron ore mining (4)	☆ Hand-operated blast furnace (1)
△ Iron foundries and smelters (9)	⌷ Glassmaking (1)
◉ Metal processing (5)	◮ Salt extracting (12)
◆ Copper smelter (1) & ◇ processing (1)	⛴ Shipbuilding (6)
✳ Potash mills (6)	■ Textiles (5)
◉ Principal fairs (7)	● Fur-trade center (9)

Map 4   Seventeenth-century industry and agriculture in Muscovite Russia

nicians were thus combined with Russian unskilled labor and natural resources. Political and military influence in the establishment and operation of these industries can hardly be exaggerated. The prototype was iron mining and manufacturing.[12]

Holland, England, and Sweden had all endeavored to obtain a monopoly on the export of Russian grain, and in 1627 Andrei Vinius, a Dutch merchant originally named Dionys T. Winius, arrived in Russia. In 1630–31 Dutch envoys opened negotiations in Moscow with the hope of securing an export monopoly on Russian grain and saltpeter, but to no avail. Legally, the tsar himself had a monopoly on the Russian grain trade, but foreign merchants in Russia had established a fixed price above which they would not purchase grain from Tsar Mikhail's reserves. With the price of grain in Western Europe substantially higher than this "purchase price" plus the cost of transport, Vinius broke the "ring" and offered the tsar a much higher price for his grain. In June 1631 Vinius was granted the right to purchase close to one million bushels of grain from the tsar's reserves, a transaction that yielded the tsar immense profits. In appreciation, Mikhail granted Vinius not only the title of *gost,* with all its attendant privileges, but also special tariff concessions on exports and imports, as well as significant commercial and personal privileges. This was the background for the organization by Vinius of Russia's first large-scale iron industry.

In 1632 Vinius, and two Dutch partners (Abraham Vinius and Julius Willeken), were granted a charter by Tsar Mikhail to construct water-powered iron manufactories. Russia, Vinius had argued, was paying unnecessarily high prices for some of its iron imports and Western armaments. These goods, he contended, could be produced in Russia, economizing on transportation costs, saving foreign exchange, and training Russian workers. Furthermore, there was urgent need for techno-logical change in the armed forces: cavalry that shot arrows increasingly had to be replaced by artillery that fired cannon balls. The tsar's charter was granted for a period of ten years, stipulating that no other foreigners would be permitted to manufacture iron in Russia. For this period, the charter also provided exemptions from import and export duties, as well as from domestic taxation. The tsar undertook to purchase such quantities

---

[12] For comprehensive discussions and bibliographies on the early history of the Russian iron industry and other forms of manufacturing, as well as geneologies of the main participants, see Erik Amburger, *Die Familie Marselis* (Giessen, 1957), esp. 11–20, 92–130, 193–214; and Joseph T. Fuhrmann, *The Origins of Capitalism in Russia* (Chicago, 1972), esp. 51–268, Appendix III, 273–6, 343–52. See also Bushkovitch, *The Merchants of Moscow,* 127–50, 177–9, 192–3.

of the firm's production as the government might require at prices fixed by the charter for cannon, plank iron, rod iron, and cannon balls. Each year Vinius was to receive an advance from the government in partial payment for the goods to be delivered to it during that year. Any goods produced that the government did not wish to purchase could be sold in Russia on the open market or, if permission were granted by the tsar, exported. After a period of four years from the date of the charter, if the firm sold any goods in the open market more cheaply than stipulated by the charter, it would be obliged to make similar concessions to the state. The charter specifically stipulated that the iron manufactories be situated in the vicinity of Tula, shown on Map 4.

Russia's financial markets were among the least developed of its economic institutions. The fear of illiquidity and political disgrace called for investment in various forms of what may be termed "insurance." Accordingly, several months after Vinius had obtained his charter, he took on two more partners, Peter Marselis and Thomas de Swain. As a further precautionary motive (and since some of the former members had left the enterprise), in 1638 Boris I. Morozov—who had already befriended the then heir to the throne, Alexei—was incorporated into the firm as a "silent partner," the first known case of a Russian nobleman participating in a large-scale manufactory principally owned and managed by foreigners.[13] In the late 1630s, Vinius and his group established four iron mills at Tula.

Between 1632 and 1662 (the year before Krizhanich began writing his *Politika*), Europeans had established ten large-scale iron mills in Russia. They built eight more in the ensuing decades of the century. Foreign entrepreneurs also played a major role in the establishment of gunpowder and copper works, glass and paper factories, and leather tanneries, as well as flax spinning and silk weaving; near the close of the century they organized textile mills and sawmills as well. *In toto,* during the seventeenth century foreigners had established eighteen (65 per cent) of the large-scale iron manufactories; the Russian state, three (11 per cent); Russian nobles, two (7 per cent); and Russian non-nobles, five (17 per cent). As regards other large-scale enterprises, in the sixteenth and seventeenth centuries foreigners had established fifteen (52 per cent); the

---

[13] A new charter was issued in 1639 incorporating these changes; in addition to Andrei Vinius, Peter Marselis, and Boris I. Morozov, the new partnership included L. Theilmann Akkema. All other earlier partners had left the enterprise. Cf. Amburger, *Die Familie Marselis,* 100–101 (and his reference to Krizhanich's views on foreigners and, by inference, their possible influence on the New Commercial Code of 1667, 143–4). See also Fuhrmann, *Origins of Capitalism in Russia,* 59–79.

Russian government, nine (31 per cent); Russian nobles, one (3 per cent); Russian non-nobles, three (11 per cent); and the church, one (3 per cent). Foreigners therefore set up a total of thirty-three (58 per cent) of the fifty-seven large-scale iron mills and other manufactories established during this period.[14] For the time, this was a modest new industrial capacity relative to that of the more advanced Western European nations, but considerable when compared to Russia's east-central European neighbors.

The foreign merchants formed a distinct and conspicuous part of the environment. Although they were not connected in any direct way with the serf-operated estates, they obtained unskilled labor through special governmental assignment of state peasant-serfs and by hiring "voluntary" workers who were eager to be employed at least partially for money wages. Working under the supervision of European technicians, an increasing number of Russians thus became skilled masters and foremen. It is noteworthy that the foreign firms were owned predominantly by private individuals, operating for profit from the sale of goods to the government, on the domestic market, and to foreign markets.[15] They helped lay the foundation of an industrial labor force, made investments in the form of real and financial capital, provided marketing knowledge and facilities for exports and imports, and established an indispensable link between foreign and domestic markets for the provision of both military and non-military goods. However, as regards the gains among different classes, the operations of the foreign entrepreneurs primarily had the effect of enhancing their own wealth and well-being and that of the Russian merchant-manufacturers and the tsarist aristocracy.[16] Understandably, when combined with frequent and gross misuse of privilege, the operations of the foreign merchants also had the effect of intensifying class conflict and social unrest.

Increasingly, archival research indicates that the contribution of domestic merchants to Russia's industrial development in the seventeenth century may have been no less than that of foreign merchants.[17] These

---

[14] Furhmann, *Origins of Capitalism in Russia*, Table on p. 244.

[15] Krizhanich emphasized, however, the particular historical context of this market behavior: "When merchants start to trade they should be made aware that they are trading at the exclusive prerogative of the king, and that all their activities should benefit the ruler and the entire nation," *Politika*, infra, 178.

[16] See Peter I. Lyashchenko, *History of the National Economy of Russia*, trans. by L.M. Herman (New York, 1949), 222–5. Though difficult to document, some economic gains doubtless accrued to the urban population, and especially to the hired workers and probably to the townsmen and peasants who made handicrafts. See *Politika*, infra, 163.

[17] See Bushkovitch, *Merchants of Moscow*, 102–50, 170–71.

indigenous contributions were associated with the evolution of Russia's
agricultural production and the household processing and manufacturing
of commodities and handicrafts on monastic and other estates. Krizhanich
explains how key Russian markets functioned in this developing environment, and his policy recommendations throw light on the existing
obstructions to substantial economic advance.

Potash, or crude potassium carbonate, was one of the earliest industrial
chemicals. A basic input in manufacturing mass-produced goods such as
salt, soap, and leather products, it was in large demand, and Russia was
well endowed with resources to supply it. A number of noblemen turned
merchant-manufacturers organized large-scale potash enterprises on their
estates. The chemical was produced by lixiviating wood ashes and
evaporating the solution to dryness, an operation carried out in iron
pots—hence the name from "pot" and "ash." The wood was practically
free. The laborers at the potash sites were mainly serfs performing
assigned work on their lords' estates and, ordinarily, a small proportion of
hired hands. The work was extremely disagreeable, bringing on cough-
ing, smarting eyes, and respiratory ailments. The serfs resented the
unconscionable demands made on them and often fled. Not surprisingly,
the hired workers performed their tasks better than did the non-hired
ones.[18] Krizhanich drew attention to the extreme variability in the supply
of potash, and hence in its price.[19] He showed how the structure of the
potash market could be improved and (more generally in the *Politika*) how
the law of supply and demand could better be taken advantage of in
economic development. And rightly so, for historically changes in relative
costs and prices have been the mainspring that has produced the necessary
incentives for economic efficiency and modernization.

Labor was scarce in Central Russia, and acutely so in the Moscow
region.[20] With the strengthening of serfdom and the attendant rise in the
supply of assigned labor, any tendency for wages to rise was held in check.
Indeed, the cost of producing potash remained low and the industry
thrived as the producers sold their increasing output to the government,
to domestic enterprises, and to merchants, who occasionally resold their

---

[18] In 1660, Boris I. Morozov recruited 346 workers from his estates in Galich and sent
them to his potash mills. According to Morozov, they turned out to be better workers than
the non-hired local serfs. See Petrikeev, *Krupnoe krepostnoe khoziaistvo xvii v.*, 120–1 and
sources cited therein.

[19] *Politika*, infra, 42–3.

[20] Hellie, *Slavery in Russia*, 11; R.E.F. Smith, *Peasant Farming in Muscovy* (Cambridge,
1977), 150; Lyashchenko, *History of the National Economy*, 201.

stocks, *seriatim,* to other merchants in ever-larger commercial centers.[21] A small amount was also sold to foreign traders for export. Generally, the large-scale potash producers managed their enterprises well. Boris I. Morozov, one of the major producers, reports that he had made a profit on his investment of no less than 50 per cent.[22]

In the mid-seventeenth century, salt production was Russia's main industry. Entrepreneurship was concentrated among Russian merchants, and the Stroganovs, whom Krizhanich had commended, were the largest producers.[23] The national and interregional markets were quite well developed, with costs, prices, and profits providing essential signals and incentives for the satisfactory organization of production and distribution. Salt was a necessity for preserving food, especially meat; it was in demand everywhere and shipped from the edges of the country to the more populous urban centers. Historically, the northern districts along the White Sea had provided the richest salt wells—the area, in fact where the Stroganovs had founded their empire. Here salt was discovered underground. The tsar had granted the Stroganovs large tracts of land in order to extract the salt and to fell the trees that fueled the furnaces. But the technology of salt mining and salt boiling remained virtually unchanged throughout the seventeenth century, with productivity depending primarily on the density of the salt found in the ground. As the richer salt wells ran dry, the Stroganovs transferred their major investments to the salt wells south of Solikamsk. By mid-seventeenth century, the north was no longer the main center for the country's salt production. This was a major economic adjustment carried out principally in accordance with market forces.

Although the government was an important potential source of land grants and commercial privileges, the Muscovite state was not the decisive factor in the development of the salt industry. It had its own salt works in the Lower Volga, which it effectively farmed out to Russian merchants. The record suggests that state enterprises were managed less efficiently

---

[21] Potash "was extremely cheap; half a ton cost 12 kopeks about the middle of the seventeenth century. At this period the demand for potash increased greatly as glass manufacturing developed . . ." Smith, *Peasant Farming in Muscovy,* 56; based on P.M. Lukianov's impressive *Istoriia khimicheskikh promyslov i khimicheskoi promyshlennosti Rossii do kontsa XIX veka,* (Moscow, 1949), vol. 2, 7. Cf. also Crummey, *Aristocrats and Servitors,* 130–3.

[22] Petrikeev, *Krupnoe krepostnoe khoziaistvo,* 124.

[23] For background material on the history of the Russian salt industry, see Lyashchenko, *History of the National Economy,* 160–3, 211–15; Bushkovitch, *Merchants of Moscow,* 127–50; A.A. Vvedenskii, *Dom Stroganovykh* (Moscow, 1962); and *Politika,* infra, 21–2, 53.

when they were operated directly by the government.[24] Several monasteries also owned and managed large salt works that competed favorably with both private and government enterprises. In regions such as Astrakhan and the Lower Volga, salt was found in marshes and lakes. Here the cost of production was comparatively low, and the producers competed successfully with the larger more heavily capitalized merchants of the commercial centers.

The rise and fall of the salt industry in Staraia Russa is particularly instructive. This industry had been destroyed during the Time of Troubles, but in the 1630s Moscow merchants resurrected it. On the basis of prevailing technology, they constructed new combinations of enlarged boilers, iron pans, and buildings. Productivity per boiler was nearly doubled and the merchants earned a high yield on their investment. Subsequently, however, salt from the Lower Volga and the Perm became available in Staraia Russa at lower prices. The Moscow merchants had no choice but to disinvest and to reinvest in other areas, a primary requisite for effective economic development. But in the rhetoric of failing markets, the experience of the salt industry in Staraia Russa is erroneously cited as proof of "instability" in the market environment of seventeenth-century Russia.[25]

Though no definitive study of Russia's state trade during the seventeenth century is yet available, recent research based on data in the Siberian archives appears to show that at about 1650 merchants, rather than the government, had conducted most of the fur trade. Furs were a very important commodity in the government's finances and foreign trade. Sable, ermine, beaver, and other valuable fur-bearing animals abounded in Siberia. As Russian rule spread the natives of Siberia were required to pay a tribute in furs (the *iasak*) to their new sovereign. At least once a year they had to supply a specified number of furs at a designated place. Traders were also assessed a tax in sable at the rate of 10 per cent of

---

[24] The Volga salt works, which were the property of the state, were managed from at least 1614 until the 1620s by wealthy merchants who were elected with the guarantee by the community for their honesty and efficiency. From about 1630 to 1680, they were farmed out to wealthy merchants. See Bushkovitch, *Merchants of Moscow*, 140. More generally, as E.I. Iarantseva wrote: "In 1662 the treasury took over the biggest metallurgical and iron founding mills, which belonged to the Danish industrialist Peter Marselis. Under the treasury's control the mills fell into ruin. Thus, in view of Marselis' ability and enterprise, Ordyn-Nashchokin decided that they should be returned to their former owner" (A.I. Pashkov, ed. of original edition), John M. Letiche, ed. and tr. from the Russian (with collaboration of Basil Dmytryshyn and Richard A. Pierce) *A History of Russian Economic Thought: Ninth through Eighteenth Centuries* (Berkeley, 1964), 226.
[25] G.S. Rabinovich, *Gorod soli: Staraia Russa v kontse XVI-seredine XVII vv.*, (Leningrad, 1973) 72, 208–20.

the value of any transaction in furs; and they were assessed many other
levies by local officials. It was the hunters of the villages and towns of
northern Russia who played the leading role in bringing the sable to
market. In certain areas of Siberia, the merchants of European Russia—
mostly of Moscow—organized expeditions of native hunters by paying
wages, loaning equipment, and even making financial advances on the
expected pelts. The receipts in sable by the Moscow government from the
10 per cent tax paid by the merchants, as compared with receipts from the
tribute paid by the natives, appear to indicate that shipments of sables by
merchants from Siberia were larger than the tribute plus tax.[26] Given the
abundance of wild furs in Siberia, it was the costs and prices facing the
hunters and merchants—more than the commands of the government or
its operations—that provided the incentives essentially responsible for the
prosperity of Siberia in the second quarter of the seventeenth century.

The merchants of Moscow, as well as those of smaller commercial
centers, furnished a form of "commercial intermediation" that was the
nexus for the economic complementarity between these centers and the
periphery. By servicing and provisioning geographical specialization—
from furs, wax, and honey to hempen cordage, tallow, and linen
products—they fused the sources of supply and demand within and
between domestic and foreign markets. Foreign and Russian merchants
prominently settled in the large and small commercial centers from
Archangel and Novgorod to Astrakhan and Kazan, encompassing numerous provincial towns and cities that also harbored military personnel and
instructors—foreign and Russian—who supplemented their pay by en-
gaging in part-time commerce. While quite a number of urban areas in
neighboring continental countries were undergoing a decline associated,
inter alia, with deteriorating terms of trade, Russian cities and towns were
experiencing a revival.[27]

Incipient Russian industry benefited from an otherwise retrogressive

---

[26] These results are based on Russian works that have drawn on illuminating information
contained in the Siberian archives, superseding some of the earlier conclusions of both
Russian and Western scholars. See Bushkovitch, *The Merchants of Moscow*, 110–26, and
sources cited on 191–2.

[27] Russian towns and cities benefited from the processing of a substantial number of export
products (e.g., leather, tallow, linen, coarse cloth), and this may have prevented Russia's
commodity terms of trade from deteriorating relative to those of East-Central European
countries. Contrariwise, referring to Poland, Bohemia, Hungary, and Croatia, Zsigmond
Pál Pach has argued that the deterioration in their commodity terms of trade—the fall in
the prices of their agricultural exports relative to the prices of their manufactured
imports—which occurred when the "price revolution" in Western European countries
came to an end by the middle of the seventeenth century, was an important cause of their
urban decline. See his paper, "The Role of East-Central Europe in International Trade,"
Études Historiques (Budapest, 1970), esp. 259–64.

factor. The system of serf labor, whereby serfs were often assigned to work on their lords' estates three or four days per week, had applied principally to the provinces of central Russia. In the 1630s and 1640s, as serfdom was intensified, the system was extended to the lords' industrial activities, marking the origin of serf industry in the Muscovite state. This provided an impetus to increase industrial production, promoting an expansion of exports, effective demand, and imports. It enhanced the unifying effect on the structure of markets; indeed, by the mid-seventeenth century, Russia's local markets had been substantially integrated into a national market.[28]

In the aggregate, Russia's major imports came from Holland, Germany, Sweden, and England. The main categories were woolen cloth, metals, arms, and silver coins, followed by a long list of consumer goods and agricultural implements: paper, herring, wines, apothecary goods, sickles, metal wares, and so forth. Archangel was the hub of Russia's northern commerce. Around 1650 it was the entrepôt for such important exports as grains (notably in years of shortage in the West), leather, skins, furs, tallow, and potash. Astrakhan was a major entrepôt for the trade with Asia and the East. Salt, leather furs, and iufti (smooth leather products) constituted the main exports; silk, cotton, and safian (finely worked goat skin) were among the significant imports. The overland trade route across central Europe to Leipzig was attracting attention, with high-quality Russian furs featured as exports and English broadcloth as the import.

The structure of Russia's foreign trade was undergoing significant change, with exports shifting from commodities based primarily on forest products (furs, leather skins, wax) to commodities based on agricultural products (grains, tallow, hemp). The exported agricultural products were to an increasing degree processed goods (e.g., meat and lard). Flax, potash, and mica were also becoming important exports. Correspondingly, imports were changing from simple to technologically more advanced products: metals, agricultural implements, more technically

---

[28] "By the middle of the seventeenth century," Lyashchenko wrote with some exaggeration, "the unifying influence of the market, no longer local but nationwide, began to be felt. It drew all regions of the land into the circulation of commodities," *History of the National Economy*, 202. Nonetheless, Krizhanich had emphasized Russia's underdeveloped market structures: the roads were long, difficult, and hazardous. In such overland trade journeys, many guides, guards, posts, and outlays of money were needed. This was an example where government "is required in business matters which private individuals cannot resolve. . . . Such assistance is greatly and desperately needed in this tsardom," *Politika*, infra, 18. Further he notes: "We should devote more attention to river transport—especially in Siberia—and do everything necessary to achieve it," ibid., 115.

advanced armaments, and a wide variety of consumer goods were growing in importance, as were gold and silver coins to supply an increasing demand for the transactions and savings functions of money.

The explanation for the expansion and structural advance of the industrial and commercial sectors rests chiefly in Russia's resource structure at the time and in its indigenous development. Her interregional trade was based to a substantial degree on the exchange of "land-intensive" commodities for one another among agents situated in widely dispersed areas—commodities that were produced with extremely limited human training and capital. Her interregional trade also reflected the exchange of "land-intensive" commodities for "labor-intensive" commodities produced by peasants on the estates and at monasteries, as well as by artisans in urban workshops. But the vast bulk of Russia's foreign trade was based on the exchange of her "land-intensive" commodities for distinctly more "capital-intensive" goods, produced with markedly greater human training and capital. Her exports were produced principally with resources she possessed in relative abundance; and the converse was true of her imports. By way of goods, therefore, most of Russia's foreign trade constituted an exchange of resources that were relatively abundant in Russia for resources that were relatively scarce. Generally, development was more consistent with modern neo-classical international trade theory, than with explanation in terms of malfunctioning markets, which is based on the belief that even after foreign trade has continually occurred, wholesale prices of the *same* commodities at home and abroad remained inordinately different from one another.[29] No substantive evidence has been presented to substantiate the latter proposition; at best, it is partially true and capable of explaining only an extremely limited amount of Russia's foreign trade. Accumulating evidence on the interdependence of Russia's price levels with those of the more advanced Western European countries would tend to refute it, as would the neo-classical theory of international trade.[30]

[29] The standard argument is as follows: "The economics of Muscovy's importation and exportation were founded to a considerable extent on the fabulously low prices of the marketed raw-material goods and the high prices at which they sold abroad. And, conversely, on comparatively low original prices of the imported goods from abroad and the high prices fetched by them in Moscow," Lyashchenko, *History of the National Economy,* 227. See also *Politika,* infra, 16, 131, for Krizhanich's views on monopoly pricing at the time. The conclusions of classical trade theory have often been robust notwithstanding important differences between its assumptions and actual economic conditions.

[30] Evidence on increasing interdependence of Russia's price levels with those of Western European countries is provided by N.W. Posthumus, *Inquiry into the History of Prices in Holland* (Leiden, 1946), vol. 1, 509, 516.

Nor were the demands of the government on the services of the merchants as preclusive of economic advance as has usually been maintained. To be sure, the prominent merchants of Moscow in particular were frequently called upon to serve as agents of the state. They bore the responsibility and tribulation of collecting tolls and taxes for the government; acted as brokers and agents for the state treasury; administered government enterprises; and, in emergencies, were even called upon to repay government debts incurred by local administrations to foreign merchants on behalf of the Moscow state. All exports and imports required permits, with government representatives always having first choice of potential sales or purchases. State monopolies had a discriminatory advantage over private merchants, and the privileged *gosti* paid no tariffs, which gave them a lucrative commercial advantage over the smaller traders. All taverns were exclusively controlled by the state, as was the production of the vodka sold by them. The state, furthermore, used the prominent merchants as its functionaries to farm out the taverns to lesser townsmen at the best possible terms. These impediments, which were ubiquitously intertwined with personal contacts at the tsarist court or at various levels of the administration, assuredly did incalculable harm to the operation of the economy. Still, many merchants found ways of eluding them; indirectly, some even exploited them. The evidence shows that quite a few amassed substantial fortunes.[31]

Nor can attempts to explain the nascent growth of trade and industry and, for that matter, the failure to achieve a significant transformation of the Russian economy, be explained convincingly in terms of rising tariffs. In the 1640s a "war of petitions" did break out among the merchants that consisted to a significant degree of special pleading for higher tariffs. Though it reflected an increase of entrants into manufacturing and a novel sense of their potential power, these protectionist pressures were constrained by the extremely limited ability of the new manufacturers to compete.[32] In 1646 the merchants were granted various forms of limited protectionism that were incorporated into the Ulozhenie of 1649. Tariffs against the Dutch in Archangel were raised from a range of 1.5–2 per cent

---

[31] For illustrative data, see Lyashchenko, *History of the National Economy*, 202, 213–14, 226–7; Crummey, *Aristocrats and Servitors*, 130–34; Bushkovitch, *Merchants of Moscow*, 151–67; Petrikeev, *Krupnoe krepostnoe khoziaistvo*, esp. 119–34.

[32] For large differences in costs of production between domestically produced goods and prices of imports, see Fuhrmann, *The Origins of Capitalism in Russia*, 327, n. 13. While costs of production in Russian iron manufacturing had declined substantially between the late 1630s and the late 1660s, and in the 1690s Russian glass, rope, gunpowder, and sawmill products were of high standard and reasonable cost (252), leather, silk, textiles, paper, and many other goods remained uncompetitive by international standards (250–52).

to 4.5–5 per cent ad valorem, and inland tolls from 3.5 per cent to 7 per cent.[33] Also, in the early 1650s the government made progress in harmonizing the tax structure and unifying the internal toll system. As the manufacturers gained experience, the government granted them further privileges at the expense of foreign merchants and domestic consumers. In the year after Krizhanich completed his *Politika,* the New Commercial Code of 1667 included an entire panoply of trade restrictions and increased tariffs of the mercantilist variety.[34] The theoretically superior device of protective subsidies, which were granted in a small number of carefully selected cases, appears to have been more successful than the comparatively indiscriminate use of protective tariffs, which was often abortive.

As regards foreign trade, from the 1630s to the 1660s it is certain that the prevailing trade barriers failed to prevent its gradual, and sometimes rapid, expansion. Understandably, the serious tensions of this period did not stem directly from the small industrial and commercial sectors: to some extent these even served as escape valves. Indeed, with only limited significant exceptions, it appears that wherever market forces were permitted to operate, economic progress was achieved. On the surface, therefore, the environment of the merchant-manufacturing class was comparatively peaceful. Krizhanich cautioned, however, that even here latent conflicts existed and were likely to erupt unless underlying obstructions to economic change were dealt with.

Transforming backward agriculture, Krizhanich realized, was the core of Russia's economic problem. But he also emphasized conflicts and harmonies in other socioeconomic spheres. Townsmen and peasants were

[33] This is stated in Dutch records: see Nikolaas Witsen, *Moscovische Reyse, 1664–1665* (The Hague, 1966), vol. 66, xxxii, n. 6. When Charles I of England was executed in 1649, Tsar Alexei showed his chagrin by expelling English merchants from all Russian cities except Archangel. The customs privileges that had been granted to the English, however, were not given to the Dutch, thus indirectly increasing Russian protectionism to a small degree. The already strong competitive position of the Dutch was nevertheless reinforced, even though the English merchants were soon permitted to re-enter Russian cities of the interior.

[34] For the complete text of the New Commercial Code, see "Novotorgovyi Ustav," in *Polnoe Sobranie Zakonov Rossiiskoi Imperii* . . . 1st series, vol. 1, no. 408 (April 22, 1667, old calendar). The preamble to the Code makes it clear that the objective of raising revenue for the treasury was no less important than that of attempting to achieve prosperity via mercantilist devices. See esp. Articles 36–37, 40–89, 92, and 94. The Code was prepared under the supervision of Ordin-Nashchokin, and has been analyzed by K.V. Bazilevich, "Novotorgovyi ustav 1667 g. (K voprosu o ego istochnikakh)," *Izvestiia Akademii Nauk SSSR. Otdelenie obshchestvennykh nauk,* no. 7 (1932), 589–622; and A.I. Andreev, "Novotorgovyi ustav 1667 g. (K istorii ego sostavleniia)," *Istoricheskie zapiski* III (1941), 303–7.

becoming increasingly incensed against the oppressive tax system. They regarded the tax-collecting merchants as their malicious enemies and believed that it was from these highly-placed tax farmers and the nobility that the "well-meaning" tsar was allegedly to be protected. Many free peasants were particularly suspicious of the foreign merchants, whose manufacturing and prospecting activities, they feared, would lead to the expropriation of their land. Russian merchants, in turn, often made ludicrous claims about the probable effects of foreign competition, inveighing especially against the "Moscow Germans." Emerging harmonies coexisted with these conflicts as partnerships were formed between Russian and foreign merchants, slowly strengthening entrepreneurship and confidence, gradually increasing coordination among economic agents, and, in a limited number of the newer industries, improving efficiency and market performance.

The transitional environment is marked in Krizhanich's own work. As can be seen from Table 1 and Figure 1, and data presented in the Appendix, the political power of Russia's "aristocrats and servitors" (or "service nobility")—as represented by their combined membership in the Boyar Duma—evolved steadily from 1613 to 1674, but these groups underwent significant changes in composition. The results of our statistical tests are consistent with the hypothesis that there was an increase in the relative importance of the "servitor" class between 1630 and 1660, and even more so between 1660 and 1674.[35] The "aristocrats," as we have observed, formed the elite of the Duma, generalists whose status and power stemmed from their geneology, leadership, and experience. Although not homogeneous, their class included almost all of the wealthiest and most powerful landlords of the realm. A considerable number enjoyed a personal, informal relationship with the tsar and his inner circle. They served as diplomats, headed the chancellories, and in the period 1613 to 1630, formed the nucleus of the army: they were the commanders of the cavalry. The servitors were mostly provincial nobles who served under the aristocrats. Traditionally, they were the warrior nobility. Diligent and often "self-taught," appointment to the Boyar Duma was a lifetime achievement for them. As the national need for technical service grew, they had the ambition and incentives to fulfill it. Members of the Duma were paid 200 rubles per year; they met at the Kremlin in an aura of *succès d'estime.* From the mid-1620s to the mid-1670s the tsar increasingly relied on the servitors to deal with the revolutionary changes in military technology, the expanding administration, and the reform cum reinter-

---

[35] The data that follow in the text are based on materials presented in the Appendix, infra.

pretation of the law. The evolution of their political power therefore denotes a national transition. Furthermore, since indigenous technology was practically invariant in Muscovite Russia, aside from wars and natural catastrophes, government decisions in regard to land grants and the control over serf labor appear to have been the principal factors affecting national output. Consequently, changes in these political factors were likely to have a more direct and greater impact on economic activity than the other way round.

As is shown in Table 1, from a base of 100 = 31.85, representing the average membership of aristocrats in the Boyar Duma during the period 1613–25, and of 100 = 3.62, representing the average membership of servitors, the indexes rose to an average of 115 for the aristocrats and of 174 for the servitors during the period 1626–59. They rose further to an index of 172 for the aristocrats and of 380 for the servitors during the period 1660–67. Thereafter the index of the aristocrats actually fell to an average of 130, whereas that of the servitors rose to an average of 762 during the period 1668–76. In percentage terms, the political power of aristocrats relative to servitors was 90 to 10 during the period 1613–25; it declined to a level of 60 to 40 by the period 1668–76; and stabilized at approximately 70 to 30 during the latter 1670s and the 1680s. From the time of Tsar Alexei's death in 1676 to the overthrow of Sophia's regency by Peter I in 1689, Russian rulers appointed an abnormally large number of aristocrats to the Boyar Duma in the false hope of influencing their political support. These opportunistic and undistinguished appointments hastened the demise of the Duma. Nevertheless, from 1613 to 1676 it served as a focus for sociopolitical transition, when from 1613 to the latter 1620s, various forms of national rehabilitation and artistic activity in architecture and painting occurred, and from around 1630 to 1676 when military technology and economic activity accelerated.

Occupying the highest ranks in the cavalry, the boyars had suffered obsolescence brought on by the new military technology. But the lower nobility, who resented the arrogance of the boyar elite, seized the opportunity for advanced training and professional assertion. Among the streltsy, the introduction of new weaponry also caused friction, for it was regarded as a means for improvement by some and as a setback by others. Still, a form of "creative destruction" occurred. The government appointed some of the displaced boyars to prestigious military and civilian positions and recruited capable members of the lower nobility to serve as leaders in the army. Similarly, in the political sphere, though most boyars had shown little interest in acquiring literary or arithmetical skills, a considerable number of the lower nobility had developed proficiency in

Table 1   Evolution of political power of Russian aristocrats
and servitors, 1613–90

Period	Group	Index	Percentage of power
1613–25	Aristocrats	100[a]	90
	Servitors	100[b]	10
1626–59	Aristocrats	115	85
	Servitors	174	15
1660–67	Aristocrats	172	80
	Servitors	380	20
1668–76	Aristocrats	130	60
	Servitors	762	40
1677–80	Aristocrats	203	70
	Servitors	754	30
1681–90	Aristocrats	290	69
	Servitors	1156	31

[a] $31.85 = 100$ (represents average number of aristocrats in Boyar Duma, 1613–25).
[b] $3.62 = 100$ (represents average number of servitors in Boyar Duma, 1613–25).

Note: A regression was run in the following way. The dependent variable used was servitor political power and the independent variables were a constant term, a dummy variable for the period 1630–60 (D1), and a second dummy for the period 1660–74 (D2). The estimated coefficients and t-statistics were as follows:

Variable	Coefficient	t-Statistic
constant	0.11	8.41
D1	0.04	2.48
D2	0.16	8.41

The R^2 for the regression was 0.56 indicating that more than half of the variance in servitor political power is explained by differences in these time periods. The results show that significant differences in the rate of change in political power were present during these times and that dividing the 1613–74 period at 1630 and 1660 is in fact supported by the data. Statistical tests for the significance of the difference between D1 and D2 reject the hypothesis of homogeneity between the two subperiods even at 0.20% level of significance. Specifically, $|D1-D2| = -0.07$, and the t-ratio of this difference is 3.76. In running a dummy variable regression, accounting for the six periods identified and plotting the residuals from the fitted model, the behavior of the residuals shows that there are differences across the periods as well as within period similarities. An examination of the plot of the residual series clearly shows that in the first and second periods the data fluctuate about a mean in a sine–cosine wave fashion and then in a more variable manner. The third and fourth intervals are characterized by rapid increases but the latter exhibit stronger growth than the former. Plots of the raw data bear this out. Finally, the remaining periods show a drop from the previous peak and then a more or less random fluctuation about a new level, which is consistent with the argument in the text.

Figure 1 Evolution of political power of Russian aristocrats and servitors, 1613–90

them. Consequently, suspicion between the two classes increased. Nevertheless, a new cluster emerged of outstanding aristocrats, talented servitors, and even townsmen—forming a single group of tsarist politico-administrative professionals who served in the higher echelons of such institutions as the Boyar Duma and the chancelleries.

No *fundamental* political transition, however, had occurred. Much new emphasis was placed on law as an instrument to define and ensure the hierarchical social structure. As promulgated in the Legal Code of 1649, the law reflected the flux of the environment and exacerbated the fundamental disequilibrium of the Muscovite state: the government was to provide or (indirectly) to ensure the occupation of each citizen (including slavery), and citizens in return were liable for service to the state. Implementing by law a hierarchical structure (*mestnichestvo* system based on geneological seniority of boyars until 1682), or "nomenclature," of this kind implies fear of displacement by some and government coercion and repression of others. In fact, one of the important legacies of this period is that "legality" was rigidly construed: neither beyond the strictest interpretation of law and contract, nor beyond the affected parties. By the completion of enserfment and deepening of slavery, the Legal Code of 1649 virtually froze the occupational mobility, earnings, and hopes of the vast majority of Russian peasants. Not only did their fury periodically explode,[36] but the mainspring of economic transformation was broken. Significant changes in relative earnings and prices were blocked by law, further obstructing the necessary incentives for improved economic efficiency in agriculture. Though short-term gains could—and did— accrue to landlords as a result of the exploitation of cheap labor, in the longer term these measures could not but forestall the transformation of Russia's agriculture and, consequently, the "modernizing" of the entire economy. Modern research has shown that poor people in developing countries are no less motivated to work hard and to improve their lot, and that of their children, than are people in developed countries. *Mutatis mutandis,* there is reason to believe this to have been true of the Russian peasants of the seventeenth century, a view consistent with Krizhanich's *Politika.*[37]

---

[36] See *Politika,* infra, 195.

[37] Krizhanich wrote: "the Russian nation has earned itself an ignominious reputation among other peoples, who assert that Russians are like donkeys and incapable of accomplishing anything worthwhile if they are not forced to do it with sticks and whips," *Politika,* infra, 201. But, he noted, "this is a falsehood." Their behavior was caused by "a cruel government, which has made their lives repulsive and without honor," ibid., 201. The modern classic on the subject is by Theodore W. Schultz, *Transforming Traditional Agriculture* (New Haven, 1964), esp. 36–52; cf. also his *Investing in People* (Berkeley, 1980), chs 2–4.

4

The classic preoccupations of the *Politika*

Two fundamental themes permeate the *Politika*: the causes of the wealth of nations and the causes of their poverty. Russia, Krizhanich believed, had in the mid-seventeenth century not yet attained a complement of population adequate to its natural resources. Moreover, he observes, the contribution of an increasing population to economic development is contingent on its "quality"—that is, on its education and training—and on the evolving institutions and structure of the nation.

Krizhanich ranks a government based on sound laws foremost among the conditions for human betterment. Next is the need for the development of an educated and industrious class of craftsmen, farmers, and merchants. The production of luxury goods also serves a useful function, he notes. Finally, he accords crucial importance in increasing the wealth of a nation to the attainment of an agricultural surplus and the availability of strategic, "exhaustible resources." He identifies the expanding wealth of a nation with the increasing wellbeing of its inhabitants. All men, he writes, are created substantially equal in ignorance, with only two basic characteristics distinguishing them from other creatures. First, they possess the capacity to think and to converse. Second, they are endowed with the ability to create new technologies, instruments, and commodities. Stripped of its archaic language, his exposition emphasizes that the earlier—and greater—the investment in these potential advantages of the human agent, the larger the private and national yield will be. The wealth of a nation, he points out, is principally contingent on the assiduous efforts of its inhabitants, promoted by appropriate knowledge and training.[1]

---

[1] Wealth and power are discernible, he wrote, whereas the benefits of knowledge are more often perceived by way of indirection. Once the desire for learning is instilled, however, it is pursued with dedication. Therefore the need for demonstrating the results of knowledge is important, as is the responsibility of kings and parents to induce the desire of its attainment on the part of subjects and children, respectively. *Politika*, infra, 87.

Every country, he says, should periodically take an inventory of its needs and resources. This is essential if it is to attain its national objectives at minimum cost. But the probability of its doing so will be greatly enhanced if the ruler has access to, and relies on, the advice of impartial experts. To be expert, however, their advice must be based on firsthand knowledge of and information about the country and its neighbors.[2] Krizhanich thus integrates, in a simple manner, qualitative and quantitative approaches to the development process.

Certain necessary conditions must, however, prevail for social well-being: honesty in government, good laws, equitable taxation, justice, and the availability of basic products at reasonable prices. Krizhanich steadfastly believed that the duty and obligation, the honor and glory, of a ruler center in the pursuit of the happiness of his people, for "kingdoms were not created for kings, but kings for kingdoms."[3] These were remarkably progressive views at that time, not only for Russia but for most European countries.

The politico-economic conditions and government policies that Krizhanich observed in Russia did not meet his criteria for the expansion of the wealth of nations. Cataclysm, he noted, was a fundamental characteristic of Russia. The country suffered from a propensity to react in—and, hence, suffer from—great extremes. Territorially, it was the largest country in Europe; economically, one of the poorest. Its grinding poverty was the result of natural, historic, and manmade impediments. Severity of climate; northern location; low productivity of the soil; isolation from the main trade routes; and hostile and backward neighbors, particularly along its eastern frontiers, were the natural constraints. But the unjust behavior of officials; lack of civil moderation among the populace; widespread drunkenness; poor roads; brigandage; and monopolistic and underdeveloped domestic markets were human and institutional hindrances to development that appropriate knowledge could help to overcome.[4]

Russia, Krizhanich contended, clearly had the potential of emerging as a major power in Europe. It was endowed with an abundance of natural resources, safe frontiers in Siberia and along the Arctic coast, excellent waterways appropriate for the building of a strong and economically efficacious merchant marine, and numerous neighbors for the development of favorable trade. He held that a well-advised Russian government,

---

[2] *Politika,* infra, 96–7.
[3] *Politika,* infra, 188.
[4] *Politika,* infra, 113, 126–7, 161–4.

especially an autocratic one, could be a remarkable instrument for economic progress.[5] Accordingly, he prepared specific proposals for Tsar Alexei's consideration, measures he deemed essential for the transformation of Russia into a prosperous and powerful modern state.

Krizhanich was the precursor of much economic thought on the development of Russia's foreign trade, manufacturing, commerce, and handicrafts. These contributions of *Politika* speak for themselves. Even more important, however, is his treatment of the roles of knowledge and agriculture in economic development, and his attendant treatment of the role of warfare in commerce. Knowledge, he insists, is the foundation of the wealth, and in the final analysis even the power, of a nation.[6] In his schema, eradicating illiteracy and providing an opportunity for education and training are given the highest priority. As the prerequisites to the attainment of all other major objectives, they are even more important than the development of military power.

Krizhanich divides the problems of education into two parts: ecclesiastical education to instill a sense of morality and moderation, and secular education to modernize the Russian language and transform the economy. The second is the more important. Krizhanich recommends the establishment of specialized schools of medicine, engineering, and military science. These disciplines, he affirms, require careful training in philosophy, mathematics, and physics. Nor does he omit jurisprudence and applied fields such as agriculture, crafts, and technical training. Book learning, he emphasizes, is the basis of civilization, liberating men from fetishism, superstition, and ridicule; advancing the arts and sciences; and bringing freedom from unwarranted foreign exploitation and interference.

Although Krizhanich advised that Russia import and adapt the required knowledge and skills from abroad, he drew attention to the related hazards. The more underdeveloped a nation, he cautions, the greater the need, but also the peril, of foreign assistance. In the circumstances, he ridicules the notion of rapid progress. The granting of privileges (especially to foreign merchants) in return for glittering gifts

---

[5] *Politika,* infra, 114, 161, 168, 173. Krizhanich's views on autocracy versus tyranny are discussed below.

[6] *Politika,* infra, 58, 99, 128, 238–9. As to the importance of education on knowledge and on all aspects of political-economic development, Krizhanich was influenced by scholars such as Philip de Commines (1447–1509), Paolo Paruta (1540–98), Justus Lipsius (1547–1606), and Maximilian Faust de Aschaffenburg. Among the ancients, Plato, Aristotle, and Polybius had a strong influence on him. He wrote: "knowledge of philosophy is indispensable to all kings, young and old, believers and unbelievers, good and bad. For God created philosophy (or knowledge derived from books) not for nothing, but to benefit people," 239.

and promises of speedy development is a policy based on quicksand. Wealth and progress can only be achieved gradually. Illustrating his arguments by reference to contemporary conditions in Russia, he repeatedly shows that both domestic and foreign merchants have a strong propensity to seek to establish monopolies. To curb their excesses, this has to be held in strict control. But there is no better alternative for an underdeveloped country such as Russia than to import more highly developed knowledge and technology and key commodities. Even the security of Russia, he notes, demands political and military alliances with more developed, trustworthy nations. As long as a country is predominantly dependent on other nations for these services, its progress is based on "artificial" (i.e., spurious) foundations. Hence the "true" causes of the wealth of a nation, he writes, are based on the continual development of its indigenous human and material resources—in modern terms, on its "tooled knowledge."[7] Krizhanich therefore devotes much attention to the requisite balance between domestic development and foreign dependence.

While he makes adequate reference to the importance of manufacturing in economic development, and emphasizes Russia's need for foreign managers and all sorts of personnel, technology, and finished products, he warns that massive foreign penetration will inevitably result both in exploitation and in the distortion of the development of a country's own resources.[8] Krizhanich therefore elaborates an entire panoply of domestic and external devices to transform the Russian economy from backwardness to a more modern state. He again calls for vocational and educational training, with special emphasis on mathematics, and recommends a state monopoly in foreign trade, principally to overcome the abuses of gross foreign exploitation and Russia's weak competitive position. He maintains, contrary to some mercantilist views of the time, that Russia should not resort to any form of warfare—military or commercial—solely for economic gain.

---

[7] *Politika,* infra, 85–94.

[8] *Politika,* infra, 130–2, 136–40. Krizhanich showed no moderation on this issue: "The Germans are the worst offenders. In quest of war and in search of military service they roam the entire world . . . receive excessive remuneration, an enormous insult to our inhabitants," infra, 130–1. Further: "They come in the name of every craft, inundate a country, appropriate resources from local inhabitants whom, in turn, they ridicule," infra, 136. Moreover: "In accordance with a general, universal law, foreigners never strive to contribute to the public welfare. They do what benefits them, put their profit in their side pocket," infra, 138. And: "Under the pretext of trade . . . bring us to the brink of poverty," infra, 142. Nonetheless, Krizhanich points out that a quality of national leadership is the single most important factor in creating the environment for successful development (infra, 67–71, 234–5).

The most striking of Krizhanich's formulations is that in regard to agriculture. It is agriculture, he maintains, that is the root and foundation of all wealth, since it provides the surplus for the enrichment of the farmer and renders possible the liberation of the wealth of craftsmen, merchants, noblemen, and kings.[9] Therefore, he advised the government should devote particular attention to this basic industry and "it should never neglect it."[10] Without an agricultural surplus, he argued, resources would not be available for the development of crafts, manufacturing, and commerce. Conversely, the neglect of agriculture could not but bring about the poverty of the nation. In consequence, he urged the tsar to order that the best available books on agricultural development be translated into Russian; to undertake a survey of the cropland and test the quality of the soil; to promote agriculture and cattle breeding; to construct storage facilities that would minimize spoilage; to subsidize the distribution of agricultural tools among the rural population; to enhance the quality of rural life; to establish experimental stations for the introduction of new varieties of rice, tobacco, grapes, and silk; and to grant tax incentives for migration to, and work in, severe environments.[11] He suggested—at least by inference—that increased agricultural productivity would raise the demand for workers, thereby increasing employment of the rural population and producing an enlarged surplus, more wealth, and increased government revenue. Agricultural advance, he affirmed, was essential to meet Russia's domestic needs and to reduce the drain of bullion.[12]

Krizhanich extended his views on agriculture to other natural resources, calling particular attention to exhaustible ores. He was Russia's first systematic advocate of a national policy on the conservation of resources, pointing out, although he had recommended the prohibition of bullion export, that certain exhaustible resources should be procured at the lowest cost, whether at home or from abroad. Concurrently, he urged the tsar to grant leases on a twenty- to thirty-year basis for the discovery and exploitation of mines in undeveloped territories, especially in Central Asia and Siberia; and to bid for mining opportunities in the Caucasus. To reduce the risk confronting merchant adventurers and the high cost of investment, he advocated the systematic, but appropriate (by implication,

---

[9] *Politika*, infra, 41.

[10] Ibid. Since most of Russia's agricultural production was not market oriented, Krizhanich's analysis of it is particularly significant. The production on the estates of the tsar, landlords, and monasteries was closely related to social status, prestige, and "the demands of lordly appropriation," R.E.F. Smith, *Peasant Farming in Muscovy*, 232.

[11] *Politika*, infra, 42–5.

[12] *Politika*, infra, 46–53.

"cost-controlled"), use of bonuses or subsidies for the successful extraction of scarce minerals. [13]

For the achievement of both military power and economic plenty, Krizhanich further integrated the functions of manufacturing, agriculture, foreign trade, and education. He insisted that the modernization of Russia's armed forces was essential. This entailed the development of construction and manufacturing, since the army had to be equipped with the most modern weapons, with satisfactory clothing, and with comfortable dwellings. Manifestly, abundant food, and thus an agricultural surplus, was indispensable. But he reiterated that effective leadership, without which appropriate training could not be achieved, was also essential. He considered increased knowledge and a balance between loyalty, justice, and humaneness to be primary requisites to instill obedience in the Russian army and obtain respect for it. In the final analysis, his major emphasis was on the excellence of leadership, and this required government investment in education—which, he insisted, was the foundation of the wealth and power of a nation. [14]

It was in this context of education that Krizhanich analyzed Russia's dire need to develop her human and material resources. He drew attention to the importance of utilizing every possible means of eliminating unemployment and its attendant misery. The adoption of such measures, he stated, would develop Russia's cities, contributing to the development of the entire nation.

KRIZHANICH'S LASTING RELEVANCE

Krizhanich wrote his *Politika* in the hope that it would attract Tsar Alexei's attention and thereby gain him his freedom from Tobolsk. He also wrote a surprisingly large number of other books during his fifteen years of detention. The first was a brief Slavic grammar, begun in Moscow and completed only five months after his arrival in Tobolsk. For a few weeks after writing it, he took copious notes on classic works of Polish history, but he abandoned this project and instead undertook a transcrip-

---

[13] *Politika,* infra, 54–6. Krizhanich applied these arguments to the efficient management of other resources as well, e.g., livestock. After he was released from Russian confinement, he wrote his *Historia de Siberia* (1680) in which he elaborated these arguments. In 1890, Andrei A. Titov edited and published this work, Latin and Russian texts, in his *Sibir v XVII v.: Sbornik starinnykh russkikh statei* (Moscow, 1890).

[14] *Politika,* infra, 238–42. The emphasis in the *Politika* on education of women, and its certification, is truly remarkable for the time. See, e.g., 38–9.

tion of the Russian chronicles, which he finished in 1662. Immediately thereafter he turned his attention to French and Russian history.

Krizhanich commenced the *Politika* in 1663, as we have noted, and completed it in early 1666. Even during this period of concentrated work, however, he revised and expanded his Slavic grammar, and in late 1665 he forwarded a copy to D. M. Bashmakov, head of the powerful Chancellery of Secret Affairs. Further, between May 1666 and October 1667, he worked on his *De Providentia Dei,* which he dedicated to Alexei Alexeevich, heir to the Russian throne. When the latter died, however, he rededicated it to Ivan B. Repnin, the *voevoda* of Tobolsk. Thereafter he wrote a volume on *Holy Baptism* (*ca.* 1669); another entitled *An Interpretation of Historical Prophesies* (1674); and a brief treatise on *Chinese Foreign Trade* (1675). He also prepared a critical tract on the Russian religious dissenters and wrote a booklet called *Mortal Predicament—A Spiritual Testament,* which he dedicated to the Russian people.[15] In 1675 he was permitted to advise the Romanian-born Russian envoy, Nikolai Spafarii-Milescu, on his diplomatic mission to Peking.

Krizhanich's prodigious output in the wasteland of Tobolsk could not have been accomplished but for Tsar Alexei's instructions that he be freed from all compulsory labor during his exile. He had been allowed to bring his books with him from Moscow. Judging from his citations in the *Politika,* on occasion understandably imprecise, his knowledge of the classics was thorough and sagacious. He cites, among others, the works of Homer, Plato, Aristotle, Plutarch, Polybius, Livy, Virgil, and Cicero. Superbly trained in the Bible, in the writings of the Church Fathers, and in the works of the medieval scholars, Krizhanich was not surprisingly acquainted with the writings of Machiavelli as well. He was also an expert on the works of Kievan and Muscovite clerics, the principal historians of Poland, and the basic works of Western European authors on the history of the Russians and other Slavic peoples.

On March 5, 1676, Krizhanich was freed from his confinement in Tobolsk. At the end of May, on the orders of Tsar Fedor III, he returned to Moscow. Siberia had taken its toll. Fragile in health and depressed in spirit, he requested permission to leave Russia, which was denied. Instead, he was assigned as translator to the ambassadorial department. Several months thereafter he wrote two letters: one congratulating the young tsar on his recent wedding, the other petitioning to leave the country. Again, the authorities denied his request. Early in 1677 he

---

[15] See Selected Bibliography, "Principal published writings of Iurii Krizhanich," *infra* 257–9.

submitted yet another petition and received a favorable response. But though he was granted permission to leave Moscow on April 1, 1677, he stayed on, for unknown reasons—and to the dismay of officialdom—until early 1678. At this time Hildebrand von Horn, secretary to the Danish ambassador, compassionately intervened by helping transport Krizhanich to Vilna. Upon his arrival Krizhanich entered the Dominican order, a surprising step for a Jesuit, and immediately wrote a comprehensive report on his experiences in Russia. It was dispatched to the secretary of the Office of Congregations in Rome. Next, at the suggestion of Hildebrand von Horn, he wrote *A History of Siberia* (1680). This brief but informative work not only displays firsthand knowledge of the place but provides an account of its historic, geographic, and ethnographic features.

Early in 1681 Krizhanich was granted permission by the Office of Congregations in Rome to leave Vilna and proceed to Warsaw. There he was to inform a Papal Nuncio of his views on Russia. Unfortunately, the meeting turned acrimonious because of a misunderstanding, and in January 1682, instead of going to Rome as Krizhanich had hoped, he was ordered by the Nuncio to return to Vilna. Krizhanich resolutely wrote to the Office, asked forgiveness for his unauthorized mission to Moscow, requested formal designation as a missionary, and pleaded that he be allowed to return to Rome. His request was granted in May 1682 and he began to prepare for his journey.[16] A year later, at the age of sixty-four, he traveled from Vilna to Warsaw. He continued thence in the company of a Polish expeditionary force on its way to relieve the Turkish siege of Vienna, where he died and was buried in early September 1683.

In 1692, all the works Krizhanich had written in Tobolsk were deposited for safekeeping in the Moscow Printing Office of the church Synod. Their rediscovery was slow and piecemeal. As the result of a remark by a Polish scholar, A. G. Bielewski, the manuscript of *Politika* was discovered in 1857 by a Russian scholar, P. A. Bezsonov, who first published the work in six installments in 1859, which was widely and keenly read. In 1860, Bezsonov republished the contents in two volumes. Reviews appeared in all leading Russian journals and newspapers, and in the years that followed, the book stimulated research in numerous languages. The literature on the *Politika* continues to expand.

We have come to the *Politika* from an interest in its insights with respect to the past no less than from a desire to discern its implications for the future. It has withstood the test of time, serving as a primary source for the history of Russia in the seventeenth century and as the herald of

---

[16] See Belokurov, *Prilozheniia*, no. 8, 265–85.

socioeconomic thinking on the need for Russia's fundamental reform. In this respect it has no precedessor, nor, more than 300 years after its composition has it had any comparable successor. In his schema, however, Krizhanich did not indicate the historical "process" that the transformation of the Russian economy would tend to take. Either he was oblivious to the contradictions between many of his economic reforms and the realities of absolute power, or he regarded these contradictions as more apparent than real. It is more for its perceptive and systematic analysis of key processes of economic development than for its policy proposals that the *Politika* deserves attention. Indeed, it was the occurrence of some of these economic processes that laid the foundation for the reforms of the future. Krizhanich's lasting relevance is thus related to his emphasis on the transitionary essence of this period. Our own analysis in this regard has basically confirmed his presuppositions.

Krizhanich's agenda, however, was alien to the Russian political environment. The success of his proposals was dependent on the existence of at least the following conditions: an autocratic ruler who was extraordinarily gifted and zealously reform minded; a substantial reduction of the power and stifling influence of the Orthodox church; an infusion of foreign experts, technology, and capital, monitored by a reasonably efficient state administration; and a confluence of interest among the various classes and the tsar's government with respect to economic development. These conditions manifestly did not exist at the time of Krizhanich's stay in Russia. They only became a reality in the early eighteenth century, when many internal and external measures that he had recommended were undertaken by Peter the Great.

On the basis of the evidence we have adduced, it is reasonable to assume that Krizhanich's ideas were known, directly or indirectly, not only to three Russian rulers—Tsar Alexei, Prince Vasilii V. Golitsyn and Peter I—but also to at least three prominent members of the Boyar Duma: Almaz Ivanov, Boris I. Morozov, and Feodor M. Rtishchev.[17] The only contemporary Russian "political economist" worthy of mention, Ordin-Nashchokin, was another member of the Duma who knew most of the preceding men well, and he, too, was probably acquainted with the *Politika*. But, *inter alia*, there was no literature of criticism and response in Russia, immeasurably reducing the contemporary impact of one economic writer on another. We have been unable to find a single contemporary Russian reference to Krizhanich's work.

---

[17] For a list of "the members of the Boyar Duma, 1613–1713," see Crummey, *Aristocrats and Servitors*, Appendix B, 178–214.

Modern research has shown, and our work on Krizhanich confirms, that it is practically impossible to determine the relevance of an author's work to the development of economic ideas (and even more so to policy) in the prescientific stage of economic analysis.[18] This follows from the fact that such analysis was characterized by the nonexistence of an integrated body of economic knowledge. Writers on economics in the seventeenth century were not an interacting group consciously engaged in a cumulative process of developing new ideas. There was no temporal sequence to economic thought in the sense of authors utilizing and improving upon the work of their predecessors or contemporaries. Characteristically, they presented their own views with various constituencies in mind. Nonetheless, an important difference occurred between the perceivable influence of Krizhanich's work and that of his contemporaries: the early English mercantilists and the early scholastics.

The most sophisticated early English mercantilists used economic concepts as analytical tools and derived conclusions from them, even though they were *simpliste* and erroneous. Specifically, Thomas Mun many be credited for one of the early formulations of the quantity theory of money.[19] He also discussed the relation between the trade balance and unemployment in theoretical terms. Gerald Malynes and Edward Misselden similarly used the exchange rate as an analytical tool in the equilibration of international accounts.[20] Sir William Petty, a vital representative of the Age of Newton, placed major emphasis on method in economics, and on free and candid discussion for its scientific advance.[21]

Krizhanich showed neither inclination nor endowment for such an approach. Nor was he a rigorous disciple of scholastic economics. In the scholastic writings of Leonard de Lessius, Luis Molina, and Juno de Lugo, the operational role of prices, costs, and profits was specifically treated.

---

[18] See George J. Stigler, "The Process and Progress of Economics," Nobel Memorial Lecture, 1982, *Journal of Political Economy* 91, no. 4 (August 1983), 529–45; Jacob Viner, *Studies in the Theory of International Trade* (New York, 1936), 109.

[19] For distinctive illustrations of comparatively more developed forms of economic analysis in mercantilist writings on the quantity theory of money, unemployment, use of precious metals, and criticism of bullionist devices, see Thomas Mun, *England's treasure by farraign trade* [written *ca.* 1630, first ed., 1664] (New York, 1903), 15–24, and 49.

[20] See Gerald Malynes, *The Center of the Circle of Commerce* [1623] (New York, 1973), esp. 64–9 on money, prices, and determination of exchange rates; Edward Misselden, *The circle of commerce, or the ballance of trade* [1623] (New York, 1968), 20–69, esp. on the mechanism of adjustment.

[21] See the *Economic Writings of Sir William Petty*, edited by Charles Henry Hull (Cambridge, 1899), vol. 1, 44–5, 242–5, 307–13, on methodology, the nature of "suppositions," and the significance of free and candid discussion for scientific advance in economics; and vol. 2, 473, for an early discussion on the specialization of labor.

These concepts were integrated in their nascent system of equilibrium analysis, with both concepts and system used to explain economic phenomena.[22] Though considerations of public welfare were central both to the scholastic system and to Krizhanich, he did not fully utilize these scholastic ideas. He combined the philosophy of scholasticism and some objectives of mercantilism whenever it served his purpose.

Primarily, Krizhanich used a historical-descriptive approach rather than an analytical one, interrelating economic reasoning, economic history, and policy formation to explain major economic events. In appraising the ways in which Muscovite institutions might be changed to break up the accumulated political restrictions, he formulated a program designed to transform the Russian economy from a primitive to a more modern state. Some of his proposals, such as those recommending a "favorable" trade balance and *dirigiste* economic controls, were of the pseudo-mercantilist variety. But his general system of thought was not mercantilist: for he rejected bullionism; differentiated between wealth as a productive process and money; and ridiculed the notion of a ruler or a nation endeavoring to accumulate precious metals indefinitely. He effectively employed not only simple economic concepts of supply and demand, profit and interest, productivity and competitiveness, but also complex concepts regarding the economic factor in class conflict. In so doing, he referred to the necessity of greater decentralization for the achievement of efficiency gains. Moreover, he emphasized the interdependence of strengthened market structures and the joint growth of trade, agriculture, and manufacturing. By drawing attention to what did not exist, he indicated the need for improved product and financial markets to benefit from adaptations of relative costs and prices. Krizhanich's analysis had more lasting relevance, albeit less theoretical rigor, than the contemporary mercantilists and scholastics. The mercantilists and scholastics, however, worked in environments with a substantial degree of open criticism and response. Notwithstanding the limitations of a prescientific period, within the English mercantilist

[22] See B.W. Dempsey, *Interest and Usury* (Washington, D.C., 1943), chs 6–8 on the economics of Lessius (1554–1623), Molina (1535–1600), and de Lugo (1583–1660); John T. Noonan, Jr., *Scholastic Analysis of Usury* (Cambridge, 1957); Joseph A. Schumpeter, *History of Economic Analysis* (Cambridge, 1963), 94–115, esp. on the scholastic treatment of welfare economics and the process of equilibrium analysis. For a brief, comparative appraisal of the mercantilist and scholastic contributions, see J.M. Letiche, "The History of Economic Thought in the *International Encyclopedia of the Social Sciences,*" *Journal of Economic Literature* 7, no. 2 (June 1969), 406–15; cf. also L.M. Morduxović, "Ju. Križanić, W. Petty, and I. Pososhkov (A Comparative Outline of Their Economic Views)," in Eekman and Kadić, 223–43.

environment a simple theory of the international mechanism of adjustment emerged,[23] and within the scholastic environment an embryonic
theory of economic equilibrium appeared.[24] Moreover, in several fields,
the English mercantilists had a demonstrable impact on government
policy, and the scholastics on the interpretation and implementation of
church economic doctrine.[25] No such contribution can be unequivocally
shown for Krizhanich.

The eclecticism of the *Politika* also complicates the problem of appraising the validity of Krizhanich's ideas and their relevance through time.
This, for at least two reasons. First, the environment in which he worked
impelled him to resort to the arts of persuasion and evasion. Second, he
suffered from a "pious bias" that confused scholastic imperatives and
economic analysis. In consequence, concerning Russia's wealth or poverty,
he writes in one place: "Our land is one of the poorest because nothing is
produced here except grain, fish, and meat."[26] In another, however, he
states: Russia's "good fortune lies in the resources of our land and rivers.
Compared with Poland, Lithuania, Sweden, and Belorussia, Russia is well
endowed and bountiful."[27] He calls attention to many goods that are
produced in this country and adds: "The bread that commoners and rural
people eat is more plentiful and delicious in Russia than in Lithuania,
Poland, or Sweden."[28] Even in comparison with richer countries such as
Greece, France, Italy, Spain, or England, Krizhanich asserts: "Our
peasants and poor townsmen who make their living from handicrafts, live
much better than do the peasants in those rich countries."[29] If allowances
are not made for the context in which these statements were made and for
Krizhanich's environment, they are at least in part contradictory. In the
first instance however, he is advocating Russia's economic development,
emphasizing the gulf between her poverty and potential. In the second, he
is describing comparative economic conditions, with the objective of
showing how economic wealth can be achieved for Russia. Still, the
arguments are *a fortiori* not free from contradiction.

---

[23] See Viner, *Studies*, 74–9.
[24] See Schumpeter, *History of Economic Analysis*, 102–7.
[25] It has been shown that several changes in taxes and the customs during the period
1660–88 were influenced by mercantilist (and anti-mercantilist) theorizing. See C.D.
Chandaman, *The English Public Revenue, 1660–1688* (Oxford, 1975), 78–9, 156. As for the
influence of the scholastics on the church's interpretation of usury, see Schumpeter, *History
of Economic Analysis*, 102–7.
[26] *Politika*, infra, 141.
[27] Ibid., 161.
[28] Ibid.
[29] Ibid., 162.

As for scholastic imperatives and economic analysis, Krizhanich intermittently resorts to "absolute autocracy" and "legal pricing" as instruments of public welfare. He writes in one place: "Autocracy is the best form of government";[30] further, in Russia's laws and customs, "the first and best is absolute autocracy."[31] Yet in another place he states: "Our greatest political problem is excessive government. Our people do not know how to use moderation. They always stray into fatal extremities."[32] Because of Russia's "inhuman laws," he continues, all European nations "unanimously call this illustrious tsardom a tyranny."[33] But he contends: "It is deceitful people who say such things."[34] He concludes by describing tyranny as the worst and most corrupt form of government, a case in which one individual seizes power and becomes a merciless oppressor of the entire nation, an executioner without a judge or laws, one who has renounced humanity and is the devil with a human face.[35] Moreover, he cites many cases in which absolute autocracy has degenerated into tyranny. How are Krizhanich's views on absolute autocracy to be reconciled with those on tyranny?

The method that Krizhanich used in the *Politika* to resolve this dilemma marks an important element in its lasting relevance. There are historical circumstances, he points out, when it is essential "to bridle" the extreme propensities of men who are inclined to misuse political power. With particular reference to Russia, he argues that absolute autocracy established by way of a social contract is the only means by which subjects can protect themselves against the "evildoings" of tsarist officialdom so that officials cannot indulge in their "vicious desires and drive the people to despair."[36] It is also the only way, he asserts, to safeguard justice in the realm. The autocrat will even have to grant these high-placed servitors and advisors reasonable privileges for them to renounce their evildoing and to prevent their inhuman counsel.

Krizhanich's views on absolute autocracy are similar to those of Thomas Hobbes, whose writings in Latin he probably knew but could not cite because of Hobbes's alleged atheism. Hobbes applied his views to the economic sphere as well, and Krizhanich's beliefs were consistent with them. In discussing the relation between civil law and econoic activity,

[30] Ibid., 206.
[31] Ibid., 161.
[32] Ibid., 127.
[33] Ibid., 200.
[34] Ibid., 200.
[35] Ibid., 185.
[36] Ibid., 206.

Hobbes advocated absolute monarchy. He believed this was essential for calculated self-interest to operate effectively in the economic arena. Only *after* a commonwealth is formed, he writes, does the liberty of subjects lie in those things that the sovereign "hath pretermitted [i.e., let stand], such as [their] liberty to buy, and sell, and otherwise contract with one another; to choose their own abode, their own diet, their own trade of life, and institute their children as they themselves think fit; and the like."[37] Absolute monarchy, he contends, is essential to bridle the extreme propensities to vicious behavior by participants in the economic arena. This is the only way in which to obtain the advantages of economic competition for individual and national wellbeing.

Krizhanich and Hobbes differed on many specific points and in degree, but these ideas provide a foundation for reconciling Krizhanich's views on Russia's need for absolute autocracy and the dangers of tyranny. Despite the high risks of tyranny, he believed that autocracy was the only feasible and efficacious alternative. Even if Krizhanich's arguments on this issue were not open to dispute, other related inconsistencies remain. In line with mainstream scholastic economic thought, he held that it was the mission of the ruler to promote public welfare and among the prerequisites for this was to keep down the prices of "necessities." Indeed, the ruler was obliged to "guarantee" the availability of necessities at low prices.[38]

Krizhanich conceded, however, that in times of serious shortage these prices would have to be raised to distribute the scarce supplies in the least inequitable manner. Similarly, he argued for economic forces to mobilize foreign exchange markets via differential rates of interest, but against the "ignominy" of usury. Such dichotomies frequently marred the quality of his economic analysis.

Notwithstanding these limitations, since its rediscovery in 1859 the *Politika* has aroused ever-increasing interest. Between 1823 and 1983, some 290 major monographs and periodical items appeared on Krizhanich in Croatian, Czech, Slovak, English, French, German, Italian, Polish, Russian, and Serbian. In celebrating in 1983 the 300th anniversary of Krizhanich's death, the Academy of Sciences of the USSR and the Academy of Sciences and Arts of Yugoslavia scheduled for publication

---

[37] Thomas Hobbes, *Leviathan* [1651] (Chicago: Great Books, 1952), 113. Hobbes had formulated the first detailed statement of his political theory in *De Cive*, published by Elzevere in 1647. Krizhanich's friend, Luc Holstenius, who was the Vatican librarian and had visited England when Hobbes was already well known doubtless knew of his work as probably did Krizhanich. For an incisive discussion of "Hobbism," see Viner, *The Role of Providence in the Social Order* (Philadelphia, 1972), 62–9.

[38] *Politika*, infra, 188–9; 238.

virtually all of Krizhanich's available works and correspondence. As noted in our bibliography, some of these books have already appeared. Many studies that have been published on Krizhanich's life and work are country- and time-specific, occasionally flawed by self-imposed or ideologically imposed intellectual blinders. Furthermore, most of the literature has neglected Krizhanich's economic thought. In the nineteenth century only two imperceptive studies appeared on the subject; in the twentieth century the number has risen to about twelve.[39]

We have endeavored to reduce this imbalance by devoting considerable attention to Krizhanich's economic ideas. They have not only had historic relevance, but in an embryonic way they are suggestive and provocative for the future as well. He maintained, by inference at least, that knowledge is a unique form of "social capital." In modern terms, he implies that knowledge is a country-specific stock of capital that varies greatly among nations. Small or large as a country's stock may be, he fully realized that knowledge is part of its human investment. Because it has an economic value, it is a form of capital, although it is neither private nor public property in any legal sense of the term.[40]

In a nascent way Krizhanich applied such views to the problems of political and ecclesiastical succession whenever the process of succession actually was in abeyance. Systematically and authoritatively, he presents the case that, *mutatis mutandis,* democracy is a method. In the ecclesiastical realm, and within its philosophical context, he argues the case that democracy is an institutional arrangement for arriving at a political decision in which authorities acquire power to govern through a responsible process: responsible both to Supreme Law and to those whom they govern by means of competitive, secret-ballot rules and laws.[41] In principle, the method is universal. In practice, Krizhanich shows that

[39] The two items in the nineteenth century were Alexander Brückner, "Ein Finanzpolitiker in Russland im XVII Jahrhundert," *Russische Revue* 1 (1891), 292–333; and Mikh. V. Vujić, *Križanićeva "Politika": Ekonomsko-politicna studija* (Belgrad, 1895). For the works in the twentieth century, see Selected Bibliography, 260–68.

[40] The concept of investment in "social capital" is still on the frontier of economic science, although Alfred Marshall appreciated its importance. "Capital," he wrote, "consists in a great part of knowledge and organization: and of this some part is private property and the other part is not. Knowledge is our most powerful engine of production. . . . The distinction between public and private property in knowledge and organization is of great and growing importance: in some respects of more importance than that between public and private property in material things . . ." Alfred Marshall, *Principles of Economics,* 8th ed. (London, 1938), 138–9.

[41] Provocative present-day discussions on these issues are presented in Kenneth J. Arrow, *Social Choice and Individual Values* (New Haven [1951], 2nd edn 1963), esp. 92–120, and *Social Choice and Justice* (Oxford, 1984), 115–32, 162–74; Amartya Sen, *Choice, Measurement and Welfare* (Oxford, 1982), esp. 1–38, 158–200, 291–317.

throughout history the principle has been applied in extremely diverse forms. The concluding chapters of the *Politika* deal with the ways in which conflicts with respect to this issue may be resolved in the ecclesiastical and political spheres. In the case of ecclesiastical succession, *mutatis mutandis,* Krizhanich accords to the "democratic process" all feasible emphasis. In the case of political succession, his advocacy is based on the realities of Russia's absolute autocracy. His argument in both cases is consistent with a fundamental scholastic dictum:

> Now right reason demands principles from which reason proceeds. And when reason argues about particular cases, it needs not only universal but also particular principles.[42]

Krizhanich applies this dictum in a pragmatic rather than a dogmatic manner. For the achievement of the general principles of both institutions—church and state—a greater degree of flexibility is required on the part of each institution with respect to its particular principles, since the likelihood of one institution influencing the general principles of the other is extremely limited. This approach, as we have seen, is also consistent with his reasoning on political and economic forms of organization.

It is in this way that Krizhanich addressed himself to the basic issues of Russian life and history. He demonstrated the different forms of insularity that have encumbered Russian views, experience, and actions. Geographic, political, religious, and linguistic insularity have intensified fears of practically all things foreign. It clearly follows from his schema that Russians would tend to interpret every defensive act by foreigners— military, political, or even purely intellectual—as a threat of aggression. In the *Politika,* Krizhanich depicts these forces incisively and in fascinating detail. English-speaking readers of his work cannot but derive insight from his analysis of Russia's exaggerated fearfulness, matched only by her excessive use of force and power; her secretiveness, matched by shrewdness; her apathy and patience, matched by compulsion and fatalism; and her national adversity, matched by steadfastness and indefatigable energy. More important, in his recommendations for tempering Russia's propensity to cataclysm, Krizhanich demonstrates abiding reasons for a degree of hopefulness with regard to the relation between the Russian people and the peoples with whom they must coexist. His vehement but mistaken

---

[42] Thomas Aquinas, *The Summa Theologica* (Chicago, 1952), Robert M. Hutchins, ed., vol. 2, 45.

views on pan-Slavism and ecclesiastical unification, however, suggest the need for humility in judging new contributions to the history of ideas, especially our own. Nonetheless, at a time in history when two fundamentally different societies are vulnerable to mutually catastrophic destruction, Krizhanich's reasons for hopefulness and his use of general and particular principles may assume major significance. In the pursuit of general principles, it emerges from the *Politika* that the way in which necessarily coexisting institutions or polities endeavor to implement their objectives is a key factor in their survival. The resolve of each society to maintain and defend its general principles and attendant institutions must be regarded as a stark reality. This calls for balance and proportion with respect to particular principles, the application of which would serve the mutual betterment of the opposing societies, as well as that of others, and thereby reduce their distrust, disequilibrium, and danger of miscalculation.

John M. Letiche   Basil Dmytryshyn
Professor of Economics   Professor of History
University of California   Portland State University
Berkeley, California   Portland, Oregon

Discourses on Government

Iurii Krizhanich

Foreword

April 15, 1663

These chapters put forth the thoughts and opinions of several well-known authors who wrote about political matters—about imperial, governmental, and national concerns and enterprises; namely, Philip de Commines, Paolo Paruta, Justus Lipsius, and others.[1]

Philip de Commines was a Parisian nobleman and an advisor to two French kings. He also served as envoy to various other kings. He is considered a good politician and political writer. Paolo Paruta was a Venetian nobleman and high government official who wrote discerningly about politics. Lipsius was a philosopher and a man of great intellect. His works are held everywhere in high esteem. Finally, Maxim Faust wrote books about the treasury, money, and minerals. He offers useful thoughts and instructions on how to collect revenue with justice, with genuine profit, and with honor for rulers and without oppression of subjects.[2]

Information has been secured for this work from other books about measures to preserve the honor and majesty of the tsar's name;[3] about the opinions of this famous tsardom other nations entertain; about what they write about it; about what they praise and what they dispraise; and about how we should interpret their charges and respond to them—should circumstances allow—during official ambassadorial visits or elsewhere.

---

[1] Philip de Commines (1447–1509) was a French historian who lived during the reigns of Louis XI (1461–83) and Charles VIII (1483–98). Krizhanich used the Latin text of Commines's principal work, *Duo gallicarum rerum scriptores nobilissimi. Frossardus in brevem historiarum memorabilium. Epitomen contractus* (Frankfurt, 1594). Paolo Paruta (1540–98) was a Venetian historian who wrote *Discorsi politici* (Venice, 1599) and *Historia Veneciana* (Venice, 1605). Justus Lipsius (1547–1606) was a Dutch scholar who edited and published several ancient classics. In Tobolsk, Krizhanich was in possession of a copy of Lipsius's *Monita et exempla politica* (Amsterdam, 1630).

[2] Maxim Faust de Aschaffenburg wrote several books, including *Consilia pro aerario civili, ecclesiastici et militari* (Frankfurt, 1641).

[3] Historically, Russian and other sources used the term *tsar* only for the Byzantine emperors, the khans of the Golden Horde, the sultan of the Ottoman Empire, the emperor

3

It is a known fact that neighboring nations deceive this glorious realm. We must learn how to deal with them during ambassadorial visits, at negotiations on commercial matters, and at war; and how to guard against the ceaseless deceits and cunning with which they take possession of all the fruits of this land and the property of this nation. Accordingly we will speak here of trade, handicrafts, agriculture or land cultivation, and of all the kinds of enterprise that serve to enrich the state treasury and well-being of the people; of the strengthening of the tsardom, the increasing of its forces, and all other military affairs; of the preservation of honor and dignity—matters that are essential to know, but about which, it seems to me, no one thus far has said anything; of laws and customs, and justice, and how they are sometimes violated; and of how to protect good order and eliminate the bad.

CONCERNING THE ILLS OR NATIONAL MISFORTUNES

St Ambrose (in Book 1, commentary 5 to chapter 7 of Luke), speaking about the dead man whom the Savior resurrected in Capernaum, said: "This dead man was brought to his grave by four principal causes, the same causes that are responsible for all calamities and that constantly draw all human bodies to their graves."[4] It is said that our body consists of four principal elements—earth, water, air, and fire. Inasmuch as they are hostile and ruinous to one another (since dry always contends with wet and heat with cold), they cannot exist in harmony and hence a combination of them cannot be permanent. Because of this, there is disharmony in our body and constant struggle among the parts. It grows sick and requires daily nourishment, and if its strength is not revitalized by food and drink (and sometimes medicine), it rapidly degenerates and perishes.

Similarly, every state consists of many contradictory parts which, by virtue of their disharmony and contention, inflict damage on and lead to

---

of China, and the khans of Siberia, Kazan, Astrakhan, and the Crimea. Beginning with Ivan III (1462–1505), the title was adopted by Muscovy's sovereigns. The word *tsar* stemmed from the Roman, and hence Byzantine, *caesar*. For a discussion of Russian perceptions of the term *tsar* in all of its ramifications, see M.F. Vladimirskii-Budanov, *Obzor istorii russkogo prava*, 6th ed. (St Petersburg, 1909), pp. 147–57; and D.I. Prozorovskii, "O znachenii tsarskogo titula do priniatiia russkimi gosudariami titula imperatorskogo," *Izvestiia Imperatorskogo Russkogo Arkheologicheskogo Obshchestva* (1877), vol. 8.

[4] St Ambrose (c.340–97), a bishop of Milan, wrote *Duties of the Clergy* (based largely on Cicero's *De officiis*), a standard work on ethics and a basic source of the Stoic tradition in early Western European thought.

the downfall or destruction of the whole. Thus the country is afflicted, now by the bad laws that inconspicuously arise therein, now by foreign invasion and trickery; these strike the state like maladies, and it sickens and decays, and it needs constant reinforcement.

Ailments, or national ills, are brought on by various causes, such as:

(1) when a monarch falls under the control of other nations, as in the case of Poland, where foreign elements rule;

(2) when a nation must pay tribute to another nation;

(3) when in treaties, and in commercial or other transactions, our nation is cheated and impoverished by neighboring nations;

(4) when there is no justice administered, thieves practice their profession freely, and the strong abuse the weak;

(5) when the kingdom has greedy individuals and godless laws or discords, or wrongs that force people to live in constant danger, and to contemplate and hope for a change;

(6) when some kind of failure occurs in our affairs that brings upon the entire nation loss and defamation, discredit and abuse.

All of this brings the nation evil, and since the sovereign should always try to prevent such evil from materializing, he must devise a program to drive it out of the state system. A good ruler should never be satisfied with preserving the status quo. He should always strive to make the state richer, stronger, worthier, and above all happier. A ruler who does not strive to improve his state doubtless impoverishes it, because it cannot remain for long in the same condition—it must either improve or deteriorate. The improvement and strengthening of the state depend much more on good laws than on the expansion of its frontiers or the conquest of new countries.

Before his death the Emperor Hadrian said to his nobles, "I inherited Rome brick and leave it marble." Given the city and the era he did well. But a ruler would have done better, and would have attained greater glory, if he could have said, "I inherited a state troubled by poor order but leave it in possession of good laws."

Philip—prince of the Czech kingdom within the Holy Roman Empire—frequently remarked:

A well-run state can be identified by three things:
First, by good roads—where there are good bridges, and where it is possible to travel throughout the country without being afraid of thieves and other dangers;

Second, by good currency—when trade does not suffer from worthless money; and

Third, by good courts—where everyone has easy access to trial and to speedy justice.

This was well said, but nevertheless incomplete—the prince left out certain necessary and basic elements. In addition to these three prerequisites, rulers also need the other essentials which, with God's help and to the extent of our capabilities, we shall describe.

THE DIVISION OF THIS WORK

Jeremiah states: "Let not the wise man boast of his wisdom, nor the valiant of his valour; let no man boast of his riches; but if any man would boast, let him boast of this, that he understands and knows me—says the Lord" (Jeremiah, 9:23).[5]

These words of the prophet show that above all it is essential to give glory to God—that is, to know Him, and to love and praise Him by means of good deeds. He speaks in one breath of the three things which the world boasts about, and which he himself considers as a source of happiness: namely, wealth, strength, and wisdom. Yet he considers worldly glory vain and ruinous to souls when they strive only to achieve it and in the process forget God. To those who are faithful to God, however, these matters are not harmful: on the contrary, they are good, quite beneficial, and in fact indispensable; they are God's gifts.

This is why we divide this work into three parts, and speak about the wealth, strength, and wisdom of the sovereign.

SOME GENERAL REMARKS ABOUT PIETY, WEALTH, STRENGTH, WISDOM, AND HONOR

In the words of the prophet just quoted, there are four pillars of the state: piety, wealth, strength, and wisdom. Piety strengthens the soul and prepares it for eternal bliss, while the rest strengthen the body and bring bodily benefit to those who use them properly and moderately.

Yet it is a surprise and a great misfortune that barely anyone seeks what

---

[5] The translations of Krizhanich's scriptural quotations are from the *New English Bible* (Cambridge and Oxford, 1970).

is better and more vital than anything else—namely, piety and eternal bliss. The entire world seeks wealth, power, wisdom, and glory, and thinks about these matters incessantly and endlessly. Moreover, a great majority seek them out through devious means, and many others do not even know what they really are.

The wealth of a ruler does not consist in how much silver and gold he has in his treasury but in how many people he has in his country. The king who has more people is rich, not the one who has more gold. For the Scripture says, "Many subjects make a king famous; a small population shames a prince" (Proverbs 14:28). The strength of a state lies neither in its size nor in the inaccessibility of its fortresses, but in its good laws. Under a harsh system the best land will become an underpopulated desert. Under a moderate system even a poor land will become populous.

A wise sovereign, one who knows the world, follows two rules: "Know thyself! Do not trust foreigners." For in the same manner that simple people are deceived by other simple people, kings are deceived by other kings and whole nations by other nations. Only a skeptic avoids deception. Consider it eternally true that no one ever does good for the benefit of his friend, only in his own interest and for his own motives. Whoever forgets this is deprived of what he aspired to, and this is especially true of our [Slavic] people. The cause of all our burdens and sufferings is that we do not know ourselves and believe foreigners.

Some see the honor and dignity of a sovereign in three things: (1) displaying to foreigners of beautiful, expensive clothing, pompous military exhibitions, silver and treasure; (2) granting to these foreigners, envoys, and merchants large and rich presents; (3) keeping many of these idle and useless foreigners on high salary for the sake of the glory they bring.

But those who think so are bitterly mistaken, and they deceive their own sovereigns as well. The glory you achieve by suffocating your own people to satisfy foreigners is vain. Neighboring nations do not praise it; they revile it, and make fun of it. Except in some special circumstances, the king gains no glory when foreigners receive rich gifts from him. His glory stems from his ability not to be deceived in commercial transactions and treaties. The king gains no glory when a multitude of foreigners wax fat and drunken in his country at his expense. These parasites, while gorging and roistering, mock at the loose order that makes this behavior possible, as others had been doing long before. And glorious will be the king whose own subjects are rich and dignified. The more proud subjects he rules, the more he is esteemed. A king who wishes to be especially respected should first elevate the dignity of his own princes and nobles.

How mistaken are those who maintain that somehow the dignity of a sovereign depends above all on the wealth of the treasury, even if the realm is poor. The dignity of a sovereign depends on nothing else but the wealth of his subjects. Wherever subjects are wealthy, the sovereign can carry on war as often as he wishes. But where only the treasury is rich and the whole country poor, the strength of the country soon evaporates, and there will be no power to wage war.

PART I

Concerning Wealth

Measures to enrich the state's treasury are well known to everyone and well applied everywhere. For this reason there is no need to expect any measures to be newly discovered or never before practiced. As it is stated in Ecclesiastes: "There is nothing new under the sun, and no one can say that this is new" (Ecclesiastes 1:10). It is better to discard some old measures for increasing the treasury than to search for new ones.

Yet it is worthy of note that in all affairs new councils prompt doubt, dissatisfaction, and easy condemnation. Only in the collection of state revenue nothing has been so new, unjust, godless and shameful that it has not been adopted. I shall not try to devise new methods of raising revenue, but only say that some methods and enterprises are unjust, dishonest, and unsound, and lead not to enrichment but to actual impoverishment. Instead I will show how to use just, honest, and useful methods, and how to preserve them.

The following are ill-advised methods: first, alchemy, or the search for gold through the devilish error by means of which people hope to make gold and silver out of copper. Countless multitudes of people from time immemorial have made claims and continue to make claims about this method, but thus far not one ruler has received enough to feed even one soldier from alchemy, and not one alchemist has created one drop of gold from copper or secured any benefit for himself without the aid of the devil or the deception of other people.

Second, coining or debasing currency—that is, profiting from coining currency and minting worthless money. This method is not only unjust, but sinful and very deceitful as well. It appears beneficial, but actually it is detrimental and harmful. No ruler can ever expect to obtain money from the debasement of currency without a hundredfold loss in the process.

Physicians speak of *remedia desperata*. Whenever a doctor determines that a sick person is dying, he cuts part of his anatomy open and sews it up

9

again, or tries to cure the body in some other way, so that the sick person either gets well or dies from the cure. The coining of worthless money resembles this deadly *remedia desperata*. And similarly, as a *remedia desperata* is used only in an extreme emergency, when there is no other means available, so worthless money should not be coined except in extreme circumstances. And this coining should be terminated as soon as possible, for if it is continued for long the people will meet the same fate as a sick person whose vein the doctor opens and then fails to close: the blood all runs out and the person dies. The same thing will happen to the nation—all wealth (which is called the second blood) will run out of it.

Third, merciless extortions, harsh systems, monopolies, shocking practices, and other excessive and unmerciful oppression of the subjects: for it is truly said: "Do not do unto others what you do not wish to have done unto you."

One of the most ruinous courses a nation can follow is when a king allows foreign merchants to remain or reside in his country and permits them to maintain warehouses and shops and to trace throughout the country. When this is done, they purchase our goods very cheaply everywhere, and reveal all of our secrets to their countrymen—not only commercial but state secrets as well. They disrupt our way of life and impose their corrupt and destructive customs on our people. They lead us into temptation and ruin our souls. For all of this the king must give an accounting before God.

In a word, these merchants are the cause of immeasurable ills to the body and the soul of the nation, and of no concrete benefits except for a few gifts to the tsar or *boyars* [landed aristocrats].[1] And these gifts are almost valueless, because foreigners export from our country ten thousand times more goods than they give us. They export goods they have purchased here during hard times, and thereby create very high prices. By contrast, native merchants must make their purchases in both good and bad times, and they are unable to export their goods because of the copper currency which has been introduced.[2]

---

[1] The term *boyar* (Russian plural *boyare*) denoted the wealthy and influential members of the Russian landed and service aristocracy. The tsar selected certain boyars to serve as members of the boyar advisory council (*boyarskaia duma*) and appointed others to high positions in the armed forces and the civil administration. For a classic treatment of the *boyarskaia duma*, see V.O. Kliuchevskii, *Boyarskaia duma v drevnei Rusi*, 4th ed. (Moscow, 1909). See also N.P. Zagoskin, *Boyarskaia duma* (Kazan, 1879); and Vladimirskii-Budanov, *Obzor istorii*, 158–74.

[2] To meet the rising cost of war in the mid-1650s, the Russian government issued copper coins. When the government began to pay its own bills with copper currency, while insisting that the people pay their taxes in silver, this form of war financing, coupled with

It is additionally burdensome when these foreign merchants act not as independent masters but as buyers for and agents of other, richer merchants, as is the case with all foreigners who trade in Russia.[3] They and their servants live and grow wealthy at our expense, and send our goods to their masters. They purchase these goods for a very low price at an opportune time. Moreover, they send a specific predetermined amount in cash or in goods to them annually. Through their cunning they deprive this glorious state of basic necessities, and there is no telling why it is necessary to pay the tribute or the *iasak* to these Englishmen, Dutchmen, and Hamburg merchants.[4]

These foreigners have thoroughly revealed themselves to us. They bought the entire fur supply for copper money and imported it back to Russia for a song, sold it for silver, and thereby inflicted incalculable harm upon the tsar's treasury and the entire nation.

Oh illustrious sovereign, do not place any trust in the wolf when he offers to feed your lambs! And never believe that a foreign merchant will bring you any benefit. It is impossible that a man who travels all lands and seas for his entire life, dedicates himself to wandering and perilous danger for the sake of money, and contemplates silver with greater zeal than the wolf does lambs, will increase your wealth. Whoever casts a line into water hopes to catch a fish. Whoever plants rye in the ground hopes to

---

harvest failures, brought about sharp increases in the prices of necessities, depreciation of copper coins in terms of silver, higher taxes, panic, and, in July 1662, bloody riots. Initially, a "copper ruble" was issued equal in value to a "silver ruble." By 1662, fifteen copper rubles were equal in value to one silver ruble. On June 23, 1663, the government returned to the silver standard, withdrawing the copper rubles from circulation at the rate of one copper ruble per ten "silver dengi." For a comprehensive discussion of this issue, see K.V. Bazilevich, *Denezhnaia reforma Alekseia Mikhailovicha i vosstanie v Moskve v 1662 g.* (Moscow-Leningrad, 1936); see also V.O. Kliuchevskii, *Sochineniia* (Moscow, 1957), vol. 3, 223–26.

[3] Krizhanich frequently refers to the "*nemtsy*" (singular *nemets*). Currently this term refers to Germans. In sixteenth and seventeenth-century Muscovite Russia the term usually designated all West Europeans (English, Dutch, Germans, Swedes, and others—except Slavs and Latins). Krizhanich used the terms *nemtsy* primarily to identify West European Protestants (Germans, Dutch, English, Swedes and Danes) who, he believed, were dangerous both to the orthodox Slavs and to the Catholics. Many of the West Europeans lived outside Moscow in a special community known as the *nemetskaia sloboda*, or free foreign settlement. For an account of this community, see Samuel H. Baron, "The Origins of Seventeenth-Century Moscow's Nemeckaja Sloboda," *California Slavic Studies*, V (1970): 1–17.

[4] *Iasak*: a Mongol-Tartar term for tribute paid by the conquered to the conqueror, used primarily in Siberia. See Raymond H. Fisher, *The Russian Fur Trade, 1550–1700* (Berkeley and Los Angeles, 1943), 49–61, and Sergei V. Bakhrushin, "Isak v Sibiri v XVII veke," *Sibirskie ogni*, no. 3 (May–June, 1927): 95–129.

harvest it tenfold. Sovereign, if a foreign merchant gives you or any of your *boyars* a silver cup or some other gift, obviously he will carry out of your land and consume a hundred times as much wealth. Baruch spoke the truth: "If you allow a foreigner [into your territories] he will ruin you."

Not everything that glitters is gold. Not everything that seems to be useful is so. Some activities seem useful but are actually harmful. There is wealth which, instead of bringing wealth, buys ruin. Enterprises can be considered just only when they provide us with the benefits from our land and neighboring nations by wise, God-fearing, and charitable and proper means—not by foolish, harsh, or vile ones.

A loss occurs when we take something and give double or more in return. We incur such losses from partnerships with foreign merchants living in our country. Losses or unjust profits also stem from tax collection, debasing of currency, and similar activities. Ill gains result from petty, insignificant, and worthless goods. [St] Paul says that "The root of all evil is greed." For states, greed and vanity are Scylla and Charybdis—perilous rocks. From these all evil and tyrannical rule stems.

Flatterers, astrologists, alchemists, debasers of coinage, and other schemers are royal sirens who seek to reap benefit either from the debasement of currency or from other methods of collecting revenues which are unjust and burdensome for the population.

No profit is reliable if it is secured without labor and sweat, or without the expense of an adequate amount of time, or unjustly, or through harsh or shameful methods. Every genuine return should be based on labor and sweat, increased gradually and patiently, and received justly and with dignity. Excessive luxury brings a body illness; excessive wealth generates ruin; excessive collections for the treasury bring poverty to a nation. Good sense brings the best gains.

In a poor and sparsely populated monarchy the king cannot have adequate wealth. In a rich and populous monarchy the king cannot be poor. Whoever fishes with moderation will always find something to catch in the stream. But whoever catches all the fish in the stream in one day finds nothing to catch the next day.

The honor, glory, obligation, and responsibility of a king are to make his nation happy: monarchies have not been created for monarchs, but monarchs for monarchies. Where laws are good, subjects are also satisfied, and foreigners wish to come to settle. But where laws are oppressive, subjects thirst for a change in government and frequently change it if they can, and foreigners are afraid to come. Oh sovereign, govern your people so that they wish no change.

We have discussed foolish, evil, undignified, and dishonest activities: alchemy, debasement of currency, extortions, and toleration of foreign merchants. The means of acquisition are beneficial and praiseworthy when they enable the treasury to fill up justly, according to God's teachings, and honestly without vile greed, without vicious extortions, and without unbearable and inhuman oppression of subject peoples. Three activities are of this sort: agriculture, crafts, and trade. They are called black enterprises, or enterprises of black [that is, common] people. The fourth enterprise is the national economy, or public service, which is the foundation and the soul of all other enterprises. These are called revenue-producing enterprises.

In a poor monarchy it is irresponsible for a king to be rich. And if any king aspires to become rich he can become very rich if his monarchy prospers. Thus if a king wants to be rich he should first see to it that his subjects become rich, and he should establish conditions that will create abundance of everything and low prices on everything in his monarchy. And a king can attain this (to the extent that it is possible in his state) if he arranges that people in his realm be engaged in agriculture, crafts, trade, and public service to the national economy with total diligence and zeal.

1

Trade

Question: When is a kingdom considered wealthy?
Answer: (1) A kingdom is considered wealthy when it possesses gold, silver, and other ores, as is the case in Arab and Hungarian lands.

(2) Richer, however, is a kingdom which abounds in things suitable for beautifying the body and for clothing: precious stones, pearls, corals, silk, cotton, fine wool, linen, hemp, and all sorts of other materials for apparel.

(3) Still wealthier it seems is the state that abounds in items suitable for eating and drinking, such as olives, grapes, honey, salt, pepper, cloves, sugar, and other spices; also rice, wheat, and all kinds of grains, beans, and fruits; edible, medicinal, and color-dyeing herbs; livestock, fish, fowl, and edible wild animals.

(4) Still wealthier and more populous and stronger, however, is the kingdom whose inhabitants either have acquired skills or have been endowed by nature with sharp minds and cleverness, where good convenient harbors and market places also exist and where, consequently, every kind of craft, agriculture, and extensive sea trade flourishes, as is the case in England and Holland.

But still more glorious and fortunate is the kingdom where, in addition to all this, there exist good laws, as we see in the kingdom of France. Kingdoms based on military might where people live by theft and the best and most useful brains neglect all other activity, dedicate themselves wholly to war and pillage, and think only about war, as is the case among the Crimean Tartars, Turks, and the Kalmucks, are never wealthy.

Although our famous [Russian] state is quite vast and immeasurable, nevertheless it is closed to trade on all sides. In the north we are engirdled by the Arctic Ocean and by wastelands. To the east and south we are surrounded by backward peoples with whom there can exist no trade. In

The west—in Lithuania and Belorussia—nothing is produced that we need, except for the copper found among the Swedes. The Azov and Black Sea trade, which would be very beneficial to this country, has been seized and is still held by the Crimean Tartars. Trade in Astrakhan is hindered by the Nogai Tartars. The Kalmucks interfere with our Bokhara trade in Siberia.[1] As a result we have only three safe marketplaces for overland trade: Novgorod, Pskov, and the Archangel harbors for sea trade. But the road to the latter is incredibly distant and difficult.

Thus it is evident, first, that this country has very few marketplaces and that it is essential that there be more; but that without the tsar's help no one can organize them.

Second, that the country possesses no gold, silver, copper, tin, lead, mercury, or good iron.

Third, that there are no precious stones, pearls, corals, and dyes at the same time that the commonest and poorest people want them.

Fourth, that there is no sugar, saffron, pepper, cloves, nuts, ginger, myrrh, thyme, nutmeg, or other spices and fragrances.

Fifth, that there are no olives, grapes, raisins, almonds, figs, lemons, walnuts, chestnuts, plums, peaches, melons, or many other fruits.

Sixth, that in addition to this there are no basic and essential items, such as cloth and other materials for wearing apparel—wool, silk, and cotton.

Seventh, that this country is devoid of stone and good lumber for construction and good clay for pottery.

Eighth, that the intellectual faculties of our people are undeveloped and sluggish. The people are inexperienced in crafts and only slightly knowl-

[1] The Crimean Tartars, a Turkic people, were once an integral part of the powerful Mongol-controlled empire known as the Golden Horde. In the fifteenth century they set up their own state in the Crimea, known as the Khanate of the Crimea, which subsequently became a vassal of the Ottoman Empire. They controlled almost the entire region north of the Black Sea, and their periodic raids inflicted heavy damage as far north as Moscow. After the disintegration of the Golden Horde, another Turkic people, the Nogai Tartars, settled north of the Caspian Sea, where they interfered with Russian attempts to reach the Caucasus, Central Asia, and Persia. The Kalmucks were a Mongol people who in the seventeenth century inhabited the area from the headwaters of the Yenisei River to the Urals. They comprised two basic groups: the White Kalmucks, or Telenguts, who camped near the headwaters of the Ob river, and the Black Kalmucks, or Dzhungars, who controlled the upper reaches of the Irtysh river. For excellent discussions of the Golden Horde and some of its auxiliaries, see George Vernadsky, *The Mongols and Russia* (New Haven, 1953), 138–332, and his *Tsardom of Moscow, 1547–1682,* part 2 (New Haven, 1969), 542–57; and Michael Prawdin, *The Mongol Empire: Its Rise and Legacy,* 2nd ed. (New York, 1961), pp. 390–464. The Kalmucks are specifically treated by S.K. Bogoiavlenskii, "Materialy po istorii Kalmykov v pervoi polovine XVII veka," *Istoricheskie Zapiski* (1939), no. 5, 48–101.

edgeable in trade, agriculture, and household management. Russians and Poles, indeed the entire Slavic population, are totally ignorant of how to carry on distant trade at sea as well as on land. Our merchants study neither arithmetic nor accounting. Consequently, foreign merchants are always able to outwit and mercilessly deceive us, all the more since they live throughout the entire Russian land and buy up our goods at the lowest possible prices. It would be possible to bear this if our people lived among them and could buy up goods cheaply themselves. But our people do not live among them, and cannot because of their natural impracticality, because of their undeveloped intellects, and especially because of foreign envy and malice, which many of our people have experienced.

Ninth, that roads in this extensive state are long and difficult because of marshes and forests; and also that they are unsafe because of attacks by the Crimean and Nogai Tartars, and by the Kalmucks and other brigand-like peoples.

Tenth, that this country abounds only in furs, sheepskin, hemp, and most recently potash. Honey, wax, caviar, wheat, rye, flax, hides and other goods exported from here are exported not because of their abundance, but out of necessity and because of the machinations of foreigners. As a result we are deprived of the fruits of our own land and suffer shortages in these goods.

There is only one way to help the people to meet many of their needs. Let the sovereign tsar, in name and in reality, resume control over the entire trade with other nations, as he has done in the past, and let him retain it for future times. Only in this way will it be possible to keep accounts in such a way that we neither export the many goods of which we have no surplus nor import foreign goods we do not need. In this way the sovereign tsar will be able to increase the number of marketplaces and customs officials essential to the state for conveyance of goods.

Then foreign merchants will have nothing to do here. Cloth and other foreign goods will pass through our own hands to Siberia, to the Bokharans and the Indians; to Astrakhan, to the Persians; to Azov, to the Turks; to Putivl, to the Ukrainians and the Wallachians.[2] Conversely, goods from these nations will flow to us and through our hands to the Germans and other Western Europeans, the Poles, and the Lithuanians.

Through such activity the entire state will become wealthy, and all of its inhabitants will rejoice. The only people who will be dissatisfied will

---

[2] The Bokharans (Russian *bukhartsy*) were merchants from Central Asia (mostly Bokhara) who served as commercial intermediaries between Russian officials in Siberia and various natives of Asia.

be the great merchants, whose revenues will be somewhat decreased. But one should pay no attention to their plight because this matter concerns the overall benefit of all the people.

Question: Is it appropriate for sovereigns to trade?

Answer: (1) Though some people maintain that it is inappropriate and undignified for kings and nobles to carry on trade, it is essential to know that by itself trade is an honorable and dignified enterprise. Only the vile greed which is usually associated with trade is undignified. When trade is conducted neither for personal profit nor for insatiable greed, but for the general public good, it is an honorable, good and wholly regal enterprise.

(2) It is stated in the Scriptures that all of Solomon's dishes and all of his apparel were made of pure gold. In Jerusalem silver was not valued because there was as much of it as there were stones in the street (3 Kings 10:21–27; 2 Chronicles 9:20). How did Solomon obtain gold? Not by mining ores, not by alchemy or the oppression of his people, but by trade. Every third year he dispatched his ships to India with goods, and they brought him four hundred talents of gold and more in addition to silver and other riches. This was 1,334 *pudy*[3] of gold, since one talent weighed 125 *grivny*,[4] or 3 *pudy* and 5 *grivny*. King Joseph wanted to revive Solomon's trade, but he was punished by God and could not fulfill his ambition.

The king of Portugal also sends out his ships to India at great profit, as do some German princes. The Danish king dispatches his ships to ice-covered wastelands for one commodity: whale oil. The kings of France, Spain, and England, and the emperors of Turkey and Germany, conduct no trade, first because their subjects are powerful and capable enough to carry on very distant and large trade; and second, because their territories are open on all sides and there is no way to prohibit their subjects from having commercial relations with neighboring peoples. Yet in spite of all this, the king of France has a permanent ambassador in Constantinople, while the king of England has a commercial envoy to serve his subjects. Moreover, the kings of Spain and Portugal, in support of their own trade as well as that of their subjects dispatch their armed forces to sea to convoy ships to India.

(3) As is evident, it is good and proper for a sovereign to carry on trade if he conducts it for the benefit and need of the entire kingdom, and if this

[3] *Pud*: a Russian unit of measure equal to 36.11 pounds, or 16.38 kg.

[4] *Grivna*: a unit of measure equal to 410 grams; also a monetary unit. From the fifteenth through the seventeenth centuries, the value of a *grivna* was about twenty *dengi*; ten *grivny* equalled one ruble.

results not in harm, but in easing and diminishing the burden of the population. This can occur, first, when the king carries on trade not with his own subjects, but only with foreigners. For it is unfair for a king to buy from one of his own subjects and then sell to another; he should purchase from his own and sell to foreigners, or purchase from foreigners and sell to his own or to other foreigners. He should not carry goods from one town to another in his own realm and retail them, but leave this activity to his subjects.

Second, it is proper for the tsar to trade when royal power is required in business matters which private individuals cannot resolve. An example would be a sea voyage requiring great expenditures which no one except the king was capable of sustaining, as during Solomon's reign, when the inhabitants of Judea were in no position to send ships to India, and only Solomon, by virtue of his royal power (and even he was not alone but in association with Hiram, the king of Tyre), was capable of doing it. Another example would be an overland trade journey, where because of long, difficult, and hazardous roads many guides, guards, posts, and outlays of money were needed. Such assistance is greatly and desperately needed in this tsardom.

Third, when a country is deprived of many goods and forced to purchase them from other nations and, as a consequence, the inhabitants are habitually cheated. If everyone is allowed to trade with foreigners, or if foreigners receive permission to live among us, the people suffer greatly; they take our wealth away from us and we starve, while they consume the fruit of our land before our eyes.

(4) The tsar's trade should be conducted and managed in the following manner:

(a) The tsar's commercial agents should not sell anything that was purchased within the state at home. They should sell everything they purchase from the tsar's subjects to foreigners for the highest profit and at the highest price.

(b) When they make purchases from the tsar's subjects they should not be stingy, but pay as much as possible generously.

(c) Whatever they purchase from foreigners they should sell to their own people at no profit or just at the smallest profit. An exception can be made in the case of hard times, when it is permissible to sell at a higher price.

(d) They should sell these goods to foreign nations for as much as possible.

(e) As I have observed earlier, these goods should not be sold at retail, only at wholesale. And they should be sold at two or three places in the country. During hard times it would be proper to retail them in many towns at a high price.

(f) During normal and good times the tsar's advisors and commercial overseers should see to it that commercial agents in no way either cheat the sovereign tsar or abuse the people; that prices on goods belonging to the tsar do not rise; and, on the contrary, that all the goods in the country are cheaper than they would be under condition of trade among private entrepreneurs.

(g) Whenever local merchants wish to purchase goods from the sovereign's agents, these agents should sell them at the same specified price. Local merchants may be granted a monopoly on one commodity or another only if they pledge to sell it cheaper.

TRADE WITH OTHER NATIONS

As we have noted, this state has very few marketplaces, and it is essential that they be established and expanded. This is because the more marketplaces a kingdom has, the richer it is. It should be possible to establish one trading outpost on the Don opposite Azov for trade with the Turks; another in the lands of the Kalmucks, along the Irtysh near the Salt Lake or some place else, to trade with India; a third in Putivl to trade with the Ukrainians and the Wallachians; and a fourth, in due time, in the Dauri territory.[5] Moreover, the Caspian Sea should be stocked with well-built tsarist ships for transporting Persian goods.

I have heard that upon reaching Moscow a certain Venetian, who was looking for a route to India said, "From India we could import pepper, sugar, and other spices into this country and capture the trade in these goods from the Germans and Spaniards who bring them by sea." Now this Indo-Chinese route is well known, and merchants from India come annually to Siberia.[6]

[5] The Salt Lake is now known as Lake Iamysh. It is located on the upper reaches of the Irtysh river. In the seventeenth century, its salt deposits played a vital role in Russian trade with the Bokhara merchants. The Dauri territory was the region east of Lake Baikal and the area north of the Amur river.

[6] In the seventeenth century, Indian merchants developed commercial contacts with Russians in Siberia, and provided the latter with detailed information about various trade routes. See N.B. Baikov, "K voprosu o russko-indiiskikh torgovykh otnosheniiakh v XVI–XVII v.v.," *Trudy Instituta Vostokovedeniia Akademii Nauk Uzbek SSR,* no. 4 (1956). For pertinent headings taken from the Register of Indian Documents in the archives of the Foreign Office in Moscow relating to Russia and India, see John F. Baddeley, *Russia, Mongolia, China* (London, 1919), vol. 2, 159–60.

A duke of Holstein conceived the idea of establishing trade between Persia and his country through Archangel and Astrakhan.[7] He failed in his ambition though I do not know why, but in his failure God revealed His mercy to our people. The Germans were not allowed to capture that country, seize our revenues, and disgrace us. This is why the Germans repeat an adage: "Russia is like a dog beside a haystack—he neither eats the hay nor lets the bull near it." The Russians appear to do the same: they do not trade themselves, and they do not allow the Germans to trade.

Trade in this country could greatly increase and improve, but it has not. Our people are still unfamiliar with the business of large-scale trade. For the cause of this, our lack of expertise and dull intellects, we need a whetstone and polishing tools, to wit: learning. Laziness hinders us greatly, since our people do not study arithmetic and consequently cannot prepare accounts in the sort of trade that involves many hundreds of thousands of rubles.

Many of them, in fact, cannot even take advantage of other nations when time or circumstances permit. They think only of collecting tribute, and see no other benefits. If we cannot subdue the Kalmucks, Persians, and Turks to our authority, many grow despondent and think that, except for the tribute, it is impossible to obtain any benefit from these people. They do not understand that although foreigners have not placed Russian land under their control, nevertheless they are collecting tribute from it, not only by various schemes, but chiefly because they maintain their agents here—officials who annually give them a portion of their profit and tribute and devour all the wealth of this land. And those who are not

---

[7] In 1634, a delegation from the duke of Holstein concluded an agreement with the Russian authorities granting Holstein merchants permission to travel through Russia to conduct trade in Persia. The secretary of the Holstein delegation was Krizhanich's bête noire, Adam Olearius (1599–1671), who, after four visits to Moscow, published a polemical and, on certain issues, perceptive work on Russian virtues and follies entitled *Vermehrte Newe Beschreibung der Moscowitischen . . . Reise . . .* (Schleswig, 1656). Krizhanich had a copy of this work in Tobolsk and was deeply and emotionally critical of most of its contents (see pp. 116–24 below). For an English edition of Olearius's work, see Samuel H. Baron, trans. and ed., *The Travels of Olearius in Seventeenth-Century Russia* (Stanford, 1967), especially pp. 56–78, and p. 74 for the terms of the agreement. The text of the agreement is in *Akty istoricheskie,* vol. 3, no. 181. For a Soviet study of the role of Persian trade in Russian relations with Europe, see E. Zevakin, "Persidskii vopros v russko-evropeiskikh otnosheniiakh XVII v.," *Istoricheskie Zapiski* 8 (1940). Russian commercial relations with Western Europe in the seventeenth century are discussed by Walther Kirchner, *Commercial Relations Between Russia and Europe, 1400–1800, Collected Essays* (Bloomington, Ind., 1966), pp. 43–131. An excellent survey of Russian foreign trade, providing much information directly relevant to some of Krizhanich's discussion, is provided in Artur Attman, "The Russian Market in World Trade, 1500–1860," *Scandinavian Economic History Review* 29:3 (1981): 177–202.

engaged in trade live on the sovereign's pay. They brag and boast about it and have even spread a rumor: "Whoever wants to eat bread at no cost should go to Russia."

Currently our own people cannot begin to appreciate or even comprehend the advantages large-scale trade brings. They think only of the great expenditures of effort required and of the danger, and they consider possible things to be impossible. They forget that great profit requires great effort.

In order to dispel these foolish notions we shall now describe the limitless benefits this state could achieve from large-scale trade. For example, if we could establish a multithousand ruble trade through the Arctic Ocean, through the Black and Caspian Seas, and along the Sukhon, Vologda, Don, Volga, Irtysh and other rivers, and if goods to and from various nations passed through our lands, the sovereign's treasury as well as the entire nation would be tremendously enriched. The reasons for this follow in the next section.

BENEFITS FROM LARGE-SCALE TRADE

If we had an *ostrog*[8] on the Irtysh near the Salt Lake we could procure thirty or forty thousand raw hides of livestock and sheep from the Kalmucks annually. To preserve them, it would be necessary to salt them and pack them in barrels. The English use this method because hides so processed are thicker and stronger. Then if we discovered a good route along the Irtysh to the sea and the portage, and across the portage during the winter overland to the Sea of Archangel, we could sell them to foreigners. If it proved to be possible, a fort should be built at the portage to handle trade in Indian and Siberian goods.

At present, when our soldiers go to the Salt Lake to procure salt, they must haul it for about half a day from the lake to the river, either on their backs or in wheelbarrows. If a fort were built there, salt could be hauled by horses. Then we would be able to procure salt in limitless quantities, not only for our own needs but also to sell to the Germans by sea. Germans currently get their salt from Portugal, so it would be easier for them to get it from here.

On the Irtysh we could also procure much livestock, salt beef and lamb meat inexpensively, and sun-dry or smoke large quantities of it. This would enable us to feed all Siberia, and to have enough left to sell to the

---

[8] *Ostrog*: a Russian term that in the seventeenth century variously meant a fort, a fortification, a settlement, or a town.

Germans. We could also procure thousands of *pudy* of raw sheep-wool useful for the ordinary cloth we desperately need. We could also procure sheepskin coats, horses, and as many oxen as we needed.

Through the Bokhara merchants we could obtain from India as many hundreds or thousands of *pudy* of cotton as we ordered and contracted for. From the cotton we could then make cloth and dye it for our own needs or for resale to other nations. Moreover, we could purchase silk and other goods more cheaply from the Bokhara merchants than from the Germans.

We currently purchase precious stones, pearls, corals, sugar, pepper, saffron, cloves, nuts, cinnamon, ginger, and other Indian products from the Germans, who transport them over long distances by sea around the world. If we could establish good relations with the Kalmucks, we could secure these goods from the Indians directly and would not have to buy them from the Germans; on the contrary, they would buy them from us. Then many of those Indian products—silk, cotton, precious stones, pearls, and spices—would also go to Lithuania, to Belorussia, to the Ukraine and to other countries. We could also mine quantities of silver, tin, and other ores, and these ores would become cheap in this country.

I do not know what to say about olive oil, rice, grapes, raisins, figs, and other fruits. If we could secure them, the Germans would willingly buy them from us.

We could obtain as many colored silk fabrics or textiles as we wanted: velvets, satins, damask, taffeta, colored cotton cloth called *aziam,* Chinese silk, and ordinary cotton. In addition to satisfying our own needs with these goods we could satisfy all the Lithuanians, the Poles, the Ukrainians, and even the Germans. In exchange for these goods we could give the Kalmucks, the Bokharans, the Mongols, and the distant Indians our Siberian furs, German goods, and all other kinds of goods.

This matter is so vital that it would be desirable to inaugurate such trade—to spare nothing in search of a suitable spot in the Kalmuck territories to build a fort. No outlay of expenditure and effort on this business would be excessive, even if we were to give the Kalmucks several thousand rubles. None of this could compare with the benefits to be expected.

Though Siberia is useful to us even now, it could become much more beneficial: first, because of trade with the Kalmucks; second, because of trade with the Bokharans, as just noted; third, because of the Mangazeia enterprise, which will be discussed in chapter 3;[9] and fourth, because of

---

[9] Mangazeia was a town on the lower basin of the Yenisei river. It was established in 1601 and for a while was frequented by Western European merchants. See P.N. Butsinskii, *Mangazeia i mangazeiskii uezd (1601–1645 gg.)* (Kharkov, 1893); Raymond H. Fisher, "Mangazeia: A Boom Town of Seventeenth-Century Siberia," *Russian Review* 4, no. 1

the Kuznetsk fort and local iron ores, since we can obtain all kinds of good weapons and arms from there.

In a word, it is essential to know that Siberia is extremely useful and indispensable to this tsardom. From these indigenous peoples we can secure goods without money in exchange for our ordinary native goods— that is, for simple textiles and cloth, for salt and grain. These goods are highly valued there.[10]

And from the Persians, if we had a sufficient number of ships on the Caspian Sea, we could obtain eventually, and at a reasonable price, all kinds of raw and finished silk and cotton goods for Siberian furs and for German textiles and manufactured products. At present we receive Persian goods, but not as many and not in the way we could procure them if we had the ships. Aboard our own ships we could visit all the towns and countries around the Caspian Sea, and if we acted prudently we could secure fine wool for the production of fine woolens. We could get unprocessed wool and sheepskins without much effort.

The Caspian Sea (notes a certain German) is 2,800 miles (or 14,000 *versts*) in circumference.[11] Under good wind conditions it is possible to sail its width in five days and its length in six days. The sea has numerous islands, inhabited and empty. The sovereign tsar could populate the empty ones with our own people, and in time collect taxes and tribute from the populated ones.

The entire circumference, or shoreline, of this sea should be surveyed; it should be ascertained where grapes grow, and if they grow nowhere, a suitable place should be found where they could be grown. With the help of our own people and the local inhabitants enough vineyards for the needs of this entire monarchy should be started there.

If the sovereign tsar had his own ships on the Caspian he could control that sea and collect tribute from the nomadic peoples living along its shores not subject to the king of Persia; he could also collect fees from merchants sailing there as the Venetians do in the Adriatic Sea. We speak without knowledge of such matters and leave judgments about it to the informed and the educated.

(Autumn 1944); and M.I. Belov, *Mangazeia* (Leningrad, 1969).

[10] Krizhanich was one of the first writers to perceive the economic importance of Siberia for Russia's development. He dealt with the subject at greater length in a pamphlet entitled *History of Siberia*. For a detailed analysis in English of Russia's conquest and administration of Siberia, see George V. Lantzeff, *Siberia in the Seventeenth Century* (Berkeley and Los Angeles, 1943), and Raymond H. Fisher, *The Russian Fur Trade, 1550–1700* (Berkeley and Los Angeles, 1943). See also V.I. Shunkov, *Ocherki po istorii zemlevladeniia v Sibiri, XVII v.* (Moscow, 1956) and V.A. Aleksandrov, *Russkoe naselenie Sibiri XVII – nachala XVIII v.* (Moscow, 1964).

[11] *Verst*: a Russian linear measure equal to 0.6629 miles, or 1.067 km. Krizhanich here gives the equivalent in terms of German or Italian miles.

From the Bokharans and Persians we could procure carpets, blankets, onions, morocco, rice, olive oil, thyme, myrrh, balsam, muscat, rhubarb, and all sorts of dyes as well as other oriental goods, so many in fact we could satisfy the needs of all of Lithuania, Belorussia, the Ukraine, and Polish, Hungarian, and Wallachian lands, as well as the Swedes and German merchants trading in Archangel.[12] As a result of such trade a certain amount of gold and silver would always remain in our hands, and there would also be an abundance of ores and other goods.

Trade on the Don could equal that of the Kalmuck and Caspian and perhaps even surpass it, because the Azov and Black Seas are linked with the great ocean. Via this route more than anywhere else, we could export all kinds of German, Siberian, and Russian goods.

After all, the Turks and Greeks are eager to purchase sables and other expensive furs which the Germans have little wish to purchase. They also purchase German textiles and manufactured goods. They also would be eager to buy honey, wax, meat, butter, wheat, hemp, and other Russian products. From them, in turn, we could obtain many oriental goods, i.e., grapes, olives, rice, raisins, figs, lemons, and other fruits. The cost of this entire trade would be far less than the exorbitant prices we now pay the Germans, and it would require less effort than we now make in transporting goods over great distances and across cold regions. Even if we could realize only a half or a third, or perhaps a tenth, of the suggestions already made this state would still soon abound in all sorts of benefits and goods.

It is essential to realize that Frenchmen, Englishmen, and Dutchmen are trading, and establishing large enterprises, throughout all the possessions of the Turkish monarch. Their ships surrounding Constantinople are literally as thick as a forest. A good portion of that trade could be diverted to us, and go through our hands.

In order to forego long discussion we shall not state here how it would be possible to reach an agreement with the Turks, Persians, and Kalmucks.

DEVELOPMENT OF DOMESTIC TRADE

Trade usually develops in the following manner:

Some governments establish marketplaces along seashores and declare them free to foreign vessels and merchants—either to all or only to some—and then ask payment of a set duty fee.

[12] Throughout his work, Krizhanich identifies Belorussia and the Ukraine as separate political entities. They were not. They were integral parts of the Polish-Lithuanian Commonwealth (*Rzeczpospolita*); Belorussia was linked closely with Lithuania and the Ukraine with Poland.

Germans and Poles usually have fairs. Once or twice a year, or even more frequently, at certain periods, all merchants are allowed to come and display their designated goods at a fair for a day, two, or more. In Italy they do not have such fairs and this is a good custom: for because of these fairs peasants leave their work, and goods become expensive from being hauled from place to place without being sold. The Germans organize these fairs as frequently as they do for their own profit, rather than for the public good. It seems that it would be beneficial to organize such fairs in large towns only once a year, and only in winter time.

Weekly trade fairs exist in all towns and of course are essential for daily needs. However, in areas where there is concern about treason or attack, rulers allow neither weekly nor annual trade fairs within towns. If the town has an adequate garrison they can, and should, be set up near it. Thus in Tobolsk, for example, fairs could be organized every second or third week provided the garrison could be strengthened. The Tartars and Ostiaks could be allowed to come to the trade fair near the town on such a day, but not inside the town or into the fort. Only the Russians should be allowed. [13]

It is essential to keep roads free from bandits, to repair bridges, river ferries, and passages across the mountains and marshlands. Ancient Romans distinguished themselves superbly in this. They paved long roads with cut stone, built stone bridges across large rivers, dug tunnels, cleared passes over mountains, and drained bogs. Today the Turks are constantly repairing roads and bridges, and building large stone structures or buildings covered with tin roofs along the roads, for the benefit of all travelers.

In every European country (except Poland) there are official couriers whose weekly duty it is to gallop on horseback from one station to another with the letters of various people. In each town they designate one day of the week for the courier to mount his horse and gallop away at full speed. He carries the letters fifteen to twenty *versts* on his route to the nearest courier. Upon receiving the mail, the next courier must immediately start on his journey, be it day or night, fair weather or rain. Whenever he approaches a town he blows his horn, and citizens must open the gates for

---

[13] Russian mistreatment and economic exploitation of Siberian natives caused much suspicion and even anti-Russian uprisings. The tense atmosphere impelled the Russians to confine themselves to their well-fortified *ostrogs*. These fortifications were off limits to all natives, other than hostages confined in the dungeons. For a discussion of this problem see Lantzeff, *Siberia*, pp. 87–115; S.V. Bakhrushin, *Ocherki po istorii kolonizatsii Sibiri v XVI i XVII vv* (Moscow, 1927–28); and S.A. Tokarev, "Kolonialnaia politika moskovskogo gosudarstva v Sibiri v XVII veke," *Istoriia v shkole* (1936), IV, 73–99.

him at any time of the day or night. Anyone may bring a letter to this courier, and for two coins the courier is obliged to accept and carry the letter. Thanks to these couriers trade is flourishing, as are mutual relations among merchants. Nevertheless, I believe there are reasons why it is impossible to have such couriers in this tsardom.

Kings provide military support to merchants on their sea voyages to accompany and protect them. The same protection is necessary for river and overland trips. And if merchants cannot hire public carriers because of hostile neighbors, then the king should strive to build fortified outposts or settlements, where hired carts and carriers can be stationed, along public roads.

It would be beneficial to have, throughout the kingdom, uniform money, weights, and measures—for cloth, grain, and liquid—set up in such a way that no one could ever change them. If possible, it would also be useful to persuade neighbors to have the same measures. It would also be beneficial if a public official was stationed in every major town to oversee measurement. His duties would include the following:

(1) To watch that merchants neither undermeasured, not underweighed, nor insulted customers, and report those who did to an official of the *oblast*. [14]

(2) To man an open shop containing all kinds of measures and weights for sale (that is, measures for solids, liquids, and cloth as well as a large spring balance and a little one with markings but not writing—that is, not a German spring balance). He should have weights for currency, and weights with scales to weigh pepper. They could be either copper or wood, so that anyone could purchase them. He should have lead and copper weight pieces (weighing one *zolotnik,* and some *poltinas,* and full *grivna*), cast as samples with emblems of the tsar. [15] If people could obtain their own weights and measures in this way, merchants would not cheat them so boldly.

(3) He should have the authority to check the accuracy of weights and measures at the fair for anyone who desired it in order to appraise the goods, or for a small fee to place them in storage for safekeeping. Some measures should be chained to a flail so that anyone could measure his goods free of charge, on the spot.

---

[14] *Oblast*: an administrative unit of territory.

[15] *Zolotnik*: a seventeenth-century Russian measure of weight equal to one-ninety-sixth of a pound. *Poltina*: a seventeenth-century Russian coin equal in value to half a ruble, or fifty *kopecks*, or 100 *dengi*.

(4) He should keep on public display samples of the various currencies that are exchanged in this tsardom—genuine and counterfeit, domestic and foreign. And for anyone who wishes to familiarize himself with these currencies, he should point out their values and shortcomings.

(5) He should also have for sale printed books on commercial arithmetic, or accounting that contain information on weights and measures as well.

(6) It should also be his duty to be well informed in all these matters—what is being sold and where, who is selling what, which goods are available in town, and which are not. And for a fee he should tell people who inquire where and what they may purchase or sell.

(7) He should also see to it that retail stores always display for sale all kinds of tools and dishes—made of iron, wood, or pottery—and that they also have all kinds of household utensils and petty items. For it often happens that people would like to buy something that they need, but cannot find it because merchants neglect to carry goods that make them little profit.

In every city let there be a tsar's merchant. He should accept any goods sent and entrusted to him by a chief merchant, or which he himself requests or calls for, and he should sell these goods as inexpensively as possible. Let the goods be hauled in hired carts, and everywhere let the tsar's merchant pay the same tax as for the goods of subject peoples. Then, having established the basic price for a product, the cost of transportation, and the tax, let the price be set as low as possible above cost, so that goods sold by the sovereign will always be cheaper than those that other citizens may sell. They should have a markup of one, two, or in some cases, three percent, or whatever is necessary to pay the merchant and the guards, and to build new retail stores. Let the goods be such that they can be sold wholesale: that is, cloth, textiles, tools, and arms manufactured to order and in great quantities; and salt, iron, cotton, honey, rye, and the like. Retail sales and the sale of unspecified goods should be left in the hands of the subjects.

Members of all social classes should be allowed to become merchants, i.e., *boyars,* lesser servitors, and commoners who can offer good security or guarantees.

The people will greatly benefit from such a system. (1) There will be neither loss nor damage to the royal treasury; indeed, trade will increase, as will taxes. (2) Goods will be inexpensive everywhere. (3) Handicrafts will develop everywhere. (4) Prices can be increased in difficult times. (5) In case of money shortages, soldiers can be paid in goods. (6) Ordinary merchants will be allowed to trade in these and other petty and trivial goods in large and small towns wherever there are no government merchants, and even to carry them to villages.

Grain purchasers and those who increase the price of bread should be fined without mercy. Under a threat of certain punishment, purchasers of other edible goods should not be allowed to travel among the people or purchase anything before noon or along the roads near the towns. All cattle dealers should be classed as idlers and drunkards. No one should be permitted to have a retail store or carry on any trade who does not perform a service, have a useful and needed trade, or haul goods from one town to another. No one should be allowed to have exclusive trading rights throughout the country. That is, no merchant should be allowed to trade throughout the entire realm in wine, beer, *kvas*,[16] grain, honey, salt, caviar, hides, hemp, flax, cloth, iron, or anything else. Such arrangements are unjust and sinful, for as soon as a major shortage arises, or the tax-farmer promises to sell a commodity at a set price, it will be sold for less than other merchants are selling it.

Because of this, no foreign merchants in Moscow are to be allowed to own homes, retail stores, warehouses, cellars—neither they nor their agents or overseers, nor consuls, nor permanent envoys. Moreover, they should not be allowed to enter the state for trading purposes. Such activities should be confined only to designated marketplaces along the frontiers.

If Germans were not in Russia, the trade of this tsardom would be in a far better state. We would sell our goods for more and purchase necessities for less. With the bread the Germans eat greedily, the more so since they send it overseas, a multitude of native Russians could be fed. In prosperous times these native people would be more useful to the tsardom; while in difficult times they would not send goods abroad, and the country would be more populous.

We should not succumb to German threats that our trade will vanish. We should experiment with royal autocratic trade. If hostile Germans do not come, others will. Perhaps the monarchy would even benefit if fewer Germans came and consumed lesser quantities of food.

There is also this to consider. The English do not allow Dutch shippers to bring anything to them except goods produced in Holland. Pepper, sugar, wine, and goods of Spanish and other origin we ourselves could bring in aboard our own vessels. The same Englishmen do not allow any

[16] An alcoholic drink made from cereals and stale bread, widely consumed in Russia and Eastern Europe.

foreign merchant to purchase their goods from them for resale. They allow him to buy a few pieces of cloth for his own use, but not to load a ship with cloth. In spite of this, many merchants come to them.

The English, Portuguese, and many other merchants have their commercial agents in Afghanistan, Bokhara, Semigrad, Mongolia, China, and other countries. Frequently, they dispatch their ships to China, and they go across Siberia to India. Neither the Persians, the Germans, nor merchants from any other nation should be allowed to stop over in Moscow. We should base this prohibition on domestic law.

If there is some benefit for the sovereign tsar or gifts for *boyars* from these Germans, there is far greater benefit for tsar and *boyar* from their own people.

All of our Slavic people are so cursed that everywhere they look they see Germans, Jews, Scotsmen, Gypsies, Armenians, Greeks, and merchants of other nations sucking their blood.

Some time ago the Poles introduced a saving device. Not one German was allowed to own a home or retail store on Polish territory. But this prohibition lasted only briefly, because the Germans soon bribed Polish officials with gifts.

Nobody siphons off the wealth of this country and ruins its people as do those Germans who live among us. They appear whenever and wherever any of our goods are sold at a low price, but they bring their goods to us, and to one place, only once a year, and by mutual agreement they set the price they want. Besides, the Germans who live among us are simply agents of others, of bigger merchants. Because they are obliged to forward their profits to their masters beyond the sea, they are forced to secure other revenues in order to feed their families and servants and accumulate some wealth. They are the true locust and lice—the worst threat to this country.

Because of this it would be desirable to promulgate an immutable law, and swear to it, that no foreign merchant, tax farmer, or agent possess the right to have a home, warehouse, or retail store in this state, or be allowed to come to any town except designated frontier marketplaces during trade fairs, where they could stay no more than a month. In order to prevent this prohibition from being violated, and in order to assure that the officials would not conspire with foreign merchants in exchange for gifts, it would be desirable to grant a privilege or authority to Russian merchants such that whenever they found a foreign merchant outside the designated city or place, they had the right to capture him, to hold him, to bring him to justice, upon proving his transgression to receive from him a substantial fine, and to expel him.

No one unable to read and do arithmetic should be allowed to own a retail store (an exception being those who sell goods that do not require accounting).

Emperor Augustus lent money to his subjects without interest or usury for good security—that is, for mortgage of stone buildings, inheritance, and commission. In this way he checked usury and theft and, surprisingly, also increased and developed trade. For the sake of the glory of the sovereign tsar it would be very useful to introduce this system in this tsardom.

In Rome and other cities of Italy, in memory of one of God's servants, well-meaning people collected a certain amount of money to loan to the poor people as mortgages without interest or usury. Such pools of money are known as "pools of kindness" in order not to insult the Jews or other godless usurers. Security usually consists not only of gold, silver, pearls, precious stones, and pewter dishes, but also of clothes—for a designated time. If the owner of the pawned objects comes before the expiration of the term and reclaims his security, he receives everything back for free and pays no interest. But if the owner does not come, does not reclaim his security, and does not request deferment, the pawnbrokers sell the security. They give any profit they make to the owner of the security or his heirs—if they should claim it—and retain only a small portion to pay the people who make the arrangements for this enterprise. The sale of goods held in pledge takes place on designated days, and buyers are summoned by the sound of trumpets. Whoever bids the highest gets the goods.

The Germans also have pawnshops to assist needy people, but because they do not return the pawned items without making a profit for themselves, they are not charitable.

In European cities, rich merchants who exchange money are known as money exchangers. If anyone requests an exchange of one currency for another, they will do it—for example, gold for silver, or copper or silver for gold—but always for a personal profit. If you wish to exchange a ruble you receive an *altyn*, a *grosh,* or a *kopek.* [17] Also, if you have a hundred, a thousand, or many thousands of rubles or some other currency, and you wish to carry it to another city but are afraid of robbers or some other misfortune, or that your money will not circulate in that town or is worthless, you go to a money exchanger and give him your money. He gives you a letter to his associate in the town you are going to, and the

[17] *Altyn*: a Tartar word for six, which in Russia was used from the fourteenth to the eighteenth centuries to designate a monetary unit equal to six *dengi*, or three *kopecks*. *Grosh* (Polish *grosz*, German *Groschen*): a small coin equal to about two *Kopecks*. *Kopeck* (also *kopeika*): a small silver coin in seventeenth-century Russia equal to two *dengi*.

associate will immediately give you the amount of money specified in the letter. This system has been so firmly established, and is so reliable, that there are no disputes or court adjudications. All that is required is the usual fee you pay the money exchanger. For one hundred rubles the charge is one, two, three or more rubles depending on time, greater or lesser risk, and the rate of exchange. Such exchanges are very beneficial and useful to people who travel, and they also benefit trade.

In some large cities of Europe merchants form associations or guilds and keep their trading money in a place called a bourse. Thus when a nobleman, or anyone, brings them his money, be it a large or small sum, they deposit the money into the general fund, pay him one, one and a half, or two rubles of annual interest per hundred, and use the money for trading purposes. On expiration of a set time, if the individual requests his money, they give it to him promptly. If they do not need money for trading purposes, they still accept it for safekeeping but pay no interest. They will return it at any time the depositor requests it, and sometimes require that he pay them a fee for safekeeping.

When Amsterdam merchants and other foreigners dispatch three, four, ten, or more ships to India, to Russia, or to Turkish or Persian lands, a merchant normally does not put all of his goods aboard one ship. Each merchant, or as many as there are, distributes his goods among all the ships so that if a ship perishes, not all of his goods are lost.

In order to assist trade and increase the population, it is useful to grant some rights to citizens, or town inhabitants. They should have the right to have their own elected *starosta* (elderman) and judges in cases involving small mutual litigations.[18] They should have easy access to the great sovereign through petition for protection from the violence and ruin which vicious officials habitually inflict on town inhabitants.

Merchant guilds or assemblies should require that their members always have on hand in their stores such daily necessities as flour, groats, malt, dried oatmeal, butter, beans, fish, and caviar—in a word, everything necessary to eat; and above all, what this land produces, namely, honey and caviar (not only ordinary but also the best quality) and similar items. Also dishes, tools, and other items made from good materials: dishes, cups, and spoons made from white pewter, cast copper, wood, and glazed clay; pots from iron, copper, and glazed clay; tubs, barrels, troughs and buckets; and finally, brooms and all sorts of small articles. And if stores are short on these items, a city official in charge of weights and

---

[18] *Starosta*: an elected official in Russian rural and urban communities who served as a local administrator and judge.

measures should notify the head administrator of the town, and the merchants guilty of this negligence should be fined.

Some goods could be entrusted to the town garrison. They could be given the right to display and sell goods all week, except on trade fair days.

High civil administrators of the region and towns, jointly with the tsar's merchant, should try to reach an agreement with the craftsmen of all manufacturing and handicraft guilds. Acting intelligently and without resort to force, they should order whatever craftsmen are able to produce for the tsar—thousands of rubles worth of knives, axes, pitchforks, locks, sickles, scythes, razors, hooks, needles, mirrors, buttons, textiles, cloths, and other useful items for the inhabitants. The tsar's merchant should sell these goods first in the town where they were manufactured; second, they should be distributed among selected large towns where local merchants could buy them to meet the needs of the local economy; third, they should be brought to frontier marketplaces for sale to other nations; and fourth, they should be issued to soldiers and other service people of the tsar in lieu of their salaries—but not forcibly, and only to those desiring or requesting them.

In addition, the tsar's officials should try to have a list in which are indicated the names and descriptions of all goods popularly used throughout the world, and they should keep pictures of these goods in order to know and identify them. Further, they should invite, and welcome, all sorts of foreign craftsmen, and give them good pay in exchange for training our youth to manufacture these goods for the tsar. Imports from abroad of goods of equivalent quality to those we have at home (as, for example, knives, herring and other fish) should be prohibited. Germans, for instance, purchase our fish very cheaply but sell us their herring at a high price. For this system to remain operative and beneficial, and not be violated by greedy local government officials, merchants, or citizens, soldiers and other service people should be granted the right, if the need should arise, to appear in public before local government officials at all times and for all cases in order to testify; they should also immediately send complaints to Moscow against those officials who violate the good order and smooth functioning of local trade or increase prices without the sovereign's decree.

2

Handicrafts

The Poles transformed an old Slavic word *premysel, premyselnik,* into *remeslo* and *remesnik,* and from Poland the word *remeslo* and *remeslennik* came to Russia. It means hand-manufacturing industry or crafts [*iskustvo*].

Crafts are more beneficial to a monarchy than the best ore deposits, or mountains of gold. In Hungary and the Arab lands there are very rich gold mines, while Holland has no ore, but the Dutch territory has a hundred times more gold and other wealth than Hungary or Arabia. Why? Because the Dutch are very skillful in crafts and trade. For this reason it would be very desirable to develop crafts in Russia.

A government office or council in charge of such matters should know what kinds of crafts there are, their principles and their purposes.

To find these things out it is necessary to translate into our language books of authors who wrote about crafts: Garzoni, Fioravanti, Sardi, and others.[1] What is useful and necessary to know can be extracted from these books.

The Venetians have transformed Venice into a noble, famous and glorious city. How did they do it? Primarily by inviting craftsmen to Venice from everywhere and then offering them large sums of money to teach their youth all kinds of crafts. Excellent craftsmen would come to us if they were guaranteed free passage back to their homelands.

It would seem that in our case they should not merely be granted such permission, but should be induced to return home so that they do not increase their numbers here. But they should not be released until they have fully trained several of our young men in their crafts.

The crafts are best developed and flourish most among the Germans. The basic reason for this is that they have privileges and laws that encourage the development of crafts. Their laws are as follows:

---

[1] Tomazo Garzoni (1549–89) was an Italian poet and writer; Leonardo Fioravanti (1518–88) a scientist; and Alexander Sardi (1520–88) a scholar and engineer.

(1) Each craft has its guild and its elder. Elders have the right, or authority, to resolve mutual disagreements pertaining to their crafts, as in the case where a master craftsman fails to pay his worker for his work, or when a member of the craft insults another member.

(2) Each apprentice must study with the same master until he completes his training, and must serve him without pay for two, three, or more years, or as many as the training for that craft requires.

(3) Upon completion of his training, the apprentice must receive from the guild a written certificate testifying that he served loyally, that he worked for a specified period of time, and that he learned the craft. Then he becomes a journeyman. He must go to other towns to inspect and study the art of other master craftsmen.

(4) After arriving at another town, a journeyman must appear before the elder of his craft. The elder will arrange for his living quarters, and will also ask his fellow masters whether or not they need a worker, and whoever needs one will accept him. If no one needs a worker with his skills, he is not permitted to live in that town and has to leave for another, soon.

(5) When a journeyman decides to become a master—to have his own shop or store, stop working for other masters, and instead work for himself—he must show his certificate of learning, give an account of his journeymanship, and create a piece of craftsmanship that serves as "evidence of his mastery." Then other masters examine this piece and approve him as their fellow master. After this he prepares a feast, gives a certain amount of money into a general treasury, and receives a written certificate of his mastership from the other masters. Then he can work in his own shop, and hang on the wall outside his house a wooden sign to tell everyone what kind of craftsman he is.

If a soldier is skilled in a craft he is not subject to the authority of the craft guild. He can work without its permission.

(6) No one is allowed to insult a craftsman or force him to do any other work. No ruler forces craftsmen to work for him without pay.

The following law would assist the development of crafts in this tsardom: when a slave has two or more sons he should be allowed, without the interference of officials, to select one and assign him to the task of learning some useful craft, such as making locks, cloth, scythes, glass, paper, or other difficult and artistic items—but not hats, clothes, or boots. And if he masters his job satisfactorily, he should be freed from slavery and/or serfdom. If he fails to learn his craft satisfactorily, he should either remain a slave or purchase his freedom from his owner.

Raw materials are items from which all indispensable things are produced (such as iron, copper, lumber, stone, wool, flax, hides, etc.). Where there are no raw materials there are no manufactured goods. Our country lacks many indispensable raw materials. It is therefore necessary to see to it that all sorts of raw materials and unfinished products be brought here from other countries—good quality iron, copper, tin, wool, dyes, and cotton—so that our craftsmen can manufacture a variety of items from them. It would be best if they could produce various metallic items and implements made from ores: iron stoves, pots, needles, caldrons, scythes, sickles, tridents, etc. From inferior quality iron which at present we completely discard, we could manufacture pots with tripods and two handles, stoves, cannon balls, small bullets covered with lead for muskets, and other items. Metallic implements [*orudiia*] are so called because they are made from metallic ores.

The law should also be firmly established—and violators of it punished—that no raw materials such as hides, flax, and hemp be exported abroad, and that our people manufacture all sorts of items at home, as many as possible, and sell the finished products abroad. For example, our people should extract oil from hemp and flax seeds; they should weave fine and heavy duty ropes for ships; they should spin hemp yarn for a firearm vent or for ornamented handkerchiefs, fine yarn for feather beds, heavy duty for sail canvas; they should also make paper for writing and for other purposes; they should produce glassware, windows, mirrors; they should bleach wax; and they should process hides to produce various items. All of this should be undertaken not only for the needs of the domestic market of this tsardom, but also to sell to the Germans, Lithuanians, Turks, Persians, Kalmucks, and Dauri.[2]

The Germans in Russia get not just a hundred but thousands of rubles for their writing paper annually, though Russia could easily sell paper to the Swedes, Lithuanians, Poles, Turks, and Persians. I do not know what devices the Germans have used to blind our people so completely that they have failed to build paper mills in Russia. It appears that they sell us their paper for less than it would cost us if we produced it, and this is sheer deception. For how could they afford to sell paper that was shipped across the sea for less than paper produced domestically, from local cloth scraps?

---

[2] The term Dauri refers to the natives of the area to the east of Lake Baikal and to the north of the Amur River. Bands of Russian cossacks reached this region in the middle of the seventeenth century. Its principal *ostrogs* were Nerchinsk and Albazin.

Obviously our paper could be cheap, white, and of good quality if it were produced from good cheap material—if it were possible, that is, to secure cloth scraps easily. This problem should also receive proper attention. In other countries poor people and orphans walk through large towns carrying needles, brimstones, spoons, and money, and buy cloth scraps from housewives and deliver them to craftsmen. Here, at first, until people got used to such an exchange, residents of large towns could be ordered to collect ten or more *pudy* of cloth scraps annually and deliver them to the tsar's officials at an appropriate price. The importation of foreign paper should be strictly prohibited, even if domestic paper is more expensive and of poorer quality. With such a prohibition in effect, our people would certainly begin to take the necessary steps to make good cheap paper immediately.

We should also start manufacturing textiles from a combination of linen and wool (which the Italians call *mezzolana,* or half-wool) and from linen and cotton. It would be desirable to learn the names of all textiles and have samples of them, especially the simple and inexpensive ones which, one would hope, could be produced in our country. And various hides (especially that of the elk) are greatly misused. We sell all of these hides to the Germans in a raw state, while at home we do not process them at all and do not use them for clothing. We sell a hide for three or four rubles, yet if we wanted to buy it back from the Germans in processed form we would have to pay thirty or forty rubles. It is very important that these hides be processed here and that our people make clothes from them, because they can be worn for a lifetime. Then we would obtain satisfaction from our clothing, and also receive more money for a few processed hides than we now receive for a great number of unprocessed ones.

In Siberia there are savages who know a good way of processing hides even though their process differs from that used by the Germans. I do not know why thus far our people have failed to learn this art from them. And it would be very easy to do. It would be very useful to learn the art of hide processing from the Germans:

(1) in order to tan thick elk—and deerskins—and fine skins for gloves;

(2) to prepare *skamot* or "velvet"—that is, hide as smooth and soft as velvet;

(3) to prepare Russian leather, as is already beginning to be done;

(4) to make parchment, i.e., thin white leather for writing purposes and colored leather for whips, implements, books, etc.;

(5) to make the kind of leather that is covered with lacquer or gold and painted with different colors—the Italians call it "golden leather." It does not cost much to produce, but is highly valued and can be sold for a high price to the Kalmucks, Bokharans, Georgians, Cherkess, and other barbaric peoples.

(6) It also would be useful to evolve a means of coloring white sheepskins red, green, or blue. Thus processed, these skins become so highly valued that nobles are not ashamed to make fur coats from them. And we could sell them to the Kalmucks, Cherkess, Ukrainians, Lithuanians, and other neighbors at a high price. We could also color Siberian white polar fox fur yellow, green, or blue.

(7) From the Persians we should learn the art of making morocco, *kremezin,* black, red, and other colors *kordovan* and *sagr* or *tsapp*—that is, leather for sabre sheaths.

(8) We should manufacture German glue from leather scraps and old boots.

Great benefit would accrue to this tsardom if gold threading and gold sewing enterprises were introduced here. Thanks to this enterprise the Germans obtain countless riches from Russia and other countries of the world. They manufacture this gold thread mainly in Nuremberg, Augsburg, and Bratislava. In Vienna I saw one spindle selling for eight *efimki,* and in Constantinople they sold it for twenty-four without any haggling.[3] In this country a great deal of such gold is consumed in sewing, in making buttonholes, in shirts, and in other items. If we maintained this enterprise here at home, all the money and goods exported annually for this gold would remain in Russia. We could also sell it to the Turks, Persians, Kalmucks, Bokharans, and Mongols, and receive substantial profit from it.

Idleness and inactivity are the enemies of handicraft. This is why, in antiquity, Roman elders questioned all the people about their occupations and enterprises—about how they made a living. The Germans, too, have town elders who do not allow any able-bodied person to solicit assistance without a special permit from authorities. The Dutch have a house of correction where they lock up recalcitrant and wilful youths and force them to make various items, and do not feed them until they have performed their assigned tasks. It would be wise to survey towns in order

[3] *Efimok* (plural *efimki*): the Russian term for a large silver coin, the Joachimsthaler, minted in Bohemia. The Russians obtained these coins through foreign trade and in the sixteenth and seventeenth centuries they circulated as part of the national currency.

to find any refugees, vagrants, tramps, or idlers in taverns or *kvas* stores along with the healthy commoners; they should either be taken to villages and made slaves of the *boyars,* exiled to Siberia, or punished in some other way.

An order should be issued to the overseers and to craft guilds that they examine all implements, dishes and clothing put up for sale and point out anything finished messily, incompletely or otherwise badly. Let them take it apart and show how it could have been produced better. For example, dirty dishes or large pitchers that show finger marks, dirty vessels and earthenware buckets without lacquer, and buckets and spoons whose handles are too small. Elders should not allow such goods to be placed on the market: should they appear, they should be either destroyed or confiscated.

In place of vessels and goblets they should produce wooden bowls, smoked or simple, glazed earthenware bowls, cups with handles and covers, and the like. Because goblets and vessels, and a few other Russian items, are grimy, these are objectionable in other nations.

Many girls get married young, before they have a chance to learn what a good wife ought to know. Moreover, the mothers of many of these girls themselves know nothing. It would be advisable, therefore, that two or three experienced widows in every town be authorized to teach young girls and new brides how to spin a fine thread, weave, sew, bleach cloth, do a clean wash, salt and dry fish and meat, prepare malt, *kvas,* beer, and mead, cultivate and grow garden vegetables, salt and preserve plants and roots, cook, bake bread, and the like. Should anyone request their services, they should go there for pay.

Initially, officials should designate these women by name: otherwise women themselves would be too bashful to start such a training even though it is a very useful enterprise. Towns that enjoy privileges should be ordered to maintain such teachers and pay them salaries from public funds. And any man who wishes to get married should be permitted to request evidence from them of what his bride knows and what her capacity for learning is. Such a system of certification would induce girls to seek education, and to receive good certificates from their teachers.

In Germany women spin thread on the spinning wheel. They spin the wheel by foot, and quite fast. One woman using a spinning wheel spins more than three times what can be spun on a spindle, and as a result they can sell cloth quite cheaply. This enterprise is necessary and beneficial, and it would be useful if our women could master it.

In addition to the things noted previously, it is essential to attract craftsmen of all kinds: craftsmen who know how to melt and cast iron, copper, tin, silver and gold; who know how to process them for all kinds of purposes and how to produce the various dishes, arms and weapons that exist in the world; who know, further, how, for example, to melt and cast iron and produce iron pots, kettles, stoves, presses, cannon balls, small bullets, etc.; how to forge iron into thin pieces and make iron and copper plates; how to produce good sabres, broadswords, harquebuses, harquebus bearings with rings, and other weapons for various purposes so that we are no longer forced to purchase useless German swords; how to make copper candlesticks, spoons, frying pans, dishes, washtubs, and kettles, and other kinds of copper household utensils for domestic use and for sale to other nations; how to produce different kinds of agricultural implements such as scythes, sickles, forks, knives, and the like. If we could produce thousands upon thousands of these items we could sell them annually to the Kalmucks, Bokharans, Dauri, Persians, Turks, Wallachians and others. Likewise all implements needed by the ore masters, by silver-smiths, by caulkers and other smiths should be produced at home and not purchased abroad.

It would also be useful to attract a variety of master craftsmen who know how to work walrus tusks and other bones and horns, and to invite master craftsmen of the textile or linen industry who know how to prepare flax for different purposes, as we discussed above, and also how to weave belts, clasps, loops, *tvezy*, and other ornaments from threads.

In Denmark and Norway they have iron stoves and pots everywhere. Some pots have tripods other have two handles, and some are straight. Such pots cost a *poltina* [25 kopecks] and can be used for fifty years, and they make these pots from brittle and otherwise useless iron.

It would be wise to commission and order samples of all kinds of implements from abroad. But above all it is imperative that our merchants and other officials bring as samples from foreign lands—from all nations—weapons, dishes and every kind of household and agricultural implement used the world over, cloths and textiles, clothes and various forms of manufacture from ore, stone, hide, wool, flax, silk, wood, bone, horn, and all other materials. Furthermore, it should be decreed that clothing of every style from throughout the world be brought in. Finally, we should invite a variety of craftsmen and tailors who could make for us, and instruct us how to make, various weapons, implements, dishes, and styles of clothing. These masters should be distributed and divided among towns, but preferably in places located close to the sources of water, forest, flax, wool, iron, and other needed raw materials. Let them manufacture their products for the sovereign in great quantities, on contract and for a proper salary.

One town should be designated to produce paper, regardless of quality; it should be promised privileges, including the prohibition of imported foreign paper even if domestic paper is of poorer quality and more expensive than foreign paper. Also any new enterprise organized in a town should be given privileges lasting for several years. For example, any town that begins producing any sort of cloth, or anything else, should not pay domestic taxes on its products, and other towns, for a specific time, should be prohibited from competing with that enterprise.

It is essential to discuss here why it has hitherto been difficult to start new enterprises in Russia. First, because Germans have well-established enterprises and hence have always been able to sell their products less expensively than our Russian masters, with their new or inadequately developed enterprises. Consequently, neither writing paper nor any other new handicraft could succeed in Russia. But now, since the tsar will control foreign trade, it will be easier to start new enterprises. Our craftsmen will be able to manufacture their products to the value of many hundreds and thousands of rubles, and the sovereign's merchants and officials will purchase needed items from them and not from the Germans. There also will be a prohibition on the importation of all foreign manufactured products of the kind that we manufacture here at home, and thanks to it our craftsmen will be able to make a decent living and to sell their products for less. Moreover, the tsar's officials will be able to sell these goods at home for less and abroad for more, the amount depending only on how fast our craftsmen produce them.

We should not believe the Germans when they say that it would cost us less to purchase ready-made scythes, sickles, and knives from them than to buy raw iron and make scythes and other items at home. If we manufactured all the goods that we are capable of producing, rather than purchasing them from the Germans, many more thousands of people could now live in this country. Also, the treasury would receive greater revenues, towns would be more populous, and the entire tsardom would be more powerful.

3

Agriculture

To repeat: poor monarchy, poor king; rich monarchy, rich king. A king who wants to become rich must see to it that his subjects become rich, in that the wealth of subjects fills up the royal treasury.

Agriculture is the foundation of wealth, for the farmer feeds and enriches not only himself but the craftsman, the merchant, the *boyar,* and the king. Agriculture is one of the best and the most essential of enterprises, and the Treasury Council should never neglect it. In some countries these statements would be superfluous—countries, for example, whose people are by nature ingenious, quick, thoughtful, and industrious, where over the years many books have been written about agriculture and many other enterprises, and where all enterprises are well developed and flourish. But for this glorious state, and for all Slavs, these statements are not superfluous at all. They are necessary.

First, because our people are mentally sluggish and unable to discover things for themselves. Second, because we have no books on agriculture and other enterprises. Third, because our people are lazy and lethargic, and will do nothing worthwhile unless they are forced to. Fourth, because under our absolute autocracy the tsar can command the entire country to take up any custom that may be useful. In other countries this would be impossible.

Agriculture is the science of cultivating or ploughing the soil and gathering and storing its products. The following are the products of the earth and the water: (1) Grains: wheat, rye, barley, spring wheat, oats, millet, buckwheat, German wheat, sorghum, rice, etc. (2) Beans: peas, green beans, kidney beans, lentils, lima beans, etc. (3) Roots, seeds, and spices: pepper, cloves, nuts, nutmeg, ginger, cinnamon, sugar, saffron, poppy seed, linseed, hemp, rape, mustard, caraway seeds, hops, etc. (4) Garden greenery: turnips, beetroots, parsnips, onions, garlic, carrots, radishes, horseradish, mushrooms, etc. (5) A multitude of medicinal herbs such as hellebore. Many books have been written about them.

(6) Grasses to make dyes: rhubarb, blueing, etc. (7) Aromatic flowers: roses or sweetbrier, marjoram, lily, mint, cloves, violets, tulips, etc. (8) Fruit trees: mulberry trees, olive trees, grape vines, apple trees, nut trees, plum trees, etc. (9) Forest trees: oak, beech, firs, pines, yew trees, birch, etc. (10) Ordinary stones: marble, marl, limestone, flint, etc. (11) Precious stones: diamonds, sapphire, turquoise, ruby, etc. (12) Ores: gold, silver, copper, tin, lead, mercury, iron, wrought iron. (13) Minerals and dyes: salt, sulphur, saltpeter, ink, cinnabar, whiting, borax, coal, etc. (14) Four-legged animals: domestic livestock and forest animals. (15) Feathered creatures: domestic fowl and wild birds. (16) Water creatures: river fish and sea fish. (17) Poisonous creatures: dragons and other snakes, flies, wasps, spiders, and other beetles and worms. Of these the most useful are bees and silkworms.

To develop a flourishing agriculture it will be necessary to translate some good books on the subject, books which identify all cereals, beans, roots, grasses, seeds, flowers, trees, rocks, ores, minerals, and living creatures, and indicate their inherent qualities and benefits: for example, how and when vegetables should be grown, and how they should be stored and used. Many of our proprietors, although engaged in agriculture, die ignorant of many useful products of the soil, of their production and use.

Aldrovandi wrote a book which identified every living creature by color, and Coler wrote a book about the cultivation of fields and gardens, and how best to preserve various products of the soil.[1]

It would be useful to dispatch observers throughout the tsardom, or better yet to command local officials to search and experiment in order to ascertain where cereals, grasses, trees or such plants as flax, hemp, hops, honey-producing flowers, cabbage, onions and the like grow or could be grown abundantly, or where the most sheep, horses, oxen, pigs, and fish are found. Peasants and other natives should be instructed to apply every effort to cultivate and develop these things so that they can sell more of them. We must note that of all the items that the Russian land produces or can produce, none are more beneficial than potash, bees, rhubarb [indigo], and livestock.

Though the benefits the country receives from potash have long been evident, two things must be noted. First, annually we produce either too little or too much of it. Whenever a bit more of it is brought to Archangel it becomes all the cheaper, so that for a greater effort and volume we receive no more than for a smaller amount. And many peasants who could

---

[1] Krizhanich refers here to Ulysses Aldrovandi (1522–1605), Italian naturalist, and to Johann Coler (d. 1639), German agronomist.

cultivate the land work at producing potash, and it would be useful to moderate the fluctuations in output of this activity. Second, the preparation of potash interferes with the gathering of honey. It would be useful to order agricultural regions to produce no potash without the government's approval. The sovereign should order as much potash as is necessary to be prepared on the territory of the Bashkir traitors, along the lower Don, and in other places where Russians will suffer no loss.[2]

There is no need to talk about honey and wax. If we learned how to bleach wax, we could sell it to the Germans. Honey, of course, we could sell to the Turks for much more than the Germans pay us for it. In some countries where honey is procured, they fence off a spot in the forest and reinforce the fencing with logs so that wild animals cannot destroy it. Villagers then set up their beehives on the spot and check up on them frequently, on rotation. They bring beehives home for the winter. It should be possible to experiment with this system in our warm regions.

Of all the products of the land, dyestuffs are the most profitable. A certain author describes them as follows. Madder or *Rubia* [*tinctorum*] is a wild grass, but it is also cultivated for profit because it brings in such great revenues. It is used to color wool and hides, and also has medicinal applications. Its stem is square, long, sharp, thorny, and flexible, and five leaves grow around its point. Its seed is green at first, then becomes red. and turns black when it is ripe. Its root is fine, long, red, and astringent, and it has a bitter taste. Indigo—*Glastum* or *Isatis* [*tinctoria*] in Latin—has a yellow flower similar to an egg yolk. Its juice, when mixed with other preparations, produces blue and green colors. I have seen dried and spread out leaves of a plant which the Turks use to color their horses' tails and manes as well as their own nails.

I do not know how to categorize Bokhara rhubarb, or indigo. In Italy the city of Tivoli has recently started to cultivate and process the indigo herb, and its citizens are reaping large sums from it. The German city of Bratislava,[3] which also makes a great deal of money by preparing this herb, has a strict prohibition on selling seeds of the herb to neighbors. Astrakhan is much warmer than Bratislava, and I think the rhubarb would grow better there. It would bring great annual profits to this

---

[2] Krizhanich is referring to a bloody Bashkir uprising against Russian rule that took place in 1662. For a comprehensive discussion in English, see Alton S. Donnelly, *The Russian Conquest of Bashkiria, 1552–1740: A Case Study in Imperialism* (New Haven, 1968). A Marxist–Leninist view of this episode is given in N.V. Ustiugov, "Bashkirskoe vosstanie, 1662–1664 gg.," *Istoricheskie Zapiski* (1947), no. 24, 30–110.

[3] Currently Bratislava is the capital of Slovakia. In the seventeenth century it was a major town in the Holy Roman Empire. For that reason Krizhanich identified it here as "the German city."

tsardom, because if we could color textiles at home we would not have to pay the Germans for their dyes, and in fact we could sell them the herbs.

It would also be useful to learn about the use of fats in the preparation of foods. Fats are produced from milk, fish, olives, nuts, linseeds, and hemp seeds. The Germans cultivate a wild root turnip, which they call *Steckrüben,* and from its seeds they extract considerable oil. It produces seeds quite rapidly. Its leaves and seeds resemble the common round turnip, but its root is oblong, thin, hard and unsuitable for eating.

Ancient peoples such as the Scythians sustained themselves on pasturing herds of cattle as the present-day Kalmuck do. In Hungary, near Buda, there is extensive treeless pasturage. The local peasants cultivate no land along the Danube, but they raise livestock and are extremely rich—annually that area exports about 100,000 oxen and many horses. It would be good to know whether in this tsardom there is such a place, one suitable for grazing and safe from robbers, where herds of cattle and horses could be kept for the sovereign.

The Bashkirs have recently rebelled, but if God enables us to subdue them again, we could arrange for some of them, together with some Russians, to take care of the sovereign's livestock in their lands. This same practice should be introduced among the Nogais, Mordva, and Cheremis, and wherever we cannot introduce it among a people, we should hire them for wages and offer gifts to their chiefs.

It should be possible to persuade the Kalmucks to allow us to graze several hundred or thousand head of livestock on their lands, and to secure hostages from them. Better yet, let us reach an agreement with their chief under which he sends us so many hundreds of thousands of head of good horned cattle and horses annually at an agreed price.

It is essential to survey the entire country in order to discover good locations, what particular advantages they offer, and where it would be possible to set up flour mills, *stupy* [grinding mills], and workshops, for example: (1) fulleries (they press cloth using water power); (2) groats-grinding mills; (3) flour mills with bellows to sift flour; (4) trident lumber mills (the water turns the trident and cuts boards); (5) glass furnaces; (6) places where it would be possible to smelt lime in furnaces; (7) places where saltpeter could be manufactured; (8) places where pitch could be produced; (9) places where bricks could be produced; (10) places where tar could be produced.

It is important to be concerned about these matters so that such places do not go to waste and so that someone be found to assume this kind of work. When they do, they should be freed from taxes for several years, and then pay only a small amount. It is also vital that the country be populous, for this will enrich the sovereign's treasury. We discuss ores and how to search for them below.

So far we have discussed extraction of the earth's products. We now discuss how to preserve these products, and how to ease agricultural toil. For agriculture to flourish it is necessary to have good buildings, good storage facilities, and good equipment. A thoughtful owner or household manager must think more about how to store than how to gather the earth's products. In other countries I have seen how they suffer shortages because ignorance has led to poor storage practices, and grain and other products have been needlessly lost. In this country the same thing sometimes happens during bad weather. It is hard to gather the harvest during rainy spells, and in any case after the harvest a large portion of the yield is lost or perishes because of the lack of covered facilities for dry storage.

It would be useful to designate builders in each town who could show people examples of good construction, and who could teach carpenters how to build substantial structures as well as cottages and other simple buildings.

Peasant dwellings in the Russian Ukraine [around Nizhin] are beautiful. Their floors are elevated, and they keep their livestock in the lower, warm section of the structure. By contrast, the inhabitants of the Dnieper [around Kiev] keep their livestock around the hearth.[4]

Village buildings should meet all the agricultural needs. Some should be for people, others for livestock, still others for chickens, geese, ducks, and pigeons. There should also be a stable or covered place to store carts, wagons, harrows, ploughs, and other farm equipment. There should also be covered storage for hay and straw and a granary for grain, beans, and flour. There should be cold storage for roots, greenery, and ice, and grain.

The Germans have large barns tightly planked with clean boards which are well closed and covered. On a winter night they hang up a lantern by a hook and thresh the grain in a room—this way they don't lose any grain. The Germans also have buildings to store their equipment. These are clean, and so large that they could store twice as much as they harvest during the year.

The Germans, as well as the Siberian Tartars, build drying structures in the form of a staircase covered by a narrow roof in their fields.[5] They

[4] The distinction made between the two separate political units of the seventeenth-century Ukraine—the northeastern region, under Russian control, and the southwestern, under Polish domination—demonstrates Krizhanich's grasp of a very complex problem.
[5] By "Siberian Tartars" Krizhanich means all natives of Siberia. In fact, seventeenth-century Russian sources identify two distinct groups of Tartars: the *sluzhilye*, or individual

spread wet or unripened grain on these structures to dry in the wind. We ought to elevate our grain on posts to dry it in the wind, and to winnow the chaff.

Useful troughlike copper dishes are manufactured in this manner. They take a copper plate a forearm or more wide and two to three forearms long. Then they hammer a five-inch indentation around its sides and fasten it on the top and everywhere with iron, creating a flat-bottomed trough. They use these troughs for drying inside the oven, on top of the oven, in sweating shells, and in the kitchen over the fire. Fruits, vegetables, fish, meat, grain, malt, and other items are dried. They also make troughs from wooden boards and twigs, but these cannot be placed inside the oven or hung over the fire. Thrifty farmers with smokey kitchens and distilleries will not allow the smoke to dissipate freely. They buy meat or fish, smoke it, and sell it.

Village officials should see that peasants building their homes also build other necessary structures, as many as they can, depending on the location and their means. If a peasant is unable to do this on his own, other peasants should help him. No villager should be allowed merely to build a home and not the essential structures noted above, unless he be so sick and so poor that he cannot cultivate the land or pay taxes.

A soldier is useless without weapons, a farmer without equipment. Our people, who have little knowledge of other enterprises, also exhibit stupidity and laziness in their aversion to agriculture. Indeed, our farmers either have inadequate storage facilities and equipment, or their otherwise adequate facilities and equipment are dirty, dull, without value, clumsy, and useless.

Village officials should visit peasants to find out whether or not they have adequate and satisfactory equipment and buildings. Those who do not should be forced to buy them, if not for cash, then by installments. District officials or the sovereign's administrators should accumulate iron agricultural equipment and sell it to peasants without interest and at a set price. Such equipment should include knives, sickles, scythes, hoes, spades, ploughs, axes, hammers, pincers, chisels, planes, lumber saws, band saws, forks, iron hoops, horseshoes, nails, pans, mill iron, buckets, flail chains, fishing hooks, iron pots, kettles, wash basins, and the like. Among containers for storage are large bins with legs to store grain in

Tartars in Russian service near Tobolsk, and the *iurtovskie,* or independent Siberian Tartars, whether friendly or hostile to the Russian conquerors. For a Soviet view of this problem, see S.V. Bakhrushin, "Sibirskie sluzhilye Tatary v XVII veke," *Istoricheskie Zapiski* (1937), no. 1, 55–80.

barns, trunks for clothes, barrels, tubs, kneading troughs, vats, buckets, pails, baskets, kettles, wash basins, and other utensils made of wood, clay, copper, and tin. Villages could use items made of clay, but it would be more appropriate for towns to have glazed pots, or better yet pots made of wood, copper, and tin.

Equipment and vessels should have an attractive appearance. Carts produced in Russia are clumsy and ugly. Axes here are all the same appearance and size, whereas in other countries they vary: small, big, wide, narrow, light, and heavy. Having the right axe for different jobs saves time and labor.

No one in Russia is familiar with tridents or carpenter's saws, and as a result much time is lost. In other countries people cut boards with saws, whether powered by water or by hand. Here, in contrast, boards are cut with axes, and poor ones at that. Annually we produce a great number of boards but lose a tremendous amount of time and effort. The number of boards which a hundred serfs can prepare in a month using axes could be prepared in the same period by twenty using saws, and the sawed boards would be much smoother. Moreover, with an axe it is possible to cut only one or two boards from a thick log. And a great deal of lumber is lost as chips. With a saw it is possible to cut as many boards as are needed— thick or thin depending on the size of the log—and nothing is wasted. Using an axe, half the lumber, or fifty out of a hundred logs, is wasted as chips, while with a saw everything is usable.

I have seen no chisels and hand planes in Russia, yet they are essential for carpenters who wish to do fine work, and they also save a great deal of time. I have seen it taking half a year to build a home which the same builders could finish in two months if they used appropriate axes, saws, chisels, and other tools.

The Germans use scythes instead of sickles for harvesting. They attach pointed beards or teeth to them and cut the grain very fast. This method is quite unsuitable for this country, because frequent rains make it necessary for us to harvest the grain as soon as possible. But I notice that we do everything here exactly opposite to the way it is done in Germany. The scythes used in some places to cut grain are so small that they barely differ from sickles.

People here are unfamiliar with the German steelyards that have numerals stamped on them, a movable arrow marker, and a small hook hanging on a line. Here only crude local yardsticks are used, and usually to cheat with. It would not require much ingenuity to make a good yardstick by copying it from a ready-made German example.

To improve the construction of buildings, builders should show peasants what kind of materials to use in the building of homes and how to make them. Namely: (1) stones with mortar; (2) rocks with clay; (3) bricks with mortar; (4) bricks with clay; (5) bricks dried in the sun, with soft clay—Hungarian peasants use this method to build their homes; (6) wicker with clay; (7) logs puttied with clay; (8) logs puttied with moss; and (9) wicker covered with straw, seeds, or ferns as used in cattle sheds.

Serbs who live between the Danube and Sava build their homes and churches in the ground like Russian cellars because of lack of timber, Turkish oppression, and—I believe—ignorance. Germans in some regions spread dirt over a threshing floor, pour water over it, cover it with straw, and use livestock to stamp it. While this material is still wet they use it to build beautiful, fireproof houses. People here could use this method, at least for fireproof compartments in drying rooms.

Roofs are made from: (1) tin and copper; (2) slabs of certain black rock; (3) glazed tiles; (4) ordinary tiles; (5) oak, beech, fir, and pine boards; (6) the bark of birch, linden, and other trees; (7) reed; (8) cane; (9) brushwood, weeds, branches, and straight straw; and (10) roofing straw— that is, straw that is not threshed. The Germans tie this straw together and weave each bundle into the roof so perfectly that even boards are no smoother. In some regions they smear this straw thoroughly on all sides with dirt so that the house seems to be covered with dirt alone. This method of roofing is best for peasants because it is convenient and easily accessible, and because the roof lasts for a long time and does not burn.

In Vienna, the Venetian ambassador Sagredo said: "In Italy we have a short winter, but here in Vienna I see no winter at all. It is always spring, because in a warm home I do not feel the chill and when I go out, dressed in a fur coat, I do not feel any cold."[6] A certain Scotsman praised Russian ovens and "bakeries" because they were more useful and comfortable than fireplaces.

Some people think that Russia can produce its own silk, but I consider this impossible. Silkworms feed on the leaves of mulberry trees and these trees can grow near Astrakhan, but worms cannot hatch there in sufficient amounts because of thunderstorms and strong winds. Still, I do not know whether they can be hatched in heated rooms. About a thousand years ago, silk was so expensive in Europe that only Roman empresses could afford to have dresses made from it. Then, two monks brought silkworm eggs from India, and silk became inexpensive everywhere, as is now the case.

---

[6] Nicolo Sagredo (d. 1676) was Venetian ambassador in Vienna from 1647 to 1651, and it is possible that Krizhanich met him there in the years 1648–50.

Rice grows in low, wet places, and also in irrigated fields that can be covered by water and then dried for harvesting by letting the water out. I do not know whether it would be possible to find such places in this country.

Near the Caspian Sea and along the Volga, tobacco could grow abundantly, and it would be of good quality, similar to the German Hanau tobacco. It could bring substantial profit to the sovereign's treasury and benefit to the entire country. Every year the several hundred or thousand rubles that are currently paid out for tobacco would remain in Russia.

Hanau has become quite rich, and is getting richer and richer every year thanks to tobacco. Large amounts of wheat grew on fertile soil around that city, but not too long ago a townsman who planted tobacco in his field reaped a great profit, much more than he could have obtained from wheat. As a result, other townsmen imitated him, and tobacco is now planted all around Hanau. They plant the herb every year, prepare it quite well, and send it throughout Germany, Poland, Lithuania, and other lands for great revenues.

Tobacco could be cultivated in this country near Astrakhan, along the Don, and among the Bashkirs. It would be good to plant several fields, and to secure a German expert who knows how to process and roll it. We could sell it to the Kalmucks and to other Siberian, Tartar and Cherkess peoples, as well as to Lithuanians and Belorussians. I saw tobacco of Greek origin growing satisfactorily in Tobolsk; in fact, it was similar to Greek tobacco. Our domestic seeds do not produce a strong herb, but Persian and Greek seeds produce good tobacco. It would be inexpensive to buy some of their seeds annually.

At first Turkish sultans prohibited the use of tobacco. I do not know why, but perhaps it was out of the belief that it was sinful to smoke tobacco as it was sinful to drink wine. I cannot see any other reason, because they grow great quantities of excellent tobacco there and its increased cultivation certainly does not hurt them. It benefits the sultan and the people. Nevertheless, Turkish sultans punished and tortured people on account of tobacco, though they have finally stopped this practice and given them their freedom.

Why is the use of tobacco prohibited in this country? Obviously not because it is sinful, because if it were, then neither soldiers on the battlefield nor miners in the mines would be allowed to smoke—but they are. It is sad that individuals often do not exercise moderation in smoking, but they do not exercise it in the drinking of liquor or in cohabitation with women either. By the same token, whoever uses moderation can drink wine, cohabit with his wife, and smoke tobacco without being a sinner. If tobacco is prohibited because of its sinfulness, then it would be even more appropriate to prohibit wine and women, because these two cause more sins.

But I think the real reason tobacco is prohibited in Russia is that otherwise the people would lose a great deal of money every year in paying for an unnecessary imported commodity—not because the sovereign's treasury would suffer any loss. This is the true, the fundamental, and the only reason. But this prohibition actually helps very little—it does not prevent the people from suffering great losses. This evil cannot be averted, because every year foreigners bring great quantities of the herb to Russia and sell it very dear. What they could get for ten or twenty *pudy* they actually get for one. A single transaction is enough for some of them to become very rich and in two or three years to rise from the status of ragged fellows to that of merchants who can afford to own homes and trade through Astrakhan and Archangel.

Ambassadors from Poland, Lithuania, the Holy Roman Empire, Persia, Sweden, Denmark, England, Holland, the Ukraine, Crimea, Georgia, Cherkassians, and Kalmucks never come to Russia without tobacco. German, Greek, Persian, Bokharan, Kalmuck, and Lithuanian merchants, as well as Russian merchants who return from Sweden, Lithuania, the Ukraine, and Persia, bring hundreds of *pudy* of tobacco to Russia every year. This is why I believe that if tobacco were planted in great quantities at home, and proper care given to it, this tsardom could obtain a threefold benefit: First, the tsar's treasury would benefit. Second, the people would retain a great deal of money which is now sent abroad for a non-essential commodity. And third, the people would rejoice at being free, because a two-pronged yoke would have been removed from their necks—the secular yoke of tsarist prohibition and punishment, and the religious yoke of a vain prejudice which defines what is not sinful as sin and makes things frightening that ought not to be.

Every year the Germans sail through desolate northern territories to the remote Arctic Ocean to procure whale fat. Their labors are well rewarded. I do not know if it is possible to undertake such voyages from this tsardom, from Mangezeia or Archangel, but I know that if the Germans controlled Siberia they would station sailors there, and distant sea routes unknown to us now would be discovered. No one knows if it is possible to find a sea route from Mangezeia to India.

A German observer, Adam Olearius, wrote of the possibility of developing viticulture in Russia. Obviously, Russian soil could develop viticulture if it were properly prepared and if vines were planted. Another

German told me that there are some hills suitable for viticulture near Kazan. I give little credence to these stories, but consider them important enough to call for experiments. Even if grapes did not fully ripen they could be used for vinegar and brandy. If the experiment was even this successful, it should be ordered that many vineyards be planted so that vinegar could be sold throughout Russia and wine brandy could be produced for the sovereign.

I heard from a man in Astrakhan that all this is pointless and impossible. Certainly, the tsar could develop vineyards for himself in Persian territories.

ORES

Adam Olearius, Ambassadorial Secretary of the Duke of Holstein, says that there are deposits of iron ore near Tula, and that the great sovereign was informed about them and about other finds and mining enterprises. He said that the tsar was afraid of deception, and would not receive the prospectors who supplied this information until they attained success on their own. The tsar did offer them aid, he said, and promised them a great reward when they succeeded.

Another German told me that during the reign of Tsar Michael Feodorovich [1613–45], mineral prospectors who were dispatched throughout Siberia brought back several ore samples and advised that mines be started there. Their proposals, however, were not accepted, because they asked for substantial backing but could promise no concrete benefits. I do not believe these fables, and I am inclined to believe that there are other reasons why no ores have hitherto been found in this enormous tsardom.[7]

These reasons are as follows. The northerly regions are cold, sandy and lacking in rocks and mountains. For this reason there is little hope of finding any good ores here except iron, and even that of poor quality. There is also some copper here, but only, I believe, in mountainous and rocky places like the sites of the Swedish mines and the mines near the Kama hills.

If there were ores in the bowels of this northern earth, they would be difficult to find. The reasons are serious, and not particular to Russia. In many countries where there are such ores as salt, sulphur, and dyes, there is no prospecting for them because the common people are unwilling to

---

[7] Krizhanich provides additional information on German mineral prospectors in Siberia in his *Historia de Sibiria* (1680).

become involved in it. This is especially the case in places where there is complete autocracy and the sovereign is absolute. People are afraid that the sovereign will appropriate their mines after they have invested their own labor and resources.

In other areas people are coarse and unskillful, and understand nothing about ores—how to prospect for them or how to process them. Sometimes a peasant finds ore, but he is afraid that his property will be ruined or that he and his neighbors will be forced to work in the mines. Also, a person sometimes finds ore and mines it secretly. Sometimes, too, the sovereign's officials have no interest in mining, or are afraid to be bold where prospecting does not reap immediate benefits, or afraid to anger the sovereign by incurring losses for him.

A man told me that silver ore was found in a mountain near Krasnoyarsk and a sample sent to Moscow, and that it proved to be one-eighth silver. He said that because of jealousy, however, the Germans treacherously concealed this information and in fact declared that the ore was useless. I do not believe this fable, but it is true that sometimes an envious expert hides the truth, or someone without expertise dashes the hopes of the sovereign and in so doing destroys a legitimate enterprise. Thus in 1662 a certain Pole, who was dispatched from Tobolsk to Ketsk to sample ores, asserted upon his return that the ore was useless. Since this individual was not an ore expert, his testimony should not have been trusted.

The same man told me that the aid of a certain magician was solicited to prospect for ores in the Kama region. He pointed to two places to dig, but they mined there with only negligible profit. This is not surprising. The fact that they invited a magician may have been the reason. God denied them success, for no enterprise will succeed if it is supported by the devil.

On November 3, 1664, a Polish prisoner returned from Kuznetsk and recounted wonders to me concerning the abundance of good quality iron found among the people there, people who since time immemorial have been known as "smiths." He said that they are savages, timid people of Tartar origin belonging to the Kondaba and to some other hordes. They extract ore and make iron pots, kettles, large and small wash basins, and anything that anyone requests, even very large tubs, and they make these for a very nominal price. If you give one of them a sack of barley he gives you an iron pot or a kettle, and their iron is of the best quality. If this is true, then the Russians are really very careless and remiss in not paying attention to them. It should be possible to extract enough iron from their mines for weapons to meet the needs of the entire nation. Siberian officials should forward to Moscow, along with furs, large quantities of this iron. Or sabres, muskets, broadswords, armor, saws, scythes, planes, and other weapons and tools could be manufactured in Siberia and sent to Moscow.

The same prisoner said that there are seas from which it is possible to extract salt. A *pud* of salt from one of them costs fourteen copper rubles because it is hauled over great distances—from Tobolsk.

On November 28, 1664, upon his return from Krasnoyarsk, Ivan Shuksta said that in Krasnoyarsk both native and Russian blacksmiths forge white iron and decorate horses' harnesses, armor, and other things with it. They also extract white and black iron ore. A certain Turk (or gypsy) is currently en route to Moscow to petition the sovereign to establish a new fort beyond Krasnoyarsk because deposits of silver and gold are said to be there. The same Shuksta said that many people are drowned in Siberian rivers. Only a few who sail down ever return. These river expeditions, and other (related) needs require great expenditures.

Olearius, describing his second journey to Moscow in Part Four of his book writes that sailors of the king of Denmark brought silver ore from the Newland or Greenland. From 100 *grivny* of ore they extracted 26 *poltiny* of good silver.[8]

---

[8] One *poltina*, or half a ruble, was equivalent to 100 *dengi*. See Table of Coinage and units of measure, p. ix.

4

How ores are mined

First, the Germans advise repeated digging and the building of experimental mines at the sovereign's expense, and they ask enormous sums of money to do those things. No sensible individual should believe them, because they clearly seek profit only for themselves. Second, it should be announced that anyone discovering silver ore and making his discovery known will receive as the sovereign's reward a set sum of money: for copper ore so much, for another type of ore so much. Third, a good number of experts should be dispatched throughout the country to search for mineral deposits. Fourth, native or foreign merchants should receive the right to exploit the mines they construct for twenty or thirty years; then the mines should be taken over by the treasury, but only after the owners have been compensated for their construction expenses.

It should be possible to take each of those approaches, but even so I maintain that all of this will bring only minor results. In fact I believe that the best way to prospect for ores is to search for them in foreign countries the way the Germans and Spaniards do. At home, an order should be issued to all local and national officials telling them to announce that no one who announces the discovery of an ore, be it iron, salt, sulphur, saltpeter, or anything else, whether he is the first to make the announcement, the second, or the third, will be punished if his discovery proves to be nothing. Further, that if something useful or valuable is found, the discoverer will receive a large remuneration from the sovereign. National officials should issue appropriate documents to guarantee the receipt of the sovereign's reward.

Intelligent people (that is, Germans, Spaniards, and Frenchmen) travel the world over searching for and visiting countries inhabited by backward and inexperienced peoples. And whenever they hear about or find an ore vein, they use every means to reach an agreement with the ruler of the country. After they do this, they pay him a rent and mine the ore for themselves. Thus, the Venetians are mining copper in Croatia and earlier mined silver in Serbia. Where they can, these enterprising people seize mining areas by force as the Spaniards and Germans did in India; but on such occasions a great deal of injustice is perpetrated and no one should imitate them in this.

We should be aware, however, that there are still many countries where neither the Germans nor the Spaniards have hitherto had access to survey the mountains and terrain. Particularly unknown to the Germans are the regions where the Nogai Tartars, the mountain Cherkess, the Georgians and other native people live. These lands are located between three great empires—the Russian, Persian, and Turkish—across which the Germans cannot move at will to inspect other lands or to prospect mountains and ores. They can come only to large towns, for trading purposes.

These Cherkess and Georgian territories are mountainous and rocky, and it is possible that they have good ores. In their songs Ancient Hellenic poets and writers praised Khalib iron as the best. The Greek [Constantin] Laskaris writes that the Khalibs were the Pontic people (that is, the Black Sea people) who lived near the Fermodon [Terma] river [in Asia Minor], and that they extracted the best iron. In that area, between the Black and the Caspian seas, the mountainous Cherkess now live, so it seems that they inhabit the area of the ancient Khalibs, from whose name apparently came the name for the Khvalyn (or Khaliv) Sea [i.e., the Caspian].

It thus seems that it would be useful to reach an agreement with these people that would allow tsarist officials and Russian merchants to prospect for ores and build mines in those mountains. Their barbarian princes should receive appropriate compensation, such as of textiles and other gifts. The same method should be used everywhere around the Caspian Sea.

An even better and more reliable method of acquiring ores is through trade. All tsarist commercial and civil officials in border towns (Archangel, Astrakhan, Novgorod, Pskov, Putivl, Tobolsk, Kuznetsk and other Siberian towns) should receive authorizations that would empower them to reach commercial agreements with foreign merchants. Under these agreements the latter could come freely to our country on condition that aboard every one of their wagons and vessels, in addition to their goods, they bring us some ore (silver, copper, tin, lead, good quality iron). Without such ores they would neither be allowed to come freely to us nor to trade here.

We can reach an agreement with the Bokharan, Persian, and Greek merchants, and with the Kuznetsk horde princelings, under which they could bring us substantial amounts of ore. In Hungary, in the region of Semigrad [i.e. Transylvania], there are good cheap ores we could obtain through the Greeks. We could reach an agreement with the Swedes that would stipulate that for the wheat and rye they order from us with the sovereign tsar's approval they should pay so much with silver, so much with copper, and so much with their own goods—that is, one half, or one third, or one sixth, or one tenth with copper, whichever is the best method for us.

If we reach an agreement with a nation to supply us with an ore, that does not mean that we should rely only on that one source of supply. We should try to procure the same ore from other nations, a small amount even if we have to pay a bit more for it. This is important for publicity purposes, so that other nations will sell us their ores more cheaply. For whatever is obtained in one place costs more, and whatever is obtained from many costs less—this is applicable to all commodities.

If a country abounds in some ore, and it becomes inexpensive, it should be mined in great quantities and stored. Ores can be stored for a long time and will neither spoil nor evaporate. One form of ore is mineral coal, or shale rock which burns. It is mined in Scotland and Courland [Latvia], and consists of two forms: one burns even when it is not dry, the other does not burn without first being dry. The latter, peat, is found in Courland, and I have heard from a knowledgeable individual that it is also found near Tobolsk and in other places in Russia.

PART II

Concerning Power

A kingdom has two kinds of fortresses: ordinary defenses and fundamental principles. Ordinary defenses are forts, rivers, weapon systems, and the like. Fundamental principles include:

(1) *Royal example*: The king should neither set example nor engender spiritual lawlessness and increase sinfulness either by his laws or by the amount of taxes he collects for his treasury as is the case in many places.

(2) *Good government*: Subjects should be content with their conditions and foreigners should wish to live under such authority.

(3) *Consensus among people*: The unity of the kingdom should be preserved and nothing allowed to break it up.

(4) *Safeguards against alien influences*: The king and the entire nation should not believe foreigners.

(5) *Advantageous alliances with other nations*: It is better to have a loyal and willing neighbor than to annex him and become one nation, since such a firm neighborhood bond creates an area free of danger for the monarchy. Nothing would be more beneficial for this tsardom than the conclusion of a firm, eternal alliance with the Poles.[1] This is because when the Austrians or Swedes seize Lithuanian or Polish lands, these lands immediately become our enemies even though they are now called our friends.

---

[1] Throughout the seventeenth century, Russo–Polish relations were turbulent, with hostility centering on the dispute over the vast and rich territory of the Ukraine and Belorussia separating Poland from Muscovy. In 1667, the two warring powers concluded an armistice at Andrusovo that provided for division of the disputed territory along the Dnieper river. For scholarly discussion of the subject, see C. Bickford O'Brien, *Muscovy and the Ukraine, from the Pereiaslavl Agreement to the Truce of Andrusovo, 1654–1667* (Berkeley and Los Angeles, 1963), and Zbigniew Wójcik, *Traktat Andruszowski 1667 Roku i Jego Geneza* (Warsaw, 1959).

5

Fortifications

Natural fortifications, or more properly, those created by God, are the seas, rivers, lakes, marshes, mountains, and forests. Artificial or manmade fortresses are *ostrogs,* forts, towers, camps, wagon trains, and ships.

It is necessary to know how to defend and utilize natural fortifications. King Darius committed an error when controlling some mountain passes, because he senselessly removed his guard and so enabled Alexander [the Great] to capture these places. As a result, Alexander emerged stronger and triumphed over him.

Thick oak groves grow everywhere along the rivers in Croatia, and the inhabitants reinforce their boundaries as follows. They erect *abatis* many yards in length, that is, they cut down the trees to make these places impenetrable to cavalry. Near these *abatis* they erect lookout towers. They place ten or more tall logs in the ground and build a hut on top. There they post two or three guards with harquebuses and mortars. When they spot the enemy they fire a shot from a mortar. Upon hearing it the next tower fires its shot, then the third, and the rest on both sides of the river. Thus in one hour the news that the enemy is in the country is spread over an area many miles in circumference.

Manmade fortresses (*ostrogs,* camps, and forts) are familiar sights in this tsardom, and they are well built. Nevertheless, they could be improved.

Blessed is the city which takes defensive precautions in peacetime. It is said of King Jeroboam that he built very strong fortresses, surrounded them with walls, installed military commanders in them, built ware-houses for supplies and armories for weapons, and ordered shields, spears, and other weapons (Chronicles 2:11). King Aza addressed his people: "Let us build these towns, and fortify them with walls, towers, gates, and locks until we organize an army, because the Lord has both warned us and given us peace on all our borders" (Chronicles 2:14).

When Lycurgus, the Spartan legislator, decreed that the Spartans build no *ostrogs* or forts, his reason was that people who depend on their

58

fortifications are neither brave nor courageous. The Poles, who do not have, or barely have, fortified towns and fortifications, usually say: "We subscribe to the law of Lycurgus and meet our enemy not behind the walls but on the plain; that is why we are called 'the plains dwellers'." But the rest of mankind does not praise the Poles or Lycurgus for this attitude. Powerful nations strengthen their territories with *ostrogs*. During the recent invasion of Poland by the King of Sweden, the Poles themselves understood the value of fortifications. The king was unable to capture two stone fortresses—Zamość and Przemyśl.

Turks who lived near frontiers or among conquered peoples whose rebellion they fear take wise precautions and live in *ostrogs* or fortified places. None of them live in an open area. If they have no fortifications, they at least erect a high and thick fence, plaster it with mud, and build their huts behind it. It would be wise for this country to imitate this system, and decree that no one should live in an open unfortified area, especially contiguous to the Nogais, Bashkirs, Siberians, and other untrustworthy conquered peoples. All settlements should be surrounded with walls, and their inhabitants should be required to carry arms. If Siberian settlements along the Tura and Iset rivers were fenced in and armed, the Bashkirs could not destroy them.

Building fortifications and *ostrogs* is the direct responsibility of the king. In this nation, stronger fortifications should be built in the south than in the north. This is because the southern region is richer and more productive, and also because southern areas of the country must be protected from Tartar attacks in order to keep trade routes clear and open. For this reason, it would be wise to dispatch an army every year to build new *ostrogs* and repair old ones near the settlements along the Volga, the Don, and in other places, and along the major overland routes. Mounted soldiers could protect the country from the Tartars while foot soldiers cut timber.

6

Weapons

Hammering weapons: the mace (*bulawa* in Polish) is a symbol of the military commander.[1] Mace with six iron flails. Flagellum—an iron with a butt end. A *haiduk* axe with a butt end. Hammer, cudgel, club, stake.

Cutting weapons: sword or broadsword, cutlass, sabre, two-handed sword or large broadsword (*multanka* in Polish), *bradva*—an axe resembling a half-moon (in foreign languages called *berdysh* and *alebarda*).

Piercing weapons: hussar lances, cossack lance or light cavalry lance (*zida* in Turkish and *wlacznia* in Polish), heavy infantry spear (*das Picke* in German), light infantry spear (*partesana* and *darda* in foreign languages and *sulitsa* in Russia and *oszczep* and *rogacina* in Polish). Cavalry dagger that hangs near the saddle (*hegester* in a foreign language), infantry dagger, German sword (*spada* in a foreign language), little dagger (*punial, sztylet,* and *tulich* in foreign languages), and Turkish knife (*khanzher* and *bichak* in their language).

Shooting weapons: bow and small cossack arrows, bow and large infantry arrows, *kusha* and large *kusha* arrows. Pistol (*pishchalka* in our language) carabine, bandoler (*pobochnitsa* in our language), *khakovnitsa* (*bradatka* in our language), musket (*peshnitsa* in our language), mortars (*kratchitsa* in our language). [Krizhanich continues to name many weapons of his time, a list which may be of interest to military historians.]

---

[1] In this brief chapter, Krizhanich identifies various weapons used in the seventeenth century. Some of the names are Polish; others are Serbo-Croatian, Russian, or German; and some are of unknown origin, without English equivalents. In the interests of readability, some of these names have been omitted here. Readers interested in military history may wish to consult Tikhomirov's edition of the *Politika,* which on page 710 lists these weapons in order of their appearance in the book.

7

Military Organization

Ancient wise men applied royal titles to two creatures in the animal kingdom: they named the lion king of beasts, and the eagle king of birds. These two, more than any other living creatures, exemplify the two critical features of strength and speed. Some animals surpass the lion in speed, but he surpasses them in strength. Some surpass him in strength but he surpasses them in speed. But not one animal is at once stronger and quicker than the lion, and for that reason the lion usually triumphs and is almost never conquered. For the same reason the eagle surpasses all other birds.

An army that wants victory must be both strong and quick. But it is difficult to combine in one human being or in a single military unit qualities that would make a soldier both strong and quick. This is why different units are armed with different weapons, and some can prevail because of their speed while others prevail because of their strength. This is one of the most important secrets of statecraft, and those who have used it wisely have gained many victories.

In antiquity, the Romans were the best military authorities and students of war. Long after they had subdued many kingdoms to their authority, they began to divide their armies into various military units: light cavalry, heavy cavalry, light infantry, heavy infantry, slingers, shieldbearers, archers, *triarii*, veterans, new recruits, and others whose names I cannot now recall.[1]

On numerous occasions the Poles fought well against the Germans because they had light cavalry—cossacks and Tartars—along with heavy cavalry—their own hussars; while the Germans had neither one nor the other. During the last war, the Tartars performed wonders in their encounter with the Swedes, capturing and killing them everywhere as if they were chickens.[2]

---

[1] Here Krizhanich uses the Roman military terms *triarii, veterani*, and *novicii*.
[2] Krizhanich refers here to the war between Poland and Sweden of 1655–59.

In a war with Gustavus of Sweden, Ferdinand II gained success because of a diversity of weapons and because his armies consisted of units from many nations.[3]

It would be useful to adopt from other nations their most famous and best military formations—namely, formations of the Kalmucks, Mongols, Samoeds, Scotsmen, hussars, dragoons, musketeers, cossacks, and shield-bearers—and to maintain at least one unit each. Whenever a need arose, the unit that appeared to be most suited could be expanded.

People tell wonders about the Kalmucks and the Mongols. The Kalmucks maintain a hussar system. They carry a spear, a bow, a sabre, and armor, and they shield their elbows and thighs with iron, or carry chain mail. In attack they drive their cattle in front.

On their horses, the Mongols carry a pistol, a bow, a spear, and a defensive weapon fettered on both ends, which they guard carefully during stops. Their harquebuses resemble muskets, but they use neither rod, flint, nor wick to fire them; they use some other firing device. Because they carry six types of weapon, in my view each man must have two horses, or an extra horse and a boy. Yet I have heard this system is quite commendable.

Scotsmen are armed as follows: each man carries a big bow and long arrows, a sword, and a pistol, a harquebus, and a knife.

Various military units must be formed, and informed as to what military units the enemy has, and what their specialities are. We should then build our own forces accordingly. Cavalry can have three units:

(1) The *hussars,* or men in armor. They have a spear, a sabre at their waist, a broadsword at the saddle, and everything else that goes with this equipment.

(2) The *cossacks,* or pursuers. They carry a bow and arrows and a sabre. They have no heavy equipment—no spiked helmet, armor, iron stirrups, or forged bridle.

(3) *Shooters or harquebusers.* They carry a harquebus or handgun, a sabre, and a helmet if they can afford one. This type of cavalry is lighter than the hussars and heavier than the cossacks; more properly, it resembles the cossacks except that instead of bows and arrows it is armed with handguns.

The Germans have three cavalry formations: (1) men in armor, who are fully covered with armor; (2) mounted horsemen, who carry swords and

[3] Reference is to the Swedish phase (1630–33) of the Thirty Years War.

short-barreled handguns; (3) dragoons or musketeers, who carry muskets and fight with the infantry.

Their men in armor and mounted horsemen are useless for our needs, because they are slow and the Tartars could defeat them easily. Their dragoons or musketeers could be used by merging them with our harquebusers. The units could be effective against the Kalmucks and the Tartars and especially in Siberia against Tartar cuirassiers and lancers. Against the Tartars a unit of mounted horsemen with muskets, bows and arrows, and axes instead of swords would be novel and very useful.

The following are infantry units:

(1) Archers. They carry a big bow and arrows, a sabre, and a shield. For the most part the ancients had only infantry. Now, following the appearance of handguns, infantry has disappeared almost everywhere, except in England and among some mountaineers such as the Scots.

Philip de Commines says that in a close combat there is nothing better than these archers, and this is really true. For this reason it is surprising that countries which have conflicts with the Tartars do not have these units. Archers were appointed by the king as his bodyguards in ancient times. For that reason guards of the German emperor are still called *Arcieri*, i.e. archers, even though they do not now carry bows, only other weapons. In Russia the *streltsy* have been so called for a long time, not because of their harquebuses, which are a recent innovation, but because of their arrows.[4] The royal guard would really be impressive if archers carrying bows and decorated shields surrounded the tsar; then there would come the *haiduks* with broadswords, followed by guards with *alebardams*, or wide gilded spears. It would be fitting for these warriors to wear black uniforms, and for the *streltsy* to have white hats and, in wintertime, three-cornered caps with red lining.

(2) The *haiduks* (a Polish term for Hungarian infantry) carry a large or small harquebus, a sabre, and, behind their belts, a small hatchet. They should be issued broadswords instead of sabres, but never swords.

(3) German foot lancers carry long spears and swords in accordance with the German system. Instead of forming separate units they are assigned to the other infantry units to defend them against mounted

---

[4] *Streltsy* (singular *strelets*) literally means "shooters," or musketeers. They were Russia's first permanent regular military units from 1550 to 1698, and were disbanded thereafter by Peter the Great. Some units were cavalry, but most were infantry. They played a vital role during several periods of crisis and in Russia's conquest of Siberia. For comprehensive discussions on the *streltsy*, cf. N.I. Shpakovskii, "Streltsy," *Zhurnal Ministerstva Narodnogo Prosveshcheniia* 319 (1898): 135–51; and A.V. Chernov, *Vooruzhennye sily Russkogo gosudarstva v XV–XVII vv.* (Moscow, 1954). See also, Lantzeff, *Siberia*, 66–7.

units. Instead of swords they should be issued broadswords or axes. Each foot soldier should also be given a sharp *haiduk* pole axe, with leather casing to prevent accidents. These pole axes are useful not only in a battle but also for other purposes.

In earlier days, warriors of each unit—cavalry and infantry—carried shields, and these shields varied: some were for mounted soldiers, some for infantry, some were broad for sieges. Soldiers rightly abandoned the use of shields in combat against harquebuses—there is little defense against harquebuses, and it is awkward to carry a shield while mounted. In Russia and Siberia, though, shields would be useful against arrows. In my view, it would be striking and impressive for the tsar to be surrounded by a detachment of shieldbearers. For open field combat, infantry spear-bearers should be issued shields. We have materials at home to make them—wood, hides, and glue—and we could produce not only shields but bows and arrows quite inexpensively; and this would undoubtedly be to our advantage.

Our worst mistake has been discontinuing mounted and infantry *streltsy* units. Because of the *streltsy*—and the use of bows and arrows in general—Russia grew and expanded, but with dragoons it will not be able to grow in size and strength again. We should organize training and competition in archery as is done in Turkey. We could assess subject peoples for a tribute payable in bows so that they could deliver a number of good bows. Our people themselves should learn how to produce bows, quivers, and arrows. They should acquire the art of arrow-making from the Persians, Tartars, Siberian Samoeds, and other natives, learning, for example, what kinds of bows they have, and how they fasten quivers to their backs in such a way that the quivers do not interfere with their walking.

No one should fully trust methods of the perfidious Germans—those of other nations should be examined as well. A reward should be offered, in fact, to anyone who comes up with a better system, both for infantry and cavalry.

Here in Russia I see battleaxe soldiers and a battleaxe system—that is, infantrymen sent into the battle with battleaxes only, no other weapons. I do not know whether there is such a system anywhere else in the world. I believe we employ it only because of a shortage in sabres and swords, or of good iron. The system seems quite useless, because our battleaxe-men cannot fight at long range since they cannot carry bows or harquebuses along with their battleaxes. Even in close combat they can only hit, not pierce or run through. Moreover, they cannot cut wood, dig trenches, or build forts.

It would be best to maintain two infantry units at all times—archers and harquebuses. These would be accompanied by lancers, not as a separate formation but as protection. Each foot soldier, regardless of his unit, should have a small axe. Instead of the fairly long German spears, a foot soldier should have a short spear, between six and eight feet long, with a sharp end and a long iron casing to reinforce it, as the German ones are made. Instead of a tassel, the spear should have a red and white flag like a hussar's. Such a spear would be easy to carry, it would be a better protection, and more terrifying to the enemy. Finally the wooden handles of hussar and infantry spears as well as the halberts of the tsar's guard should be painted white and red—and should be straight and strong.

If music is necessary for anything in the world it is in battle. The sound of music will encourage valor among our own forces and instill fear in the enemy. For this reason we should see to it that we develop the finest of military bands. Copper kettledrums are a bit too heavy for our horses, and in any case inappropriate for our mobile units and for combat with the Tartars. It would be sufficient to have wooden drums for our infantry and cavalry units.

It is difficult to blow into copper horns, and besides we do not know how to make them. In any case, our armed forces need only a few trumpeters. But we should have an adequate number of pipers, for there is no more appropriate music for cavalry, infantry, and sailors. When a skilled piper played on his instrument, Alexander the Great was seized by emotion and leaped from behind the dining table to grab his weapons. Played on the battlefield by a good number of skilled pipers, pipe music creates incredible fear and confusion in the enemy. Common soldiers (in addition to the usual number of pipers) should be taught how to play pipes, and camp wagons should have extra pipes to distribute among them before battle to increase the sound.

The *pomort* is one of the largest of the horns. In Warsaw I saw many such horns taken from the royal treasury, and was told that they were played during the feast King Stefan Batory prepared for the Muscovite embassy. About twenty players played the high notes on small horns, others played the low notes on big horns. It sounded like real battle music. The *shtort* is a large horn. In its appearance, construction, and sound it resembles a large horn, though the latter is even larger and has a more powerful sound. For a description of various horns consult Julius Solinus, chapter 11, and [Julius] Pollux, Book 4, chapters 9 and 10.[5] The *shalamai* is attached to large horns for better sound.

[5] Krizhanich obtained much of his information about musical instruments from G. Cnapsius, *Thesaurus polono-latino-graecius* (Cracow, 1643), and from the works of the third-

I. Valtrini (Book 3, chapter 4) maintained that when trumpets, flutes, horns and other instruments played in harmony before a military commander, it was battle music. Polybius writes that the Praetorian guards usually ate their meals to the sound of horns and organ music. It would also be useful to issue a general invitation to good flute players and skillful trumpeters, build a school for them, give them full support, and encourage them to perfect their art. Nothing would add more to the splendor of the tsar's court than good music played on wind instruments. An orchestra should give restrained concerts for the people from the Florovskaia Tower of the Kremlin, but on major holidays it should play really loud and clear. Musicians should have the following privileges: trumpet and flute players should be allowed to learn to play on string and other instruments, and they should be allowed to play for pay at weddings and other festivals. Anyone who cannot play a wind instrument is useless for military service, and if they cannot obtain a written certificate from the masters of Moscow testifying to their musical skills, they should be barred from musical performances and from deriving an income from them.

Hypocrites and ignorant people read the words of St John the Golden about the Maccabees that "they played neither on their horns nor on their drums, but they prayed to God," or the words of another Holy Father— "David loved music and during his reign Israel was secular, but now Israel has become religious"—and say that it is sinful for Christians to play music. But some teachings of Christ and the Holy Fathers (such as these) refer to the road to a higher degree of perfection. For example, "if there should be anyone who feels hatred toward his father and mother and his own soul, he cannot become my pupil; he must sell off his property and distribute his income among the poor." These words do not apply to those who wish to follow only Christ's commandments; they apply to those who wish to follow his teachings as well, those who wish to take the road of perfection.

---

century Roman writer Julius Solinus; the Greek historians Julius Pollux (second century), Plutarch (*c*.46–*c*.120) and Polybius (*c*.205–*c*.125 BC); the Italian scholar I. Giannantonio Valtrini (1556–1601); and the Italian musician Giovanni B. Doni (1593–1674). During his stay in Rome between 1651 and 1657, Krizhanich became interested in the theory of music. He was a member of the Baroque Circle, which included the musical theorist and mathematician J. Caramuel. In 1656, Krizhanich published a musical work of his own, *Asserta musicalia*; he also had occasion to prepare other musical works and to supervise the publication of musical materials for King João IV of Portugal. See Ivan Golub, "O. sačuvanim primjercima Križanićevih Asserta musicalia," *Arti musices* 2 (Zagreb, 1971): 31–41; and the comments by J. Sidak on "Das Problem 'Križanić als Musiker,'" in Thomas Eekman and Ante Kadić, eds., *Juraj Križanić (1618–1683): Russophile and Ecumenic Visionary* (The Hague, 1976), 44–49; hereafter cited as Eekman and Kadić.

As the Holy Pope Gregory says, the saints have performed acts which we cannot imitate, only be astonished and carried away. St Vincent of Ferrara says the same thing. Thus, for example, David advanced against the enemy with a sling shot; Joseph triumphed over the Maccabees by singing a hymn praising the Lord. But we cannot invoke God and expect miracles: we should pray first, then go to battle carrying every weapon we have.

The same can be said of music. It would be best if we had no music, or swords, or slingshots and if we turned the other cheek when anyone hit us. I repeat—this would be best. But as it has been proclaimed and prophesied, the best is not for everyone. It is only for the elect, those predestined to receive God's blessing. In war we should use weapons and music, because for *ordinary* mortals they are necessary, to say nothing of useful.

Any intelligent person who sees two stone houses, even if he is neither a builder nor an architect, can judge which of the two is better built and more suitable for human habitation. Any intelligent person can also judge weapons, and military units, and decide which is better and more effective. But spelling out how military matters are to be resolved—that is exclusively for military commanders and experienced soldiers, not for the author of a book. Similarly, any intelligent person can judge which of two musicians plays better even if he knows nothing about music. But only a musician who has been trained to play a wind instrument can do so. This is why I cite the views of several intelligent writers on a variety of weapons and different military units. To treat these matters in detail is neither my purpose nor that of these other writers—and besides, it would be immodest.

Skillful craftsmen know how to make cannons, shot, battering rams, gabions, and the like. The commanding officer [*ban*], the *voevoda,* and the rest of the officers know military principles, lead their troops, prepare camp, fortify it, protect their forces during their march, defend the army in open field, ready their troops for battle, encourage them by speeches and other means, transport them across rivers, and handle similar problems. I remain silent about all of this, though I have one thing to say about Alexander. No water could stop him, and he crossed the widest and swiftest rivers with unbelievable speed. Yet the same thing can be accomplished today if the army has knowledgeable men and appropriate equipment.

There are several ways to transport a small number of men across a body of water. In some countries soldiers use leather sacks to carry drinking water. When a sack is needed for floating, they pour out the water, inflate the sack, and seal it, and sail across the river on it. Others have leather rafts with two sticks across and one at the bottom for sailing across rivers. In still other places calabash trees that are quite useful for sailing are grown. I do not know whether these trees could be made to grow in Astrakhan, but they could be imported from the Persian border.

8

The military personnel

You will have fine soldiers if they are provided with good food, uniforms, and weapons; brave and alert if they are kept in fear. First, soldiers should concern themselves with strengthening their bodies—that is, with securing food, clothes, and weapons—then with improving their spirits—with training, discipline, study and courage.

This tsardom shows more concern with food supplies than any other state in the world with which I am acquainted. Its people use biscuits, dried mushrooms, oatmeal, various groats from oats, buckwheat, millet, rye, barley; a very tasty pork, melted butter, flax and hemp oil, caviar, salted fish, meat, and *kvas*. People in other countries are either unfamiliar with these foods or unable to prepare them so tastefully. The Tartars boil, roast, and eat barley and wheat—a dish they call *kurmych*. The Ostiaks dry their fish in the sun and air but do not salt it. The Germans, after salting meat and fish, smoke it. Directions how to salt and pickle, and how to prepare various greenery, roots, kidney beans, and other varieties of beans, belong not here but in a book on agriculture and home economics.

It is even more critical that soldiers be adequately uniformed, for though few soldiers die of starvation, many die of the cold. Citizens of all towns near a line of march should be ordered to prepare for sale an adequate quantity and variety of ready-made clothing, namely hats, fur coats, gloves, trousers, underwear, and boots. They should sell all these items to soldiers at the usual price, with no mark-up. The military commander and the town administrator should determine the price for these goods.

The purpose of military training is to teach soldiers how to shoot well with a bow and a harquebus, and how to keep order under the colors. Soldiers must know how to use not only the harquebus but the bow, because the accuracy and speed of firing of the bow is useful and in some circumstances essential. We should not encourage, and in fact not even allow, the introduction of the sort of drill and goose-stepping introduced by the Germans, because this exhausts the troops uselessly and distracts them from their real work. Drills have no application to real battles, and German goose step is of no use in battle with the Tartars.

Bravery is inspiration and daring and also a certain self-confidence thanks to which a soldier thinks that he is stronger than his enemy and consequently marches boldly into the battle. Some people are mistaken about the source of bravery. They argue from nature, which has endowed the eagle with the ability to fly and walk on two legs, and the ox only with the ability to walk on four legs, not to fly or walk on two legs. They think it equally true that nature has endowed some nations with bravery, and that in no way can other nations come up to their standard in this. But they are badly mistaken. Bravery and military valor are not natural gifts. They depend on effort, skill, prolonged training, and above all on good government.

In bravery and in valor our nation compares favorably with any other nation. For we can see that many nations, under the sway of good kings and generals as well as of good and free—not slavish—governments, emerged from insignificance, debasement, and illiteracy into power and glory. But under poor governments, these strong and brave nations again became dishonored, outcast, and insignificant.

Some people think that wealth, luxury, and abundance are responsible for the loss of nobility. They are mistaken, for though nobility is not lost, desire, willingness, and even readiness are forfeit. In their place what emerges is foreign influence, which is detrimental to everything good.[1]

Once upon a time the Romans (or Italians) lived under free and responsible governments, and were braver than any other nation. But now the Italians have lost all their valor because they are divided into numerous states, controlled by foreign nations, and more preoccupied with trade than with military matters. The Turks and the Tartars were once insignificant and unknown nations but now they are a threat to the entire world. Thus bravery is not given to nations at birth, but develops thanks to effort, good government, and experience.

Bravery will emerge when the following prerequisites are present: (1) soldiers have good weapons; (2) soldiers are well trained and experienced in military matters; (3) music is beautiful, resounding, cheerful, and inspiring; (4) military commanders are good and wise—and native rather than foreign; (5) the terms for all military equipment are in the native, not a foreign language; (6) soldiers' names are dignified, not ridiculous or

---

[1] Throughout his work, Krizhanich uses the term *xenarchia*, rendered here as foreign rule or influence.

exotic; (7) the hair and beards of soldiers are properly groomed; (8) they wear proper uniforms; (9) separate units receive special names; (10) soldiers are certain they will be paid for their labor; (11) they are assured they will be respected; (12) soldiers are allowed to dispose of their salaries and to maintain their honor; that is, without strict prohibitions or restrictions a soldier can freely dispose of the fruits of his labor—salary or material goods—which he has acquired in adverse weather, in dangerous situations, and through suffering.

But above all, to arouse bravery it is necessary to have a benevolent government. Without that all these other means will be useless, and soldiers will never become skillful; they will always be cowardly and desperate. God's blessing should be a shield of hope, a fortress, and a foundation of the bravery of Christian kings as well as soldiers. But—and here is our problem and our sorrow—people concern themselves least about the things that are most needed.

9

Commanders

The importance of a good commanding officer to the army is indicated by the saying that an army of deer led by a lion is more powerful than an army of lions led by a deer. There is no way to make soldiers brave if the commanding officer is without substance.

The Chinese in this respect arrange things poorly, indeed stupidly, when they pay no attention to experience, bravery, intelligence, knowledge, and family background, and instead appoint commanders who know how to write better than they know how to speak. They appoint all their military and civil leaders this way. This is why the Chinese are not a warlike people, and their commanders are taught more about civil than about military matters and resemble scribes rather than soldiers.

The Turks pay no attention to family background (since they do not have any nobility), but say that they value expertise, knowledge, and bravery. The facts are different. Usually their leaders are unworthy men who have learned how to insinuate themselves: in one move the lowest becomes the highest, and the highest the lowest. Such a process deprives people of their bravery, and gives birth to nihilism and despair because no one is content with his status, material possessions, or degree of security, and no one has any reason to work hard to attain high honor or glory.

European kings do better because along with other attributes they consider family background. Men with a family background, those who have enjoyed illustrious names and extensive landed estates for years, will be more concerned to protect and maintain their own noble status, the monarchy, their own estates, and the glory of their family, than the common people will be about the achievement of high success. Hereditary nobles are more concerned about their wealth, estates, and the upholding of their own glory than the poor or common people are about new wealth and fame. Moreover, nobles have more time and opportunity earmarked for study in their youth than common people. Yet if a commoner who possesses true nobility appears, the door is not closed to him: the king first appoints him a colonel, then a nobleman, finally a military commander.

In order to inspire the people, they should be promised that all those allowed to accompany the tsar as his personal bodyguard will be Slavs.

The famous military leader Attendolo Sforza[1] said:

> The following are the obligations of a good military commander: first, to fight for a just cause; second, to save innocent people; third, to protect churchs and young maidens; fourth, to spare the blood of your own soldiers; fifth, not to rejoice and brag about the defeat of an enemy; and sixth, to believe that every victory is a deed of God.

The German slow march and cavalry formation requires more officers than a mobile system. For this reason, we should not increase the number of officers beyond the normal number if a war with the Tartars or another nation develops. We should increase the number of officers only if we fight the Germans, and then only in the infantry. The Germans fight standing firm, hence our infantrymen would have to fight them standing up. Officers should urge them on from behind, not allowing them to flee.

The following are my thoughts concerning the qualities of a good commander.

(1) Everything required of a good soldier should be expected of a good commander. That is, he should be a loyal, brave and experienced soldier.

(2) He should be vigilant, quick, zealous, thoughtful, ever preoccupied with his duties, never idle, and good at saving time.

(3) He should be resolute, persistent, and stern in arousing fear and maintaining discipline.

(4) He should be a just judge, impartial, above taking gifts, and not greedy. On these matters, he should be willing to take an oath.

(5) He should be generous and humane, for if anyone in the world needs generosity and humanity, it is the commander. In peacetime, excessive, extravagant generosity is not praiseworthy, but in war it always is, and seldom turns out to be wasteful.

(6) The commander should be cool in battle and not panic at rumors.

(7) He should be high born, or have some other special distinction.

(8) He should be native born, not a foreigner or the son or nephew of a

---

[1] The Italian military commander Attendolo Sforza (1370–1424).

foreigner. This is because soldiers lose all inclination to fight bravely when they see that the wages to which they are entitled go to foreigners. Not just once or twice, but actually as a general rule, officers are chosen from the foreigners and the natives supply only common soldiers.

Here in Russia something takes place that has not happened and will not happen anywhere else in the world. The Germans are in charge of fortresses, and have obtained almost the entire authority and command over the army, while our people cannot even dream of ever receiving a high post.[2] There is cause for apprehension in this; in fact, one can look forward with certainty to the time when this issue will bring about revolt, treason, and bloodshed.

The Roman empire fell because foreigners were granted citizenship and nations were mixed. Monarchy is dying now in Poland for the same reason. It would be a wise stroke for the sovereign tsar to agree secretly with the Poles to limit the number and influence of foreigners, pledging at the same time not to infringe on their freedoms.

(9) The commander should be skillful. He should know how to prepare and inspire the army for battle; how to build fortifications; how to lay out a camp, etc. For reference purposes he should have a manual on the making of artificial fire or fire balls, on the conduct of court martials, and similar matters.

(10 The commander should also know about the history of warfare, because he can learn many useful things from the past and apply them to his own needs.

(11) He must also have a map and a good descriptive account of the territory on which he is waging war, and be well versed in the past and present conditions of his own country and its people.

(12) the commander should also contemplate, and prepare private memoranda, on our land and its people. For example, how many and what kind of nations are our neighbors? What kind of good, or ill, can we expect from each of them? When and why did our people suffer their worst disasters, and when and how did they attain their greatest triumphs? Why did we win or lose various battles? What weapons should we use and how should we use them, to conduct a war against this or that nation? What reasons we have to be at war or at peace with every other nation? And anything else that comes to mind.

[2] In the second half of the seventeenth century, many Western European mercenary units (German, Swedish, and English), captained by soldiers of fortune, sought and received employment in Russia. Though costly and often unreliable, they contributed to many Russian successes against the Ottoman Turks and paved the way for the modernization of the Russian military establishment under Peter I.

10

Languages, titles,
appearance, and uniforms

It would make our soldiers braver if they felt and believed that our nation yields to no other nation in military valor and is indeed braver than many of them. But the use of foreign terms in military matters gets in the way. Soldiers lose their nerve if they have to parrot incomprehensible foreign terms to identify their weapons, duties, and activities. The foolish mixing of languages is useless anywhere, but especially harmful in the military, because when soldiers hear every military item called by a foreign term, they begin to think that foreign nations are exceptionally brave and that they, and their own nation, are not brave enough. They think the terms for military matters must come from the same places as military prowess and valor.

Therefore throughout the entire tsardom it would be wise to prohibit the use of foreign terms in official papers, petitions, and camps, in formations and under banners. See table 2 for example.

Golova (from Turkish *hash*) should be properly called *zapovednik*, or better yet, *glavar*.

Where we have no name for something, then of course from necessity we must borrow from our neighbors; as, for example, *shereg*—a Hungarian term.

It would also be proper to prohibit certain inappropriate Russian expressions, as for example:

(1) "The sovereign tsar is in service." Whom, except God, does the sovereign serve? A correct way to put it would be "The sovereign is at war or on a military expedition."

(2) The tsar's living quarters are called *dvorets*, implying a small court. It would be more correct to call the tsar's or a *boyar*'s living quarters *dvor*, and the living quarters of common people *khorom*, or *dom*.

(3) A *pogreb* should be called *pivnitsa*.

(4) A *krestianin* should be called *kmet*, *rab*, or *kholop*.[1]

---

[1] In Krizhanich's view the term *krestianin* meant a villager or an agriculturist; *kmet*, a dependent peasant; *rab*, a slave; and *kholop*, an indebted individual. It should be noted that

Table 2 Russian military terms

German terms	Our terms	Alien terms	Our terms
Reiter	Konnik	Dobosh	Bubnar
Soldat	Pekhotinets	Barabanshchik	Bubnar
Sergeant	Poruchnik	Vitiaz	Ratnik, boets
Rotmeister	Sotnik konnyi	Shiposh	Svirelshchik
Major	Pervyi sotnik	Husar	Kopeishchik
Hetman	Polevoi ban	Amanat	Zalozhnik
Ataman	Hlavar, sotnik	Baraban	Buben
Captain	Hlavar, sotnik	Kulbak	Tatarskoe sedlo
Lieutenant	Podvoevoda		
Esaul	Poruchnik		
Musketeer	Pishchalnik		
Dragoon	Konnyi pishchalnik		
Sahaidak	Kolchan		
Kantar	Uzda		
Bakhmat	Tatarskii kon		

(5) It is incorrect to consider and call a *krestianin* a *kholop*, or call a *boyar* a *poddanyi* or *sluga* [i.e., subject, servant]. Some time ago the Germans had this expression: "Der Ritter und Knecht stechen un turnilren." The Scots even today, call their cavaliers "knights." All subjects of the king, including great princes, were called "vassals"—that is, "orphans." One can call one's own slaves pejoratively: "my man" or "my people." But when referring to others in official papers or in laws, one should not write *chelovek* in place of *kholop*.

(6) Instead of *golova*—say *voevoda*.

(7) Instead of *polkovoi voevoda* say *voennyi ban* or simply *ban*.

(8) "Service people" is a vile, undignified expression that diminishes the manliness of soldiers. A more dignified expression would actually make soldiers manly and brave. Thus you should not say "Russian servitors" but say instead "Russian warriors," "young Russian men," and "Russian military."[2]

---

the meaning of these terms changed during the course of history. Thus, for example, *kmet* in the Kievan period identified a military servitor. In the Polish–Lithuanian Commonwealth (sixteenth–seventeenth centuries) the same term meant a peasant. For a discussion in English of these distinctions, see Jerome Blum, *Lord and Peasant in Russia* (Princeton, N.J., 1961), 219–76.

[2] Among the various groups making up seventeenth-century Russian society, Russian historians have distinguished (1) *sluzhilye*, or *sluzhashchie liudi*—servitors, or service people; and (2) *tiaglye liudi*—tax-paying people. The first group, to which Krizhanich

Another cause of cowardice is the fact that here in Russia soldiers are called by unintelligible Greek, Hebrew, and sometimes monastic names such as Feofil, Avramii, Pakhomii, and Pafnutii. They would be braver if they were called by the well-known apostolic names—Peter, Andrei, Ivan, Pavel—as well as by local names in their language: Khervoi, Belai, Dolgosh, Iarosh, Novak, Debeliak, Tretiak, Vladimir, Branimir, Skorovoi, Liutovoi, Radosav, Vladisav, Berisav, Iarosav, Bogdan, Dragan, Dragavan, Radvan, Vukashin, Grubisha, Gruitsa, and others. They could also have two names: Peter Khervoi, Andrei Bogdan, Ivan Radosav, and Pavel Liutovoi, one name always of a saint, another from our own language. For every day of the year we should add a Slavic name alongside the Greek names. In this way we may be able to eliminate the drunkenness that prevails on name days. Moreover, our language may eventually enter the church calendar where, God willing, it will be dignified by the sainthood of someone from our midst. Rulers can also glorify our nation and our language, because kings of other nations are more often known by their local names than by their Greek names.

One of the basic causes of cowardice in soldiers is the unkempt, undignified appearance of their hair, beards, and uniforms. Beauty arouses love, and a face that manifests good grooming also reveals bravery, and stimulates respect and fear in those who see it. A horse decorated with trappings kicks and jumps. By the same token, a soldier who has a handsome, skillful haircut, a fine beard, and a fancy uniform inspires admiration and indeed becomes a new person.

The Russian face is distinguished neither by beauty, grooming, nor independence. Indeed, to the observer it reveals a slave-like state, poverty, and cowardice. Our soldiers march wrapped in tight uniforms as if they were packed and sewed up in sacks, their heads are shaved hairless, like the heads of young calves, and their beards look neglected, so that they actually resemble savages of the forest more than brave dashing warriors.

A tree that loses its leaves in the winter looks small, ugly, pitiful, and insignificant; but in the summer it puts on its curls again, and looks large, beautiful, and happy. The same applies to a man who has, though

---

refers here, included those in government service (military and other) who performed various services instead of paying taxes, receiving landed estates or payment in cash in return. The *tiaglye liudi* included townspeople and state peasants who had obligations to the government that were met by payments in cash, in kind, or in labor. For discussions of this differentiation and its implications, cf. N.P. Pavlov-Silvanskii, *Gosudarevy sluzhilye liudi* (St Petersburg, 1898); M. Diakonov, *Ocherki obshchestvennogo i gosudarstvennogo stroia drevnei Rusi*, 2nd ed. (St Petersburg, 1908), 249–397; Vladimirskii-Budanov, *Obzor istorii*, 127–47; V. Sergeevich, *Drevnosti russkogo prava*, 3rd ed. (St Petersburg, 1909), I, 422–559; and I.D. Beliaev, "Sluzhilye liudi v Moskovskom gosudarstve," *Moskovskii sbornik* (1852), I, 357–82.

not a fluffy woman's hair style, properly groomed hair; who wears smartly fitting clothes; who looks imposing seated on a horse; who can walk at a brisk pace; who looks handsome and dignified; and who is well protected from frost, rain, slush, wind, and sun, and consequently is braver and more skillful, and hence more dangerous to the enemy.

The Italians and Spaniards are better looking than we are, and they also live in a warmer climate. However, they have full heads of hair, and do not shave their heads. They get haircuts only for appearance's sake. But for us, living in a cold climate and not naturally handsome, hair is more important: it would hide the roughness of our faces, make us more attractive and dignified, cover our ears from bitter cold, and arouse the bravery of our soldiers. But we prefer to imitate barbaric peoples—the Tartars and Turks—rather than the noblest of the Europeans. In fact we do not even follow the barbarians fully, and act worse than they do. They cover the baldness and ugliness of their heads with small—and sometimes large—caps, without concealing their faces; whereas we walk around bald-headed like pumpkins. A shaven head is a sign of captivity and slavery. Indeed, owners shave the heads of captives and oarsmen aboard seagoing vessels.

A Tartar tuft of hair on the parietal bone or a Polish tuft of hair atop the forehead are the same as baldness. The customary Russian hair style is disorderly because it hides the person's face and projects a savage appearance. An ungroomed beard gives soldiers an old look, older than they actually are and not so frightening to the enemy. The Wallachians have a beautiful hair style. They cut their hair back, and leave as much hair as necessary on the parietal bone to cover the rest of the head. Their hair hangs down to the middle of their ears. This hair style is a genuine ancient Slavic haircut, and gave rise to an expression still used today by all trans-Danube Slavs, "cut the hair." In Russia nowadays they do not "cut the hair" but shave the entire head except for a little tuft of hair, so it would be more appropriate here to say "shave the head."

The Venetian hair style is also beautiful. They do not shave their hair on the parietal bone; they cut it low with scissors and leave a wreath of hair around the head—a thick sheaf over the ears, a little hair at the back and still less in front, on the forehead. The Germans make this wreath of hair even on all sides. The Spaniards style their hair the same as the Venetians do, except that they cut the hair close behind their ears and at the back, and do not leave the entire wreath. All of these hair styles are beautiful and becoming.

I cannot praise other hairstyles. Some Germans let their hair grow, some down their shoulders and some even farther down, the same as women. Still others pull their hair to one side and interlace it with silk.

This is dissolute and overindulgent. Things that are neither too much nor too little are always good. Moderation is good; while both insufficiency and excess cause problems.

The Czechs and Hungarians wear round beards, shaved and scissor-cut. Among some nations, young men and soldiers, especially those who cannot grow thick beards, wear a moustache, and cut their beards with scissors, leaving hair only half a finger long. Among the Germans, every man trims his beard as he wishes and as he thinks best for himself. On this score they are right, because not all men grow the same beards. Some are thin, others bushy. Some men have hair all over their faces, others only on their cheek bones. Consequently, each man should trim his beard as he thinks suits him best, but not whimsically, since we cannot approve of the sharp goatee worn by some Europeans. Single Turks shave their entire beard, leaving only the moustache, but once they get married they cannot touch the beard. But soldiers need not concern themselves about this Turkish superstition because a married soldier can shave his beard off. He should trim it with scissors and not shave it off with a razor, however, in order to appeal to women.

The first objection to these concerns is that it is inappropriate for Christians to engage in such pursuits as music, shaving, and wearing long hair. The rebuttal is that this business about beards and hair being prohibited was for the Jews, but does not apply to Christians. This simple answer is enough, and there is no need to document its truth since here we are not talking about faith. We shall say only this much: whoever wishes to lead a monastic or hermitic life should renounce marriage, meat, music, and every concern over his clothing, beard, and haircut. It would also be good for him to abstain from wine, mead, sugar, spices, fish, fruits, and even bread, and eat only herbs and drink water. But to demand from those who live in wordly surroundings such abstinence, and to transform soldiers into monks, would be not an act of piety but of superstition, and a violation of the established order.

A second objection is that ancient Romans, under their first emperors, shaved their heads, beards, and moustaches but nevertheless were still brave. Our answer is that Roman soldiers wore strange helmets made to resemble a snake, a wolf, or a bear, and their uniforms were made to cause shock during battle and to frighten the enemy. Besides, not all of them shaved off their moustaches. Still, it would be best for us to trim our beards and hair nicely rather than to squander huge sums of money on uniforms intended to frighten the enemy.

A good suit is one which protects the wearer from cold, rain, mud, wind, and sun without restricting his mobility; which can be worn for a long time; and which can be purchased cheaply.

11

Wages and honors

A soldier's bravery is stimulated by his wages, glory, honors, and freedom; that is, freedom to dispose of his wages.

(1) Soldiers receive their wages in money.

(2) The Romans sometimes gave wine the same way it is now given in this state on holidays.

(3) The Romans also issued salt, and for that reason every soldier's pay was known as "salarium," or "solnitsa" [salt reward]. Here, too, salt is issued.

(4) The German emperor issues a monthly food provision, or baked bread, in frontier outposts. But poor soldiers are actually insulted by the officers who issue them this bread, since even dogs do not want to eat it.

(5) Siberia, which has a better system, distributes various grains, flour, groats, and oatmeal.

(6) The Turkish sultan distributes fabrics among his janissaries—any color they desire.

(7) Here, as in other countries of Europe, the tsar's bodyguards, or the *streltsy,* receive cloth of various colors for the uniforms of various units. This practice is known as "diuisata" or distribution.

(8) Here, as in other countries, soldiers who perform some special assignment receive as gifts fur coats, textiles, gold, silver, gold chain, silver cups, gold kopecks, and other reward money especially minted.

(9) A deserving old or invalid soldier receives lifelong subsistence, i.e., a specified amount of money or grain per year.

(10) Deserving soldiers, non-invalids who can still perform service, receive a written promise of favor; that is, they are promised the first

available official position that may occur in any town or region. Such men are known here as head or chief scribes.

(11) The wounded receive a specified monetary gift for medication.

(12) Some kings have special estates which they distribute to hereditary nobles—but only to single men—who are known as cavaliers, knights, and crusaders.

(13) Polish kings do better, in that they also distribute such estates to married nobles, whom they call elders.

(14) But nowhere in the world does there exist a better, more desirable and beneficial reward for soldiers than that which exists currently in this illustrious tsardom and among the Turks (and previously among the Romans); that is, some soldiers receive landed estates while others receive only titles. Those who do not receive estates live in Siberia, and receive remuneration in food and money from the sovereign.

(15) The *vysluga,* or retirement from meritorious service, is also a reward. The janissaries enjoy such a privilege. Whoever has participated in a specified number of military expeditions is not required to go on any further expeditions, and subsequently serves in the imperial guard, or performs some civil service in a town, unless the sultan personally orders him into an expedition.

(16) Ancient Romans granted freedom to loyal and meritorious slaves and called them free men. The Germans free some of their soldiers from guard duty, but there is nothing praiseworthy about this.

Soldiers receive glory and honors in different ways.

(1) Ancient Romans gave wreaths to soldiers who performed exceptional acts of heroism: (*a*) a wreath of flowers for freeing others from siege; (*b*) a wreath of oak-leaves for saving a Roman citizen in battle; (*c*) a wreath of gold and feathers for being the first to climb the wall of a fortress; (*d*) a toothed gold wreath for being the first to enter into the enemy's camp; (*e*) a gold wreath with booms for being the first to conquer the enemy at sea; (*f*) a triumphal wreath, laurel, and later gold, for victorious military commanders; (*g*) a myrtle wreath during ovations; and (*h*) an olive wreath for organizing triumphal processions.

(2) The Romans also gave their units impressive names or titles to commemorate great actions or defeated enemies, as for example: the mighty unit of Augustus; the loyal unit of Trajan; the British unit; the

Parthian unit; the iron unit; the thunder unit; the unit of victors; the strong and happy unit; the loyal and stubborn unit.

(3) The Turks have units with a special name, "the janissaries." Their members wear striking headpieces, which make them look arrogant and brave, and consider themselves superior to other soldiers. In this way units vie with each other for honor. The Wallachians and the Turks also have "semens," i.e., court guards. The Romans had tertiars and veterans.

The German words for infantry and cavalry, when used in Russia, lose their meaning. If these units had special Slavic names they could be more frightening to the enemy. For example, the Turkish names "janissaries" and "semens" are frightening. Thus, for instance, our *pishchalniks* [harquebusers] could be called *stanovniks,* while a mounted unit could be called *khervois* (instead of "cossacks"). Such names would be terrifying.

(4) The Romans, after every great victory, prepared celebrations, which they called "triumphs," for their military leaders. On such occasions the leaders entered the city to the sound of trumpets and pipes accompanied by demonstrations and orations from the entire army and town. But this was before imperial times, during the republic. Under imperial rule such spectacles were prohibited.

(5) The Athenians celebrated victories in the same way during their republican era. In honor of their military leaders, they erected marble posts with inscriptions, which were known as trophies. They also built marble and bronze statues and beautiful marble tombs. The Venetians do the same thing even now. The Poles erected a monument to their Swedish King Sigismund III.

(6) It is little wonder that young boys and youths of nobility, reading of the great achievements of famous military men in their books, are excited. The famous Athenian general Themistocles, when asked why he stayed awake every night, replied: "Praises for Miltiades allow me no sleep." In Poland and elsewhere in Europe many noble familes proudly boast that they have written evidence of the great achievements of their ancestors in chronicles. This is why they so ardently wish to preserve intact the glory left them by their ancestors. We could cite many examples and corroborations of the fact, but it is clear and requires no proof.

In ancient Rome the son of a noble did not move automatically from the status of youth to that of soldier. A general gave the son a belt which symbolized that he was no longer just a young man, but a soldier and a

Roman knight. Among the Croats it is still possible to hear the expression *pisany vitez* [honored hero], or better yet *pisany iunak* [honored youth]. But who these Croatian honored heroes were, and how they were designated, I do not know. German emperors and princes strike the youth on his back, place a sword in his hands, and strike his face, exclaiming: "Henceforth bear such blows from me and no one else, and with this sword defend your honor."

Some kings and princes distribute titles of honor to their nobles calling them, for example, cavaliers of such and such a kind. Among such titles the most illustrious is Cavalier of the Golden Fleece. Only kings and princes are so called, and the King of Spain bestows this pompous title. Each recipient receives an insignia consisting of a flail with a fleece, both made of gold. Others are called the Knights of Malta and Crusaders, and as a sign of this designation wear a white cross sewn on a grey coat. They cannot be married; all must remain single. Still others are called the Cavaliers of the Golden Spur. As a sign of this honor, the prince gives the recipient golden spurs, and such individuals are subsequently known as Golden Cavaliers. These and many other cavalier designations are empty and useless.

The Romans had no way to glorify their soldiers, and did it differently on every occasion. Victors and deserving or exceptional soldiers received rings, belts, necklaces, various kinds of wreaths, bracelets, medals, coats, weapons, land, titles and the like. Here in Russia landed estates, official positions, and silver cups are distributed as rewards.

Feather decorations attached to helmets and to soldiers' hats have been known since time immemorial, and were already in use in the Trojan War. The Germans wear ostrich feathers, white and colored, and anyone who wishes to is allowed to wear them. Among the Croats and Hungarians, anyone who wishes may wear crane feathers. But ordinary Turks are allowed to wear no feathers, only the most powerful and distinguished soldiers, or those who have performed some heroic deed.

In my view soldiers look better and more dignified in crane feathers than in ostrich feathers. It would even be appropriate to decree that no one wear feathers except by permission of the military commander or the tsar himself. Also, feathers of different colors would be a nice touch—so that some wore white feathers, others red, still others blue, and yet others green. Some could wear one feather, others two, and still others three. Thus, for instance, the commander could wear three white feathers; the next in rank, two; and the captain, one. Soldiers who had performed some heroic deed could wear one or two red feathers, or red and white, or a similar combination, so that it would be possible to identify the achievement of the individual on the basis of the feathers he wore. On the battlefield, of course, no one should be allowed to wear any feathers.

The practice of the ancient Romans was to have their helmets resemble lions, snakes, tigers, or wolves. They also painted the same animals on their shields, both to frighten the enemy and to arouse their own bravery.

In place of gifts, German kings have begun to distribute symbols, or pictures with symbolic meanings, to their nobles and soldiers. These symbols, which are an expression of their loyalty and valor, promise eternal glory for themselves and their descendants and distinguish them from the rest of the population. Some nations call these symbols "coats of arms," because kings portray their signs on their shields and banners. The Poles call them by a German name—*Herb*—while in our language we should call them, more accurately, *znakovina*. These *znakovinas* cost the king nothing, but subjects greatly treasure them as evidence of their bravery and nobility. They carve them on seals and silverware, and also paint them on their homes and in other places.

It would seem proper that such *znakovinas* be distributed in this tsardom to nobles and others who distinguish themselves by their valor. This way their dignity would be enhanced, and they would be considered equal to the nobles of other kingdoms who now hold them in contempt because they have not such signs. Moreover, the sovereign tsar would thereby gain great honor, because the distribution of such signs is really a royal prerogative.

Military commanders and units should not be designated by the number of soldiers; that is, one should not speak about *desiatnik, piati-desiatnik, sotnia, sotnik,* and *tysiatskii.*[1] Such names are ugly and simple, and do not express the grandeur which is the essence of military affairs.

---

[1] *Desiatnik*: a Russian term for the leader of a squad of ten cossacks, or of *streltsy,* before 1700; *piatidesiatnik*: leader of a group of fifty men; *sotnia*: a formation of a hundred men, led by a *sotnik*; *tysiatskii*: commander of a thousand men. In Novgorod before 1478, a *tysiatskii* was an elected official in charge of the city militia. While the psychology of language practiced by the military is an important phenomenon, Krizhanich's illustrations in the text appear unusual to the modern reader.

PART III

Concerning Wisdom

12

The indispensability of learning

From birth, lower creatures have clothes—hair or feathers—and weapons—horns, teeth, sharp claws. Even without teachers they know what is essential for their existence; and what is most astonishing, they all know how to swim. Human beings alone are naked, weaponless, unable to swim, and totally ignorant. They have no clothes or weapons, or any other essential items for their existence, unless they obtain them with their own sweat and toil. They know nothing unless they learn it.

Yet from birth human beings have two gifts which the lower creatures do not possess: reason with which to acquire knowledge, and hands to make useful or beautiful things.

Furthermore, all individuals are born stupid and incapable of doing anything. They grow slowly, and become intelligent even more slowly. Many begin to comprehend the world around them only at the age of forty, or even much later. Only when they get old do a great majority of people, perhaps all of them, growing wise, acknowledge that they have lived in vice and vain delusions; but when they begin to understand how they should live, life leaves them. This gives rise to a saying: "Seek wisdom from the old and intelligence from gray heads." Old people often voice the desire to return to earlier days, because they regret their youthful ambitions and actions. Hence, when the famous commander Nestor, who lived for 300 years, was approaching Troy, he said, "Oh, if God could only return my former years." Similarly, Emperor Charles V regretted that in his youth he had not wished to study Latin. And Boris Ivanovich Morozov, the later tutor of Tsar Alexei Mikhailovich once asked, "Why am I no longer young, so that I could learn something?"[1]

In this respect, many kings are no happier than their subjects. This is because kings, like all other mortals, live in delusion, vanity, and ignorance which they come to regret at their dying day. Some point to the fact that kings have their advisors, but we would reply that they also have flatterers, men who fill them with vain hopes and false ideas and inspire

---

[1] During Krizhanich's stay in Moscow, the *boyar* Morozov (1590–1662) was, in fact, the head of the government of Tsar Alexei Mikhailovich (1645–76).

them to be greedy, fierce, and godless, and truly the worst enemies of kings are those whose counsel hurts their subjects and erodes the monarchy. Among advisors are simple flatterers who try only to please and indulge the tsar. Others are greedy and unscrupulous, and thus incapable of offering good counsel. Some are good, thoughtful people who would like to give good counsel but do not know how to do it, and still others are afraid to tell the truth. But as has been said, "dead advisors," through their books, are the best and most loyal of friends. Books are not motivated by greed, hatred, or love; they do not flatter, and they are not afraid to tell the truth. Which is why from the very threshold of life one should strive to acquire knowledge from those "dead advisors," who freely reveal the truth to us and enable us to live life commendably, for God's glory and for the benefit of ourselves and our entire nation.

Any common person can acquire wisdom through personal experience, but this method is dangerous for the highest leaders. There is a saying about such a form of learning, "They learn by their mistakes," but royal mistakes bring enormous unfair harm to the nation. That is why kings must learn their wisdom from teachers, books, and advisors—not from personal experience.

Wealth and power are tangible objects; they can be both seen and touched. That is why everyone perceives and desires them, and strives for them with methods which are often intolerable. But wisdom is intangible and therefore goes unrecognized by many people, while some even despise it. We must know the benefits of wisdom if we are to perceive it and ultimately search for it. Kings should encourage their subjects, and parents their children, to strive for knowledge.

What was said earlier about bravery is equally true of wisdom: it moves from one nation to another. Some nations (for example, the Egyptians, Jews, and Greeks) were expert in several branches of knowledge in ancient times, but today they are ignorant. While other nations (for example, the Germans, French, and Italians) were once crude and savage, but now, surprisingly, they are expert in craftsmanship and in all branches of learning. Marcus [Terrentius] Varro, a Roman man of letters, once wrote that industry, craftsmanship, and learning were invented and developed by the Greeks not in one year, but over thousands of years. While [Marcus Tullius] Cicero, a Roman, writes about his nation as follows: "I have always thought that our people are more ingenious than the Greeks, and whatever we have adopted from them we have corrected and improved."

In the last centuries, the Italians have invented a number of important items, such as bells, the magnetic compass, the harmonized singing. The Germans have invented the printing press, the clock, cannons, and copper engraving, among other things. Let no one say that we Slavs have been denied access to the road to knowledge by the will of heaven, or that we cannot or should not study. Other nations did not acquire wisdom quickly, but passed down knowledge through the generations, and we too can acquire wisdom if we invest our desire and our determination through the years.

Moreover, we believe that now the time has come for our nation to study. Now, through His mercy and generosity, God has elevated the power and greatness of the Slavic monarchy to such a height that there has never existed such a glorious kingdom. And considering the experience of other nations, we see that as a kingdom reaches such a peak, a flourishing of learning begins in it.

The greatest Jewish kings were David and Solomon, and during their reigns the Jews reached the pinnacle of their craftsmanship. They had superb architects, blacksmiths, musicians, and other masters. David himself was an exceptional musician, while Solomon was a philosopher educated by God Himself. Under Alexander, the Greek Empire reached the apex of its glory. Plato, Aristotle, and other learned men, as well as many superb craftsmen, lived in his time. Alexander himself was educated by Aristotle in philosophy, and in addition was a musician. The Roman Empire was strongest during the reign of its first Caesars—Julius and Augustus. Some of the wisest Romans lived at that time, such as Cicero, Cato, Virgil, and Seneca, and the most gifted of craftsmen, sculptors, and other masters. Augustus favored and supported all scholars, and Julius was himself a philosopher, rhetorician, poet, and chronicler—one who during his battles and travels wrote many books which are still renowned.

Among Christian emperors, none was greater than Constantine. During his reign and that of his sons, the most learned Holy Fathers lived, while Emperor Julian the Apostate prohibited Christians from reading books or studying philosophy, so that St George the Divine wrote accusations against him. Charlemagne was one of the most famous of the German kings. In his time the Germans were uneducated and unskilled, but he tried in every possible way to compel them to study the sciences and improve their language. This enabled the Germans to attain the wisdom and glory that we see now.

All this shows that we too should study, and that we should hope that under the noble rule of the pious and great Tsar Alexei Mikhailovich we will be able to break the mold of ancient barbarism, study the sciences, and introduce more civilized customs among our people.

Among the monks of a certain monastery there lived a learned man who was ready to teach younger brothers written Greek so that they could understand the teachings of the Holy Fathers, foster their own study, and teach others. But local monks rejected this, saying, "We need bread, not study." They were afraid that the younger brothers, once educated, would lose their respect for the older monks, and also the respect of the people. I do not know who introduced this silly notion in Russia, or who introduced the anti-intellectual sentiment that theology, philosophy, and the knowledge of foreign languages are heresy. Certainly the Holy Scriptures and Holy Fathers teach us exactly the opposite.

God said to Solomon: "Ask whatever you wish and I shall grant it to you." Solomon asked for wisdom and God replied: "Because you have asked for this, and not for long life for yourself, or for wealth, or for lives of your enemies, but have asked for discernment in administering justice, I grant your request; I give you a heart so wise and so understanding that there has been none like you before your time nor will be after you. I give you furthermore those things for which you did not ask, such wealth and honour as no king of your time can match" (1 Kings 3:11–14; 2 Chronicles 1:11–13). The Book of Maccabees (1, 8:1) says: "The Romans . . . were renowned for their military power and for the welcome they gave to those who became their allies; any who joined them could be sure of their friendship."

The Romans expanded their empire through countless battles and much bloodshed. Nevertheless, the Holy Scriptures attribute their valor and triumph not to weapons, but to wisdom and patience, and with good reason. The Romans made certain that they never started a war without a reason, and they always explained that reason through a courier. Also, they never insulted or detained any enemy ambassador or courier, even of those nations who had insulted or killed Roman ambassadors.

The Holy Scripture abounds with praise of wisdom. It says: "Happy he who has found wisdom, and the man who has acquired understanding; for wisdom is more profitable than silver, and the gain she brings is better than gold" (Proverbs 3:13–14). "Wisdom and understanding build the temple. A wise man is mighty, a man of understanding is powerful and firm. One should start a war with the brain; victory will go to the side on which there is more understanding. Through wisdom emperors rule and rulers make just laws. Wisdom brings happiness, glory, prosperity, and truth" (Proverbs).[2] "The desire of wisdom leads to kingly stature. If, therefore, you value your thrones and your sceptres, you rulers of the nations, you must honour wisdom, so that you may reign for ever." (The Wisdom of Solomon 6:20–21).

Objection: Since heresies develop among the educated, one should not strive to attain wisdom.

---

[2] Krizhanich's references to Proverbs do not correspond with proverbs 2:8, though they are so designated in the original.

Answer: Among uneducated people heresies also develop. Mohammed, for example, was uneducated, possessed no wisdom or common sense, and wrote real nonsense in his books. Still, he gave birth to one of the most widespread heresies in the world. Moreover, has not a heresy recently originated in Russia among illiterate peasants who could be called "fasters" and "new cathars," since they want to fast until death and consider themselves the only clean people? And did not the current religious schism start on account of silly reasons, such as replacing the shroud with the altar cloth and adding "Glory to you, Lord" to the "Hallelujah"? I do not even mention superstition, which is no better than heresy and which prevails among the illiterate people of Russia.[3]

Second, wisdom eliminates heresy, while the ignorance of illiterate people keeps heresy and superstition alive for ages.

Third, heresies develop not because of true wisdom, but because of the false wisdom caused by carnal desires. The Holy Fathers were wise and did not start any heresy; rather, they fought and triumphed over them. Arius and other instigators of heresy appeared wise, but were really ignorant. St Catherine was a learned person, who because of her learning was able to convert pagan philosophers wise enough to recognize the truth.

Finally, fire, water, and iron kill many people, but nevertheless people cannot live without them. In the same way, people desperately need wisdom. Wisdom does not currupt, nor does it lead astray. On the contrary, deceit and ignorance lead people astray, because the cunning man can deceive and tempt the ignorant man, but not the wise man. Besides, if the deceitful man were wise he would not try to deceive.

---

[3] Krizhanich opposed the Russian religious schism: he was "a messenger of religious concord in a period when Russia was in the throes of its greatest religious discord. . . . Krizhanich believed that the reforms of the patriarch Nikon simply were making the Russian church more subservient to the Greek; and he thought it far better to retain the old, corrupted texts than to yield them to the scrutiny of the Greek churchmen. In his stand, Krizhanich was almost as violent in his vituperations against Nikon [in his *Oblichenie na solovetskuiu chelobitnuiu*] as was Avvakum, the leader of the Old Believers." (Cyril Bryner, "The Political Philosophy of Yuri Krizhanich," *The New Scholasticism* 13 (January 1939): 139–40). Nevertheless, in his letters of 1674–75, Krizhanich also fervently criticized the views of the Old Believers. The "new Cathars," to whom Krizhanich refers, were Christian "heretics" active in Western Europe during the twelfth and thirteenth centuries, also known as Albigensians. Krizhanich here uses the "new Cathars" as analogous to the "Old Believers." For a careful appraisal of Krizhanich as a theologian and a provocative discussion on the controversy regarding the relative import- ance he attributed to the union of the two churches and Slavic unity, see I. Golub, "Križanić theologien—sa conception ecclésiologique des événements et de l'histoire," 165–79, and Thomas Eekman, "Vatroslav Jagić on Križanić," in Eekman and Kadić: 323.

13

Wisdom, knowledge, and philosophy

Since the third part of these discourses deals with wisdom, it is essential, first of all, to define wisdom, knowledge, and philosophy.

Wisdom is knowledge of things of utmost importance, namely, God, the heavens, earth, human customs, legal orders, and other noble and absolutely vital matters.

Knowledge is the understanding of reason, which also means understanding the causes of things. He who does not know the causes does not understand the problem.

Philosophy, or the love of wisdom, is a Greek word. In our own language it should be properly called a desire for wisdom, and a philosopher should be called a zealous pursuer of wisdom.

Since things are understood by their causes, let us look at the example of solar and lunar eclipses. Anyone who witnesses an eclipse of the sun or moon without understanding its cause is alarmed, and expects some misfortune. But whoever understands the cause is not alarmed and expects no misfortune. He knows that the phenomenon occurs as a result of normal celestial movements and not because of a miracle. He knows, for example, that the moon and all the other stars do not emit light but are illuminated by the sun. Thus, whenever the earth moves between the sun and the moon, the sun's rays cannot reach the moon, and the moon appears dark until it emerges from the earth's shadow. The sun goes into eclipse when the moon moves between the sun and the earth. Then the moon blocks the sun's rays, preventing them from reaching the earth. Some might think that the sun has darkened, but the moon only hides our view of it. Hence it follows that an eclipse of the sun never occurs except during a new moon, and a lunar eclipse always occurs during a full moon.

The cause is that which is responsible for the existence of an object. The effect of this object is what stems from the cause. For example, clay is the cause and pottery is the effect.

There are four principal causes: the creative, material, formative, and purpose. Secondary causes include tools, condition, etc.

The creative cause is that which creates or produces. For example, the potter is the creative cause of a pot, the blacksmith of the sword, the builder of the house. The material cause is that matter from which an item is produced. For example, clay is the basic material of the pot, iron of the sword, and wood of the house. The formative cause is the appearance or quality which gives an item its essential identity. To illustrate, the uniqueness of the pot is its round shape and its suitability for cooking food; the uniqueness of the sword is its length, sharpness, suitability for cutting; the uniqueness of the home is its suitability for human habitation. The final cause is the purpose for which any item exists. For example, the purpose of the pot is to cook; of the sword to cut; and of the home to live in.

The productive cause is any tool, weapon or utensil with which other items can be produced. For example, the potter's wheel is the productive cause of the pot, a hammer and pincers of the sword, the axe, the saw, etc., of the house. The contributory cause is what provides an inducement or condition to create anything. For example, the battle is a condition that enables soldiers to exhibit their bravery; the condition for a lunar eclipse is the position of the earth between the sun and the moon; the condition for a solar eclipse is the movement of the moon between the sun and the earth.

A zealous seeker of wisdom through the study of causes can thereby understand effects. Thus, when he knows about the movement of the moon, he understands that when the sun darkens, it is only being hidden from our view by the moon. In addition, where the cause is unknown it can ultimately be discovered by means of the effect. Thus the effects of alchemy show that it is a false discipline. One would doubtless be able to say "From time immemorial alchemy has made no one rich, and has ruined a great multitude of people. Consequently, alchemy is not a true source of wealth, but a deception and a temptation."

From what has been said it can be seen that to philosophize or intellectualize is to ponder the causes of things and to explain from where, from what, for what purpose, and how each one originates. Every wise man should be a philosopher in matters that concern him, especially if he is a politician or some sort of leader. If a leader wishes to judge things properly he must truly understand the causes of many, very many things. No one can judge anything accurately if he does not know its principal causes.

In short, philosophy is not a special art or science; rather, it is considered reasoning, and experience in judging problems. Philosophy teaches how to assess things without making errors. A philosopher knows

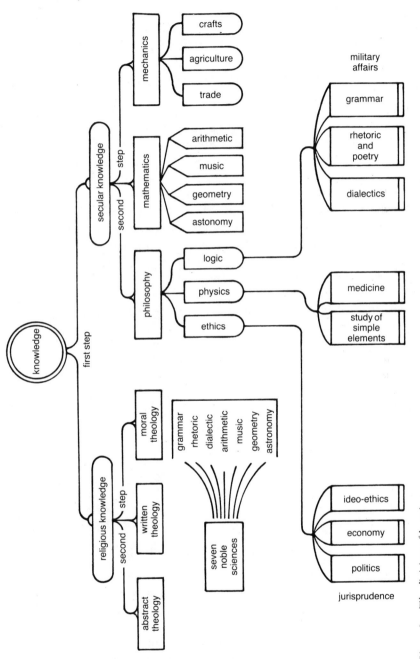

Figure 2 The divisions of learning

both nothing and everything. A real philosopher can do nothing, but can pass judgment on everything.

Wisdom can be divided into two parts; spiritual and secular. Spiritual wisdom is called theology, which has subdivisions that we will pass over here. Secular wisdom is divided into three parts:

Mechanics (or crafts and industry) includes manufacturing, agriculture, and trade.

Mathematics (or "the marvellous study") includes music, arithmetic, geometry, astronomy, accounting, land surveying, and study of the stars.

Philosophy includes logic, physics, and ethics.

Logic (or the study of discourses) includes grammar, dialectics, rhetoric, and poetry. Physics includes medicine and the study of various bodies: ores, rocks, trees, grasses, and all other visible things. Ethics is the study of personal morals, which teaches how every man should conduct himself; economy, which teaches how to manage a household and servants; and politics (or the study of governing and of royal policy), which teaches how to govern justly, honorably, and with dignity.

The divisions of learning described above can be presented in a chart (see figure 2). We think it useful to note all of this before we start talking about political or governmental wisdom, its ingredients and its origin.

14

Political wisdom

The principal and most useful of all the secular studies is politics, or royal policy. It is also the most appropriate for kings and their advisors. For as human strength is centered in arms, speed in legs, and wisdom in the head, so in the spiritual realm of the nation, various attributes are distributed among various parts. Strength is the prerogative of soldiers; wealth of merchants; and state affairs center primarily with the king and his advisors.

The foundation of political wisdom rests on two proverbs: "Know thyself" and "Do not trust foreigners." Among the ancients, "know thyself" was considered a great enough axiom to be inscribed above the doors of the temple of Apollo, the Greek God of Wisdom. Solomon says the same thing (Proberbs 14:8): "A clever man has the wit to find the right way." For just as a doctor who does not understand an illness cannot cure a person, a politician who does not know himself—his strengths and weaknesses—cannot judge his own actions or properly conduct his own affairs. And sometimes, like the doctor, what he considers to be a cure turns out to be a poison. Whatever he thought of as medicine he will come to think of as poison.

The first obstacle to national wellbeing is the failure to know oneself, in other words, to consider oneself as strong, rich, and wise, although one really is not. Plato wrote about this as follows: "Excessive self-love is the cause of all human ills. For if people love themselves more than the truth, they never can understand what is ignorant and what is good."

Apostle John explains this even better: "Saying that I am rich and that my wealth is abundant and that I do not need anything, you are unaware that I am wretched, poor, blind, and naked" (Apocalypse 3:8). St Bernard said, "Many know a great deal, but they do not know themselves." St Augustine emphasized all of this in these words: "What does the understanding of truth mean? First, it means to know oneself, to become what one is supposed to be. Then to know and love one's Creator, for therein lies the whole of human well-being" (*Handbook*, 26). Knowledge of truth and political wisdom from first to last means that we must know ourselves—that is, our nature, our customs, and the condition of our people and country.

How does a statesman come to know himself? Above all, a royal advisor should know the natural qualities of his people, their customs, capabilities, and shortcomings. He should evaluate, compare, and contrast the appearance, character, clothes, customs, and wealth of other nations with ours. Second, he must familiarize himself with the natural conditions of our country, with its wealth and poverty: what our land is abundant in, what it is deficient in, what it can and cannot grow. Third, he must get to know our way of life: what it lacks and what it is famous for. And, after a comparison with other nations, he should ascertain whether our ways are poorer or richer than those of neighboring nations. Fourth, he must evaluate our relative power: where we are stronger, where weaker, than other nations. Fifth, he must understand public administration, national laws and customs, as well as the past and present condition of the people. He must ascertain what is good, what bad, in the laws and decrees promulgated by sovereigns. Sixth, he must be aware of the overall strength and weakness of the entire realm; where dangers lie, and who our neighbors are. He must ascertain who are friends, who enemies; what forces they have, what their ambitions are, and what benefit or threat they currently pose or may pose in the future. Seventh, he must devise a method for utilizing the wealth which nature and God have granted our land. But he must also know how to conserve that wealth, for both the minds and hands of our subjects must be made to serve our national wellbeing. The land should be cultivated so that we can harvest all its potential products. Eighth, he must know how to conceal our state secrets from other nations; how to conceal our lack of certain skills and other general vices; and how to preserve national dignity and glory. Ninth, he must know how to interpret and weigh various counsels. For some advice that would be good for any other nation could also benefit us, but other counsel good for them could be harmful to us, or vice versa. All this can be understood using the cause-and-effect method.

If our ancient Slavic rulers had been able to understand the power of their people, and if they had known the nations against which to direct it, they could have performed miracles. Our people are among the most simple-minded of peoples, and therefore less arrogant and less opposed to their leaders. It is easier to convince them to participate in devastating wars than the people of any other European nation.

If we had understood our own ignorance, of course, we would never have become involved in the multitude of negotiations, marriages, and trade relations with other, cleverer nations. We would not have been so often deceived and ridiculed by other nations, and we would have been able to escape many of the troubles we currently experience. Further, a wise individual must judge things in two ways. First, what things are or usually are. Second, what they should be. On the one hand we should be as simple as pigeons: we should believe everything, expect everything, allow everything, suffer everything, and consider all people as our loyal brothers. On the other hand, we should be as alert as snakes; we should neither trust nor rely on foreigners, not allow them to come to us, never think they can become our brothers.

To the best of our abilities we have discussed the first maxim of politics, "know thyself." We have also said a little about the second maxim, "Do not trust foreigners," which will be discussed in some detail later on. Now we must turn to the appearance, language, clothes, and other attributes that enable us to judge the natural qualities and capabilities of nations.

15

The human visage

A handsome face is a sign of a good sharp mind, while a coarse face is a sign of a dull mind. To the extent that the people of one nation are more beautiful than those of another, they are also more intelligent. However, there are also some peoples who are quite good-looking, but are not distinguished by any particular intelligence. Their beauty is unvaried. They seem as alike as if all of them were children of the same father. Such, for example, are the Armenians, the Georgians, and the Cherkess. In addition, they have neither a comely language, nor skill, nor other attributes with which to acquire wisdom.

Some peoples have especially beautiful features. The Greeks, for instance, have big, round, sparkling eyes; the Spaniards have white skin, black hair, and long moustaches. The French, Germans, and Italians also have their specific features, and all of them are distinguished by their beauty.

Other nations are known for their deformities. The Tartars, for instance, have small, sunken eyes. The Kalmucks have flat noses; the Mari [Cheremis] are as black as coal and their lips protrude. The Indians have black hair, flat noses and no beards. The Samoyeds are short, broad faced, and have small eyes, short legs and no beard. The Arabs have dark skin, but faces that are not too bad; they are therefore neither at the top nor at the bottom intellectually.

Our people are distinguished neither by special beauty nor special ugliness. No one among our people is so ugly that there could not be found uglier people among the Gypsies, Tartars, Samoyeds, Finns, Indians and Siberian natives. At the same time, no one among us is beautiful enough to compare with the most handsome among the Greeks, Italians, Spaniards, French, or Germans. I think that in beauty we yield to the sons of Japheth but do not descend to the Rhom tribe. Our people have large bodies and light blue eyes. Their hair is neither too thick, nor very dark, nor very red, but ash colored. Because almost no one has hair on his face, we admire the rare thick, long beards.

Neither the Spaniards nor the Italians treasure their beards; they shave them off. In Italy and Spain every person would have a thick, long beard if he would let it grow. The Germans have quite varied beards. For that reason, the Germans groom their beards differently. Some shave them more, others less; some trim them with scissors; others let them grow long. It would be good if our people did the same, especially soldiers.

Some people have beautiful voices, very fine, high and resounding, or very deep and low. Our people do not have beautiful voices. They are neither especially high nor extraordinarily low, but are in the middle range called tenor—soft and pleasant enough, but weak and not audible over a long distance.

From all this we can see that we occupy a modest middle ground. In beauty and intelligence we are neither first nor last among nations. Thus, if we should be confronted by nations who are inferior to us in intelligence and strength, we can place our trust in God and God's gifts, and boldly and clearly act against them. But if we should have a confrontation with nations that are more intelligent than ourselves, we should not allow ourselves to be outwitted. We should counter their intelligence, cunning, and strength with great caution, always watching for the opportune time to act. Medium intelligence and strength used with great caution are much better than keen intelligence and strength used with imprudence and lack of discipline.

16

Language

The perfection of language is the most unmistakable sign of wisdom—indeed, perhaps its principal sign. The more improved a nation's language, the more successfully it engages in crafts and other enterprises. An extensive vocabulary and care in articulation help tremendously in devising wise plans and in skillfully realizing various peaceful and military affairs.

Among the Germans, there are many individuals who know Greek and Latin very well, and the German language itself is quite rich in vocabulary and adequate for expressing any thought. It is especially suitable for songs and stories. No wonder, therefore, that the Germans surpass all other nations in skills.

Some languages have particular attributes: some are easy for conversation; others are concise; still others are suitable for songs and poetry. Some languages, as for example Turkish and Hungarian, have a loud and harsh sound, characteristics that serve to inspire soldiers.

Our language is poor in all of these attributes. I cannot find anything in it worthy of praise. It is miserable, undeveloped, sibilant and unpleasant to hear, corrupt, and poor in all respects. This applies to all the dialects of our languages: Russian, Polish, Czech, Bulgar, Serb and Croat. We do not have terms for the arts and sciences, for government departments and military matters, for city administrative units, or for the virtues and vices. We do not have any of the indispensable grammatical parts called prepositions, adverbs, conjunctions, and interjections. Our language is less suited than any other for songs, poetry, music, and other complex or artistic expressions.

Other languages abound in insulting and abusive curse words. The one distinguishing mark of our language is that it does not have any insults or abusive terms that have entered into use except "son of a bitch." But this is not because our people avoid bad words; rather it stems from the poverty of our language. Our language also has numerous other short-comings. It is not proper to discuss them here since they have already been dealt with in my grammar.[1] In those publications I document the fact that in the translation of religious works our language was corrupted and moved out of its track.

As a result of the beauty and richness of other languages and the shortcomings of our own, we Slavs, in contrast to other nations, are literally like mute guests at a feast. We are incapable of developing any great and noble thoughts or ideas, and we also cannot carry on an intelligent conversation. Hence, if any of our people live abroad, they try to conceal their origins, because they are ashamed of being Slavs. Some Poles boast about their freedoms, but I personally have met some who lied, saying they were Prussians in an attempt to conceal that they were Poles.

Accordingly, we should strive to correct and improve our language so that we can avoid ill repute and devote ourselves more diligently to science and statecraft. It would be desirable, especially in military matters, to create appropriate native expressions since a soldier's morale and bravery increases if he can talk about military affairs in his own, rather than a foreign language.

Our writing is so rough and imprecise that it has been awkward for the study of the sciences. I believe that no one will ever be able to bring enough order into it to achieve anything concise, beautiful, or elegant. As a result, those of our people who would like to study ancient chronicles or any other sciences must learn another language.

---

[1] *Gramatichno izkazanie ob russkom jeziku* (1666–67) and "Objasnenje vivodno o pisme slovenskom" (1660–73).

17

Style of clothing

There are five reasons why people make and wear clothes: to cover their nakedness; to protect themselves from the elements; to protect themselves from weapons or to frighten the enemy; to decorate or adorn their bodies; and to enhance a sense of dignity.

Four qualities characterize good, useful clothing: proper fit, availability, durability, and lightness. By availability, we mean clothes that can be purchased for a reasonable price. Durability refers to clothes that can be worn over a long period of time without falling apart. And light clothes are those that do not constrict the human body or interfere with its mobility.

The following custom is practiced by the Spaniards: a festival is held where young men compete for awards. One award is given to the person who is best dressed, but has spent the least money on his clothes. As a result, young men compete not in wealth, but in wit, seeing who can devise the finest clothes at least expense.

St John says that everything that exists in the world is a carnal temptation and an enticement (1 John 2:16). The temptation of the eye is a beautiful body and the glitter of precious stones, metals, and dyes that adorn it. People love beauty in others and like to consider themselves beautiful. For that reason, they dress up as much as they can and, in choosing clothes, pay more attention to their appearance than to their suitability.

It is ironic that things that are necessary for existence, such as bread, water, wood, and iron, are for the most part inexpensive. But things that are not vital (except to please the eye or enhance the appearance) are much more costly. People are almost willing to give the apple of their eye for them. They would give away whole villages and entire estates for one pearl, and still seek further for gold, silk, and expensive furs. Because of this, the realm is ravaged and all or our wealth goes to other nations. Anyone who could design pleasing, inexpensive clothes for us would therefore be making a great contribution to the stability of the realm.

What clothes do the Slavs have? Emperor Constantine in his book calls the Serbs, in his own language, *servuli*.[1] In Latin *servul* means a servant or a young slave. Mockingly, he also writes that they call the *servuli* (or Serbs) *chrevli* because they wear poor shoes called *chrevli* that are no more than pieces of rawhide tied by a string to their feet. The Russians weave their sandals from bark. Both of these styles of footwear are poor and dirty in wet weather. We sell a great variety of hides to foreigners and yet walk barefoot.

The trousers that Slav men wear are long and tight, reaching to the heels and tearing quickly around the knees. Their clothes are unbelted, making them look half-naked, effeminate, and weak. They look as though they were sewed up in sacks. Handkerchiefs are carried in hats and lost easily. Knives, papers, and other little items are kept inside the top of their boots, which looks ridiculous and uncomfortable. They hold coins in their mouths, which is revolting. All of this is done out of necessity, since, thanks to the tightness of their clothes, it is impossible to have pockets.

Sable furs are valued more than sheepskins because they are more beautiful. Yet while Turks, Greeks, and Poles wear this fur on their hats and suit collars as adornment, Russians line their suits, hats, and coats with it, so that nothing is seen on the outside. Even the lower classes buy sable to line their clothes, and thus spend a great deal on fur that is never seen. Still more incomprehensible is the fact that even the lowest class of people wear shirts adorned with gold threads and pearls. This is not only a waste, but looks ridiculous: peasants wearing gold that is hidden under their outer clothes!

They decorate their hats and collars with *tvez*, beads, bands, and laces made respectively from pearls, gold, and silk. They buy only cloth dyed in flowery colors. They do not do this out of need, because the hats and collars in themselves are so lacking in style that, unadorned, they would be quite ordinary and inexpensive.

When the Germans dress according to their own style they all wear gray; when they put on Russian dress, however, they always wear colorful fabrics, for the clothes are so lacking in any style that a person wearing gray would look like a peasant.

Among other peoples, pearls are used to adorn women and would be considered inappropriate for men. Our men wear this foreign feminine ornament without moderation on their hats and collars, yet we hide our

[1] A reference to *De administrando imperio . . .* by the Emperor Constantine (913–57).

native decoration—sable—inside of our garments as though we were ashamed of it.

Russian women wear very tight sleeves of expensive foreign fabric, and uselessly make them long—for the sleeves wear out so quickly, being tight, that it is impossible to see whether they are long or short. Women also attach large pieces of silver lace to their bodices, which resemble a horse harness, and wear four-cornered square hats that are noticeable from all sides. Some women cinch their belts below their stomachs, while others go around without a belt or any other support, thus accentuating those parts of the human anatomy that should be concealed.

A THOUGHT ON CLOTHING

Human attire is diverse, but can, nevertheless, be divided into two general styles. One is Eastern—adopted by the Persians, Greeks, Slavs, Turks, Tartars, and Hungarians. The other is Western—adopted by the Germans, French, and others. Both of these styles change; sometimes for better, sometimes for worse. It is therefore impossible to willfully create a style of clothing for any nation, because fashion so frequently changes. It would be best for us to appropriate from each style that which appears to be the most suitable and design clothes that are adapted to this country.

Both Eastern and Western monks wear loose clothing. It adds honor and dignity to the individual. In a tight suit, a person appears weak and insignificant; the body is poorly covered and almost all parts of the anatomy are visible. Fatness or clumsiness, protrusions both back and front—all of these are on view and quite unattractive.

When an individual dressed in a tight suit comes to a gathering where everyone else is wearing loose clothes, he becomes ashamed, realizing that his body is inadequately covered and looks naked. A Hungarian feels this way when he meets Germans. A smart decently loose suit contributes to human beauty and dignity. Thus, when an Italian, German, or Spaniard appears among Hungarians, or among our own people, he seems like a lion, moving his body freely and powerfully. Yet his suit costs him far less than that worn by a Russian or Hungarian because, unlike our own clothes, it has no need for excess color or trimming.

A man's civilian clothes should thus be neither too long nor too short; neither too loose nor too tight, but moderate in size and comfortable to wear. It is impossible to describe this appearance in words, but it has much to do with the four qualities of good clothing previously mentioned: proper fit, accessibility, durability, and lightness.

Clothes should be light so that they do not restrict the mobility of the body. German boots, because of their width, impede walking. Russian clothes, because they are so tight, make it impossible to wash one's face or dress without great difficulty. One cannot run or count on riding comfortably—one's legs hang down and one sits there, literally, like a stump tied in the saddle.

Clothes are durable if they are reasonably loose and properly made. Among the Russians, Croats, and Hungarians, one sees new clothes with the sleeves torn because of their tightness. The loose sleeves of the Italians last as long as the rest of the suit. The Italians also have the custom of sewing patches of cloth to the sleeve that are of different color or material. For their clothes it is quite wise, but it would look wrong on ours. Kryliak hats and overcoats are quite comfortable. Their longevity saves considerable sums of money for the home, which is very useful for soldiers. And, instead of wearing long trousers, it would be more advantageous to wear short pants and socks. Wearing such pants, one might wear out two or three pairs of socks, but the pants would last. These are some of the many useful ideas that could be adapted to our clothing.

The style of clothing determines its cost. Smart Western-style clothing does not need to have buttons made of gold or precious stones; nor long transverse buttonholders; nor gold *tvez,* lace silk, and gold tassels, or pearls attached to it. Their clothes are attractive and smart in themselves, and a man wearing them looks dignified.

The Spaniards, Italians, and distinguished Germans wear suits of black and gray material. They use textiles with decorative patterns only for church ceremonies, for women's dresses, and for other purposes—but never for men's suits. Our clothes, on the other hand, do not have the above-mentioned decorations and patterns and are considered unworthy by nobles. For what one of our *boyars* must spend on his clothes here, in those countries three princes could be clothed. There, nobles, princes and kings also refrain from such ornamentation and wear simple clothes not because of monastic humility, or contempt for the secular world, but because the style of their clothes does not require colorful textiles, furs, pearls, precious stones, pieces sewed on, or tassels. If anyone were to wear colorful clothes (except at a wedding or in wartime), he would be considered a fool. But here among us even peasants must have gold threads in their shirts, something that kings do not have in other places.

Style is of the utmost importance. Those nations that have more attractive faces and bodies than we do prefer a style of clothing that by itself (without artificial decoration) adds beauty and dignity. We, on the other hand, who desperately need added means to hide the roughness of our appearance, prefer clothing that is useless without its expensive artificial decorations.

The Germans endure bitter frosts without wearing fur coats, but we cannot live unless we are clothed in furs from head to toe. Even the Germans cannot endure the frost without fur when they dress in our clothes. Why is this so? Undoubtedly, style is again the culprit. Thus, style is the principal factor that determines whether or not clothes are beautiful, smart, elegant, inexpensive, dignified, and appropriate. Because of unsuitable, clumsy, ugly styles, we are forced to seek beauty and smartness in expensive and womanlike ornaments. The Germans, Italians, and Spaniards live in warmer and sunnier regions than we. Nevertheless their clothes are wisely styled to protect from cold, rain, dirt, and wind. We on the other hand, who live in cold regions, wear clothes that are useless in bad weather.

The above-mentioned nations have in their countries silk, wool, dyes, gold, and other adornments, except pearls and precious stones. But whatever they lack, they import from India. We do not have any of these items, and we do not know how to import them. We consider whatever they give us a good thing and pay whatever they demand from us. We purchase from them all kinds of apparel and decorations, for which we give the apple of our eye, but we do not want to learn from them for free the styles of clothes (which more than anything else determines beauty). Foreigners see all of this and consider us stupid. Because we wear such uncomfortable clothes, they scorn us and have no respect for us.

The Spartans had a law according to which only prostitutes were allowed to wear colorful clothes and gold ornaments. Venice and some other city republics have special laws on clothing that stipulate how much a nobleman may spend on his clothes, and members of the lower classes are prohibited from wearing silk, pearls, gold, and the like. In kingdoms or autocracies such laws are not necessary. We do not need laws on clothing. What we need above all is a good style.

My heart was bursting with shame when in a foreign town I saw the ambassadors of his tsarist majesty going to an official reception in clothes adorned with pearls and other precious stones. Despite this finery, their tight clothes made them look far from majestic, and people looked at them not with wonder but with pity.

It seems, therefore, that the problem of clothing is worthy of the concern of royal officials. Let them decide who should devise a new, more appropriate style of clothing. For whatever is foolishly dreamt up by commoners, tailors, and willful youths, in time tends to become a part of life even for landowners and kings. Common people should follow the custom of higher officials rather than the reverse.

Such a royal decision about clothes can be put into effect in this way. Let the new clothes be tried out by one of the sovereign's regiments. It is not uncommon for royal guards to wear distinctive costumes. Turkish janissaries wear unusual hats. The bodyguards of other European kings wear uniforms that differ from the clothes of the rest of the population. This enhances the majesty, honor, and dignity of the king. It also cuts down on expenses, for if the guards' uniforms do not differ from the clothes of commoners, they will need expensive ornaments to set them apart. A special uniform maintains dignity.

If we cannot introduce anything new, then at least we should correct the situation in the army and give our soldiers a uniform that will enable them to be stronger and quicker and protect them from the cold and damp. Although this is one of the coldest and rainiest of countries, our clothes are the least adequate for cold or wet weather. To put it succinctly, if someone had tried intentionally to devise the most worthless, expensive, non-durable, and ridiculous garb of all, he would have created what is now worn in Russia.

Presian, the king of Bulgaria (as told in a story) invited his *boyars* to a feast twice a year—once in summer and once in winter. On those occasions he wore clothes that had nothing foreign about them. His clothes were smart and beautifully tailored from local wool, flax, skins, and other native materials. By this example, the king sought to convince his *boyars* that they should not scorn clothes that were native to their country. During great festivals and at receptions for foreign ambassadors, the *boyars* put on foreign clothes, but did not wear any pearls or gold ornaments.

The emperor Augustus (according to Suetonius) wore no clothes except those made for him by his wife, sister, daughter and servants. He had nothing royal and dressed with great simplicity. Everything was inexpensive and similar to the clothing of his subjets. The Lithuanian grand duke Jagello,[2] who became king of Poland, never wore any furs except sheepskin. I cite these examples more in exhortation than for imitation. It would be very useful if we could develop varied processing of hides so that people could wear more clothes made from them. Thus, all raw materials could be processed here at home, as described in Part I of this work.

If anyone should say that it is unfair to violate old customs, we reply

---

[2] The Jagellonian dynasty, to which Krizhanich refers, ruled Poland from 1386 to 1572. Its founder was Jagello (1386–1434); it came to a close with King Sigismund (1548–72).

that it is also unfair to maintain old misconceptions, especially when those misconceptions cause great expense, when all of our wealth goes to foreigners, and when our kingdom is being deprived of the best products of its soil.

In addition to doing away with the harmful custom of everyone wearing pearls, it would be proper to decree that pearls be worn only by the tsar's guards on their uniforms. These pearls could be issued from the treasury, and landowners should be compelled to get rid of their pearls and also to stop wearing other precious stones and superfluous collars. In order to distinguish them from noblemen, it would also be quite appropriate to prohibit commoners from wearing silk, gold thread, and expensive scarlet cloth. There is nothing more inappropriate than when a low scribe wears the same clothes as a distinguished *boyar*.

Whoever does not believe that our clothes look ridiculous to other nations, let him look at some engravings that bear pictures of the kings of various nations standing or on horseback, and let him then compare the "beauty" and "dignity" of Russian attire with the rest.

After Alexander the Great had conquered Persia and Media, he reviewed the attire of those peoples and decided that he did not want to adopt either Persian or Median clothes exclusively. Instead, he contrived a third style, which was a mixture of the two. Being a king and a statesman, he wanted to secure the friendship and loyalty of the nations he had conquered. But he also wanted to demonstrate that he would not copy his dress from his subjects and that they should rather copy theirs from the king. Also being a philosopher, moreover, he wanted to set a good example by showing his new subjects that their own styles of clothing could be made more useful to them.

Those who hunt animals (as Plutarch notes) dress in deer hides; and those who hunt birds wear clothes made of feathers. In an effort to pacify conquered nations, this great king humored them with respect to their native costumes, while also gaining their good opinion. Thoughtless individuals reproach him for this instead of seeing the wisdom of his actions.

18

Russia in the eyes of other nations

Boris: Brother Khervoi, I often think about the sad situation of all of our Slavic nations: Russians, Czechs, Poles, Bulgars, Serbs, and Croats. I wonder why we became the laughing-stock of all peoples, who either insult us, haughtily disdain us, and devour our wealth in front of us. They call us barbarians and consider us more as animals than human beings.

Khervoi: The first reason why other nations treat us contemptuously is our illiteracy and our lack of interest in education. The second reason is our stupidity, which causes our suffering under foreign domination and trickery. It is for these reasons that they call us barbarians.

Boris: What do they mean when they call us barbarians?

Khervoi: Oh, Boris they mean every stupidity that a person may imagine. But to understand it properly it can be divided into three parts.

First, people who are savage are called barbarians; people who live in the forest, who resemble animals, who have neither homes, nor bread, nor salt, like some Siberian natives. Some, like the Samoyeds or cannibals, eat raw flesh; and some do not believe in God, like the Indians of Brazil, who are naked and whose language does not include the three essential letters: R, L, and F, which commence the three Latin words, *Rex, Lex,* and *Fides* (King, Law and Faith). These people have no sovereign, no law, nor faith in God.

Second, barbarians are people who have some moral shortcoming, who are capable of perpetrating any evil. They are exploiters, oppressors, and thieves, who bitterly torment and viciously scheme against others; who

---

[1] In this use of Socratic dialogue, as elsewhere in the *Politika*, Boris connotes a Russian seeking instruction, while Khervoi is a Croat (perhaps intended to represent Krizhanich himself) who imparts knowledge.

violate oaths and commit heresies; and who think nothing of the life to come having no fear of God and no respect for their fellow man.

Third, barbarians are uneducated people who are ignorant of the noble sciences (political and philosophical knowledge) as well as of handicrafts. They are those who are lazy, careless, and unskilled, and who are therefore poor. They worry only about today and cannot visualize the future. Cicero wrote of them: "To live from day to day is a barbarian custom. In our decisions we must have eternity in view." Finally, barbarians are also those who are easily outwitted and deceived.

Boris, of all Christian nations the Europeans consider two as barbarian: the Slavs and the Hungarians. This is not because of the first reason, for we are neither cannibals nor primitives; nor because of the second reason, for the same nations who criticize us also surpass us greatly in cruelty, falsehood, heresy, and all other vices and excesses.

We are called barbarians, savages, beasts, thieves and cheaters only because of our illiteracy, laziness, and stupidity.

Thanks to their cleverness, they move all of our wealth to their own countries and leave us hungry and destitute. They also prepare all kinds of snares for us. They twist us around at will, and at the same time disgrace and insult us. Because of our ignorance, we do not know how to protect ourselves or how to reply to their abuses. We cannot determine what is best for ourselves—what should be preserved and what corrected. We feel obliged to bear all manner of ills, when our own ignorance is their cause.

Boris: Oh, how bitter is our life when we allow foreigners to cheat us and to lead us around by the nose!

Khervoi: Brother, they not only lead us, they drive us, they ride on our backs while they take our wealth. And we allow them to dominate us, as is currently the case in Poland.

Boris: Khervoi, please explain to me in more detail what the reasons are behind the judgments and accusations against us by foreigners.

Khervoi: Foreigners judge us by superficial standards—they judge us only by what they can see and hear: our appearance, our language, our clothes and customs, and the way we build our houses and make our tools.

Our *appearance* is neither first nor last. Therefore, our intelligence is neither first nor last, and is adequate for the study of science if we put great effort and determination into it. It has been said that a moderate intelligence used with great effort is better than a great intelligence used carelessly.

Our *language* is very poor and inadequate. We are ignorant of our history and legends. We are incapable of sophisticated political discourse. Because of this, we lose the respect of other nations.

The *style of clothes* is a vital sign of human intelligence. Those who have devised the most appropriate style clearly surpass others in natural intelligence. An attractive style of clothing often helps a man in achieving his life's ambitions. Conversely, a poor style of clothes does little to help anyone.

The poor style of our dress results in excessive expenditure for decoration, undermines the spirit of our soldiers and decreases the honor of our ambassadors. In addition, long hair, beards, and shaved heads make us look ridiculous. We resemble a tribe of wooden goblins let loose among human beings.

Laws and custom determine what will be virtue and vice, justice and injustice, but we are not concerned here with these fundamental customs. We speak only of daily customs and the ruder aspects of life that manifest themselves in conversation, in types of food, in cleanliness, and similar matters.

Foreigners criticize our food as dirty, attributing it to our generally coarse and untidy way of life. This is because we put coins in our mouths, and because a commoner filling a pitcher with liquid will stick his two fingers into it before offering it to his guest. *Kvas* looks dirty when it is sold, and the dishes in which other foods are sold often are dirty.

The king of Denmark once made the following remark about our ambassadors: "If these people come often I will have to build a pig-shed for them, because any place in which they stay becomes uninhabitable for half a year, thanks to the smell they leave behind." In another country, the following was written mockingly in a popular weekly newspaper about our ambassadors: "If they go into a store to buy something, no one will enter it for a whole hour after they leave on account of the stench."

Our houses in some places are unfit for habitation. The windows are small and there is inadequate ventilation, so that people are blinded by the smoke. They nail boards under the benches, causing debris to collect indefinitely because it is impossible to sweep it out. Our carts are very poorly made, while other implements are completely worthless.

Because of all this there can be little wonder why foreigners condemn us. They also invent a great deal that does not exist. Yet the harm that stems from the inadequacy of our appearance, language, clothing, customs, and housing is still not that great. Far greater harm stems from the cause of these inadequacies, which I call *xenomania*, or craze for all things foreign. We admire every foreign item and we despise and reject our own things. We take in all foreigners, admire their beautiful appearance, resounding language, and free (but more accurately licentious) way of life, and we grant them authority over us in our own country, enabling them to devour all of our wealth and dominate us.

Other enlightened nations study only one learned language—Latin or

Greek—because it is necessary to understand philosophy; they do not study other languages. But our Poles and Croats, in addition to studying Latin, roam across Europe studying German, Italian, French, and Hungarian. They consider anyone who does not speak at least one of these languages unworthy of his class. Thus they belittle themselves, their own language, and their nation. Seeing this, other nations invent vile expressions about us, like the following.

Whenever the Greeks speak about a slave, a servant, a prisoner, or a galley oarsman, they always use the name of our people, *sclavos*—that is, Slav. "This is my Slav," that is, "he is my slave." Instead of "enslaving," they say *sclavonin*—that is, to "make a Slav." They also have a saying: "Greek is beautiful; Albanian is young, Bulgarian is not human." Hungarians also say: "A Hungarian is a wolf, an Italian is cunning, a German is a pig, a Pole is a thief, and a Slav is not human." Italians say: "Either a tsar or a Slav," that is, either the top or the bottom of humanity. When they bargain and a merchant asks too much, the purchaser usually says: "I am not a Pole," meaning "I am not stupid." Germans say: "Guard your things so that Poles will not steal them," or "A Hungarian and a Croat support each other, when you add a Czech to them you will have three thieves." They refer mockingly to their Croat subjects as lice and pig-herders and speak of them not as "Croat" but as "a little Croat." When Frenchmen spot a Pole, they usually say "a Polish bear."

Such insulting expressions prevail among other nations as well. Ignorant Poles contribute to such views when they say: "A Pole is an ox, a Lithuanian is a snake, and a German is a rose." We should not malign ourselves. On the contrary, we should realize what is being said about us and strive to correct it.

Boris: But I would say instead, "Whoever barks is a dog." Our neighbors show their envy when they malign us, and we should therefore ignore them. Those who despise should be despised. Whoever thinks I am a barbarian, I consider him a barbarian.

Khervoi: Brother, you are mistaken. It is easier to say than to do, for whoever ignores the view of the outside world knows neither shame nor honor. He is like some ancient fool who considers himself a philosopher, but who is merely a cynic.

19

The Russian land

Hitherto, we have spoken about all the Slavic peoples in general. Now we shall examine the causes of the poverty and wealth—misfortune and good fortune—of the Russian people in particular.

CAUSES OF MISFORTUNE

The first cause of misfortune and poverty is *luxurious dress*. Shirts are decorated with gold and silk, boots with copper wire. Pearls are worn even by men. Nowhere in Europe do such disgraceful practices exist. Even the lowest common people wear silk clothes. Their women cannot be distinguished from the leading *boyar* ladies. Our country has no pearls—yet everyone wants to wear them. Our country has no dyes—yet everyone wants to wear colored textiles.

The second cause is the *lack of natural resources*. The country does not have any of its own precious stones, pearls, coral, or dyes; it does not have gold, silver, copper, tin, lead, mercury, or good iron. There is no silk, cotton, or wool for textiles. There is no rice and no pepper, saffron, sugar, cloves, myrrh, thyme, muscat, or other spices and aromatics. There are no fruits like grapes, olives, almonds, raisins, figs, or lemons. We lack balsam, camphor, amber, and other medicinal drugs, herbs, and roots; and we lack raw materials like limestone, clay, and good forest land.

The third cause is the *long winter*, which necessitates an enormous amount of firewood and hay and supplies for both people and livestock. The summer is short, cold, and rainy, so that abundant crops cannot be grown; and what survives is difficult to harvest because of the rains and the lack of time. As a result, it is possible to feed only a small population and to keep only a small number of livestock which, by the way, is smaller than anywhere else. Moreover, not only in Russia but among the Poles, Bulgars, Serbs, and Croats—wherever the Slavic tongue prevails—only small horses can be found. Yet everyone around us—Tartars, Turks, Hungarians, and Germans—has big, fast, powerful horses. Because our bodies are large and our horses are small, we appear clumsy on horseback. The Tartars are small, but their horses are large and strong, which is why Crimean horsemen seem to be better than our own.

The fourth cause is *evil neighbors and merchants*. The Crimean [Tartars], the Nogai [Tartars], and other barbaric peoples frequently devastate and despoil this country. At every favorable opportunity, the Swedes use deceit to take something away. The Greeks persuade us to trade much of our wealth for false gems and glass. Finally, German merchants and military officers clean out the remainder of our wealth.

The fifth cause is the *scanty population* and sparsely inhabited land. This stems from drastic and cruel laws, which will be discussed later.

CAUSES OF GOOD FORTUNE

Whoever does not value the good things God has given him is unworthy of them. If we wish to receive new national benefits from God (such as peace, security, and prosperity), we should understand and acknowledge all the benefits that God has already bestowed upon us. (We speak here only of worldly benefits.) Just what benefits has God bestowed on this tsardom and why, as a result, should it consider itself fortunate?

The first, most important, and leading benefit is *absolute autocracy*. This is "the rod of Moses" with which the sovereign tsar can perform all necessary miracles. Under such a system of government, it is easy to correct all mistakes, shortcomings, and distortions and to introduce all kinds of beneficial laws. We will attain this if we obey the sovereign tsar, the lieutenant of God, in everything; and if the sovereign gives each layer of society appropriate privileges. In addition, we should maintain dignified relations with peaceful nations, offend no one without cause, conclude alliances with like nations, and take advantage of happy circumstances, opportunities and divine grace.

The second cause is *safe frontiers*, because this tsardom needs fear no enemy from the Arctic Ocean. Moreover, there are no powerful kings in Siberia; only the Kalmucks and other nomadic peoples, whom we need not fear.

The third cause is the presence of *good neighbors*, such as the Persians, with whom we can trade and whom we need not fear will violate our dignity. The Poles and Lithuanians are also good neighbors. We need not fear that they will start a war provided we ourselves do not precipitate one. We can also conclude a very advantageous alliance with them. More will be said about this later.

The fourth cause is the presence of ideal *circumstances for large-scale trade*. We are capable of receiving goods from various nations and transmitting them to various other nations, as do the inhabitants of Danzig (from which practice they get rich year after year). We can carry goods from the Germans to the Turks, Persians, Cherkess, Kalmuks, Bokharans, Chinese, and Dauri, and transport the goods of these nations to Germans, Poles, and Lithuanians. We could build new marketplaces similar to Archangel, first along the Don, second in Astrakhan, and third near the Kalmucks. Lesser marketplaces could be established in Putivl, along the Lithuanian and Swedish frontiers, adjacent to the Dauri territory, and in appropriate places along the Caspian Sea. We could also dispatch our merchants to live and trade throughout the Bokharan and Persian realms, as noted earlier.

The fifth cause of good fortune consists of *favorable conditions for shipping*. We have ports on the Arctic and Caspian Seas as well as on the Black Sea. We have navigable rivers: the Northern Dvina, Don, Volga, Irtysh, Ob, and others. We possess an abundance of hemp, tar, and timber suitable for ship building, and have boats and all sorts of sailing craft; but apparently we are unfamiliar with marine transport. We should fill the Caspian with our ships.

We should devote more attention to river transport—especially in Siberia—and do everything necessary to achieve it. The value of Siberia is contingent on the use of its rivers; whoever is the master of these rivers is the master of the entire territory.

It would also be useful to discover if water routes exist from Siberia to Dauri, or China, or India; and from Magazeia and Ob to Archangel.[1]

Clearly, we are also blessed with *domestic products*: furs, reindeer hides, colored hides, hemp, potash, caviar, fish, honey wax, grain, meat, and flax among other things. We should conserve these divine gifts, not squander them. We certainly should sell to foreigners, but not deprive ourselves of these riches. On some goods, an annual export quota should be imposed. This can be achieved only if all foreign merchants leave the country, and if the sovereign tsar takes over the whole import and export trade.

---

[1] For other comments by Krizhanich on this subject, see his "Istoriia Sibiri, ili svedeniia o tsarstvakh Sibiri i ledovitogo i vostochnogo okeana . . ." in A.A. Titov, ed., *Sibir v XVII veke. Sbornik starinnykh russkikh statei o Sibiri i prilezhashchikh k nei' zemliakh* (Moscow, 1890); John F. Baddeley, *Russia, Mongolia, China* (London, 1919), vol. 2, 212–15; and Albert Parry, "Juraj Križanić's Views on Siberia and China of the Seventeenth Century," 245–60, in Eekman and Kadić.

20

German slander about Russian customs

The duke of Holstein, in an effort to capture the Astrakhan and Archangel trade, sent an ambassador to the shah of Persia in 1633 and the three following years. The secretary of this ambassador, one Adam Olearius, described our glorious empire, and wrote the following about Russian customs and habits:

If one were to analyze the nature and customs of the Russian people, one would justly call them barbarians, because they have neglected the noble sciences and have remained in their natural state of ignorance. The Russians possess fairly sharp minds, but, by placing them solely at the disposal of personal profit and temptation, they often become vicious and immoral. That is why, in his description of the Russians, Jacob, the ambassador of the king of Denmark, calls them obstinate, violent, and treacherous.[1]

Simply stated, they are shameless and capable of committing any evil; they rely on force rather than reason. Their vices are especially evident when cheating in trade or when, through loans, they place something in someone's hands and then accuse him of stealing it. Such deceit is quite frequent among them. Individuals of the more important class are so arrogant and haughty that they flaunt themselves at every opportunity. The courseness of their customs is evident everywhere. Moreover, personal contact with them is hard to bear because of the continual smell of garlic and onions, staples of their diet. Dissoluteness, lechery, shamelessness, and dishonesty prevail everywhere. We can thus agree with Jacob of Denmark that the Russians have rejected all honesty and humility.

The cause of all these shortcomings and vices is the idleness and drunkenness that engulfs the Russians. Drunkenness is widespread among people of all ranks and classes, ecclesiastic and secular, men and women.

---

[1] Jacob von Ulfeld, ambassador of Frederick II of Denmark to Tsar Ivan IV in 1578–79; he wrote a volume entitled *Hedeoporicon Ruthenicum* [Journey to Russia] (Frankfurt, 1608).

The corpses of drunken persons are found daily on the streets and lying in puddles. This widespread drunkenness also affects the treatment of foreign guests. When a person goes anywhere he is treated to a glass of brandy. This process is repeated so often that in due course his soul necessarily takes leave of his body. There have been several cases where individuals of high rank, and even ambassadors visiting foreign nations got drunk. In 1608, a Russian ambassador to Sweden consumed such an excessive amount of strong brandy that he was found dead in his bed the following day, when he was to have appeared before the king.

Punishment with rods and whips is widespread among them, and after a thrashing with rods they praise the person who ordered them to be beaten. Their servile character is also evident in their manner of bowing, when they touch the floor with their foreheads.

Subjects of all ranks and classes must call themselves "slaves of the great sovereign." Princes and *boyars* also are required to express their submission by signing their petitions with diminutives: Fedka, Ivashka Pashka, Vaska, instead of Feodor, Ivan, Pavel, Vasilii. The great sovereign addresses them with these diminutives, and whenever a *boyar* commits any wrong he receives barbaric punishment.

The *boyars* have many slaves on their estates. Some have fifty, or even a hundred, in one mansion. These slaves receive payment that barely covers their essential needs. Seldom does a night go by without someone being murdered, especially during big celebrations or on the eve of a fast, when everyone drinks like mad. During our stay in Moscow on December 11, fifteen people were found dead in the Zemskii courtyard. At harvest time, these slaves are sent to cut hay and, near Moscow, they commit violent crimes. Their masters can be considered accomplices, since they give their slaves barely enough to feed and clothe themselves.

In spite of their coarse and slavish nature, they are cordial, diligent in war, and brave enough at times (the ancient Romans, however, would not have allowed such people to enlist in the army, because in those times soldiers were concerned about national power and wealth, while these soldiers think only of pillage and their own personal profit). Being slavish, these Russians readily submit themselves to foreign officers if native ones are unavailable. They exhibit great bravery and courage inside forts, but not much in the field. There have been instances when they considered burning their uniforms or starving to death rather than surrendering a fort. In the town of Padis, in Livonia, when they finally abandoned the fort, the Russians could not meet the Germans at the gate because they were half starved. The chroniclers considered this worthy of wonder. They can truly be called warriors in their defense of forts; they wil suffer great privations on behalf of their sovereign. But in sieges of forts and in battles they do not exhibit any special bravery. They have always suffered defeat at the hands of the Poles and Swedes and were always more ready to flee than to attack or pursue the enemy.

Nobles and leading merchants live in mansions made of stone. They started building them some thirty years ago. Before this, they lived in small wooden houses with only a few insignificant furnishings. Even now they use only three or four earthenware pots, and the same number of wooden dishes. Silver utensils are rare, except for a few cups for wine or mead. What silver they do have, they make no effort to clean, so that even the silver and pewter dishes of the great sovereign, used to entertain our envoys, looked as though they had not been polished for an entire year.

Their walls are not decorated with pewter utensils, as is the custom in German lands, but are either bare or covered with spiderwebs. Their beds are filled not with feathers but with wool or straw. They wear the same clothes to bed that they wear during the day. In the summer they sleep on benches, and in the winter they sleep on top of the stove. Husband, wife, children, and servants, and sometimes even chickens and pigs, sleep together.

In eating, they have plain tastes and are content with porridge, sauerkraut, cucumbers, and salted fish. They always use onions and garlic, an aroma that fills the homes of common people and princes alike. During feasts they serve marvelous viands and drinks. But feasts are used not to attract new friends or to maintain old ones, but for personal advantage. In accordance with established custom, guests are supposed to come the following day to give the host valuable gifts. Heads of various departments usually organize three or four such feasts at the expense of the invited foreign merchants.

The great sovereign frequently dispatches large embassies to the Holy Roman Emperor, to the kings of Sweden, Denmark, Persia, and others (i.e., to Poland, England, Turkey, France, and China; to the Crimea and Georgia; to Florence, Prussia, Courland, Holstein, and Cherkassia; to Bokhara, the Kalmucks, Holland, Hamburg, Venice and Malta). With these embassies he dispatches great gifts. For example, in 1595 the following gifts were dispatched to the emperor of the Holy Roman Empire: 206 sables, 1,038 martens, 240 black foxes, 674,000 red foxes, 6,000 beavers, 2,000 wolves, and 148 elks—a grand total of 683,632 furs.

Various ambassadors also come to Moscow. They are kept there for a long time and accumulate expenses. Others live there as consuls, agents, and residents (that is, officials representing various entrepreneurs). These have special quarters or homes where they live at their own expenses. From the Kalmucks, from the Southern Siberian Tartar *murzas* [tribal leaders or nobles], and from other savage Tartar Hordes, ambassadors come for no other reason than to receive gifts. Russians adopt whatever is shown to them by foreigners. Consequently, if anyone wishes to obtain advantage from an invention, he should not show it to the Russians.

This—and many other false charges in foul language—were written by Olearius.

21

Replies to foreign slander

West Europeans write very little about our other Slavic peoples, such as the Poles, Croats, and Serbs. They only make caustic remarks about them, since they live alongside them, associate with them daily, and know their ways without books. They have written not one, but many special books about the Russian people and this illustrious state, because this country is located far away and its customs are less well known, as well as because God in His mercy has recently allowed this great and powerful kingdom to rise to prominence.

The first to write a book about Russia was Sigismund von Herberstein, the ambassador of the German emperor to the great prince Vasilii Ivanovich. He was followed by Phillip Pernisteri, ambassador of the same country to Tsar Ivan Vasilevich. The third was Antonio Possevino, the papal legate. These envoys did not write slanderous accounts. Indeed, Bishop Paolo Giovio, in his historical works based on an account he heard in Rome from Dmitrii, writes favorably about this empire. The Bishop refers to Tsar Ivan as the "illustrious defender of the Christian faith."[1]

I do not have these books now and I cannot completely recall what was said in them. I only know that they do not write about our customs and way of life as maliciously as the above-mentioned critic [Olearius]. They do not exaggerate our weaknesses and they do not ridicule our customs because they know well that all nations have an equal share of sins and

[1] Sigismund von Herberstein (1486–1566) served as ambassador to Moscow of Maximilian I (1493–1519) and Charles V (1519–56) in 1517 and 1526. Upon his return, he wrote a description of Russia and its people entitled *Rerum Moscoviticarum Commentarii* (Vienna, 1549), which Krizhanich read in 1640–41. Phillipi Pernisteri was an envoy of Rudolf II (1576–1612) to Moscow in 1579, and the author of *Relatio de Magno Moscoviae Principe* (Frankfurt, 1579). Antonio Possevino (1534–1611) was a Jesuit priest who served as legate of Pope Gregory XIII to Tsar Ivan IV. Upon his return, Possevino wrote *Moscovia* (Vilna, 1586), a book that deeply influenced Krizhanich. Paolo Giovio (1483–1552) was an Italian historian, author of *Libellus de legatione Basilii magni . . . ad Clementem VII* (Rome, 1525), a collection of tales about Russia told by Dmitrii Herasimov, an interpreter attached to the embassy sent by Vasilii III (1503–33) to Pope Clement VII (1523–34).

shortcomings. Moreover, they do not criticize our simple things and our modest, unhappy way of life, for they know that a simple way of life is more worthy of praise than is luxury. Nevertheless, not all of them praise the Russians, and some recommend changes. For example, they maintain that the people should study. And, when speaking of the cruel laws of Tsar Ivan [the Terrible], they do not extol them. But, as I have said, I cannot adequately comment on these writers because I do not have their books in hand.

Peter Petrejus, a German, wrote a sizable book about this tsardom.[2] Each page abounds in malicious insults and false stories. He calls his book Russian history but it would be more appropriately called Russian "libel." It is a spiteful and abusive book. There is no need to cite even one example from it; there is not a single page that is free of malicious abuse. No one could depict even the demons of hell more vilely and more gruesomely than he portrays our people. He makes us look worse than the Turks, Tartars, Samoyeds, and other hellish devils. Concerning himself, he writes that he lived in Russia for about four years in the pay of the great sovereign and that he travelled through almost the entire Russian empire and saw everything with his own eyes.

Foreigners in Moscow possess this book and value it because it describes in detail the violent rule of the False Dmitrii and the Polish occupation of Moscow [1610–12]; it makes reference to the entire country—including towns and rivers, distances from place to place, and everything else that is considered vital. Foreigners therefore think that everything this slanderer writes is true and think badly of our people.

The Danish envoy Jacob wrote a book, but I have not seen it. Heidenstein wrote a large book about the gruesome suffering under Tsar Ivan. He gives a day-by-day account of those the tsar ordered to be executed and how. Solomon Henning, author of *The Livonian Chronicle,* wrote about Russian affairs. Hammelmann, author of the *Oldenburg Chronicle,* also wrote about Russian affairs. Atsernus wrote a book about Russia. David Chyträus, a German writer, published a work entitled *Vandalia* in 1589; Paul Oderborn, a German historian, published in 1585 a work on the reign of Ivan the Terrible entitled *Johann's Basilidis, Magni Moschaviae ducia vita*; and J. Abelin wrote a work called *Archontologia cosmica,* which was published in 1628. All these books were, at least in part, about Russia, but I do not have access to them now.[3]

---

[2] Peter Petrejus was in fact not a German, but a Swedish traveller and author, who in 1620 published a volume entitled *Historien und Bericht von dem grossfürstenthum Mushkow.*

[3] The works referred to are Jacob von Ulfeldt, *Hodeoporicon Ruthenicum; De bello Moscovito commentariorum libri* by Reingold Heidenstein (1555–1620), a secretary to the Polish kings Stefan Bathory and Sigismund III, published in Cracow in 1581; *Lifländische-Churchländ-*

In short, when these authors write anything about Russia or any other Slavic people, they write not history, but biting satire. They exaggerate our vices, inadequacies, and natural shortcomings, and whenever there is no sin to be found, they invent one. They also write false histories. For instance, Petrejus wrote that at one time Russian sovereigns were required by necessity as well as agreement to meet the ambassador from Crimea, who travelled on horseback, and to bring him some mare's milk.[4] The ambassador, while drinking that milk, would deliberately spill it on the horse's mane, and the great sovereign was allegedly required to lick that milk from the mane. These dear writers present such fables not as jokes but as the "truth." Such stories resemble those the Germans tell in their fables about the Swabians, saying that seven Swabians killed a hare with one spear. Or that the Silesians eat eagles instead of hares, etc.

We should note that the first four authors—Herberstein, Pernisteri, Possevino and Giovio—were members of the Roman Catholic faith. For that reason, they do not curse us, they do not shame us, and they do not exaggerate our sins. On the contrary, they praise what is good and tell honestly what they have seen. Pernisteri writes that people here eagerly attend church services and remain in churches for a long time praying: at matins, at mass, and at vespers. Thus, good people say good things and are silent about silly matters even if they know about them. And, conversely, evil people never mention good things, but strive to exaggerate things that are silly.

As for Adam Olearius, Petrejus, Jacob the Dane, and the rest of the writers, they belonged to the Lutheran heresy, and as a result they have spoken libelously in accordance with their custom and teaching. For it should be known that Luther and his followers were never able, and are unable now, truthfully to accuse the Roman church of anything, apart from citing the sinful life of its churchmen. Consequently, by writing about sins of the priests they lead the followers of the Roman Catholic faith into heresy.

If we ever talk with the Lutherans, we should ask them: "Why do

---

ische Chronica [The Livonian Chronicle] by the German historian Solomon Henning, published in Rostock in 1590; and the *Oldenburgisches Chronicon* (1599) by Hermann Hammelmann (1525–95). Asternus was the pseudonym of the Polish poet Sz. Klonowicz (1551–1608) who wrote the poem *Roxolania* (Cracow, 1584). David Chyträus (1531–1600), a German writer, published a work entitled *Vandalia* in 1589. Paul Oderborn (d. 1604), German historian, published in 1585 a work on the reign of Ivan the Terrible entitled *Johann's Basilidis, Magni Moschaviae ducia vita*. J. Abelin was the pseudonym of J. Gotofredus, author of *Archontologia cosmica* (1628).
[4] *Historien*, p. 159.

Roman Catholic writers not write the nonsense that you Lutheran authors write? Luther and all of your preachers cannot find anything concrete to divert people away from the Roman faith except the exaggerated descriptions of Papal sins." Since birth they have been conditioned to smear and abuse, and they cannot be different in their attitude toward us. When they describe and magnify our sins, they wish to destroy our Orthodox faith.

Second, it should be said, "By being eloquent and loquacious, you subdue us with your language and thereby persuade us to accept anything. The absence of eloquence among us prevents us from inventing any histories about you in response."

It should be pointed out that the Greeks once considered themselves the only civilized human beings and viewed all other peoples as barbarians—or cattle. It has come to pass that those whom the Greeks once called barbarians now use that term to describe the Greeks.

Third, you curse our humble way of life and consider it to be rude, barbaric, and filthy. Yet you explain that your own wasteful, haughty, and empty way of life was ordained by heaven and is therefore pure. But if we were to follow your licentiousness, gluttony, and luxury, if we were to drown in feathered beds and sleep until noon, and if we were to eat food prepared with thousands of spices, then you yourselves would curse us as wasteful and licentious, and you would hail your own "humble" way of life as saintly. When it is us who have few luxuries and live simply, you call this simplicity filthy and barbaric.

As for sins, we acknowledge that we are sinners. But you describe those sins as if sin were our own invention. But if we had public inns like those found in some of your towns, where you hang pictures of various prostitutes, with fees attached, what then would you say of us? The Saviour was correct when He said: "Oh, hypocrite, first remove the beam from your own eye before you remove the mote from somebody else's eye."

We should respond to our enemies with these words, but among ourselves we should be aware that not all of these revilers speak falsely. This is especially true with regard to our drunkenness, for truly nowhere does such vile drunkenness exist. We also have a great inclination to lie, to distrust others, as well as some other vices. We should ascertain what causes them: for they are not caused by natural factors or by faith (as foreigners would like us to believe). The same Slavic people and the same Orthodox faith prevail elsewhere, but there are no such vile habits among the Serbs, the Greeks, and in Belorussia. What then causes these vices? Clearly, stupid laws about which we will say more later.

Whenever the Greeks, Germans, or Poles receive wagons officially

assigned to them in this tsardom or in Belorussia they usually beat the
poor peasant drivers mercilessly, saying: "These people are barbarians,
and barbarians must be beaten if one hopes to derive benefit from them."
We should respond to this abuse not by words but with cudgels. These
soft-headed and haughty politicians should be taught a lesson as to just
where they had encountered "barbarians"!

The Poles praise their freedoms and liberties. They also criticize
autocratic systems of government endlessly. They are pampered, spoiled,
and licentious. Poles glorify their chaotic state and repeat over and again:
"The Polish Kingdom is maintained by disorder." This problem, however, requires long discussion at another, more appropriate place.[5]

There are so many sorcerers and sorceresses among the Germans that
sometimes entire cities teem with them. They are even found among high
city officials. According to my recollection, in the town of Hamburg the
judges had decreed that the executioner extract the names of their
accomplices under torture, and the executioner replied: "Gentlemen, you
will never discover all of them. For if we were to place in the square a large
beer tub full of water, and if all the town sorcerers and sorceresses were to
come and moisten just one of their fingers in it, be assured that by evening
there would be no water left in the tub." Eventually, almost all the judges
and their wives were burned for sorcery.

[5] In his manuscript, Krizhanich crossed out the following passage: "Olearius and other
Germans reproach us for the fact that Russian commoners share their bread with the
executioner. But the Germans do not wish to recall the fact that in antiquity all of their
princes were executioners who cut off the heads of their criminals with special knives, and
they now glorify those who can trace their family to those executioners. Among us, thank
God, the princes have never acted as executioners and no nobleman will seat an executioner
at his table."

22

Characteristics and shortcomings of the Russian people

When merchants wish to ascertain the quality of a piece of gold or copper, they lay a sample on a stone alongside another piece. By comparing the two, they can see the variations and clearly recognize the piece of best quality. A royal adviser should use the same rule of comparison. If he wants to judge the customs of our people, he should compare them with those of other nations and, further, should understand the reasons why some problems exist among us, but not elsewhere.

Khervoi: Brother Boris, I am always ashamed and angry whenever I think about the arrogance of our people.

Boris: What arrogance are you talking about?

Khervoi: An example of this is that we take pride in comparing ourselves to the Samoyeds, Ostiaks, and Kalmucks who are coarse and barbaric. This should serve as a reason not for arrogance, but for humility and compassion. For, to the same degree that these people appear to be savage when compared with us, we appear rude and ignorant when compared with other nations.

Boris: That is a strong condemnation. We should not slander and berate ourselves. A bird that fouls its nest is a reprehensible creature.

Khervoi: You are right. I would never say such things before foreigners. On the contrary, I would try in every way to conceal our shortcomings. But among ourselves, we should not conceal a public evil and deceive ourselves. One does not hide one's wounds from a doctor if they are to be healed. Also, there is no benefit in hiding from ourselves what the entire world knows. Foreign books abound in stories of our ignorance and shortcomings.

Boris: How do you explain these matters?

Khervoi: I consider the Tartars, Kalmucks, Ostiaks, Gypsies and similar peoples as savages because they have neither permanent dwellings nor political systems. We are superior to them in humanity; but on the other hand, some of them are superior to us in adroitness, others in quickness, and almost all in trickery or cunning.

The Italians, French, Germans, Spanish, and ancient Greeks transcend us in humanity, intellect, and beauty; and also in truthfulness, devotion, sobriety and other good behavior. They also transcend us in bad features and vices, especially foul language, cursing, anger, and brutality. These nations have many gruesome swear words, curses, and a multitude of filthy and shameful words which our language does not have. This particular deficiency can be viewed as a blessing, as was noted long ago by the Papal ambassador Possevino. Once these foreigners are angered, they carry their anger with them until death. In their search for revenge, they know no mercy.

Compared with these nations, we are not very clean or well cared for: stupid, ignorant in science, and almost completely impoverished. More-over, we are burdened with several nation-wide vices; especially laziness, wastefulness, poor speech, and what is most ruinous, the entire nation drinks—young and old, laity and clergy, the lowest and the highest.

Compared with these nations we lead an especially dissipated and wasteful life. Our ancient pagan forefathers considered Radigost (patron of feasts and festivals) as their principal idol. They perpetually feasted and drank in his honor. Today, in place of the feast of Radigost, we celebrate two weeks in honor of St Nicholas and Shrovetide; plus every holy Sunday, christening, birthday, funeral, and special holidays. In the past there were court feasts for foreign envoys and there still are court festivals to honor *boyars,* priests, and nobles. On all these occasions, we always drink ourselves to a stupor.

Drunkenness is the most gruesome of all vices and sins. it makes us unacceptable before God, repulsive to all other nations, and unsuitable for anything. It transforms us into animals. An Italian, Spaniard, or Turk, when seen drunk in public, loses all the respect of his fellow men and is considered unworthy of holding any public office.

Boris: What are the reasons for such gruesome and staggering drunkenness among us.

Khervoi: Let us speak about it later. Now let us finish the topic at hand.

As we have observed, the shortcoming of our people is their love of feasts and their vain hospitality; both cause waste and ruin. Accompanying this is brutality toward subordinates. Few people among us would consider it dishonorable to feast a great deal or to squander their property without reason. When they are left without means, they mercilessly oppress and exploit their poor subjects, their own compatriots; but toward ungrateful, cocky foreigners they are always generous and spendthrift. Jesus, son of Sirach, speaks thus of this sort: "They give food and drink to ungrateful individuals and hear bitter words in return."

We do not have a naturally cheerful disposition or a noble or proud bearing that would enable us to view ourselves and our people with dignity. People who possess such attitudes cannot tolerate foreign rule unless they are forced, but our people-willingly invite foreigners to their throne.

Tartars and Turks, even when deserting, will not submissively allow themselves to be killed. They fight to their last breath.. But our soldiers will not defend themselves. When they desert they allow themselves to be butchered. Good military commanders must bring these facts to the attention of our soldiers and instill bravery in them.

Our greatest political problem is excessive government. Our people do not know how to use moderation. They always stray into fatal extremities. In one place overly undisciplined, willful, and disorderly government prevails; while in another there is overly firm, stern, and brutal government. A more disorderly and undisciplined kingdom than in Poland is not to be found anywhere, nor as stern a government as the one that exists in Russia.

Our tragedy centers in the fact that other nations—Greeks, Italians, Germans, and Tartars—involve us in their disputes and cause divisions among us. Because we are ignorant, we allow ourselves to be deceived, we fight for others, we consider foreign wars as our own, we cannot stand one another, we quarrel to the death, and brother advances against brother without any need or reason. We trust foreigners in everything and maintain alliances with them, while at the same time we are ashamed of ourselves and our own people.

Once upon a time the Greeks tempted a great Russian ruler into dispatching a joint military expedition against the Bulgars.[1] Following the defeat of the Bulgars, they even established a commemorative day in memory of this allegedly great event when brothers killed brothers. At present, the Turks and the Crimeans would similarly like to tempt the Poles, while the German emperor and the Swedes wish us as much good as the wolf wishes the sheep. Nevertheless they try to tempt us.

For years the Greeks and Romans had political differences that caused hostilities. They falsely portray this as a religious struggle, and each side accuses the other of heresy, even if there is none. Unable to comprehend this, we imitate them and kill one another without rhyme or reason. Matchmaking with foreigners leads to civil strife. This harms us more than anything else.

---

[1] This refers to the expedition of Prince Sviatoslav of Kiev in 968.

23

Xenomania

Xenomania (*chuzhebesie* in our language) is an obsessive love of foreign people and things. This deadly plague has infected our entire nation. It is impossible to list all the losses and disgrace we have suffered because of this rage for foreign things. Because of this undeserved trust, we fraternize and intermarry with them, putting ourselves at their mercy.

Foreign degeneracy impresses us as much as foreign eloquence, beauty, and adroitness. Using their knowledge, cunning, and unsurpassed flattery, as well as their rudeness and viciousness, foreigners have deprived us of our reason and order us around as they wish. They extort our wealth with greed and gluttony. Their insincerity often places us in desperate situations. Their devilish arrogance humiliates us and exposes us shamefully to all nations. From the beginning, no nation under the sun has been so insulted and disgraced as have we Slavs. No other nation thus has more need to avoid close contacts with foreigners than we do. But how well are we protecting ourselves?

Nowhere in the world do foreigners have half the honor and revenue they do here in Russia and Poland. Foreigners are responsible for the famine, thirst, sorrows, oppression, enslavement, and frequent public disorder in this Russian nation. Our tears and sweat are given to German merchants and military commanders, to Greek merchants, to Crimean bandits, and to envoys from various nations. Everything that is forcefully taken from a Russian is devoured by a foreigner.

There is ample evidence of their deceit, because they have deceived us in almost every circumstance. An enormous multitude of foreigners live in Poland: Gypsies, Scotsmen, Armenians, Jews, Germans, Tartars, and Italians. They all preserve their own customs, attire, and laws; they all are rich and powerful; and they are respected and elevated to the status of princes and even kings. In Poland there are so many of these residues that it is less appropriate to say "foreigners live among the Poles" than to say that "the Poles live among foreigners."

Of all nations, we alone seem to have this strange and unhappy fate, we alone are the laughing-stock of the entire world because we willingly invite alien rule. We have allowed ourselves to be conquered by sweet words alone rather than by weapons. As a result, foreigners sit on our backs, drive us, and beat us as if we were animals. Others play practical jokes, leading us about like a bear with a ring through its nose. They set up kingdoms among us, appoint kings, and portray themselves as gods. For instance, a German emperor appointed a king in Bohemia and designated that king as his "principal cup-bearer."[1] Like locusts, they devour our wealth and consume the fruits of our land.

Boris, never forget these precepts:

Vain acts from which we hope to derive honor bring us the greatest dishonor: this pertains to the excessive welcoming and feasting of foreign envoys.

Wasteful policies from which we expect to acquire wealth, bring us loss and ruin: this pertains in allowing foreign merchants to live profitably in Russia. They are one of the principal causes for the misery of this land.

Acts from which we hope to gain power bring us ruin: this applies to using German military commanders and instructors, as well as seeking Swedish assistance. Kazan, Astrakhan, and Siberia were conquered by Russian military forces with God's blessing. By the continued use of German forces, we may lose these territories.

---

[1] Emperor Henry IV so appointed the Bohemian king Vratislav in 1086.

24

Ways in which the employment of foreigners is detrimental to nations

Foreigners interfere in our wars. They promise aid, but they bring destruction. During a civil war the Greeks requested Turkish aid: they came to help one side and conquered both.[1] The Swedes offered aid to Tsar Vasilii Ivanovich against the Poles; upon coming, they betrayed the tsardom to the enemy near Klushino, and helped themselves to Novgorod.[2] The Swiss-Germans who were hired by the French King Francis I did not wish to fight, and therefore turned the king over to his enemy near Pavia [in 1525]. Foreigners involve us in their own wars and cause internal discord.

Through trade, the Italians spread throughout Greece and seized control of several cities. German merchants came to Poland and bought the best of everything. The most distinguished Poles eat wheaten bread only three times a year, because the Germans have exported virtually all the wheat. They have flooded Poland with copper coins, but accept only gold and silver for payment from the Poles. By promising to pay high taxes, the Jews have inundated and defiled Poland. The Gypsies, Scotsmen, Armenians, Jews, and Germans are itinerant people. They do not wish to cultivate the land or to defend it.

The Germans are the worst offenders. In quest of war and in search of military service they roam the entire world. The kings of France and Spain and—even—the Pope have selected them as bodyguards. These rulers have gained neither glory nor benefit from this: they have only offended

---

[1] Reference is to the bargain struck by the usurper John VI Cantacuzenus (r. 1347–54), an ambitious Byzantine nobleman, with the Turkish Sultan Orkhan in 1350. Cantacuzenus requested Turkish aid in order to gain the imperial throne, offering the Gallipoli peninsula in return. A hundred years later, the Turks captured Constantinople.

[2] Here Krizhanich refers to the reign of Tsar Vasilii Ivanovich Shuiskii (1606–10) and relies on information contained in two works by a Polish writer, Szymon Starowolski—*Polonia, nunc denuo recognita et aucta* (Cologne, 1632) and *Reformacya obyczajow Polskich* (Cracow, 1649).

their own people. Here in Russia these transients are used during reviews only for display. Further, they receive excessive remuneration, an enormous insult to our inhabitants.

In the treaty of peace with Sweden, Russian merchants were permitted to live in Sweden and Swedish merchants in Russia.[3] This was detrimental to us, because our merchants for various reasons were not allowed to live in Sweden. Bokhara merchants live among us, and if our merchants could live there, it might well be beneficial.

The Germans bring small gifts for the tsar and *boyars*. In return they have been allowed to have commercial agents in Russia. They have been granted leases on ore mining and glass manufacturing and on many hereditary estates and properties in Lithuania.[4] In Poland and Lithuania, all taverns, tax collecting, flour mills, and many hereditary estates have been farmed out to the Jews. Consider the kind of life that exists there for poor Christians!

Foreign envoys throughout the world use as much cunning as possible. But here in Russia they are especially zealous. This is partly because of our ignorance, and partly because nowhere in Europe are so many useless envoys received. On the other hand, when our envoys are sent to Europe, they bring indescribable disgrace upon their people by reason of their coarseness and lack of education. A certain German interpreter named Lazarus has written a whole book about it.

The Poles, too, travel without purpose through foreign lands. For all the money they spend there, they bring home nothing but abuse and contempt from all Europeans.

The Germans once entrenched themselves in Hungary in great numbers, and German kings distributed Hungarian towns to their German friends. As a result, the Hungarians introduced a law banning "foreigners" from controlling any Hungarian city. But because of the connivance of German kings, many Germans were registered as Hungarians. Accordingly, Germans still control Hungarian cities.

---

[3] The treaty of Stolbovo, 1617.

[4] Russian historians believe that Krizhanich was correct in maintaining that foreign merchants had greater access to Russian markets than the other way around. For a discussion of this problem, see P.P. Smirnov, "Novoe chelobitie moskovskikh torgovykh liudei o vysylke inozemtsev, 1627 g."*Chteniia v istoricheskom obshchestve Nestora-letopistsa* (1912), book 23, part 2, 3–32, 97–104; and K.V. Bazilevich, "Kolektivnye chelobitia torgovykh liudei i borba za russkii rynok v pervoi polovine XVII veka," *Izvestiia Akademii Nauk SSSR. Otdelenie obshchestvennykh nauk* (1932), no. 2, 91–123. "In general, Russian foreign trade in the seventeenth century, as in earlier times, showed very considerable export surpluses . . ." that "were covered by massive shipments of bullion from western Europe" (Artur Attman, *ibid.*, 184); the issue of Russia's "access" to foreign markets therefore appears extremely nebulous.

In Poland, the Germans began to purchase many properties. The Poles introduced a law under which no foreigner was allowed to purchase property in Poland. But here, too, the Germans found a loophole. Now they purchase property under the disguise of mortgage (which they call *Widerkauf*); under its terms, after a specific period of time, the buyer cannot sell the property to anyone except the seller, and the seller cannot mortgage it to anyone else. He can only repurchase the property for his own use. Other Germans [in Poland], as in Hungary, have been trying to organize their own landowning associations, which the Poles call *indigenat*.

Why did the Roman Empire collapse? Some writers have thought that it fell because of waste, pride, and luxury. But other empires have survived for many centuries with all of their wastefulness, such as the Persian, French, and English empires. The principal cause of the downfall of the Roman Empire was, in the prophet Daniel's words: "So shall men mix with each other by intermarriage, but such alliances shall not be stable" [Daniel 2:43]. In an attempt to increase their population, the Romans bestowed citizenship on various peoples and made Roman citizens out of the Greeks, Jews, and Persians. Other nations thus began to set their own leaders on the throne.

Once the Turks eagerly accepted any runaway or unfrocked monk who wished to become a Turk. They gave such individuals high honorary positions in that empire. Even now they continue to accept many refugees, and we call such people turncoats. They have recruited the janissaries from among Christian children. Because of this practice the Turks have gained such infamy that they are ashamed of their own name. Moreover, thanks to the acceptance of these turncoats, the Turkish empire has fallen into the control of alien hands.

The Russian empire somewhat resembles the Turkish, because it too receives anyone wishing to come; in fact, it even begs them to come. Many foreigners are compelled to be baptized. But this is done for opportunistic reasons, not from a wish for salvation. Some of these newcomers manage the most important affairs of state; others conclude peaceful commercial treaties with foreign nations—and, little by little, they transfer Russian and tsarist wealth to their compatriots. If the Russian tsardom should ever perish, it will be because of these "converts" and their descendants. They intermarry with us, but they will never accept us as partners in their ambitions. More than once, a foreign aspirant has been chosen to receive the crown of this tsardom, but their plans have always been frustrated, not by human but by divine design. Now let us briefly discuss this problem.

25

Seekers of the Russian crown

In an attempt to become a German, a Scandinavian, a Roman—anything except a Russian or Slav—Tsar Ivan Vasilievich sought a foreigner as his son-in-law. He married his brother's daughter to Magnus, the duke of Holstein, and appointed him king of Livonia (so writes Petrejus, the liar).[1] But it was a wrong thing to do. In trying to govern Livonia, Magnus angered the tsar, and then fled to Poland.

Under Tsar Feodor Ivanovich, concern developed in Moscow over the policies of King Stefan[2] and over the fact that Tsar Feodor turned out to possess a weak mind and was incapable of governing. The burden which Tsar Ivan inflicted pressed heavily on the people. Some, indeed, decided to invite to the throne a certain Austrian prince, or relative of the German emperors, who might ease their oppression, and a German was dispatched to discuss this matter with the emperor.[3] But where man failed to find a solution, God found one. Kind Stefan died, the Muscovites got rid of their fear, and Boris Feodorovich Godunov was entrusted with the affairs of the tsardom.

In 1599, Tsar Boris Feodorovich invited Gustav Erikovich, the son of the king of Sweden, to come to Moscow, hoping to marry him to his daughter Xenia, provided he would agree to convert to the Orthodox faith.[4] He came, but refused to be converted as he had promised. He

---

[1] A brother of the Danish king Frederick II, Magnus married Maria Vladimirovna, a relative of Ivan IV, in 1573, and was proclaimed king of Livonia. In 1578 he deserted to Sweden and fought against Russia.

[2] Stefan Bathory (1533–86), king of Poland (1576–86), defeated Ivan IV's attempt to gain access to the Baltic Sea for Russia.

[3] Krizhanich based this on a rumor that circulated in Poland in 1584–85 to the effect that a Russian delegation had gone to see Emperor Rudolph II seeking approval for the candidacy of his brother Maximilian.

[4] The son of the Swedish king Eric XIV, Gustavus was exiled from Sweden and lived in Italy. In 1599, Tsar Boris Godunov (r. 1598–1605) invited him to Russia to marry his daughter Xenia, but the marriage did not take place because Gustavus refused to convert to Orthodox Christianity.

insisted on leaving and threatened to set Moscow on fire. On that score, Gustav was exiled to the principality of Uglich, and he died in Russia. In 1602 Tsar Boris invited prince Johann, the brother of the Danish king, to come to Moscow in an effort to make him his son-in-law. But, with God's help, this threat and danger to the people was quickly removed. The groom lived in Moscow less than six weeks and died before the wedding in 1602.

In 1605, bandit Grigorii the monk came to Moscow, and for eleven months disgraced the Russian crown and tsardom. He was eagerly assisted by foreigners and by the offspring of foreign converts, such as Peter Feodorovich Basmanov and others.[5]

In 1610, after the ill-fated Klushino disaster, foreign allies deserted Russian armies to their enemies and exposed the tsardom to ruin. After they had conspired with the enemy, three rebels incited the people to overthrow Tsar Vasilii Ivanovich Shuiskii, and replace him with the Swede, Wladislaw, heir to the Polish throne. There again, God saved our people from foreign domination that we ourselves foolishly tried to establish. Sigismund, Wladislaw's father, delayed his son's departure from Poland to claim the tsardom, and those who were deeply concerned with the national honor utilized this time to elect the noblest and the most illustrious Tsar Michael Feodorovich Romanov of blessed memory.[6]

In 1611, after he reached an agreement with the Novgorodians, Vasilii I. Buturlin informed the Swedish military commander that the *boyars* and other Russian classes wanted Carl Philip, heir to the Swedish throne [son of Charles IX], as their tsar. In 1613 Philip came to the border, hoping to become the tsar. However, God in his infinite mercy again turned away misfortune. He opened the eyes of the Russian princes, and they would not succumb to the cunning of this seeker, or place upon their necks the shameful yoke of foreign domination.

In 1644 Count Volmar Christianovich, an illegitimate son of the king of Denmark, arrived in Moscow. He had neither princely nor royal title at home, or among the Germans, and was simply known as "Count

---

[5] Krizhanich is mistaken in identifying Basmanov as a foreigner: the son of Feodor Basmanov, one of the principal henchmen of Ivan the Terrible, Peter Basmanov was a *voevoda* (military commander) under Boris Godunov, but deserted Godunov for False Dmitrii, whom Krizhanich describes as "bandit Grigorii the monk."

[6] In 1610, a group of Russian *boyars* chose Wladyslaw, son of the Polish king Sigismund III (1587–1632), as tsar. Sigismund's failure to approve the arrangement caused many problems, including a brief Polish occupation of the Kremlin, which incited Russian patriotic feeling and led to the election of Michael Romanov (1613–45) as the new tsar. Wladyslaw subsequently succeeded his father as king of Poland (1632–48).

Volmar." This count almost succeeded in his schemes, but God again revealed his mercy and turned Volmar's schemes into dust. Still, when he left Russia in 1645, he took with him 100,000 rubles in gold and 50,000 furs.[7]

In 1660, at a propitious time, Nikolai Davidovich, heir to the Georgian throne, left Moscow.[8]

In addition to all of these, the English princess of Chestershire was brought to Russia. I do not know which grand prince was interested in her, but she died before the marriage.[9]

These then were the number of foreign aspirants to the Russian tsardom and princely throne during such a short period of time.

Our people have been assigned a fatal destiny (as punishment for our sins) to bear eternal disgrace. For, if the fable about the Varangians is true, for over 1,000 years—or since the time of Gostomysl—the Russian land has not had more than four rulers from among its own people: Tsar Boris Feodorovich Godunov, Tsar Vasilii Ivanovich Shuiskii, Tsar Michael Feodorovich Romanov, and our present noble sovereign, Tsar Alexei Mikhailovich. And even during the rule of our own tsars, the danger of foreign domination has kept increasing substantially.

For the past 300 years, the Poles have had thirteen kings and all of them have been foreigners. Some of them, in fact, were begged to accept the throne, especially Kasimir Jagello.[10] According to the liar Petrejus, the Russians also once pleaded tearfully with the Varangians so that the latter would allow three of their princes to come and govern Russia.

---

[7] Volmar (or Waldemar), illegitimate son of Christian IV of Denmark, came to Moscow in 1643 to marry Irina Mikhailovna, the daughter of Tsar Michael, but the marriage did not take place as he refused to covert to the Orthodox church. He left Moscow in 1645.

[8] Nikolai, a nephew of the Georgian king Teimuraz, lived in Moscow from 1653 until 1660, and Krizhanich may have met him before being exiled to Siberia.

[9] There was no princess of Chestershire. Krizhanich doubtless had in mind a projected marriage between Ivan the Terrible and Mary Hastings, a relative of Elizabeth I. The English never seriously considered the arrangement, and for the sake of politeness intimated in 1583 that Mary was in poor health. See Iurii Tolstoy, ed., *Pervyia sorok let snoshenii mezhdu Rossieiu i Anglieiu, 1555–93* (St Petersburg, 1875).

[10] Krizhanich exaggerates. Jagello was a Lithuanian, but all his reigning descendants until 1572 were Polish born. The same was true of the descendants of Sigismund III, Wladyslaw IV (r. 1632–48) and Jan Casimir (r. 1648–68).

26

Foreign domination

All nations despise foreign domination. We the Slavs, are the only ones who do not share this feeling. The Poles have been called pigs and dogs by some of their queens—their names were Riksa and Christina. According to a story I heard from a well-informed German, when the present king Casimir Sigismundovich was returning from France and reached Gdansk, the Poles met him, but he responded in anger: "I treasure a German dog more than ten Polish nobles." And when the Tartars captured the Germans—who are Polish enemies—the queen ransomed many Germans, but not Poles. There is nothing to add to this. If one were to list all the insults the Poles alone have suffered from foreign rulers, an enormous book would result. It would take more than a year, more than a hundred tongues to describe all the misfortunes that result from foreign domination.

In antiquity the practice of trading of kingdoms by marriage, conspiracy, or open invitation did not exist. This evil practice has appeared only in modern times and was begun by Germans. The Germans were the first to dare secretly, and then openly, to seek the royal thrones of the Romans, Hungarians, Czechs, and Poles. Through marriage alliances they also seized the Spanish throne.

No nation has been so ignorant as to accept the yoke of foreign domination without the use of force. What would the ancient Assyrians, Chaldeans, Persians, or Greeks have said if some foreigner had expressed an interest in their thrones? They would have plugged their ears and quickly killed the seeker. The Germans have protected themselves so well that no foreigner has ever ruled them. But they have brought under their own control almost all the kingdoms of Europe, sometimes by resorting to war, sometimes by cunning. And in those places where they are not considered masters, they still dominate as hired mercenaries or by way of trade. They come in the name of every craft, inundate a country, appropriate resources from local inhabitants whom, in turn, they ridicule.

For that reason we should beware of Germans, keep them at a distance, and spurn those colonels, parasites, and worthless gluttons, who teach us how to make war, beat us insolently, despise us, and consistently call our nation a herd of pigs.

Any nation that voluntarily places its destiny in the hands of a foreign ruler is like a herd of cattle. An ox cannot herd oxen. Only humans produce their own shepherds or kings, who should stem from their own midst. Among the Poles, however, the shepherd is not a Pole but a foreigner.

It is less disgraceful to be subdued by weapons than to be persuaded. Weapons subdue only the flesh, while the heart remains free, but words subdue the heart as well. The Russians are not without blame. First, because they write uncomplimentary fables about themselves, alleging that they once invited the Varangians to their throne; second, because early in the seventeenth century they invited prince Wladislaw of Poland and prince Philip of Sweden to rule them. We do not possess the noble pride that holds it better to die than to become subject to foreign domination.

Senseless people are doubly unfortunate. First, because they run around naked and fight among themselves; second, because while everyone else discerns it, they alone cannot perceive their misery and disgrace. Our nation suffers from this kind of senselessness. Foreigners have confused us so much that we submit to them.

Jeremiah well understood the disgrace of foreign domination, when he lamented: "We were put to shame by the reproaches we heard, and our faces were covered with confusion when strangers entered the sacred courts of the Lord's house" (Jeremiah 51:51). And further: "they say in Jerusalem that enemy forces from distant lands will come" (Lamentations 4:12). And again: "Our patrimony has been turned over to strangers and our houses to foreigners" (Lamentations 5:2).

The French, too, understood this when they prepared their legal code known as the Salic Law, which requires that royal wives or daughters receive neither hereditary estates, nor hereditary rights, nor have any association with the throne. This was done to prevent those foreign kings who marry the daughters of French kings from claiming any rights to the French throne.

The Athenians also understood this when the Persian king attacked the Greeks with an enormous army and many cities submitted to his rule. A certain citizen named Kirsil then advised the Athenians to capitulate to the Persian king; the Athenians became so angered at this Kirsil and his disgraceful advice that they stoned him to death, and even that did not appease them. Athenian women stoned Kirsil's wife to death. On another occasion, when the Athenians were besieged and had reached a critical point, they resolved that whoever counseled surrender would be killed.

St Thomas Aquinas, the great theologian, says: "God has decreed that foreigners should not be set over us as sovereigns, because such sovereigns usually care little about the nation they govern."[1] The Sicilians also understood this when in 1282, at the sound of the bell ringing vespers, they murdered all the French who were in their kingdom. The Sogustinians likewise understood this when, during a Roman siege [in the course of the second Punic War], they could not defend themselves. They set their wives, children, and property on fire, and then themselves, rather than fall under the foreign yoke.

Finally, the Amazons understood it: in order not to be forced to obey husbands, they decided to live without them. They governed themselves, went to war, and allowed their husbands to come near them for only a few days a year. They sent their sons away and kept their daughters at home. If women, treasuring their honor, could not bear man's authority, alleging it to be dishonorable, what can one say about men who endure foreign domination without compulsion? Truly, they are unworthy of either a manly or a womanly name.

Paul Piasecki speaks about his fellow Poles as follows:

These people obviously have been completely deprived of their natural mental qualities and judgment and, in addition, have violated God's commandments and all the rules of politics. For one of God's commandments stipulates: "Do not appoint any foreigner as your king if he is not your brother." All political sciences declare unanimously that the customs of various nations are rarely similar; because there exists a diversity of virtues and customs, confusion results in affairs. In accordance with a general, universal law, foreigners never strive to contribute to the public welfare. They do what benefits them, put their profit in their side pocket, and are concerned only about how to turn their new kingdom into the personal property of their family and how to decrease the determination of the nation to maintain its hereditary property. If anyone wished to enumerate various arguments that prove foreign domination is dangerous and harmful to every state, there would be no end to the list. For that reason, enlightened Christian nations, as well as barbarians, have kings from their own midst. Only the

[1] St Thomas Aquinas, *Summa theologica,* I, chapter 2, 105, 1 and 2.

Poles, contrary to the human inclination toward individuals of one's own blood and the general trend prevailing among nations, not only accept foreigners on their throne, but offer this honor indiscriminately, so that once even Tartar ambassadors seeking that throne for their sovereign were received and heard by the *sejm* [Diet].[2]

In conclusion, we say that it is better to have the worst of the native candidates on the throne than the best foreigner. It is better to have a vicious native tyrant than some sweet David among foreigners. For it is improbable that a fellow national, even if he were to be a bandit or a murderer, would abandon his affection for his own people. It is equally improbable that a foreigner would love his subjects more than he does his own nation.

In concluding this discussion, I wish to tell you, Boris, about a meeting between our Russian people and the Poles. As is customary at negotiations and frontier meetings the Poles praised their licentious freedom and belittled us and our state. During this conversation, a certain Pole tried to convince everyone that their nobles were worthier than ours because they were free. Our Russian responded: "My friend, on the contrary, we are more noble than you, because should our tsar expire, any suitable man from among our *boyars* can become our leader, while none of you can do the same." Then the Pole responded: "Every one of our noblemen considers himself qualified for the throne and therefore no one wants to yield his place to another. Also, everyone thinks that it is undignified to become a subject of his own brother. Because of this rivalry, foreigners acquire our throne." To which the Russian replied: "Forgive me for saying so, but in my view you resemble pigs gathered around a trough full of forage. Each pig tries to push all others away from the trough with his snout so that he can have it for himself. Thus they fight until they turn over the trough and lose the lot. Similarly, because of vain rivalry, you upset national authority. You don't see your own disgrace. You say that every one of you is worthy of the throne, yet you do not want to bow to any of your kinsmen. Instead you bow to foreigners. Thus you reveal your own lies, and in essence, confirm that none of you is worthy of the throne."

But another Pole, who was a bit older and wiser, added: "It is not true that every one of our noblemen considers himself worthy of the throne. If

---

[2] Paul Piasecki (1583–1649), a Roman Catholic bishop and a historian, wrote a detailed account of contemporary events in Poland and in Europe entitled *Chronica questorum in Europa singularium* (Cracow, 1648).

this were so, it would be stupidity in the extreme. During elections a great deal is required to be worthy of the throne. It is also untrue that our people believe that nobody from their midst is worthy of the throne. It would be easy for them to bow to one of their own countrymen if he were elected king, because they are already bowing to less worthy foreigners— to open enemies and offenders. Earlier, when we were ruled by native kings, they were highly esteemed by their subjects, much more than are the current foreign kings. The real cause of our misfortune lies in the fact that for the past three hundred years we have not found among our people any individual who considered himself worthy of the throne. Examine all the royal elections and you will discover that there were never any individuals from among us who sought our honor. People are often so affected by bad precedent that there is a change in their very nature. Prior to Jagello the Lithuanian, our people aspired to the royal throne and they ruled excellently. Thereafter our national sense of honor died and was forgotten."

To this must be added another cause—namely, greed. The authorities offer the honor of our nation for sale to the highest bidder, like a prostitute, and transform the royal throne into a place of ill repute. The poet Virgil commented of such a merchant: "He sells his fatherland for money and imposes on it a mighty master." It is clear to everyone that foreign-born kings bring with them the causes of new and unnecessary wars. Thus, for example, Sigismund [III] forced upon the Poles a prolonged war with Sweden. The same thing is done by foreign-born fiancés and foreign-born queens. But what is the most disgraceful of all is that the custom of foreign domination has become a habit with the Poles, who no longer even notice their degradation.

27

The disgrace foreigners inflict
upon the Slavs

It would be best if we guileless Slavs were to have nothing to do with foreigners, knowing how much harm they can cause us. But this is impossible, because as long as we live in the world, we must live with people. Therefore we must decide how to live in peace with them and carry on trade, while still protecting ourselves from the injuries they usually cause us.

Our land is one of the poorest because nothing is produced here except grain, fish, and meat. Moreover, since we have been unable to develop any knowledge of value, we must learn all sciences from foreigners and acquire samples of all kinds of goods from them. In addition, we have been compelled up to now, and must continue voluntarily, to learn not only piety and Christian faith but correct behavior from other nations. Consequently, since we cannot live without having contact with foreigners, we should recall the precept: "Whoever distinguishes the true good conducts himself well." Thus we must distinguish good from evil; that is, accept from foreigners the good (the true and not the artificial good) they offer. We should seek it out.

Foreigners bring us four benefits: piety, numerous goods, paths of scholarship, and various forms of political arrangements.

Yet we should know that the bulk of their wealth is not real, but artificial. Neither do they do good deeds *gratis,* but seek to sell all of this at a substantial profit. Even this does not fully satisfy them, for they always try to add some harm to everything they sell us.

Using piety, some foreigners teach us useful things, and do not seek our wealth. Profit-seeking foreigners, however, roam needlessly across our countries, perpetrate many transgressions against the Holy Commandments and violate church rules. They turn every holy shrine into a commodity, and try to sell Christ many times over—whereas even Judas sold Him only once. For money, they appoint vagrants as soldiers and pig tenders as priests, people whom our bishops in Belorussia would not consecrate. For money, they annul marriages, allowing the husband to divorce sometimes as many as five or six wives by sending them to a nunnery. For money, they absolve people's sins without confession or penance and sell indulgences. Although they are not bishops they pretend that they are and consecrate priests. Eastern pastors practice such things in Russia.[1]

For money, Western or Roman pastors among the Poles falsely curtail or expand the authority of our bishops, and for money they appoint them. For money, they used to proclaim "jubilees" or years of grace for entire countries, but they did not abolish confessions. Instead, whoever wished to receive forgiveness confessed his sins and offered money which was then forwarded to Rome. Out of this practice developed the Lutheran and Calvinist heresy and as a result this sort of offering does not exist anymore.

Under the pretext of trade, foreigners bring us to the brink of poverty. Germans, Scotsmen, Armenians, and Jews have seized all the wealth that exists in Poland. They live there in idleness, nourish their bellies, and enjoy all sorts of luxuries, while they impose on the native inhabitants additional agricultural work and engender family disputes, court difficulties, and even warfare. Here in Russia one does not hear about any wealth (outside of the tsar's treasury). Poverty and misery prevails everywhere. Foreign merchants or thieves consume the fruits of this land before our very eyes.

Under a disguise of crafts and services they also siphon off our wealth by working as doctors, exploiting the mines, manufacturing glass, weapons, gunpowder, and the like. Yet they never try to teach these crafts to our kinsmen. Others receive enormous largess and promise to teach us military skill. But they teach us in a way that keeps them as teachers forever and our people cannot ever reach the level of the teachers. Some even hint that they have important secret information, unknown in Russia. But if they did not reveal anything new during the long Russo-Polish War, it follows that we should not believe they are hiding anything. Moreover, they teach us some military skills that are not only useless but even harmful to us.

According to Aristotle, whenever foreigners are allowed to come into a

[1] It is possible that attacks such as this on the Eastern (i.e. Greek) clergy, first made while Krizhanich was in Moscow—at a time when the Russian church was headed by the Patriarch Nikon and sought close ecumenical cooperation with the Greeks—were responsible for his exile to Siberia. This has been suggested by several authors. See S.A. Belokurov, *Iu. Krizhanich v Rossii. Iz dukhovnoi zhizni moskovskogo obshchestva XVII v* (Moscow, 1902), 21–30, 97–104.

country with their armies as allies, they end by subjugating those whom they have come to aid; the Turks have done this to the Greeks and the German Crusaders to the Poles.[2] Whenever we have triumphed over foreigners with our army, they have immediately conquered us with words. De Commines tells us how during one negotiation a certain Englishman said to the French, "When you Frenchmen meet us on the battlefield, we always defeat you, but when we enter into negotiations with you, we always emerge defeated." Likewise, earlier the Greeks and now the Germans invariably drag us into long discussions and during these dialogues confuse us into concluding disadvantageous agreements with them. This happened in the last two agreements made between this tsardom and Sweden.[3] Consequently, we should not wage war with these more developed nations. For, if we take anyone prisoner, they will in turn imprison us in our own home by means of their beauty, eloquence, and graciousness. For beauty is a silent eloquence which is capable of transcending even the intellect. This is how the Jews, with the help of Esther, once dealt with Emperor Artaxerxes [Ahasuerus], and with the help of another Esther, mistress of Casimir Jagellonian, dealt with the Poles.[4] Blinded by her beauty, he granted extensive privileges to the Jews, who migrated to Poland in large numbers. The Germans and the Greeks have achieved even more with the help of handsome, knowledgeable, eloquent men. There are many examples of this in the Polish chronicles. Whenever they have their own reasons for a war with the Turks, they always pretend to wage it on behalf of the Christian faith, and they drag us into their alliances in order to place the burden of that war on us.

The Venetians are particularly cunning in these matters. Once they deceived the king of Spain and the Pope, who had persuaded them to become their allies, but as soon as the Venetians achieved a major triumph over the Turks they immediately abandoned the alliance, concluded peace with the Turks, and turned Turkish forces against the Spaniards. The Venetians also persuaded King Wladislaw to join them in an alliance against the Tartars. This resulted in the devastation of the Polish and

---

[2] Here Krizhanich refers to the invitation Prince Konrad of Mazowsze extended to the Teutonic Knights in 1226 to help him pacify the pagan Prussians. The Teutonic Knights rendered the assistance, but also established a foothold in the region, subsequently known as East Prussia, and became a menace to Poland. This episode was brilliantly described by Henryk Sienkiewicz in his historical noval *Krzyżacy* (1900).

[3] Here Krizhanich refers to the treaty of Stolbovo of 1617 and the treaty of Kardis of 1661.

[4] See below, p. 152.

Russian countryside in 1651. The same Venetians, using their cunning tales, persuaded the great sovereign to send his ambassadors to them.[5] They exploited this to their own advantage by spreading a rumor that the great sovereign had concluded an alliance with them against the Crimean Tartars; this angered the Crimeans against the tsardom, and the Turkish sultan ordered them not to seek peace and to fight against Russia.

The Germans deceived us and made a mockery of peace when they reached an agreement with us stipulating that Russian merchants could maintain their commercial establishments among the Swedes and Germans if the Germans were allowed to maintain their agents, good, and dwellings in Russia. Since our people do not have large sea vessels they cannot sail the seas, and therefore will never be able to establish their own enterprises among the Germans. Besides, it is disadvantageous for them to travel there. Those few who have done so, returned home with losses. Hence it is both silly and foolish for us to enter into such an agreement. Whatever we do out of friendship, humanity, and respect, they consider a joke. They maintain permanent ambassadors called "residents" or *sugerere* here, while others are called "consuls" or overseers of trade. They are all simply traitors, mockers, and enemies sustained in our homeland. Some of the merchants, interpreters or translators, soldiers and other foreigners—converts and non-converts—who live on salaries from the great sovereign are hired spies of foreign kings. Some we could identify by name.

Foreign kings insult and humiliate us in many ways.

(1) Some act cunningly and are elected to the Russian throne; then, when they are summoned, they decline to come, as happened in the case of prince Wladislaw.[6]

(2) Henry of Anjou served as king of Poland for a brief period, but was then invited to ascend the French throne and secretly fled, causing the Poles much embarrassment.[7]

---

[5] Here Krizhanich refers to the alliance of king Wladislaw of Poland with the Venetians in 1646–47 and to the ambassadors sent by Tsar Alexei Mikhailovich in 1657, when the Russian envoys I. Chemodanov and A. Postnikov visited Venice to discuss the possibility of an anti-Turkish alliance. Evidence suggests that Krizhanich met and talked with some members of this embassy. See S.A. Belokurov, *Iu. Krizhanich*, 71.

[6] A reference to prince Wladislaw of Poland, son of King Sigismund III, whose personal ambition upset Wladislaw's election to the Muscovite throne in 1610.

[7] In 1573 Henry of Anjou, brother of the French king Charles IX, was elected king of Poland. Upon his brother's death, he left Poland to become Henry III of France.

(3) Others, using money, attract followers and spread discord among the Polish nobles and whenever any minority illegally declares them to be their king they come with weapons to gain control of the throne, as did Maximilian of Austria.[8]

(4) Queen Christine not only stole the crown and funds from the treasury, but kidnapped the heir to the Polish throne. Elizabeth also stole the crown from the Hungarians.[9]

(5) Louis [king of Hungary from 1342 and of Poland from 1370] appointed a Polish Parliament in Buda, the Hungarian capital.

(6) Wladyslaw, the Jagellonian, squandered the Polish treasury for Hungarian needs.

(7) The Swedish King Sigismund and his sons involved Poland in prolonged wars with Sweden.

(8) Under King Stefan Bathory only the Hungarians were accorded any honor. The Poles were not appointed to office and one Polish official named Melecki resigned because he was unwilling to put up with Hungarian insolence.

(9) The insults to the Poles by the Jagellonians could fill a book. Foreign rulers always interfere in our affairs and appoint themselves as our mediators, arbitrators, and conciliators. They create an impression that they wish to arrange reconciliations but they never consider our own conciliatory efforts. On the contrary, they sow personal discord among us, search after our secrets and discover means to achieve their own designs.

Whenever the ruler of one of the great nations becomes king among us, foreign princes, nobles, councilors, military officers, and other court officials immediately appear. These kings do not allow any Pole or a Russian to get close to them.

The Poles and Hungarians, having once sensed this, adopted laws prohibiting foreigners from purchasing immovable property or hereditary estates in Poland and Hungary, and laws providing that no foreigner

[8] Between 1573 and 1575 Maximilian II, the Holy Roman Emperor (1527–1576), expressed an interest in the throne of Poland; he was elected by the Polish Senate to succeed Henry of Anjou (Stefan Bathory being elected by the Diet) and died in 1576 while preparing to invade the country.
[9] This passage refers to Queen Christine of Poland (d. 1163) and to Elizabeth of Hungary, who seized the crown in 1439–40.

could become a prince, noble, or official. But these laws accomplished nothing: because if the king wished to grant hereditary estates to foreigners he merely insisted that they be granted citizenship.

Here in Russia, heretics, exiles, and traitors pretend that they would like to become converts and are baptized in order to acquire hereditary estates and large salaries. German military leaders who have inundated Russia have benefited our nation only in one small respect: they have shown our infantrymen how to fire handguns and how to carry long lances. But our warriors could easily have learned this without them. The Germans are really performing an injustice when they organize our forces according to their ways. What we need is light cavalry and hussars.

We want our soldiers to be brave and experienced in military matters but instead they lose the eagerness they previously had because they are deprived of all hope of promotion. They acquire useless knowledge while forgetting the old, tested weapon system and the Russian art of war.

Through influx there and settlement among us, the Germans have pushed us out of entire regions: Moravia, Pomerania, Silesia, and Prussia. In the Bohemian towns there are now very few Slavs. All Polish towns are now full of Germans, Gypsies, Scotsmen, Jews, Armenians, and Italians. In their own homeland, the Poles beg mercy from their guests and perish before their eyes from hunger and shame. And what is happening here in Russia? Foreign merchants, Germans, Greeks, and Bokharans, rake up all the wealth and revenues of this realm.

In troubled times, foreigners remove their goods and money from the country. Those who can also leave. They reveal our secrets, commit treason, and join the enemy. Whenever these merchants and craftsmen settle in any town and increase to the point where they become sufficiently strong, they drive our people away, fortify the town, and become the sole masters. They have done so in Danzig, Torun, Riga, and in some Russian towns, while the Saxons have gained in Hungary, in all of Bohemia, and in Pomerania. And, particularly, wherever there are suitable places for trade, such as harbors, the Germans have taken them away from us. They have driven us away from the sea and large navigable rivers on to the prairie. [10]

[10] According to M.N. Tikhomirov, Krizhanich deleted two paragraphs. Their content is as follows. Whenever foreigners gain control of any town or small territory, they immediately call themselves Slavic kings in order for it to appear that they are kings of the entire Slavic people. Thus, Hungarian kings in former times, and German emperors at the present time, call themselves kings of Dalmatia, Croatia, and Slovenia and use three different coats of arms that they themselves have designed. Similarly the Venetians, because they control four or five of our seaports, call themselves "sovereigns of the Slavic land." Likewise those Jagellonians call themselves kings of Poland.

These foreign buyers, residents, consuls, merchants, colonels, ore experts, doctors, jewelers, craftsmen, bellmakers, and other artisans entice us with their luxuries. They also teach us their vices and sins, such as sodomy. They teach us heresy, and little by little they infect us with disbelief. They transform our laws, violate our wonderful church rules, and deprive us of all piety. And now, under the pretext of holiness, they bring us superstition and erroneous sanctity, and in a pharisaical manner impose unbearable burdens on us.

Today they entice us with vain academic titles, high institutions of learning, privileges for local scholars and elevation to the rank of doctor (or teacher). This interferes with the learning process, with the result that the country now abounds in useless clerks or scribes. Many, taken in while young, do not wish to study useful crafts and instead seek to become scribes, with the result that they are incapable of making a livelihood for themselves.

These learned masters teach us only grammar, while hiding useful disciplines from us. I cannot make any comments on other branches of learning, because I do not know of any doctor, mathematician, musician, or architect who has emerged from our people. Others take enormous sums of money from us to teach us how to dance (which has absolutely no usefulness) and boasters receive money for fireworks displays and promise that they will bring us great benefit, but in our time not one town has been captured nor one country conquered with the aid of these wonder bombs and fires.

Finally, others bring us the cursed devilish crafts: astrology, alchemy, magic, and cabala, which contain nothing but witchcraft.

CONCLUSION

It is incredible that the uncontrollable love of foreign things has made so many of our rulers behave foolishly. All our Slavic kings, princes, and sovereigns have stumbled over this rock, yet not every one to the same degree. The Polish King Casimir the Great distinguished himself by inundating Poland with Jews and Germans, while among the Russians

---

Our name, "Slav," is translated into German as "Wennish" or *Wennen*. In their language this means racing dogs. On the coat of arms of their mythical "Slavic kingdom," German emperors portray three animals, but no one knows which ones. To ignorant Slavs, they say that these are three martens, but they themselves do not consider them martens but dogs—to conform, as I have already noted, to the meaning of the term *wennen*.

Ivan Vasilevich and Tsar Boris Feodorovich Godunov and above all the pretender Dmitrii performed the same service.

Thus as Delilah conquèred and subdued Samson, so the neighboring nations, if they are not conquered by our weapons, will conquer us by their beauty, intellect, eloquence, deceitful talk, and comic plays. It would have been better if Samson had run away from the Philistines than to have been their conqueror or sovereign. The same holds for our people. It would be more beneficial not to know foreigners than to triumph over them and occupy their homes because, thanks to their eloquence and cunning, the vanquished soon govern the victor.

The most astonishing and worst of all is the fact that even our wise teachers have been influenced by this deception: even our sage Starowolski suggested that the Poles should invite the Germans to come to our land to build forts against the Crimeans and to settle there.

We have been victims of the same experience as the Jews. The Jewish language was rough, squeaky, and undignified. Their music was also simple and rough. The idol-worshiping Greeks had a beautiful and eloquent language. Their good-natured humor, their music, and various ingenious, wonderful dances transcended those of the Jews in their beauty. As a result, the Jews were deceived and became entirely captivated by these Greek dances, ceremonies, and flattery, and in the end they become infected by their idol worship.

This applies to us. Our language is the most undeveloped and least articulate. Our intellect is weak and we command no eloquence. We resemble birds who follow the footsteps of a hunter and become an easy prey. For this reason, it would be good to close our eyes to their beauty and to plug our ears to their talk, in order to save ourselves as Ulysses saved himself from the Sirens.

28

The harmful effects of royal marriages with foreigners

We would like to describe briefly how marriages with foreign rulers have always been a cause of great disaster for a nation. Using this device, the Lithuanian Jagello bypassed and conquered the Poles, while Hungarian kings did the same to the Croats, and Germans to the Czechs. For the same purpose the Swedes, the Danes, and other suitors have approached the Russian throne.

Out of a hundred intermarriages there are perhaps one or two that do not in time cause some war or bring some other misfortune on a nation. Philip the Fair of France, who died about 1315, had three sons and a daughter named Isabella. After their father's death, all the sons ruled in succession one after another and died without leaving a male heir. Isabella married Edward II of England and gave birth to a son who later became King Edward III.

As Philip's grandson, Edward had pretensions to the French throne as his grandfather's inheritance. But French authorities rejected his claims, arguing that their crown was not inherited by the female line but in accordance with their own law. They bypassed Edward and the daughters of Philip's three sons and selected as their king [Philip of] Valois, a nephew of Philip [the Fair], that is, his brother's son. Edward therefore declared war on France. He and his successors fought so fiercely that Paris and a large portion of the French kingdom were captured and held by the English for many years, until they were driven out by King Charles VII. Still from that time on, English kings have considered France as their patrimony and call themselves kings of France—even though it all happened 300 years ago. This is the kind of disgrace and indescribable bloodshed that the French suffered because of a foreign marriage.[1]

---

[1] Krizhanich based his account of the events leading to the Hundred Years War between England and France (1337–1458) on a *postcriptum* to Philipp de Commines's *Duo gallicarum rerum scriptores* . . . (Frankfurt, 1545).

And how many crises have occurred in Europe resulting from marriages with the Austrian dynasty [the Hapsburgs] (whose members now vainly call themselves Roman Emperors)? Anyone desiring to recount all the crises, wars, deceptions, misfortunes, disgraces, and ruins brought on by these Austrian marriages to Germany, Hungary, Bohemia, Italy, Spain, England, and France could fill not just one but ten books. A certain flatterer once wrote as follows on the subject: "Let others fight to gain a throne; you, Austrian dynasty, intermarry and thus acquire other thrones."

Now let us cite a few examples of what happened among the Poles.[2]

(1) The Polish king Popel had a German wife named Blanka. This Blanka seized power, poisoning Popel's uncles and the leading nobles. But the corpses gave birth to mice, who devoured Popel and his wife.

(2) The German emperor Arnulf was married to the sister of king Sviatopolk of Moravia who was the first of their kings to be baptized.[3] Arnulf then invited and incited the Hungarians against his relative Sviatopolk, and they killed him. This German Arnulf proved the truthfulness of the German saying: "You have as many wolves as you have relatives."

(3) Emperor Otto, upon arriving in Poland as a guest of Boleslaw the Brave, offered his niece Riksa in marriage to Boleslaw's son Mieczyslaw.[4] When Mieczyslaw assumed power his wife was so greedy, insolent, and bold that he ruled his kingdom in accordance with her decrees. The Moravians and other Slavic princes who lived beyond the Oder River refused to obey, appropriated royal revenues for themselves, entered into friendly relations and intermarriage with the Germans, and finally openly courted treason, submitting themselves to the German emperor.

After Mieczyslaw's death Riksa began to rule even more sternly than before and succeeded in postponing the coronation of Kasimir, the young royal heir. During this time she came up daily with new methods of getting money. She constantly humiliated the Poles and appointed her Germans to responsible posts. Finally, after she had accumulated immense wealth, Riksa fled to Germany and took with her the royal heir, the

---

[2] Here Krizhanich's comments on events in Poland are based on a volume by Martin Cromer, *De origine et rebus gestis polonorum* (Basel, 1555).

[3] Emperor Arnulf ruled from 887 until 889, and Sviatopolk was king of Moravia from 870 until 894.

[4] Reference is to Emperor Otto III (983–1002), the Polish king Boleslaw the Brave (992–1025), and Boleslaw's son Mieczyslaw II, who succeeded to the throne in 1025 and died in 1034.

entire treasury, and both crowns: the kings and the queen's. Then she persuaded the German emperor Conrad [II] to send an army to ruin Poland.

(4) When king Boleslaw Krzywousty triumphed over emperor Henry, the latter, thanks to his cunning, succeeded in getting Boleslaw, the victor, to come to the tent of Henry, the loser, to seek peace.[5] The emperor made it known to Boleslaw that he offered his sister and daughter in marriage. Boleslaw allowed himself to be deceived and wed Henry's sister Adelheide, while he married Henry's daughter Christine to his son Wladyslaw. He also released all prisoners of war, of whom he had an enormous multitude without ransom.

In accordance with Krzywousty's will, his four sons divided the kingdom among themselves. But Christine, the wife of the eldest son, Wladyslaw, was a greedy vicious woman. She openly considered all Poles pigs. She did not permit them even to come into her sight. She told her husband: "I am an emperor's daughter. I married you hoping to gain the entire kingdom. I now see we have only a quarter of a kingdom." Using these and similar words, this devilish witch ignited a fratricidal struggle. Wladyslaw went to war against his brothers, but they defeated him and drove him out of Poland. Emperor Conrad came with his armies to place Wladyslaw and Christine back on the throne, but he did not succeed. Subsequently the emperor Frederick advanced with the same intent, and the following agreement was reached: the widower Mieczyslaw (Wladyslaw's brother) was to marry Adelheide, the emperor's niece, and Wladyslaw was to return to the principality of Silesia. However, because of other factors, Wladyslaw did not return to the Silesian throne. He died with his Christine in exile.

Emperor Henry V went to war against King Koloman of Hungary. Frightened, Koloman sought a meeting and discussion with Boleslaw Krzywousty. After they met, the kings concluded an alliance and a marriage bargain. Koloman's son Stephan married Krzywousty's daughter Judith. As a dowry, she received the small territory of Spish [Spiska Nova Ves], including some fortified towns. From then on, that area was severed from Poland, and came under the authority of Hungary.

As the dowry of Salome, sister of Leszek the White, the Poles gave Galicia to Koloman the Hungarian. But the Russian prince Mstislav

---

[5] This passage describes the victory of king Boleslaw Krzywousty (1102–25) over the emperor Henry V (1106–25); the succession struggle that followed Boleslaw's death provoked the intervention of the emperors Conrad II (1027–39) and Frederick I, Barbarosa (1155–90).

defeated the Poles and the Hungarians, and captured Koloman and Salome. King Andrew, Koloman's father, with the aid of his ambassadors, succeeded in making a deal whereby Mstislav's daughter Mary was married to Koloman's brother Bela. Koloman was to be freed and within three years was to return Galicia to him. But in due course the Hungarian magnates forgot about Polish and Russian good deeds and sold Galicia, Vladimir, and the entire frontier region to the Lithuanians for cash.

Wladyslaw Lokietek married his daughter Elizabeth to the twice-widowed Hungarian King Charles, but without any dowry.[6] And for his son Casimir he sought a wife from the Lithuanian prince Gedymin, also without any dowry, simply on condition that Gedymin free Polish prisoners.

When Casimir married his second wife Adelheide, daughter of a Czech prince (who, however, was a German) two thousand Prague *Kop* were promised as a dowry but were never paid. This Adelheide was unattractive, and when he saw her Casimir instantly despised her and sent her back, so he could live freely with his concubines, who led him into many sins and disgraces. But most trouble was caused by a Jewess named Esther. Thanks to Esther, Casimir granted the Jews enormous privileges: they came in great numbers and infected the entire territory of Poland. Similarly Wladyslaw, son of Sigismund,[7] left his wife and began to sin with prostitutes when they brought him a bride from far away who was not as beautiful as he had expected. Oh, how much better it would have been for those kings to marry a woman from among their own people, and select her in accordance with their own wishes and thus not violate the Lord's commandments!

The emperor Charles married Elizabeth, daughter of Boguslaw, Prince of Szczecin, niece of King Casimir the Great. Casimir then [1363] prepared a sumptuous wedding in Cracow at enormous expense. Present at the wedding were: (1) Emperor Charles; (2) Louis, king of Hungary; (3) Sigismund, king of Denmark; (4) Peter, king of Cyprus; (5) Otto the Bavarian; (6) Zemovit of Mazurie; (7) Boleslaw of Svidnik; (8) Wladyslaw of Opolie; and (9) Boguslaw of Szczecin—all independent princes. The tenth was King Casimir himself. The wedding lasted twelve days. As a dowry Casimir gave the bride 100,000 rubles.

Casimir's administrator, a German named Warinck, was the instigator of the entire affair. This lecher was richer than the king himself (because

---

[6] Wladyslaw Lokietek was king of Poland from 1320 until 1333, and his son Casimir I (Casimir the Great) succeeded him and died in 1370.
[7] Sigismund king of Poland (1632–48).

his power over the kingdom was greater than that of the king over him). In an attempt to show off his wealth, acquired at the price of the blood of poor farmers, he invited all of these kings and princes to his home, entertained them, and gave each rich gifts, especially Casimir, to whom he gave presents worth more then 100,000 rubles. While these foreigners feasted, shouted, and danced in Cracow, poor Poles throughout the country suffered hunger, wept, and grieved.

Casimir, son of Wladyslaw Lokietek, on account of some distant marriage relationship appointed Louis, king of Hungary, as heir to his throne. After Louis's death, the Poles were forced to dispatch their ambassadors five times to his daughter Jadwiga before they were able to reach an agreement with her. After they had done so [in 1385], they married her off to a Lithuanian, Jagello, with the royal throne as a dowry, thus forever depriving their nation royal honors.

It is essential to recall that the Old Testament prohibited intermarriage between the various tribes of the Jewish people, and even more so among various nations. It was then stipulated that a convert could never become king. Besides, membership in the priesthood was exclusively reserved to the Levite tribe. For this reason, new converts were denied any religious or civil positions. This is clearly stated in Exodus 34:16 and in 3 Kings 11:2, which stipulate that the Jews shall neither take foreign wives nor marry their daughters to foreigners, "so that they will not divert your hearts to their gods." But because we are more inclined to worship foreign ways than the Jews were to worship paganism, we must be more alert than the Jews. Solomon, the wisest among the Jews, was greatly mistaken and forfeited his wisdom when he married the daughter of the pharaoh and other foreign women, who diverted him towards paganism (see 3 Kings 2). Vile, too, was the attitude of Solomon, who had 700 wives and 300 concubines.

Turkish sultans take as many wives as they wish and they take them from various tribes as well as faiths, both noblewomen and slaves, free and captive. Their only consideration is that the wives be beautiful, and therefore they pay no heed to honor. I do not know whether the Persians and other Mohammedan rulers subscribe to the same practice.

It is even more surprising that Artaxerxes, ancient king of Persia who though having a legal wife and granting her royal dignity nevertheless made Esther his queen because of her beauty, without knowing her background and without realizing that she was a Jewess. Such marriages are vile and differ little from common sin, because they do not occur for any reason but sexual satisfaction.

The best law existed among the Roman emperors, both the ancient heathens and, subsequently, the Christians. Each of them had only one legal wife who enjoyed royal dignity. They married neither slaves nor prisoners, nor foreigners, nor daughters of other kings or princes, but only Roman maidens. Neither did they consider beauty alone. They selected the daughters of the highest Roman aristocrats and married their daughters to the noblest and most loyal of their subjects. Their prestige thus always remained so high that nobody could transcend it.

Such loyalty prevailed throughout Europe until German rulers started to aspire to kingdoms among the Moravians, Czechs, Poles, and other Slavs. To attain their goal, they began to wed the daughters of native rulers and to marry their own daughters to the latter. The German autocracy began to weaken as princes and rulers gradually secured more rights and privileges for themselves and became less dependent on their own kings. They contracted marriages with more powerful monarchs in order to acquire more power against their kings. In time, this practice became so customary that the princes regarded it an insult if any one of them took to wife a woman who did not stem from a royal house, or if he did not marry his daughter to a king or prince.

This practice spread through France, Italy, Spain, and, finally through the medium of foreign kings, to Poland. Thanks to God's grace, however, it has not yet engulfed Russia. Our most merciful tsars do not consider it dishonorable to take daughters of their subjects' lords as their wives. Concerning the marriage of the tsar's daughters, it seems best to follow the ancient custom of the Roman emperors, and the ancient general law of Slavic peoples and of all Europe, rather than adopt the German custom, recently conceived to benefit them alone. Even if all nations saw advantages in marrying the daughters of their kings to other rulers, or keeping them single rather than marrying them to their own lords, this practice would never benefit Russians and other Slavs, for we are too easily deceived.

Emperor Augustus and other Roman and Persian emperors were in no way inferior to the Germans, yet Roman emperors sought their wives among their own nobles, not from the families of other emperors. German kings long ago lost the respect and fear of their subjects. Actually, they were never respected or feared and for that reason they have always tried to increase their authority and gain the respect of their subjects through intermarriage with neighboring rulers. But rightful kings and rulers, who by divine right possess full authority, have no reason to seek assistance from foreigners to maintain their power.

29

How foreigners besmirch the royal authority of Poland

Some idlers have invented a fable: Once upon a time the Polish prince Mieczyslaw (who was the first of these princes to be baptized) sent an ambassador to the pope asking that he grant him a crown and a royal title.[1] The pope consented and ordered the jewelers to make a crown, but while he slept an angel instructed him to give the crown not to the Pole but rather to another ambassador, who was to come to him on the morrow for the same purpose. The following day a Hungarian ambassador arrived. The Pole was therefore denied the crown, which went instead to Stephen [997–1038], prince of Hungary.

Other liars speak as follows: Once Emperor Otto III visited the Polish prince Boleslaw [the Brave]. Boleslaw entertained the emperor lavishly and gave him many gifts, and the latter proclaimed Boleslaw a "king" and "friend of the Holy Roman Empire" and released him for the payment of tribute and from all allegiance to the emperors.

German braggarts tell another story: "When he became haughty, Boleslaw the Brave appropriated royal title and refused to pay tribute to the emperor; accordingly the emperor Conrad subdued him after numerous battles. In trying to attain Boleslaw's ambition, his son Mieszko was overthrown, and in his place his brother Otto was appointed. Mieszko threw himself on the emperor's mercy and renounced his royal ambitions. He was allowed to divide the principality with his brother, and was satisfied with a princely title. Poland thus remained a tributary fief of the German emperors."

King Boleslaw [II] murdered the great miracle-worker St Stanislaw [in 1079]. Pope Gregory VII therefore imposed on the Poles an interdict taking away the royal title from Boleslaw. He instructed the bishop not to crown anyone to the throne without papal permission. As a result, for the next 215 years the royal throne was unoccupied.

---

[1] This entire chapter is based on Cromer's *De origine et rebus gestis polonorum.* Mieczyslaw ruled as Mieszko I (966–92).

A German named Mutius writes as follows:

Emperor Henry [V] and his princes assembled in Frankfurt and declared war against the Poles who refused to pay tribute and had elected and crowned a king for themselves—an act the emperor considered an affront. The emperor advanced against them with his armies. They fought several times and both sides shed much blood. Finally, the emperor won, accepted the Poles as his subjects, increased their previous tribute, and returned home.[2]

But if the German emperor is affronted by anyone who calls himself a king, then all the rulers of the world, except the Polish and Czech monarchs insult and disgrace this kind of emperor, because he has not designated any of them as such.

It is very easy to recognize German boasting whenever the Germans speak of the alleged Polish payment of tribute to their emperor. Which portion of Polish territory do they consider as the entire country and people? There never was a time when all Poles were German subjects and there is sufficient evidence to prove it. There has not been a single emperor who called himself the king of Poland. But during the civil wars among the Poles, whenever the Germans captured any portion of Polish territory, whether in Pomerania or Silesia, they boasted that they had conquered the entire territory of Poland. And whenever any petty prince paid them tribute they simply called it "Polish tribute" as if that tribute was paid by the entire Polish nation. We Slavs are also treated in the same manner by Hungarian kings, by the Lithuanian Jagellonians, and by the Venetians.

Emperor Frederick II gave the Crusaders a charter in which he granted the country of Chelm everything that they might conquer from the Prussians in the future. Yet the Germans never had any authority over these Polish territories. Prince Przemyśl II, who united the previously divided Polish state, restored to the nation the royal title which had not existed for 215 years. Prince Przemyśl was elected king in 1295 and was legally crowned. Within seven months after ascending the throne, thanks to the deception of the German princes of Brandenburg, in 1296 he was ambushed and killed during a hunt.

For unknown reasons, Przemyśl's successor Wladyslaw Lokietek did not wish to be crowned, or to be even referred to as king. During the twenty years of his rule he called himself the "inheritor of the Polish kingdom." Nevertheless, in 1320 the Poles sent ambassadors to Pope

[2] H. Mutius, *De Germanorum primi origine* . . . (Basel, 1539).

John XXII to request a royal title for Lokietek because they thought that Przemyśl ill-advisedly appropriated the title without papal consent. The Pope did not wish to grant a royal title to Wladyslaw openly, which would have offended John, king of the Czechs (who appropriated the title of Polish king for himself), and his father-in-law, Phillip [VI], the French king.

The pope therefore informed the embassadors secretly of his consent, stating that he did not wish to interfere with the Poles in the exercise of their rights. Wladyslaw Lokietek was thus crowned king of Poland.

Sigismund of Hungary, a German, sought to secure the vacant and at this time vain, title of emperor of the Holy Roman Empire. To appease the German princes, his electors, he violated a previous oath and by adopting many cunning devices, assisted the German crusaders in fighting the Poles. He conceived a clever plan designed to alienate Vitold, prince of Lithuania, and his brother Jagello, the king of Poland, eventually setting the Poles against both of them. He dispatched a courier to Jagello requesting a meeting and negotiations.[3]

The kings came to two nearby border towns: Jagello to Sudec and Sigismund to Kesmar. Jagello sent his brother Vitold to Sigismund. Along with other more open discussions, Sigismund held a secret talk with Vitold, whom he promised to appoint to the kingship of Lithuania should he become the German emperor.

In 1429, after Sigismund was chosen as emperor (but not yet crowned), he renewed his scheming and again proposed to start negotiations. These were to be held in Lutsk. There Sigismund reached an agreement with Vitold, now aged eighty, to whom he offered a royal crown. King Jagello, deceived by flattering words, failed to perceive the approaching danger and consented to this arrangement.

However, Zbigniew, the bishop of Cracow, strongly reproached Vitold and in a major address showed how his opportunistic ambition would be detrimental to the Lithuanian and Polish nations. "Prince, please be aware how poisonous this offer is which you are about to accept from the emperor, the common and eternal enemy of both of our nations," he pleaded. He also expressed many other strong sentiments and immediately thereafter all advisors counselled Vitold to abandon his plan.

Later, however, at the *sejm* [legislative assembly] in Korczyn,[4]

---

[3] This passage refers to the dealings of Sigismund of Hungary (1387–1433) with Vitold of Lithuania (1384–1430) and Jagello of Poland (1386–1434).

[4] *Sejm*: the Polish term for the Polish parliament as a whole, which in Krizhanich's time had two chambers: the Senate, consisting of the wealthiest and most influential nobles and leading churchmen, and the *sejm*—the lower chamber, or Diet—made up of lesser nobles and townsmen.

Vitold's ambassadors, unable to gain any concession from the Poles, declared: "Whether you like it or not, Vitold will be king." And, in fact, through his couriers, Vitold did continue to ask the emperor to fulfill his promises. After they had detained several such couriers, the Poles assembled in a *sejm* in Sandomierz, and sent their ambassadors to Vitold with the following offer: If they were unable to persuade Vitold to abandon his intentions, they would offer him the throne of Poland, since King Jagello was agreeable to abdicating his authority to his older and childless brother, after which it would probably revert to his sons. To this Vitold responded as follows: "I do not wish to be so shameless and despicable a person as to deprive my brother Jagello of his throne."

[Vitold] was so determined to commit treason against his brother and the Poles, however that he made all Lithuanians take a new oath of allegiance, and designated August 17, 1430, as his coronation day. Meanwhile, the emperor Sigismund did not lose any time. He bragged to his friends, "I have thrown a bone to two dogs, and it looks as though they will devour each other over it."

The Poles intercepted two of Sigismund's couriers with letters to Vitold. In his letters the emperor implored Vitold to cast off all doubts about his intentions, but Vitold did doubt whether the emperor had any right—inasmuch as he was declared, but not yet crowned—to create new kingdoms and appoint kings, as Sigismund was intending. These couriers carried the imperial letters by virtue of which Vitold was designated king of Lithuania. The emperor promised to send the crown with other ambassadors at an appropriate time.

Then came the news that a splendid embassy carrying the crown was on its way. As a result, without instigation, the nobles of Greater Poland, as though hearing a danger signal, armed themselves and went as far as they could into the forests, seizing control of all the roads, so that the imperial ambassadors, upon reaching Frankfurt on the Oder did not dare to proceed and turned back. With great disappointment Vitold dismissed the ambassadors from Moscow, Tver, and Odoevsk, as well as those of the Tartar khans and two Teutonic crusading chiefs whom he had invited to his coronation. Shortly thereafter he died.

I thought that this problem should be discussed here at some length (even though much pertinent information concerning this matter has been omitted) in order to be able to convey the devilish malice and cunning the Germans have used to dishonor our people.

The real truth centers in the fact that God alone, and neither emperor nor pope, established the legal foundations of the Polish kingdom. For if emperors can create kingdoms, they can also destroy them at will. After the fictitious creation of the Polish kingdom by emperor Otto, the pope and two emperors withheld the royal title from the Poles. At the final reaffirmation of the Polish kingdom, Lokietek requested the title from the pope, not the emperor. The pope granted it to him saying: "I do not deny the Poles the use of their authority." With these words, the pope acknowledged that every nation has the right, without papal or imperial authorization, to select a king for itself. This creation, in which neither the pope nor the emperor took any part, was—and remained—strong.

Nevertheless (deceived by such Polish chroniclers as Cromer, who was a German by birth) the Poles continue to trace their royal dignity to alien, illegal, and simply erroneous source. Even if this source were the true one, it would be advantageous to hide or modify the fact. Yet they continue to praise and glorify this insult to them as if it gave them honor.

30

Foreigners who have besmirched the royal authority of Czechs, Bulgars, and Serbs

In 1087[1] the emperor Henry IV appointed prince Bratislav, the Czech, as king and granted him all of Poland, over which neither had any authority.[2] By this evil act, Henry ignited war among alien nations.

In 1159[3] the emperor Frederick bestowed a royal title on Vladislav, a Czech prince. But in the course of sixty years Vladislav's descendants—Czech rulers—did not use this title.

Přemysl or Otokar, a Czech prince, accepted the royal crown from the emperor Phillip [in 1198]. His relatives had lost this crown earlier, in a civil war. Otokar bestowed it to his descendents.

In 1002 the emperor Otto III, together with Pope Gregory V, designated six German princes and bishops as electors of the emperor.[4] Much later, the emperor Rudolf I added a seventh elector, the Czech king, and in addition designated him "the cupbearer of the Roman emperor." He also imposed on him the obligation by which this poor king acknowledged himself an imperial servant, whose duty was to pour wine for the emperor sitting at a table and to bear him the cup. In this way he transformed an independent prince into his subject and the royal cupbearer became the laughing stock of the world. Because no one can conceive anything more ridiculous than to be a crowned king and at the same time to tend to another king at the dinner table. These amiable king-makers ridicule us in this way.

George of Podebrady,[5] the last Czech king to emerge from among the Slavs, was legally and justly condemned by the pope [Pius II] for heresy and, together with his children, was deprived of all royal and princely dignity not only in this world, but hereafter as well. . . .

[1] Actually 1086.

[2] Krizhanich left this chapter unfinished. It is a rough outline of his thoughts on the matter.

[3] Actually 1158.

[4] This statement contains two errors. Pope Gregory V died in 999, and the electoral system only came into existence in the thirteenth century.

[5] King of Bohemia 1458–71.

31

Concerning the good fortune
of our nation

Nature has given us a prime advantage. *Our people are not ambitious.* They do not yearn for power and therefore readily submit themselves to anyone who knows their nature, who can thus easily force them to do hard work or engage in war. Most other nations are different. We are content with *simple food and drink* and do not make any special effort to prepare it. The Germans, on the other hand, never stop boasting about their gastronomic delights and their luxury. But we should neither envy them nor seek out ways to import such viands from India. *In preparing their beds,* our people do not exert any special effort either. All Germans in contrast drown themselves in feather beds.

The first major good fortune of this country is the fact that is has secure borders along the Arctic Ocean. Our second good fortune is our good neighbors: the Persians, Cherkessians, and Poles (if we could discover how to utilize them). Our third good fortune is our weak neighbors such as the Kalmucks, Samoyeds, and other Siberian natives, who pose no danger of major attacks.

A fourth good fortune lies in the resources of our land and rivers. Compared with Poland, Lithuania, Sweden, and Belorussia, Russia is well endowed and bountiful. Here grow large and delicious garden fruits, cabbages, radishes, beets, onions, turnips, and so on. In Moscow, turkeys, chickens, and eggs are larger and tastier than those available in the above-mentioned countries. The bread that commoners and rural people eat is more plentiful and delicious in Russia than in Lithuania, Poland, or Sweden. Fish, too, is available here in abundance.

A fifth good fortune of this land is the navigability of its seas and rivers, as well as the availability of various materials for shipbuilding. We, too, are capable of starting and developing an extensive overland trade system that would transport goods from nation to nation.

There also are some very good things in our *laws and national customs.* Of these the first and best is absolute autocracy. A second good custom is the closure of our borders. We deny foreigners free entry into our country and prohibit our own people from wandering outside the borders of the realm without vital reasons. These two customs are the pillars—the heart and soul—of this realm and should be preserved by all available means. In effect, they should be reinforced by the expulsion of all foreigners, a matter that will be discussed later.

Another beneficial custom is that no one is allowed to lead an idle life—that is, no one can free himself from public and national service, be it at court, in government offices, or in the military. In contrast, many German nobles and burghers live in idleness and luxury, like the ancient Sardanapalu,[1] or like weaned-out pigs who bring no benefit to anyone.

Still another good custom is that no one is allowed to spread heresy. A further beneficial custom and national good fortune, centers in our spiritual Palladium: we maintain sacred vigils, attend matins, participate at the Holy Liturgy, sleep little, rise early, eat late, and restrain our bodies through a multitude of genuflections and fastings. It seems to me that this is the most vital factor in the preservation of our realm. This is the true and lofty fortress. For that reason our kings and pastors should especially see to it that strict preservation of the well-established rules of the church are in no way violated by any modification.

A final useful custom is the method of punishment used in this tsardom—namely the exile system, under which those who have been exiled receive means to live, or even salaries from the ruler. In this way the tsar can punish any guilty person without causing a popular uprising.[2] It is bad when a well-known and previously useful person is punished for some transgression by being completely abandoned, as the emperor Justinian did when he blinded Belisarius (once his military commander) and confiscated all of his property, forcing him to live by begging.

Those who counsel that exiles should receive no sustenance, counsel poorly. It may perhaps be that they are now useless, but providing them with food is not useless.

Knowing our national advantages (both bestowed and acquired) we can now compare our life with that of other nations and conclude that Russia is richer than Lithuania, Poland, and Sweden because our people can live in greater prosperity. Although Sweden has copper ore and Poland some silver, these advantages cannot compare with the combined good fortunes of Russia. However, when we compare ourselves with other, richer countries (such as Greece, France, Italy, Spain, or England) that have

[1] Assyrian monarch of the seventh century BC.
[2] Krizhanich refers to "king" and "tsar" interchangeably; we have used the term "tsar" whenever it applies to the Russian context, and "king" when it applies more generally.

vineyards, wool, silk, dyes, and other expensive goods, and where there exists better political organization and more developed industry, it is essential to acknowledge that the nobles and burghers are much richer in those countries than in Russia. Even the richest of our Russian people do not live in such luxury as do their more common people. Any town, there, has more gold and silver—and all other goods—than all Russian towns.

It is a fact that in England, Germany, France, and other countries there are many cities which have more wealth than our entire nation—excluding the tsar's treasury. If Russia were as populous, as naturally productive, and administratively as well organized as France, it, too, would have a seat among the leading nations.

From the preceding account, the following conclusion can be drawn. We should not compete with these very affluent nations either in hospitality, dress, the splendor of our silverware, or the hiring of foreign mercenaries.

We can boast before the Poles, Lithuanians, Belorussians, Tartars, Siberians, and similar peoples about our food, drink, clothes, and silver. But if we boast about food and drink to Germans, Frenchmen, and Italians, they would simply ridicule us and consider us fools. We support this impression by getting stone drunk in front of foreigners.

For that reason, the Polish king Casimir, son of Lokietek, deserves a great deal of reproach, for when preparing a wedding that was attended by five kings and five princes, he entertained them with wine bought in their countries and transported for long distances.

Even more foolishly, the Polish archbishop of Gniezno threw a great party in Paris to which he invited all the teachers and students of the local school and treated them to their own wine. Thus, the guest entertained his host in the latter's home! He was properly rewarded. The teachers presented him with an insulting book written by a German that ridiculed the entire Polish nation. The bishop later complained of this affront to the Council of Constance [in 1414]. He not only failed to obtain redress but, on the contrary, lost his good name.

Finally, let us remember that although some people in these other countries live more comfortably than we do, nevertheless our peasants and poor townsmen, who make their living from handicrafts, live much better than do the peasants in those rich countries. For there, in many places, the land has been set aside for vineyards, specialized crops, cultivation of dyes, mining of ores, and similar uses, so that grain cannot be cultivated. The agriculturists and craftsmen engaged in these enterprises cannot grow grain and thus live quite poorly. Sometimes for the entire year they drink only water. All wine produced is sold. They eat bread sparingly and know nothing about *kvas*. Some eat bread made from chestnuts, sorghum, or Turkish wheat that resembles gravel more than true bread. Many regions, sometimes whole countries, consist of mountains. There grain does not grow at all, and the people must eat bread that is scant and tasteless. This is the case in Switzerland, the Tirol, and Salzburg.

Thanks to God's grace, here in Russia all people, both rich and poor, eat rye bread, fish, and meat, and they drink *kvas* if they do not have beer. As a result, peasants and poor craftsmen live far better in Russia than do their counterparts in Greece, Spain, and other countries where meat and fish are quite expensive and where firewood is sold by weight. People who live in those warm countries also suffer more during the winter from cold. They sleep there in cold rooms without ovens or fireplaces, while here we have heated rooms.

32

Three ways the Germans corrupt
other nations

There is no limit to the insults that other nations, especially the Germans, pay us Slavs. It seems appropriate to identify the three principal contagions with which the Germans infest us and our neighbors. These maladies are: (1) heresy, (2) waste, and (3) the destruction of autocracy.

There is no need to say much about heresy. It is well known that the Germans have infested and continue to infest the whole of Europe with this devilish plague. All that is required is to view briefly their Sardanapolian luxurious and licentious life. The Germans have never stopped emphasizing the sins of the Italian and Russian peoples, and especially those of the pope. By offending and insulting them, they try to portray themselves as perfect. But actually their condemnation of the sins of others serves more as self-accusation than justification; for, like Pharisees, they accuse their brothers and neglect their own sins. The Italians and Russians confess their sins. But the Germans, after having rejected and tramped on the Church's laws, do not even consider their vices and transgressions as sinful.

The Germans say that no one should live without a wife, and they have condemned and rejected the monastic way of life. Sexual intercourse between men and women is open and free among them. The Germans maintain that other places have more licentious men and women than they do. Yet if one were to examine the problem, it is clear that where there exists a greater cause there is also a greater result.

There has never been in the past nor at present any nation so concerned about food, drink, and other bodily pleasures as are the Germans. The daily dinners of German nobles and merchants are prepared more meticulously than the royal wedding feasts of other nations.

Throughout the world, people, and especially monks and nuns, are allowed to wander and to ask for food. But the Germans allow the right to solicit alms only to some, in the form of a privilege. They cannot tolerate monks.

Whatever the Germans do at home is not our concern, but it harms us when they instill their boundless luxury into our people. We should not imitate their excesses. On the contrary, we should rejoice that we prepare our food simply. And we should work to ensure that in the future we will always have enough of such easily obtainable supplies as onions, garlic, *kvas, kissel,* oat flour, dry-crusts, crust flour, buttermilk, solid non-fat cheese, and so on, products which the Germans consider coarse and unappetizing. We should not dream about exotic German drinks, but should be content with those to which we have become accustomed.

Everything that is not expensive and luxurious, the Germans consider to be filthy. They write as follows: "The Russians like salted fish, which can be smelled even before it is seen. The Russians seem to like this stinking fish very much." Thus these Pharisees write of us. But they do not write anything about the cheese they serve that contains worms, which they eat with a spoon, and they do not mention that this cheese also smells horribly.

What is to be said about their venison? I know well that the Germans age it so long that its smell is unbearable. I myself have left the table in a hurry on many occasions when they placed this food before me.

The Germans also criticize us because we, allegedly, talk with the executioner and eat bread with him. But it must be known that when a German executioner has dispatched a specified number of the guilty the town councilors pay him very well, and then appoint him to their council. Thereafter he makes a living either as a doctor or a merchant. They also criticize us because all members of our society are called "the sovereign's slaves." But they see no fault in calling themselves "vassals;" this term is German not Latin, and means "orphan." Once the term "knecht" was also quite dignified among them, and even today the Scots call their distinguished cavaliers "knecht"—that is, "servant." In old German books we read that: "Knights and knechts (that is, more distinguished military leaders and ordinary soldiers) fight with lances."

The Germans have quite abundant and luxurious food, drink, beds, homes, weapons, servants, carriages, horses, and other items. The Tartars, in contrast, live in filth and mud. We should avoid luxury and filth and follow the middle course, which might be termed "clean living" or "moderation."

Overindulgence expresses itself in such things as decorating rooms with rugs or silk, putting great amounts of sugar and other spices in food, using a great deal of ceruse, perfume, and rouge in makeup, wearing of pearls on men's clothing or shirts, gilding beds, and dying textiles. All of these things are vanities; they lead to sin and bring ruin to a kingdom.

One can avoid these overindulgences without being filthy; that is, keeping dishes poorly washed, allowing debris to accumulate under benches, putting coins in one's mouth, filling a glass brim full and handing it to a guest, and sticking one's fingers in the drink.

If we have the material to make household products and do not need to purchase it from other nations, we should make them attractive and practical. This would not be overindulgence. For instance, we have forests and flax, and therefore ought to make good, smooth, handsome tables, cover them with white table cloths, set out wooden cups, and place cloth napkins near them to clean one's hands.

Another evil with which the Germans infect the world is the destruction of autocracy and royal authority. It is essential to remember that once all the kings in Europe enjoyed full authority and were autocrats in their respective kingdoms. Only with time did German princes and nobles gain such unbridled freedoms and liberties that they finally undermined the power and authority of their kings and became subject to no one.

To some extent they have now infected neighboring nations like the Italians and the French with this evil, but most of all the Poles—so much so that there is no way it could be made worse. Indeed, it seems that the Poles have lost their senses. Inasmuch as we have many contacts with the Poles they, more than the Germans, cause our people to lose their senses. Both the Poles and the Lithuanians glorify their chaotic, tyrannical system, while heaping a great deal of abuse on our autocratic government.

33

The superiority of Russian to Polish government

Let us assume that an advisor to the tsar delivers a major speech before a national assembly. The title of his remarks is *An Address to the Entire Nation: Concerning Good Government and Autocracy*.

Distinguished prelates, lords, *boyars* and representatives of all classes and ranks of the glorious Russian tsardom. Humans have developed various forms of government. These include autocracy, *boyar* rule, and popular (or citizens') rule. All Greek philosophers and all of our Christian holy fathers believe that autocratic forms are the best and praise them. They explain and document their conclusions by the following irrefutable arguments.

First, because autocracy provides somewhat better accountability in justice. Second, because autocracy makes for peace and tranquility. Third, because this form of governent offers better protection against disasters. And fourth, and most important, because autocracy resembles God's authority. Indeed, God is the first and true autocrat of the universe. Accordingly, every true king in his kingdom is—next to God—the sole autocrat and God's lieutenant.

But you will say: What crime did the Israelites commit when they appointed themselves a king? The answer is simple. A long time before, God had promised to give the Israelites a king and told them how to appoint him (Deuteronomy 17). The Israelites thus sinned not in appointing a king but in appointing him at a time when it was more appropriate to be silent—that is, when they were already being ruled by a saintly and just man, the Prophet Samuel. For that reason God told Samuel: "They did not reject you: they scorned me and my authority." They did not want to listen to a prophet sent by God. It is also said that autocracy is the oldest, the strongest and the most widespread form of rule among nations. In addition, it also survives longer than any other type of rule.

We fully subscribe to the views of the ancient teachers and approve the reasons why autocracy or royal authority deserves praise and glory. But even if we were to dismiss these and other reasons, there is the vital fact that under autocracy it is easy to correct the mistakes of government. Because whatever correction the autocrat wishes to make, he does so without any delay. In other governments, or when the king does not enjoy full authority, or where many rulers exist, once errors have become part of the law, they remain uncorrected for ever.

This orthodox, illustrious kingdom of our beloved tsar, sovereign, and grand prince Alexei Mikhailovich, the autocrat of Great, Little and Belorussia, is highly respected, fortunate and happy, because it is governed by absolute autocracy. Consequently, it is possible to correct all mistakes and damages that may have been introduced by the carelessness of administrators and under which the people suffer.

The Germans and Poles are especially critical of autocracy. They praise their disorder saying: "Poland is held together through anarchy." The Germans maintain: "The king of Spain is king of slaves; the king of France is king of nobles: the king of Poland is a royal king; while the German emperor is lord of the entire world." This is because the king of Spain is an absolute autocrat and can fully order about all of his lords. The French are less submissive to their ruler, while in Poland and Germany almost no one obeys the king.

In order that our people do not become infected by this Polish illness, it would be wise to explain to them in detail why Russian autocracy is so much more dignified than the chaotic rule of Poland. In Russia it is possible to correct all harm and mistakes of government; it is impossible to correct them in Poland. Here in Russia we have only one lord who controls the lives and deaths of his subjects. The Poles, in contrast, have as many lords as they have kings and tyrants, and as many nobles as judges and executioners. Anyone can kill his peasants, and no one will punish him for it.

If burdensome monopolies exist here in Russia, they belong only to one great sovereign. In Poland and Lithuania far more burdensome monopolies exist in towns and villages belonging to nobles. Everywhere there sit either Jewish leaseholders or noblemen themselves, who distribute smelly drinks to slaves—a beverage that even slaves pour away rather than consume, but for which they are charged.

In Poland it is possible to devour other human souls with heresies and still flourish. Banished heretics and servants of the devil from all nations come to Poland. To Russia they can neither come nor live, and, thanks to God's mercy, the Orthodox faith is preserved. Polish territory is a refuge for people the world over.[1] As aboard a ship, where every kind of filth

---

[1] From about the middle of the fourteenth to the middle of the seventeenth century, Poland opened its frontiers to all persecuted minorities, especially Jews and various

trickles down into the hold, in Poland are assembled thieves, murderers, pilferers, traitors, heretics, and other transgressors of the law from all nations. In addition, entire transient groups come there. A Latin poem has been written on the subject:

> Poland resembles the new Babylon.
> It is a colony of the Germans, Gypsies, Armenians, and
>   Scots.
> It is a paradise for the Jews and hell for peasants.
> It is a hidden treasure for foreigners and tramps from
>   all countries.
> Its territory is a refuge for people the world over.
> It is an inn as well as a home for all squanderers.
> Parliaments are elected continuously there.
> People are agitated there constantly.
> It is governed by foreigners
> And it is despised by all nations. [2]

Young Polish nobles travel abroad and roam the world over. All Europeans consider them stupid. They ridicule them because they waste their wealth abroad and bring home nothing except personal ruin, insult, vice, and disgraceful diseases. And, during their wanderings, they pawn off their poor Christian peasants to the Jews, who torment them as the devils of hell torment lost souls.

In Russia, by contrast, such wandering is prohibited to young nobles. The wise Italians and Spaniards, though having the right to travel abroad, do not. Besides, whenever such travel is neither permitted nor practiced by kings and their sons, their subjects certainly should not have greater freedom to do so.

In Poland no class of people—neither agriculturists nor townsmen—can be content with their destiny because their masters torture and kill them, the Jews torment them, and soldiers devour them. In Russia, no one is so oppressed. Soldiers cannot be content in Poland, because no one ever pays them; they cannot survive except by stealing, killing, and robbing peasants. In Russia, soldiers always receive a set wage.

Protestant sects. It was simultaneously the most tolerant country in Europe and a wealthy nation. Bigotry and intolerance slowly emerged in the second half of the seventeenth century when, seeing Poland's military weakness, foreign powers (Russia, Sweden, and Prussia) began to champion their "persecuted co-religionists" and invaded Polish territory.
[2] The sentiments expressed in this poem were apparently widespread in Poland in Krizhanich's time. See S. Kot, *Polska rajem dlia Żydów* . . . (Warsaw, 1937), a work published when anti-Jewish sentiment in pre-World War II Poland was at its height.

Local merchants in Poland also cannot be content, because all the cheaters of the world (Gypsies, Scots, Armenians, and Jews) carry on trade freely alongside them. The Jews mint counterfeit money, and bad currency from neighboring kingdoms is accepted. Neither the Gypsies nor the Jews are allowed to live in Russia.

Neither can churchmen be content in Poland, because heretics from all countries and advocates of all heresies can freely move among them. But heretics cannot live in Russia.

Nobles themselves, who boast about their unbridled freedom, cannot be content, because of the Diet. They never enjoy tranquility as a result of constant sessions. They are always traveling and must purchase food and poor drink at high prices from Jewish innkeepers. When they arrive at the Diet, they must pay the Italians, the Scots, and Germans for housing, wine, and so forth. There are no Jewish inns in Russia, and there are no ruinous expenditures.

Polish magnates, too, and even the entire Polish nation, cannot be content with this chaos, for they suffer from the rule of foreign kings and can never select their own ruler. In contrast, our Russian nation has pious tsars and sovereigns from among its own people in accordance with God's commandment as stated in Deuteronomy 17:15: "You must not appoint a foreigner, one who is not of your own race." In Russia, with God's grace, we have no foreign rulers. This is one of the greatest pieces of good fortune with which God has endowed our people. For to have a foreign king brings misfortune, evil, and shame.

Finally, foreign kings who have intermarried in Poland cannot be content either, because the Diet usually shouts them down and the people ignore their decrees. The conclusion is self-evident. If anyone were to travel around the world in search of the worst government, he could not find a more appropriate candidate than that which presently exists in Poland. Of all the misfortunes that befall mortals, none is worse than being governed by a foreigner. For one who treasures his honor, it is better to die a hundred times than to accept foreign rule.

34

Royal dignity and authority

The people need a king as much as a body needs a heart: "For want of skilful strategy an army is lost" (Proverbs 11:14). The king is a human shepherd: "He chose David to be his servant, to take care of Israel, his patrimony" (Psalm 78:70–71); "I say to Cyrus, 'You shall be my shepherd to carry out all my purpose'" (Isaiah 44:28).

All lawful kings have been appointed neither by themselves nor by the people, but by God. "Through me kings are sovereign and governors make just laws" (Proverbs 8:15). "Every person must submit to the supreme authorities. There is no authority but by act of God and the existing authorities are instituted by him; consequently anyone who rebels against authority is resisting a divine institution" (Romans 13:1–2).

The ruler is a deputy, a servant of God, and a judge over thieves. "It is an obligation imposed not merely by fear of retribution but by conscience" (Romans 13:5–6). The king resembles God on earth. "This is my sentence: Gods you may be, sons all of you of a high God" (Psalm 82:6). Whenever the king makes a judgment, God guides him so that he does not commit an error. "Let judgment in my cause issue from thy lips, let thine eyes be fixed on justice" (Psalm 17:2).

ROYAL RIGHTS AND PREROGATIVES

Samuel explained royal rights to the people of Israel as follows:

This will be the sort of king who will govern you. . . . He will take your sons and make them serve in his chariots and with his cavalry, and will make them run before his chariot. Some he will appoint officers over units of a thousand and units of fifty. Others will plough his fields and reap his harvest; others again will make weapons of war and equipment for mounted troops. He will take your daughters for perfumers, cooks and confectioners, and will seize the best of your cornfields, vineyards, and olive yards, and give them to his lackeys. He will take a tenth of your grain and your vintage to give to his eunuchs and lackeys. Your slaves, both men and women, and the best of your cattle and your asses he will seize and put to his own use. He will take a tenth of your flocks, and you yourselves will become his slaves" (1 Samuel 8:11–18).

Note that the king is entitled to take away one tenth of the harvest, vineyards, and livestock. It is also just that the king enjoy a reputation as a sovereign and that his subjects be his slaves. However, it is unjust to appropriate all this by force. Yet everything that kings do, be it just or unjust, Samuel calls a royal prerogative.

The judge could not do anything he wished, or anything contrary to the written law, whereas the king could. The king is the lawmaker, or more accurately, he is God's living means of legislation. Moreover, sons of judges do not inherit the authority of their fathers, but royal sons do.

Once the king is annointed and crowned, there exists no other judge above him in the world. No one is allowed to curse the king, even if he should be unjust. "You shall not revile God, nor curse a chief of your own people" (Exodus 22:28). No one can refuse to serve the king or commit treason even if the king should be unjust. "Servants, accept the authority of your masters with all due submission, not only when they are kind and considerate, but even when they are perverse" (1 Peter 2:18–19). No one can punish the annointed king or raise his hand against him. The king is God's deputy, the Lord's annointed, and a saint. "Touch not my annointed servants, do my prophets no harm" (Psalm 105:15). Canon law also proclaims that no person can pass judgment on the supreme authority.

What should be done should the king be a bitter oppressor, an offender, and a torturer of the people? The answer is simple: the people should ascribe this misery to their sins, should correct their way of life, ask God for help, and implore the king to have mercy. God sends bad kings as a punishment for human sins. "He makes a godless man king over a stubborn nation and all its people" (Job 34:30). "I will appoint mere boys to be their captains, who shall govern as the fancy takes them" (Isaiah, 3:4). "Woe betide the land when a slave has become its king, and its princes feast in the morning. Happy the land when its king is nobly born, and its princes feast at the right time of day, with self-control, and not as drunkards" (Ecclesiastes 10:16–17).

OBLIGATIONS OF ROYAL SUBJECTS

The king is entitled to royal tribute. "Discharge your obligations to all men; pay tax and toll, reverence and respect, to those to whom they are due" (Romans, 13:7–8). "Then pay Caesar what is due to Caesar, and pay God what is due to God" (Matthew 22:21–22). All citizens must obey the king. "Submit yourselves to every human institution for the sake of the Lord, whether to the sovereign as supreme, or to the governor as his deputy for the punishment of criminals and the commendation of those who do right. For it is the will of God that by your good conduct you should put ignorance and stupidity to silence" (1 Peter 2:13–15). "Whatever you tell us we will do; wherever you send us we will go. . . . Whoever rebels against your authority and fails to carry out all your orders, shall be put to death" (Joshua 1:16–18).

Citizens should pray for the king's health. Paul says: "I urge that petitions, prayers, intercessions, and thanksgivings be offered for all men; for sovereigns and all in high office" (1 Timothy 12:1–2). Baruch counsels: "Pray for Nebuchadnezzar king of Babylon, and for his son Belshazzar" (Baruch 1:11). Citizens should be absolutely loyal and obedient to the king. Paul says: "Slaves, obey your earthly masters with fear and trembling, single-mindedly, as serving Christ. Do not offer merely the outward show of service, to curry favour with men, but, as slaves of Christ, do wholeheartedly the will of God. Give the cheerful service of those who serve the Lord, not men" (Ephesians 6:5–8). "Tell slaves to respect their master's authority in everything, and to comply with their demands without answering back; not to pilfer, but to show themselves strictly honest and trustworthy; for in all such ways they will add lustre to the doctrine of God our Saviour" (Titus 2:9–10). "All who wear the yoke of slavery must count their own masters worthy of all respect, so that the name of God and the Christian teaching are not brought into disrepute. If the masters are believers, the slaves must not respect them any less for being their Christian brothers. Quite the contrary; they must be all the better servants because those who receive the benefit of their service are one with them in faith and love" (1 Timothy 6:1–2). But to explain the obligations of citizens more clearly, it is necessary to examine different classes and ranks of people separately.

35

Concerning classes

The various classes of people are determined by their separate obligations. As the apostle says, nobody lives only for himself. Every individual should work for the good of all, and thus earn his daily bread. This is called "obligation." Based on the different obligations of human beings, there are three classes of people, namely churchmen, nobles, and commoners.

The obligations of churchmen consist of praying to God and taking care of saving souls. The obligations of nobles consist of explicating the will of the king to other classes and assisting in government. The obligations of commoners consist of fulfilling their different tasks and serving their superiors.

Churchmen consist of three categories: bishops, priests and monks. Nobles consist of three categories: princes, government officials, and military commanders. Commoners consist of four categories: salaried people, merchants, craftsmen, and peasants.

Salaried people are those who live on public salaries, who have no authority but are under an obligation to serve. These include scribes, servants, soldiers, and so forth.

Slaves or non-free people consist of various groups. For example, one category—those of the household—enjoy considerable respect and can be compared with salaried people. Others do heavy work (shepherds, military servants, etc.) and resemble peasants, but in fact are inferior to peasants.

Almost all of the above categories also include many other sub-groups, which we need not discuss here. The head of all of these categories is the tsar, who is God's deputy.

When speaking about nobles, it is essential to know that the princely group includes those who assist the tsar as his councillors in every branch of administration. Government officials are those who head civil matters and who serve as judges. The category of military commander includes those who are in charge of military affairs.

All of the above categories include some important positions that should not be held on a permanent basis. That is, no one should keep a position for his entire life. Such high administrators, important leaders, and military commanders should be replaced frequently. For, when they retain authority for a long time, it becomes easier for them to resolve problems in a way that is contrary to good laws and ancient customs. Germans can be cited as an example. At one time, the Germans had legally established categories for nobles. That is, they did not have permanent authorities, but changed them periodically. At the time, the Germans were strongest. Then they controlled Gaul, Italy, Spain, and England. Since then, because their emperors are elected, public order has deteriorated and the power has diminished. Princes seeking the throne promised extensive privileges to nobles, in order to be elected emperor. First, they granted them lifelong authority and rights, then they permitted them to transmit these to their heirs. In this way, the German emperors deprived themselves of all authority. The nobles completely disregarded their obligations. They trampled on God's commandments and human laws, and spread all kinds of heresy and devilish deception. They now do not consider that it is their inborn duty to obey the king and to administer the nation in accordance with his orders, or to encourage virtue. They think that their only responsibility is to eat, drink, and be merry.

Rotation of responsibility is both useful and necessary for monks too. For, where no rotations exists, a good monastic order weakens very quickly.

Thus far we have examined society in terms of what it ought to be, which is the ideal. Now let us examine it as it usually is, when good parts are intertwined with bad.

Just as the human body consists of its parts—head, arms, legs, and so on—so the imaginary body of the state has its parts, which can be divided into three groups: the protective, the protected and the unproductive (see table 3). The protective parts guard and procure all things necessary to life. The protected parts, for various reasons, require protection. The sick parts infect the state with vice and consume its wealth. The king is the head of the entire structure.

Peasants, craftsmen, and merchants (in the realm of public well-being) produce everything that other citizens use and consume. They are called *chern* and are tax paying people.

Lords, *boyars,* and soldiers dispense justice, fight in wars, protect public peace, and the health, life, and wealth of citizens from internal villains.

Table 3 Division of the state into three groups

	Protective	Protected	Unproductive
privileged	*boyars* leading nationals soldiers	churchmen women children	heretics and magicians foreigners who live in enclaves
commoners	merchants craftsmen peasants and slaves	poor people teachers essential guests	foreign merchants, second-hand dealers, hirelings, etc. squanderers, idlers, gamblers, drunkards usurers and grain speculators thieves, murderers

They also defend their people from foreign enemies. For that reason these classes are protective.

Protected members are needed because people cannot exist without them. Churchmen, bishops, and priests give people their spiritual education. Monks and nuns pray to God for His forgiveness of the sins of the entire nation. We must protect poor people and those who are blind or crippled, on account of our love for humanity and because of God's commandment.

Masters are those who are engaged in learned matters which in the life of any particular individual may not appear significant. But they are essential for the nation as a whole. These include painters who paint pictures, casters who cast bells and cannons, engineers who design good weapons, grammarians who teach language, historians who compose chronicles, mathematicians who teach the art of accounting, astronomers who calculate the appearance of stars, and philosophers who deal with morals and politics or statecraft.

Essential guests are those from whom we cannot escape. We need to allow them to visit our country in accordance with international law, so that our people can receive reciprocal treatment in case of need. Such are ambassadors, prisoners of war, indigent foreigners, some merchants, and the like.

The unproductive are first those who harm the nation, such as heretics, magicians, foreigners, thieves, and murderers; and second, those who contribute nothing to the national well-being, namely idlers, gamblers, and beggars, useless nobles like those among the Germans, usurers, second-hand dealers, and all other merchants who concern themselves exclusively with trade. Anyone who does not contribute to the national well-being in agriculture, crafts, armed service, or a position in the administration must be considered an idler who is after his own interests. For that reason it is necessary to remove their right to trade so that only honest people will be able to benefit from it. When merchants start to trade, they should be made aware that they are trading at the exclusive prerogative of the king, and that all their activities should benefit the ruler and the entire nation.

Commoners (i.e. peasants, craftsmen, and merchants) supply items that are essential for human consumption and therefore indispensable. Furthermore, kings, lords, nobles, and soldiers have differing perceptions of their duty. Many stay single because they have neither means nor adequate property to maintain a household on a level to match their status. Commoners pay no attention to honor. They think only of profit and their bellies; therefore they easily find a companion, marry young, and produce offspring early. For this reason, the Romans called the commoners "proletarians"—that is, people who proliferate.

The *boyars* are sent to war and possibly to their death: they serve at the royal court, and remain single for many years. They rise early, retire late, and keep vigil over governmental and national affairs. In contrast, no one inquires when commoners rise. Nobles are also dispatched on ambassadorial missions and on special assignments from one place to another. They spend much time outside of their homeland, and many die in battle or on assignments. Commoners, in contrast, always stay home near the oven and close to their wives, and therefore enjoy the fruits of their labor in peace and multiply.

Consequently, let the commoners know that, in fairness and right, they are under an obligation to feed the king, lords, *boyars,* and soldiers and to serve them. First, lords and *boyars* hold court and dispense justice, and together with soldiers defend the state from foreign enemies and local bandits. Commoners would never be able to accumulate wealth if the king and the *boyars* did not protect it. Second, it is more important and dignified to work by using one's head and hands than one's legs. The *boyars* spend whole nights in councils and in other government concerns, while the commoners snore beside their wives. Third, it is more dignified to shed blood for the nation, as the *boyars* do, than to sweat as do the commoners. In a word, lords, *boyars,* and soldiers experience constant anxiety, are subject to deadly dangers, and bear a very heavy governmental burden. This contrast has resulted in a Greek proverb: "Whoever does not pay the tax does not know its value."

It is evident that commoners should not complain about the king, lords, and *boyars.* They should be ready at any given time to obey a royal order and willingly pay taxes to sustain other free classes. It is wiser to contribute one's entire annual income, or even half one's property, while preserving one's home, rights, and the rest of one's property, than to lose the house and entire property.

Correspondingly, the king, lords, and *boyars* should always treat the commoners so that they would be able to appropriate something from them. They should not increase the customary taxes and obligations of the commoners excessively to avoid disrupting agriculture, crafts, and trade. It would be best to discover and teach them ways of increasing their production. Those states where the enterprises of the common people are allowed to develop are populous and rich, as is evident in Holland and France. (We should not try to imitate them though, because it is impossible under our present form of government.) Wherever commoners are numerous and rich, there too the king, lords, and *boyars* are rich and powerful.

It is necessary by every means to assist the commoners in their enterprises: agriculture, crafts and trade. In return, the commoners should refrain from requesting freedom from taxes and public obligations. They should be ready to pay tribute and obey the king. No one can predict a time when the state may face a problem, be it small or large. For that reason, there cannot be any fixed rules. What is necessary is sound reason and the generosity of the king. Secondly, if a good citizen is always ready to die for his country and his people, what can be said about property? If the *boyars* die in dangerous times, it is not too great a sacrifice for the commoners to give up their wealth.

In this illustrious Russian realm one must keep in mind three reasons peculiar to this tsardom why lords and *boyars* are more necessary for public well-being than are commoners. First, this tsardom has many evil and rampaging neighbors: the Crimeans, Nogais, Mordva, Kalmucks, Cheremis, Bashkirs, Samoyeds, and others. Threatened by brigands, our commoners could never accumulate wealth. Second, there is no kingdom where common people can live as well and can enjoy as many rights as they do here. Third, our Russian merchants do not travel anywhere by sea and therefore do not experience maritime dangers or suffer from pillage on sea or land. For these reasons, common people everywhere in the world, but most of all in Russia, should always pay taxes to their ruler, provide transport and supplies for public needs, perform every service, and do every task required.

Among the commoners, merchants are less necessary than peasants and craftsmen, because they bring the nation fewer benefits. Merchants do not work with their hands, do not die for the nation, and shed neither blood nor sweat. They only transport goods from one place to another, and not with their own efforts but using hired peasants. This is not for the public good, but for their own gain, and quite often to the detriment of the nation. These idlers fill their bellies, live in luxury, cheat, and resemble the locust that ravages the land. Therefore if the sovereign tsar wished, he should in justice and by law appropriate all commercial profits. By doing so he would not cause any harm or injustice either to public wellbeing or to the nation. On the contrary, he would be performing a great service because he would be removing a burden to the state, and would also be gaining considerable wealth. If this action should help all other classes, the ruler should not worry that the merchants grieve. Such a misfortune benefits the whole nation. Public wellbeing is more vital than the profit of a few individuals.

36

Royal obligations

Since we already have indicated what obligations citizens have towards the king, it is now necessary that we learn what royal obligations are. Here, above all, it is necessary to know the royal commandments and rules that God has especially set up for kings, and which he has decreed they obey.

The first rule is: "He shall not become prouder than his fellow countrymen" (Deuteronomy 17:20). The second rule is: "He shall not acquire many horses" (Deuteronomy 17:16). That is, the king should forgo luxury in his travels, and in all other displays of his majesty.

Boris: What are you saying: Can the king commit a sin just by trying to dress properly and by enjoying some luxury?

Khervoi: You already have heard God's commandment and have understood that he can.

Boris: I consider this surprising. How can the king sin just by trying to dress up?

Kervoi: The king sins when he tries to have many horses and servants (especially foreign ones), when for that reason he harms and oppresses his subjects. However, when the king acquires many horses, servants, and other things necessary to uphold his honor and dignity without harming the nation, this does not constitute luxury. The third rule is: He shall not "acquire great quantities of silver and gold for himself" (Deuteronomy 17:17). This rule should be understood the same way as the preceding one—that is, the king should not increase his treasury exorbitantly and ruthlessly. Let him rely more on God than on his treasury. "By just government a king gives his country stability, but by forced contributions he reduces it to ruin" (Proverbs 29:4). "Like a starving lion or a thirsty bear is a wicked man ruling a helpless people" (Proverbs 28:15).

The fourth rule states: Everyone who rules over people must honor wisdom. "The desire of wisdom leads to kingly stature. If therefore, you value your thrones and your sceptres, you rulers of the nations, you must honor wisdom so that you may reign for ever" (Wisdom of Solomon 6:20–21). "A wise king sifts out the wicked" (Proverbs 20:26). "Shame on you! You who make unjust laws and publish burdensome decrees depriving the poor of justice" (Isaiah 10:1–2) 'He reckons our life a game, and our existence a market where money can be made; "one must get a living", he says "by fair means and foul"' (Wisdom of Solomon 15:22). "Hear then, you kings . . . lords of the wide world . . . it is the Lord who gave you your authority; your power comes from the Most High. He will put your actions to the test and scrutinize your intentions. Though you are viceroys of his kingly power, you have not been upright judges. . . . Swiftly and terribly will he descend upon you, for judgment falls relentlessly upon those in high place. The small man may find pity and forgiveness, but the powerful will be called powerfully to account. . . . Small and great alike are of his making, and all are under his providence equally" (Wisdom of Solomon 6:1–8).

"Your very rulers are rebels, confederate with thieves; every man of them loves a bribe and itches for a gift" (Isaiah 1:23). "Her [Israel's] officers were lions roaring in her midst, her rulers wolves of the plain that did not wait till morning" (Zephaniah 3:3). "You devour the flesh of my people, strip off their skin" (Micah 3:3). "Her [Israel's] officers within her are like wolves tearing their prey, shedding blood and destroying men's lives to acquire ill-gotten gain" (Ezekiel 22:27–28). "Listen to this, leaders of Jacob, rulers of Israel, you who make justice hateful and wrest it from its straight course, building Zion in bloodshed and Jerusalem in iniquity" (Micah 3:9–10). "Empire passes from nation to nation because of injustice, insolence and greed" (Wisdom of Jesus son of Sirach 10:8). "How long shall the wicked, O Lord, how long shall the wicked exult? . . . they beat down thy people, O Lord, and oppress thy chosen nation" (Psalm 94:3–5). The Lord says: "For the ruin of the poor, for the groans of the needy, now I will arise" (Psalm 12:5). "Shall they not rue it, all evildoers who devour my people as men devour bread" (Psalm 14:4).

O king of Judah . . . and your courtiers and your people . . . these are the words of the Lord: Deal justly and fairly, rescue the victim from his oppressor, do not ill-treat or do violence to the alien, the orphan or the widow, do not shed innocent blood in this place. If you obey, and only if you obey, kings who sit on David's throne shall yet come riding through these gates. . . . But if you do not listen to my words, then by myself I swear, says the Lord, this house shall become a desolate ruin (Jeremiah 22:2–5).

Study and remember this well. God orders the king to protect the offended. Consequently, does the king rule according to God's commandments if he himself offends all of his people by merciless extortions?

37

The mission of the king:
royal authority and tyranny

The human body contains one soul, but it has three vital elements: reason, feeling, and health. In a state, the king represents the soul. The king and his advisors have three vital elements: wisdom, power, and wealth. Through them, the king alone rules over the will, the wisdom, and the life of his subjects. Using his wealth, the king controls the aspirations of his subjects. he concerns himself with the general well-being of his subjects rather than his own gain. When his subjects prosper, the king earns their devotion and in turn, prospers. Nothing is more desirable to a king than prosperous subjects who adore him. Conversely, the king who offends many, with merciless tyranny, in order to enrich a few, can never gain the admiration of his subjects.

Using his power, the king controls the life of his subjects. He tames the unruly with fetters, dungeons, fasts, tortures, and laws, and protects the kingdom from attack by external foes.

Using his wisdom, the king above all controls himself and his own aspirations and, if he truly fulfills his obligations, he also controls the wisdom of his subjects. In the final analysis, the obligation of every king is to make his subjects content. If his subjects see that the king is concerned about this, they realize that it is good to live under such government. They praise the acts of the king, place at his disposal their insight, and respect him not just for appearance's sake but from the bottom of their hearts. In this way, the king commands the will, the life, and the wisdom of his subjects.

Every human being should render All-Merciful God the highest honor, which in Greek is called piety. There are three forms of piety: fear, love, and respect. Because the king is God's viceroy on earth, his subjects should render him a slightly lesser, human honor, immediately after God, compounded by the same fear, love, and respect. To be able to create fear, the king must have power: to command respect, he needs wisdom; and to be loved, he must be able to promote prosperity—not his own royal riches, but the general wealth of his subjects.

Reason teaches us this, but flatterers turn everything around. They give the king deceptive advice and, in effect, impoverish him. They say that the king's dignity consists in having enormous wealth, which must be gotten by merciless plunder. They say that he will be strong, because with the plundered wealth he will be able to hire many mercenaries and will be valued and feared by other kings. But those who advocate such measures are infinitely mistaken. A treasury gained by brutality represents not wealth, but poverty, because it is the inevitable cause of future misery. Such a kingdom can never be strong, because not one of its classes is satisfied with its fate, and all crave change.

Power based on plunder is unreliable. For anyone who places aspirations on money alone—has no means of regaining his authority once his treasure is exhausted. His subjects will desert him. In consequence, excessive preoccupation with such revenue reflects neither wisdom nor honor, but extreme ignorance. History indicates that at all times and among all peoples those rulers who mercilessly filled their treasuries were hated by everybody, and gained neither glory nor honor, but only the curses given to tyrants.

Thus far, nothing has existed that attracts the human heart more than gold, and there is no sweeter song and no advice more appealing than that dealing with how to become rich. Consequently, those who devise various means of accumulating treasure are always to be found around kings. Some of them are good people. Unfortunately, they do not always know whether their advice is beneficial. Others concern themselves only with flattery that might win them royal favor. They devise means of sucking the last drop of blood from subject peoples and hence bring ruin to the entire nation. Such counsels are contrary to justice and to honor. Royal dignity suffers, and the kingdom becomes poor, weak, and desolate.

God has commanded kings: "You shall not increase your wealth excessively" (Deuteronomy 17:17). This commandment, however, does not mean that kings are not allowed to accumulate great wealth. God himself promised and gave Solomon enormous wealth. Wealth is a gift of God. It is good provided it is used properly. Prohibited, however, are greed, viciousness, or injustice in filling the treasury.

The king should not resort to the continual accumulation of treasure. He should stop once he has reached a certain level. Moreover, he should not collect wealth that would remain idle or bring him no benefit. He should collect only what is required for pious efforts, for the upkeep of royal dignity and for other state needs. In his effort to realize his ambitions, the king should put more trust in God than his treasury.

Boris: But how can the king introduce good government and make his state flourish?

Khervoi: Whenever he creates conditions in which all classes are content with their fate. When no one desires any change and all prefer to live under such a government rather than that of their neighbors.

Boris: How can the king achieve this?

Khervoi: Let him introduce in his own kingdom whatever works well elsewhere and make it a firm law of the land.

There exist three ways of establishing a good government, the best being autocracy. There are, however, several forms of corrupt government, the worst being tyranny. And of these, there are five forms. The first is the republican, in which the populace is agitated, and everyone aspires to become a ruler. This situation breeds anarchy. The second is oligarchy, a corrupt form of government in which a small group of individuals, such as nobles or others, seize power illegally. The third is tyranny, a case in which one individual seizes power and becomes a tyrannical merciless oppressor of the entire nation. The fourth is gynecocracy, female rule, where women possess the right to inherit the throne. And the fifth is xenocracy, or alien rule. Of these, tyranny is the easiest to correct, because only one person is responsible.

Boris: But how would you define a tyrant?

Khervoi: A tyrant is a brigand who is afraid neither of courts nor punishment. He is an executioner without a judge or laws, one who has renounced humanity. He is the devil with a human face. He is capable of creating infinite good but does not do so. In our language a tyrant is called "*liudoderets*," a destroyer of human beings.

Holy Scripture refers to kings as shepherds. Because of greed, however, the king becomes a wolf—a tyrant. Ezekiel has stated: "Princes of Israel are like wolves who capture the prey" (Ezekiel 22). A ruler should not ruin his people but provide them with an adequate amount of the goods necessary for a decent life. Aristotle says: "It is required that the ruler be a guardian. He sees that the wealthy do not suffer harm and that the common people do not suffer oppression" (*Politics*, Book V, 8, 5). Cicero, a Roman civic administrator, writes as follows: "Those who govern people should follow two rules. First, everything they do should serve the public good. Second, they should consider the entire body of the state, never favoring a single unit to the neglect of the rest. Authority over the nation resembles the care of orphans. It should benefit those who are governed and not those who rule" (*De Officiis*, Book 1).

Royal honor is higher than any honor under the sun. Therefore the king should cherish his honor and fear the name of tyrant, because tyranny is the greatest and the worst disgrace to kings. The king is not subject to any human laws. Nevertheless, he is subject to God's commandments and to the public's judgment. These are the two bridles which constrain the king. The first is the respect of God's commandments; the second is humility before the people. He who does not fear God, has no humility before his people, or sense of responsibility to future generations is a real tyrant.

38

A mistaken view about possession
of goods and unlimited power

Rich people believe that any property they legally own belongs to them completely, and that they can lose it, distribute it, and squander it according to their will, and no one may ask "Why are you dressed so pompously?[1] Why do you have so many dogs and falcons? Why do you waste so much money on feasts and games?" To this they usually respond: "It is none of your business. I can do with my property as I wish." But this is a grave mistake; for wealthy people are masters of their property only in relation to other people. In relation to God, they are not masters but administrators. And this can be variously demonstrated.

When David and the princes of the tribes of Israel offered many thousands of pounds of gold and silver to construct God's temple, David said: "Thine, O Lord, is the greatness, the power, the glory, the splendour, and the majesty; for everything in heaven and on earth is thine; thine, O Lord, is the sovereignty, and thou art exalted over all as head. Wealth and honour come from thee; thou rulest over all; might and power are of thy disposing; thine it is to give power and strength to all. And now, we give thee thanks" (1 Chronicles 29:11–13). Psalm 24:1 states: "The earth is the Lord's and all that is in it, the world and those who dwell therein." In Psalm 50:10–11 God says: "All the beasts of the forest are mine, and the cattle in thousands on my hills. I know every bird on those hills." And through the prophet Haggai, He said: "Mine is the silver and mine the gold" (Haggai, 2:8).

In chapter 16 of the Gospel According to Luke, there is the story of a certain rich man who suspected an administrator of squandering money. The rich man commanded: "Give an account of your administration." The term "rich man" here means God, and the term "administrator" here means a wealthy person. Such interpretation is offered by the

---

[1] This chapter appears to be a paraphrase of a book by R. Bellarmino, *De arte bene moriendi* (Cologne, 1626).

following Holy Fathers: St John Crysostom (cited by St Thomas Aquinas in "The Golden Flail"), St Augustine, St Ambrose, Bede, Theophilus, and Euphimeus. Consequently, if any wealthy man squanders God's property, God eventually will demand: "Give account of your administration or you will no longer administer it." This means that God may either deprive him of his life, punish him with an incurable disease, or reduce his wealth, and subsequently, assign him to eternal damnation.

There are some individuals who, after they have accumulated a great deal of wealth through deceit, think that they can earn forgiveness by offering the poor some comfort. For example, he who has stolen 1,000 rubles thinks he can settle his account by giving back ten rubles. But as Christians, we should clearly understand that ten rubles will not justify the 1,000 stolen rubles. Even two or three thousand rubles would not be sufficient, for the Holy Fathers say that, "The sin is never forgiven if the item taken away has not been returned." Yet every day we witness oppression, force, and pillage, and we do not hear anything about compensation.

For these reasons the Savior said of man: "Many are called upon, but only a few are chosen." And of the rich, He noted especially that: "It is easier for a camel to go through the eye of a needle than for a rich man to enter the kingdom of heaven." These words apply above all to the king and his royal officials. At the same time, our faith teaches us that no individual, as long as he is alive, should despair of God's mercy, for he can always confess and repent. True repentance redeems all our sins. Redemption is possible because of the great mercy of God. Yet it happens only with great effort, and so rarely that we are reminded of the words: "It is easier for the camel to pass through the eye of a needle than for a sinner (especially a rich one) to express real repentance."

Some kings and princes consider themselves to be the ultimate and sole masters of their kingdoms, but they should consider the following. First, kingdoms were not created for kings, but kings for kingdoms. They should ever remember: "God gave me these peoples not to oppress them or torture, but to shepherd and govern for their well-being." Second, "God, the Lord Most High, is fearful. He is the great sovereign over all the earth!" (Psalm 47:2). "Jesus Christ who is the Lord of lords and King of kings" (Apocalypse 17:14). God is the only true master. The king is His deputy. Third, from every individual God eventually demands an account of his property and possessions, and He punishes the individual who squanders his wealth foolishly. Fourth, the mission of the king is to make people content, which is to cherish virtue, to dispense justice, to maintain the peace, to keep down prices on necessities, and to uphold the honor of the nation and promote public well-being. Because of his goals, the king is called the head and the shepherd. What the head provides to the human body and the shepherd to his sheep, the king should provide his people.

As stated in the code of the emperor Justinian [*Corpus juris civilis*], harm will not transpire where justice and truth prevail.

Nobody owns anything which he has not received from someone else. As [St] Paul stated: "What do you possess that was not given you?" (1 Corinthians 4:7). All kings received their authority not from themselves but from someone else. They received everything from God. "There is no authority but by act of God" (Romans 13:1).

However, God gives the authority to kings through human agency, that is, first, through a prophet, as happened to Saul and David, who received their authority from Samuel; second, through selection, as is the case among the Turks, the Tartars, and other nations.

In these four ways, God appoints kings for the people. A nation that elects a king does not give him unlimited authority, which he can then use for his own caprice, be it good or bad, to the detriment of public well-being, and to oppress, plunder, rob, and ruin the people. They grant him authority over the people so that he can govern them and make them content by dispensing justice, conducting war, and striving to secure the abundance of everything that national life requires.

The king who governs by virtue of inheritance receives the throne by the right of inheritance from his father or a predecessor. But that predecessor leaves him that authority which he himself possessed and nothing more, because no one can give anyone anything that he himself did not possess. Consequently, a hereditary king does not have more authority than his father or grandfather or a more distant ancestor whom the people willingly elected with a stipulation that he be succeeded by his descendants.

Such a hereditary king might expand his authority by reason of some new circumstance. For example, if the people were to commit treason without cause, and the king were then to subdue and curb them, he might deprive them of some liberties and introduce laws that were more severe than those that had existed before. However, he may not introduce laws contrary to God's commandments and to natural honor and justice. Yet such are the laws of vicious and avaricious tyrants.

Finally, a ruler who governs as a result of some just or unjust military victory does not have authority contrary to divine and natural law. God does not grant authority to anyone for destructive purposes, but only for creative purposes. St Paul says as much: "The Lord gave me authority to create and not to destroy" (2 Corinthians 13:10).

Depending on the seriousness of the crime, the king may confiscate an entire property; he may even impose the death sentence, if such a step is demanded by justice, or is necessary as a warning, but only on those who have committed treason and who are more guilty than anyone else. He cannot, however, oppress the entire nation with eternal tyranny.

Objection No. 1: You say that the first selectors granted the king unlimited authority to use his kingdom as he wished, both for good and evil—to sell it, alienate it, devastate it, and ruin it.

Answer: The selectors never could have granted such a right, because they themselves did not have it. No one has the right to burn down his house, throw his money into a river, kill his horse, or above all, kill or sell his children. To acquire the stigma of eternal tyranny for oneself and one's descendants is a crime equal to someone's burning down his property or murdering his children. Even if some nations do not punish people for such transgressions, still they are guilty before God. Furthermore, if any nation has granted the king such unlimited authority, it was probably forced to do so, and such forcibly extracted consent is illegal.

Objection No. 2: Samuel explained to the Israelites the essence of royal authority and said: "Such will be the rights of the king. He will take away your fields and will give them and everything else to his servants." Such unlimited authority denotes royal, not national, benefit.

Answer: The Israelites at that time were pleading that God give them a king, being dissatisfied with Samuel, the judge, prophet, and holy man whom God had appointed over them. Therefore, He became angered and decided to enlighten them as to the burdens, just and unjust, that the king may impose on them. The forceful seizure from people of their harvest, vineyards, and livestock is clearly an unjust burden.

Example: If the king were entitled to take a vineyard away from one of his subjects, then king Ahab had the authority to expropriate the vineyard belonging to the Israelite named Naboth. Ahab had said to Naboth: "Give me your vineyard since it is close to my home; let me have it for a garden; I will give you a better vineyard in exchange for it, or, if you prefer, its value in silver" (1 Kings 21:2). Naboth wished neither to sell nor exchange his vineyard. If the king had had the authority to confiscate property, he doubtless would have confiscated the vineyard, but Ahab did not do so, because he did not have such authority. On the advice of his wife, he sent false witnesses who accused Naboth of blasphemy. Then the unjust court punished Naboth and the king took his vineyard.

I do not know what present-day kings would do if a *boyar* were unwilling to sell them property adjacent to the royal court. I think that they would not even ask him, but would instantly seize his property.

Neither David nor other Jewish kings enjoyed such authority, which shows that God did not give unlimited authority to kings.

Objection No. 3: Turkish and Persian rulers possess unlimited inhuman authority, and for them everything comes easily. Does this mean that such a government is just?

Reply 1: These rulers also suffocate their own sons as if it were legal, and say that it is right. Should we imitate this? Precisely because these bloody murderers of their own sons maintain such a government, we Christians should be suspicious of and avoid it. David says: "Do not envy the evil people who are favored by good luck." If these murderers of their sons have been selected to enjoy happiness in his life, then it is possible that God has selected them to serve as a whip to punish us Christians for our sins. For (so speaks St Augustine): "Every thief lives either to reform himself or, through his activity, to teach true believers."

Reply 2: Those kings are not as happy as they may appear, for they have turned their kingdoms into great wastelands. They would have ten times the inhabitants that they now have if their rule were more just.

39

Dreadful government and inhumanity

Some rulers never notice injustices and pay no heed to the problem of easing the people's burdens. They only wish to collect every revenue authorized by their treasury, regardless of the methods used in collecting it. Other rulers consider themselves innocent when their officials cause people injury in collecting revenue. They believe that nothing can be sinful if it causes the treasury to grow. No one has ever heard of a king punishing or fining his officials for unjust collection of revenue. Throughout the world, new ideas of any sort easily arouse doubt. Humans do not accept novelty with ease. Only in the collection of revenue is ill-advised counsel—unfair to both God and man—readily accepted by a majority of kings, despite its novelty.

Some people maintain that tyranny exists when innocent people are tortured to death (as pagan kings once tortured saintly Christian martyrs), but not when there are rapacious, inhuman laws. Hence, when kings have godless laws introduced by their predecessors on their books, they regard their predecessors, the ancient kings, as being responsible. They never consider correcting the old laws. But such a rationalization does not help in the eyes of God; even a human court punishes not only the initiator of a robbery but also his accomplices, those who have been persuaded into committing the crime.

Just royal authority develops into tyranny not because of torture, but rather because of extortionate laws. Any king can be a tyrant without extortionate laws and still the system of government may be a just one. Where extortionate laws prevail, however, both the system of government and the king are tyrannical. Thus if any king openly pillages the rich and murders the powerful, but does not undermine beneficial national laws, then, although he himself is a thief and tyrant, the state system itself is not a tyranny. After the death of the tyrant, good administration will reassert itself.

But if a king imposes extortionate laws and unjust fees and exactions on commerce and agriculture, he will not only be a tyrant but will make his successors tyrants, and the government structure will change from royal authority to tyranny. Moreover, should any successor of such a king become generous, merciful, and just without, however, eliminating old inhuman laws, he will remain a tyrant. The king is obligated to know and to understand the laws on which his realm is founded, and if he does not he is guilty.

Inhumanity is one of the three sins that bring down the vengeance of heaven. According to the Scriptures, when the Egyptian pharaoh started to oppress the people of Israel with cruel works, they appealed to God and He listened to their groans (Exodus 2). David asked: "How long shall the wicked exult? . . . they beat down thy people, O Lord, and oppress thy chosen nation" (Psalm 94:3–5). And God replied: "For the ruin of the poor, for the groans of the needy, now I will arise. . . ." (Psalm 12:5).

How does God punish inhuman individuals? The answer is: He takes the throne from them and their descendants. Solomon ruled peacefully for forty years without wars and disasters but imposed an unnecessary tax on the people. After him his son Rehoboam ruled. The Israelites came to him and pleaded with him: "Your father laid a cruel yoke upon us; but if you will now lighten the cruel slavery he imposed on us . . . we will serve you" (1 Kings 12:4–5). Rehoboam called an assembly where wise elders and loyal advisors urged him to listen to the people, to spare a good word for them and to ease their burden. But some greedy, foolish young flatterers recommended that he tighten the yoke, and Rehoboam replied to the people: "My father laid a heavy yoke on you; I will make it heavier" (1 Kings 12:11). As a consequence, God sent the prophet Ahijah to a nobleman named Jeroboam instructing him to commit a treason. This he did. Ten of the twelve tribes of Israel, in turn, committed treason by electing Jeroboam as their king, and they never again returned to the House of David. In this way, God punished Solomon's and Rehoboam's inhumanity.

Here in Russia, the entire nation knows very well the damned and bitterly remembered example of Tsar Ivan Vasilevich. For he was not only vile and mercilessly inhuman but also a vicious, godless butcher. For that reason, as God once sent Jeroboam to compete with Rehoboam, so, too, He made the *boyar* Boris Feodorovich Godunov a rival of Ivan IV, and predetermined that Ivan kill one of his three sons. God then deprived the second son of his senses and his ability to have heirs. And Boris, the rival, killed the third son in his childhood. The kingdom was thus taken from the dynasty of tsar Ivan and the line expired.

The new tsar, Boris Feodorovich, failed however to improve the government. He increased the tax burden of the farming-out system and built churches and towns with the stolen money. God sent a rival against him who was neither king nor *boyar,* but a deserter and a defrocked monk. This defrocked monk, with a handful of people and 6,000 mercenaries (using not his own strength but God's consent), seized the throne from Tsar Boris, compelled him to die a bitter death and extinguished his dynasty. He himself then committed treason before God by violating his pledge to become a monk and died a terrible death.

God's scourge was not removed from our nation until this ill-gotten revenue, covered with blood and with orphans' tears, was pillaged by foreigners and godless heretics, and until this godless inhumanity was redeemed by the burning of the entire city of Moscow. The towns that were built with peasant blood did not fall into the hands of foreign rulers.

Kings who are pious (for example, David) are usually blessed with many descendants. As St Leo teaches us, the father's glory does not fade even under unworthy descendants.

All the states of the Russian nation (Ukraine and Belorussia) returned to the realm from which they were severed several centuries ago. First, they drove out the Poles and then, when the latter regained control over them through deception, they defeated them again.[1] They thereby reaffirmed that they will never return to Polish authority. Once re-assembled, they pledged allegiance to the sovereign tsar.

Some people then correctly suggested that no new burdens be imposed on the new [Ukrainian and Belorussian] subjects of Russia—that it should be considered resource enough that the sovereign tsar should always have them at his disposal as a large army that would literally form a barrier, like a wall along that entire frontier. However, because of the old laws of Tsar Ivan IV and Tsar Boris, the *Boyar* Council chose otherwise and as a result the cursed drinking inns were introduced there.

Those advisors who believe in the sale of liquor, in taverns, in infamous revenues, and in other measures oppressive of poor subjects, are silly young men who think only of today's benefit, have no concern for the future, and do not understand what is worthy and honorable. They

---

[1] Here Krizhanich refers to a complex situation. In 1654, the Ukrainian Cossack hetman Bohdan Khmelnytskii and representatives of the tsar reached an agreement under which the tsar assumed protection of the territory under Khmelnytskii's control, but the Cossacks retained many of their rights. This arrangement engendered discontent among the Cossacks and was the cause of a Russo–Polish war. In 1657, Khmelnytskii's successor, Ivan Vyhovskii, joined forces with the Poles, while Khmelnytskii's son, Iurii, backed Moscow. In 1660, however, the latter also joined forces with Poland. For excellent, extensive discussions on the subject in English, see O'Brien, *Muscovy and the Ukraine,* 28–125; and Vernadsky, *The Tsardom of Moscow, 1547–1682,* part 1, 482–556.

thought that they were delivering great wealth to the tsar, but actually they brought upon him great ruin and indescribable harm.

Since the reign of Tsar Ivan Vasilievich, who originated this cruel government, affairs in this kingdom have been identical with those in ancient Israel. If one were to gather together all the money collected in this kingdom by forceful and inhuman methods since the time of Tsar Ivan Vasilievich—excluding lawful royal revenues—and, if it were ever to be put in one pile, that vast hoard could not compensate for one-tenth of the harm inflicted upon this kingdom by this brutal method of government.

I do not pretend to be a prophet, but I am firmly convinced that if human nature does not change, there will come a time in this tsardom when the entire nation will rise against the godless, inhuman laws of Tsar Ivan and Boris Godunov, and their inhumanity will not disappear without violence, clashes, and heavy losses. This is clearly evident from the omens and signs—the three recent upheavals, one in Pskov [1650] and two in Moscow [1648 and 1662], and the three treasons, along the Dnieper [1657], among the Bashkirs [1662], and near Berezovo [1663].[2]

It would be better if the sovereign tsar himself were to examine the problem and correct those inhuman laws. And to correct, it is necessary above all to uproot—that is, to decrease the ruinous expenditures on foreigners and to learn from the proverb: "Bread is always wasted in vain on strange dogs and somebody else's children."

Generous kings (whose fame is known throughout the world) shied away so much from greed and inhumanity that they often neglected to take advantage of dignified means to enrich themselves. Alexander the Great was once asked: "Where is your treasury?" And he replied: "Among my friends." Constantine the Great also cared little about his treasury, and, when his friends suggested that he pay more attention to it, replied: "A good ruler who is loved more than feared by his subjects possesses everything that his subjects possess."

Alfonso of Aragon, noted: "The responsibility of the king centers, above all, in making his subjects wealthy. For when his subjects are wealthy, their king cannot be poor." King James of England wrote a book to instruct his son, wherein he urges: "My son, do not try to enrich yourself by imposing new and burdensome taxes on your people. Instead, consider the wealth of your subjects as your own wealth."[3] The Roman

[2] This series of violent uprisings shook Russia in the mid-seventeenth century. They were a manifestation of widespread discontent against the oppression and injustice of the entire tsarist system.
[3] James I, *Basilikon doron; or, His Majesties Instructions to his dearest sonne, Henry the Prince* (London, 1603), 110.

emperor Trajan assented: "The treasury is the spleen of the nation. For whenever the spleen expands, the rest of the body grows thin and perishes and whenever the treasury becomes overfilled, the entire nation seems to plunge into despair."

Since the beginning of time, there has been no city that could stand on its won without being either conquered or occupied by an enemy, except Venice, which from its inception to the present day has remained free. The Venetians are considered exceptionally wise in governmental affairs. They have, for example, a law calling for capital punishment for anyone who suggests the formation of a public fund that would lie idle. As a result, the Venetians do not collect more from their citizens than is necessary to cover the customary annual expenditures. But if they are pressed in wartime, or if they need money in any crisis, the people willingly pay any levy that the authorities impose, because they trust that it will be repealed at the end of the war—thus treason is not committed.

40

Greed is the root of all evil

These are not my words. These are the words of St Paul and of God, the Holy Spirit: "Greed is the root of all evil" (1 Timothy 6:10). But since it may happen that someone may not be able to comprehend this expression, it is necessary to explain it briefly and to demonstrate how great and inexpressible harm results from inhuman behavior.

First of all, kings and their servants should know that because of their inhuman behavior, they destroy their souls and condemn themselves to eternal suffering. For as Christ says: "What benefit will a human gain when he gains possession of the entire world and loses his soul?" What benefit do you gain when you steal property that belongs to someone else, property that you should return and, for not doing so, will be condemned to eternal suffering? Your sin will never be forgiven if you do not return that which you have stolen. If those who have failed to share their wealth with the needy will go to the eternal fire, where else will those go who, using force, have seized property that belonged to others?

Moreover, greedy kings should know that through their requisitions they not only commit a sin, but are also the cause of countless other sins. This is because the officials in charge of requisitions always violate their oath of office by cheating the populace and stealing from the treasury. The poor, meanwhile, either curse the king, sound a warning, or perpetrate treason. All this in turn causes bloodshed, murder, perjury, other crimes, and ruin to the country. For all this, the king must give an account before God, because he has instigated everything and has oppressed his people by his godless tyranny.

Two of these arguments should be sufficient to turn every ruler away from this hideous inhumanity. Yet it would also be useful to recount those ills that greed and harsh government cause.

Among the vicious tyrannical laws of Tsar Ivan [the Terrible] the first and the most important was that which compelled all government officials and servants to take an oath to the sovereign tsar and swear as follows: "I,

[name], on every occasion, by every means at my disposal, will seek ways to increase the sovereign's treasury and will not let any opportunity pass to increase it."[1]

It is obvious that so illegal a law and so damning an oath caused great evil, because these officials, in the tsar's name, and for their own and the tsar's benefit, used every conceivable means, torture, and torment to pillage helpless subjects and allowed no opportunity of plundering them to pass.

Another such destructive law was this. High advisors bound by the above-mentioned oath did not give any salary to the lower officials, or if they did it was so little that these officials could not live on it. At the same time they were ordered to wear colorful, expensive clothes. They were sternly prohibited from accepting any bribes. What then was left for the poor people to do? Nothing but to steal. High state officials and other servitors were forced to adhere to the law and thus became partners of thieves.

Here is an example. One state official, shortly after he arrived in his territory, proclaimed: "During the entire period of my stay, I will not punish anyone." Simply stated he meant: "Brothers, steal freely, be brigands, pilfer and bring a portion to me, and everything you do will be forgiven." Local thieves practiced their trade for four years. There were frequent reports of murder and theft, and people were afraid to sleep in their homes, but not one thief was punished. This official and others like him maintained that this showed the tsar's mercy. Actually this is not mercy, but vicious torture, because wherever thieves and bandits have freedom, other people live under heavy oppression and are confident neither about their property nor their lives. And the reason for this, as we stated, is that officials do not receive adequate pay. A poor scribe is required to spend every day of the year in his office, without missing a single one, and often he is there the whole night too. The treasury pays him one *altyn* per day, or twelve rubles per year. But on festive occasions he must dress up in bright clothes, which cost more than twelve rubles. How can he feed and clothe himself, his wife, and the members of his family? Yet people live. But how can they live? They live by trading in the law.

---

[1] In a comment on the original Russian text (p. 722, n. 2), A.D. Goldberg observes that this oath only bound government officials to be loyal to the tsar, and that no other obligations were implied regarding the tsar's treasury. This is incorrect, however, since throughout the seventeenth century, and subsequently, all Russian officials were under obligation to advance the tsar's interests, including economic and financial interests, wherever possible. This was especially true with respect to collection of tribute from the natives in Siberia.

It is therefore not surprising at all that in Moscow there are so many thieves and so much banditry and murder. What is even more surprising is that honest people still live in Moscow. Constantinople has twice as many people as does Moscow and people there are of a far greater diversity and are hostile to each other's faiths and nationality. And, besides, the sea is near the city, so that it is easy for a murderer to dispose of a dead body in the water and thus hide his tracks. Nevertheless, years go by in Constantinople when one does not hear of a single burglary of a store, pillage of a home, or any other crime. In Moscow, by contrast, not a week passes without such news.

Why does this happen? Because of the connivance of officials. And what causes this vice among the officials? The unsatisfactory pay or remuneration that makes it impossible for them to exist.

An example: Bayezid I, the Turkish sultan, after hearing many complaints about the maliciousness of his judges, ordered them to appear before him, and allegedly resolved to lock all of them in one building and set it on fire. Ali Pasha then coached a certain Negro—a talkative fellow who was a royal jester—in what he should do and say, and he sent him to see the sultan. The Negro put on bright, fancy clothes and appeared before the sultan, who asked: "Negro, what news do you have? Why are you so strangely dressed?"

Negro: "So that you will send me as an ambassador to the Greek emperor."

The Sultan: "Why do you want to travel to our enemy?"

Negro: "In order to bring you several monks so that they can serve as our judges here since you plan to kill all of our judges."

The Sultan: "Oh, my little Negro! But do these monks know our laws?"

Ali Pasha answered *that* question. "Oh, sovereign! They do *not* know. Why, then, do you wish to kill the people who do know?"

The Sultan: "But why do they pass dishonest sentences?"

Ali Pasha: "Sovereign, I will reveal to you the reason. Our judges do not receive any pay from the treasury and therefore take money from the people. Designate their salaries and they will reform."

The Sultan liked this advice, and instructed Ali Pasha to do what was necessary. In this way judges were saved, and with them justice, which until then could be purchased. Since then Turkish judges have judged better and more justly than anywhere in the world. This, it seems, is the main reason why God has so long tolerated and permitted the impiety of the Turkish people and other sins, and has allowed them to dominate and insult Christian nations for so long.

But why waste words on correcting unjust courts when the laws of Tsar Ivan [the Terrible] themselves are clearly unjust? For what could one conceive to be more unjust than collecting such enormous court fees and tithes for the treasury? Nowhere in the entire wide world do kings receive any profit or gain from courts except here in Russia, where a practice so godless, inhuman, and destructive to justice has evolved.

Because of just courts, God has forgiven the sins of the Turks. It is little wonder, therefore, that God constantly punishes the Russian nation because of the existence of so many unjust courts. God's whip does not leave our backs because we are unwilling to pursue justice.

Not only do the judges and clerks lead a difficult life, but other servitors of the tsar's and administrators are often entrusted with affairs they cannot handle adequately on their own, for which they receive no assistance from the treasury. Ambassadors receive no adequate provision for their needs, nor do others for other needs. This causes a great deal of embarrassment and disgrace. For many, when pressed by necessity, forget their own personal honor and the honor of the nation and, in return for gifts, allow foreigners to drag them into all kinds of disgraceful criminal affairs. A German named Olearius boasts in his book that anyone who has money can obtain copies of even the most secret matters from government offices in Moscow.

In addition, in order to obtain gifts, ancient advisors to the tsar arranged that foreigners in Russia received whatever rights and freedoms they themselves requested or wished to enjoy. Accordingly, in return for trivial gifts and for a small (anticipated but not real) gain for the treasury—and at considerable loss—they have transformed this kingdom into a German tributary. These freedoms for foreigners cannot be maintained without enormous disgrace in the eyes of the entire world. Because of its inhuman laws, all European nations unanimously call this illustrious tsardom a tyranny. And, in addition, they say that the tyranny here is not a common one, but the greatest.

On July 26, 1663, I had a conversation with a deceitful German who said:

> It appears that all principal Russian *boyars* carry poison with them so that they can take it when they discover that the tsar is angry at them. The *boyar* who was near Kamenets [Podolskii], they say, took poison in Kiev. And another one, who investigated the pilfering of the treasury in the Ukraine, showed him his poison saying: "Look how slavishly we live."

There will be time and the appropriate place to reject this German lie. This German every day came up with thousands of fables, as for example that in his homeland along the Rhine the sun sets forests on fire, and so forth.

In the Turkish and Persian empires, with the exception of their practice of killing sons and their custom of strangling rulers, oppression is less cruel and tyrannical than that which exists here in Russia. Those who have visited those countries will verify these facts.

Because of this, the Russian nation has earned itself an ignominious reputation among other peoples, who assert that Russians are like donkeys and incapable of accomplishing anything worthwhile if they are not forced to do it with sticks and whips. Olearius writes thus. Yet this is a falsehood. The Russians speak the same language, belong to the same family, and have the same habits as other Slavs—Poles, Ukrainians, Croats, and others who are not donkey-like, but have other more refined characteristics. At present, many Russians do nothing out of respect for authority, and everything only because of fear of punishment caused by a cruel government, which has made their lives repulsive and without honor.

There is no doubt that if the Germans, or, for that matter, any other nation, had such a cruel government, they too would have similar habits to our own, perhaps even worse. I do not say worse idly, because they transcend us in intellect and cunning, and whoever has a sharp mind can come up with more crimes and deceptions.

As a result, this nation has developed so many revolting habits that other nations consider Russians cheaters, traitors, merciless terrorists, and killers, foul mouths, and slovens. What causes this is the fact that taverns, monopolies, prohibitions, tax-farmers, sworn-in deputies, tax collectors, dues collectors, and secret informers are everywhere, so that people are always constrained, and cannot do what they would like or freely enjoy what they have secured with their sweat and work. All of them are required to trade secretly, with fear, trepidation, and deception, and they must hide from the multitude of these government servants, robbers and thieves, or, more accurately, executioners. These sworn-in deputies and torturers of peasants, in consequence of not getting a sufficient salary, cannot behave justly, because need forces them to seek profit and to receive gifts from thieves.

And so, the people, who have become accustomed to do everything secretly and thievishly with fear and deceit, abandon honor, are deprived of martial spirit, and become rude, discourteous, and careless. They do not know how to distinguish one person from another, and their first question, when they encounter a stranger, is: "Do you have a wife?" Second, they ask: "What salary do you receive from the tsar, how much wealth do you have, and are you rich?" They are not ashamed when someone sees them naked in the public bath. And if they need help from anyone, they disgrace themselves badly, humiliate themselves, plead, and bow their heads almost to the floor almost loathsomely.

For that reason, all nations have an aversion for this tsardom and for the Russian people. Not long ago the Dnieper cossacks showed theirs. Although they speak the same language and profess the same faith, they prefer to be under Polish authority rather than ours, because of the viciousness of this government. During uncertain times, local inhabitants and leading individuals easily incline to commit treason, as was evident during the Time of Troubles [1598–1613].[2]

Cruel government is responsible for the fact that Russia is sparsely populated. Twice as many, or even more, people could live in Russia than is the case now, if the government were moderate. As already noted, nowhere in the world does there exist such revolting, hideous, and terrible drunkenness as here in Russia. And the cause of it is the government monopoly on taverns.

Boris: How can taverns be responsible for drunkenness?

Khervoi: Let me tell you how. First, because of that monopoly the people cannot brew their own drink without an official permit. Government regulations stipulate that private brewers must consume their beverage in three or four days after they had finished the brewing process, and after that they cannot keep it in their homes. Thus, in order to finish what has been brewed as soon as possible, the people drink excessively and become drunkards. And neighbors, who do not have any of their own drink at home, and cannot buy it anywhere, sit down without embarrassment and do not leave until they know that there is not a drop left in the barrel. As a result, the monarch is the cause, the participant, and the real promoter of this national sin.

Second, lower-class people do not have the means to prepare beer or wine at home for their own needs, and there are no taverns where one can drink except the tsar's taverns. These places and their utensils are dirtier than a pigsty, while the drink itself is repulsive and is sold at a devil's price. Moreover, these hellish taverns are not handy. In a large town there are one or two. I repeat, as a result, poor people are almost always deprived of drink, and consequently they become desperate for wine, shameless, and frenzied, so that regardless of what amount of wine they receive, they consider it God's and tsar's commandment to finish it in one gulp. Whenever they get some money and come to one of these hellish

[2] See introductory analysis, pp. xix–xxi.

taverns, they grow wild and they drink away all their household property and the clothes off their backs.

Third, it is impossible to brew intoxicating beverages without permission. Permission is not, however, given to anyone who does not show some reason or need. People therefore try to devise all sorts of reasons in order to receive a permit to brew an intoxicating beverage. This has contributed to the development of feasts, and in addition to the Holy Resurrection and other great holidays, the absurd custom was introduced of feasting, celebrating, and drinking for a week or two during the holiday of St Nicholas. This, in turn, has led to celebrating the last day of eating meat before a fast, and celebrating the name day and birthday. This, too, has led to giving gifts so often, that they contribute more frequently to the ruin rather than the saving of souls. Through drinking and new sins one cannot atone for old ones. Finally, this has also brought on court feasts, which great sovereigns prepare for foreign ambassadors or for their local lords and courtiers. Thus, when Tsar Ivan realized that his oppression was unbearable, in order to sweeten his oppression he introduced court commemorative feasts. I think, therefore, that all regular court feasts were organized on a grand scale and became part of court custom either during or after Ivan's reign.

These feasts or entertainments (especially those to honor foreign ambassadors) carry with them a general and open sin. For we invite foreigners to witness our disgrace, and we force our guests to commit a sin in every possible way. This is because a guest is required to accept a cup from the tsar's hands or from the tsar's table. He is placed in a dilemma, because he is forced to sin either against God or against the tsar.

These occasions, which at first were conceived arbitrarily, have in the end, inconspicuously entered into custom and become indispensable—a kind of immutable law. Hence, anyone who failed to prepare gifts and plenty of food for a name day, christening, birthday, or St Nicholas's day would lose respect and would be considered an offender. Therefore, many are forced to prepare these feasts not because they want to, but because of the general custom and to preserve their own respect.

Indeed, guests are invited not to a feast but to a sinful occasion, not to love but to degrade. Many of the guests return home hungry, without having eaten a meal, or even a slice of bread. Nobody ever returns home sober from such feasts. The host does not join his guests (as is customary the world over). He only goes around, as a servant, with bottle in hand.

These feasts never bring satisfaction or joy to an impoverished host. They bring only a threefold harm. First, his soul is harmed, because he angers God by the fact that through his craftiness and cunning he gets other people drunk. Second, his purse is harmed. And third, his body suffers and is tortured, for he walks around like a servant, instead of sitting and visiting with his guests as is customary in other countries.

Boris: You earlier said that to a considerable degree we Slavs are squanderers and hospitable by nature. It seems to me that our disgraceful drunkenness stems not from the monopoly on taverns but from our nature.

Khervoi: It is true that our people are squanderers and like to put on feasts. In contrast, the Italians, the Spaniards, and the Turks are moderate in their expenditures, do not waste money foolishly on drink, and never get intoxicated. The Germans, on the other hand, although they do not like to waste money foolishly, nevertheless, as far as drinking is concerned, quickly lose their balance the same way we Slavs do. For that reason, the Italians and the Spaniards consider Germans to be greater drunkards than ourselves. Let us also remember that all nations of our race both beyond the Danube and this side of the Danube—Serbs, Croats, Poles, and Russians—are alike by nature and all suffer from the squandering and feasting sickness.

Yet it is a fact that neither among the Germans, the Belorussians, the other Slavs, or anywhere else in the world, except in this single Russian state, does one encounter so much senseless drinking, nor find drunken men and women, laypeople and clergy, in the streets, and filth where so many die because of drunkenness. Nowhere else can one see so many forced feasts and so many diverse reasons for them. Nowhere else do there exist such means and pressures to drinking, except where devilish taverns exist. Boris, you can safely believe me that when you do away with taverns and court feasts, Great Russia will become like the Ukraine and Belorussia, and the drunkenness here will not be more excessive and more hideous than it is there.

Boris: But people in the Ukraine drink, and considerable drunkenness is found there too.

Khervoi: Brother Boris, it is true, and there is also much sin. But still, our drunknenness, is much more disgraceful. Besides, when people get drunk in other countries, they alone sin; the rulers and the national law do not promote it. Among us, however, Boris, rulers and national laws are the cause, the perpetrators, and the enforcers of the entire evil. For that reason, God is so angry with us, because those who are God's lieutenants and who should obey God's commandments openly violate them because of the weakness of their will.

41

Correcting tyranny and bad government

There is one piece of wisdom of which it is worthy that kings always be aware: "Rule over the people so that they will never seek a change." Because whenever any king rules by adhering to moderation, without resorting to inhumanity and expropriation, and willingly dispenses justice to everyone, all his subjects are contented and do not desire a change, and such a government is everywhere considered to be worthy. But if his successor should be greedy and inhuman, a squandering debauchee, or an enricher of foreigners, every good will turn into evil and the happiest kingdom will be transformed into a vicious tyranny. Consequently, any king who, upon his death, wishes to be a benefactor of his people and to gain glory for himself in subsequent ages, must not only be good himself, but ought to introduce good laws and grant proper privileges and rights to every category of people. Why? Because otherwise he cannot control the unrestrained greed of his successors and the bad habits of servitors who offer inhuman counsel.

Whatever the root, so the plant; whatever the tree, so the fruit; and whatever the laws, such is the order of things in a state. We may wish that seed which in other places sprouts into darnel [tares] would produce wheat here. But it is impossible to obtain wheat from darnel, because darnel always produces darnel, and vicious laws always and everywhere produce bad results—that is, godless inventions of officials and the pillage and devastation of the country. Even if the king were an archangel, if his servitors are not restrained by good laws (that is, by privileges appropriate to every segment of the population), it will be impossible to prevent them from perpetrating local and unaccounted thefts, offenses, and other inhuman acts.

The worst of all is the fact that rulers become open co-conspirators of thieves. When officials, in return for bribes, agree with thieves, ordinary citizens do not have the right to punish the thieves. This means that there is only one way by which the king can soothe his conscience, terminate the thievery of his·servants, and escape the association of brigands. He should grant every segment of the population appropriate, reasonable, and just privileges, which we will soon discuss.

Boris: Autocracy is the best form of government. Moreover, where subjects have no privileges, autocracy is firmly maintained. Conversely, where subjects enjoy privileges, autocracy is ruined. This implies that it is improper to grant privileges to subjects.

Khervoi: You are right when you say that autocracy is the best form of government and that it should be preserved by every available means. However, it is not true that autocracy would perish if reasonable privileges were granted to its subjects.

Wherever unlimited and unnecessary privileges exist, autocracy will perish, and will be replaced by dissoluteness (anarchy), as we now see among the Poles and the Germans, where no one obeys anyone and there are as many rulers as there are tyrants. Wherever there are no privileges, autocracy will not succeed, and inhumanity (tyranny) will evolve. Only where reasonable, appropriate, and just privileges are granted can true autocracy be preserved, strengthened, and maintained.

The king himself may be good, but his successors may be bad. The king may be good, but many of his servitors may be bad and unworthy. If royal servants and kings themselves were God's angels, and could not commit any mistakes or abuse their authority, there would be no need for privileges, and the autocracy would be preserved without them. But kings themselves and their servitors can easily abuse their authority, and usually do. In addition, the [wicked officials] always contribute to great lawlessness, because they ravage the country, disgrace the people, lead the king to commit awesome sins, anger God, and invite God's punishment.

However, when the people are granted reasonable privileges, a bridle is placed on royal servitors, so that they cannot indulge in their vicious desires and drive people to despair. This is the only means by which subjects can protect themselves against the evildoing of servitors. This is also the only way to safeguard justice in the realm. If there are no privileges, then no prohibitions and no punishments by the king can cause his servants to renounce their evildoing and prevent his high-placed advisers from offering him godless, inhuman counsel.

Rehoboam's subjects requested relief because the construction of God's temple had been completed and there were no wars but he increased their burdens. Rehoboam favored sternness and inhumanity instead of justice, and for that reason lost almost the entire kingdom.

Many kings in the world resemble Rehoboam, and every king has many close advisers similar to those Rehoboam had. The obligation of a wise man and of an advisor is to look forward and back and to be concerned not only about today's needs but about tomorrow's. If one does not remove the load from a camel's back but rather constantly increases it, the animal will fall down under the weight and will not be able to carry anything. If a bow is constantly drawn and never unstrung it will lose its elasticity. A human who works constantly without sleep or rest will expire. The same applies to a kingdom when its subjects are never allowed a reprieve but instead receive increased burdens and therefore suffer many misfortunes and disgrace. Such a country becomes a wasteland: foreigners devour and carry off every commodity, unrest and treason prevail, kings are dishonored, expelled, murdered, and turned over to the enemy, and the entire nation sins against God.

Who was the Russian Rehoboam? Tsar Ivan Vasilievich, who introduced cruel and merciless laws in order to rule his subjects. Another Rehoboam was Tsar Boris Feodorovich Godunov, who not only approved but greatly expanded these laws.

One of the principal causes of bad laws, as well as their mainspring, is the oath accompanied by the kissing of the cross that all tsarist officials and servitors take, wherein they pledge that in all affairs and under all circumstances they will always try by every means available to seek out and increase the profit of his tsarist majesty's treasury. This godless oath leads not only many bad, but also many honest individuals to sin. Because of this oath, many consider it their duty to come up with all kinds of vicious ideas that may somehow bring profit to the treasury. And those who are naturally inclined toward greed and inhuman behavior (and there are plenty of them at any given time) do not waste any opportunity or sit by idly. They skillfully take advantage of the authority given to them and use every means to harm and to oppress the poor.

Boris: But, on the other hand, all officials are strictly prohibited from harming people without cause and from ruining the tsar's patrimonies.

Khervoi: Neither this prohibition nor any punishment will help, because all government officials justify their actions by this oath directed at increasing the tsar's treasury.

In place of the current pledge which affirms, "I will increase the tsar's revenue by all means at my command," it would be better to obtain from them an oath wherein they swore: "I will not unjustly harm any subject, nor will I ruin the tsar's patrimonies."

Illustrious tsar, you resemble God's angel. But the generosity of your greatness cannot benefit the realm as long as there exists the demand for the unjust oath and the excessive power of your servants. Moreover, all of your descendants, even if they were archangels, will be unable to free themselves from the malignant gossip of the entire world, and will be considered tyrants by all European nations, if they should maintain these laws. As we had occasion to note, it is impossible to stop or to prohibit outrages by your servants as long as such laws exist. It is not enough to tell your servitors that they will be punished mercilessly. Under tyrannical laws, there are always many opportunities to commit crime, and wherever there are so many opportunities, no punishment is adequate to deter people from doing so. It will be necessary to keep whips and gallows ready constantly. As soon as the executioners stop torturing thieves, servitors will resume their evildoing—as happened recently with respect to the official debasements of our coinage [in 1662]. There is no other way to improve conditions in the realm than to repeal bad laws and introduce good ones. By this means, the kingdom will forever be preserved for the descendants of your majesty and your conscience will be clear before God and the world. Your subjects, indebted for such good deeds, will be eternally loyal to you, and will willingly and gladly pay taxes and extraordinary levies.

As far as current events are concerned, the *boyars*, merchants, and all those who receive these privileges, will assist with all of their efforts (given the current deficit of the treasury) to restore the value of the silver coinage and normal conditions. The Poles, too, will seek peace with us more readily, and will accept the lord sovereign tsarevich on their throne.[1] And those people who now are afraid of this government as if it were a devil, will henceforth wish to live, illustrious tsar, under your so benevolent, wise, and merciful authority.

We shall outline the way to handle this problem, and what to do before laws are corrected and the sovereign tsar grants privileges to his people, in the hypothetical address which follows. The sovereign tsar can deliver this address, or some more appropriate one, to the nation in person, or can delegate a *boyar* to compose it.

---

[1] The Polish king Jan Kazimierz (1609–72) had no heirs, and the Russian regime hoped to have a Muscovite prince elected as his successor. For discussion in the broader context of Russo–Polish relations, see N. Bantysh-Kamenskii, *Obsor vneshnikh snoshenii Rossii* . . . (Moscow, 1902), part 3, 131–33.

42

The Tsar's draft address
to the realm: preamble

Our honorable beloved fathers, princes, *boyars*, nobles, and the entire Russian people, our loyal subjects! We, as well as our late father of blessed memory, have always taken care of, and have been concerned about, tsarist responsibility—that is, that all of you, and our entire realm, abound in everything, that you be rich and content, that everybody cooperate with everybody, that the country be powerful against its enemies, and that it enjoy God's mercy and the respect of the entire world. In a word, the general welfare of the country has always been close to our heart.

There is no need for us to recall this because you yourselves understand it very well. Compare the present situation and that which existed in earlier times during the reign of our father. And if, by chance, not everything has turned out the way we wished, we hope that all of you will acknowledge that this was not because of our unwillingness or lack of concern, but for other reasons.

If, however, there should be found an uninformed person who even now is unfamiliar with our fervent desire to promote the public good, then henceforth (inasmuch as by God's mercy peace has been granted to us) we have firmly resolved to proceed in such a way as to enable the entire world to know that which none may conceal—that we nourish toward our entire nation not only royal, but real fatherly affection.

In order that you may understand the reason for our address and why we have invited you here, please know that we have discovered that conditions exist in our realm that interfere with the well-being of the people and about which all segments of the population—clergy, *boyars*, nobles, young people, soldiers, townsmen, and peasants—complain. In a word, not one group is satisfied with its fate and circumstances. This is not surprising.

You well know that from time immemorial this realm has experienced grave problems and discord. After the reign of Vladimir the Great [980–1015], endless turmoil divided the nation. Later we were overwhelmed by the Tartars, who easily conquered a kingdom in such desperate circumstances, they held it in subjugation for a long time, and almost annihilated it. Thanks to God's mercy, Grand Prince Dmitrii Ivanovich [Donskoi, 1359–89] started to cast off their yoke, and then Tsar Ivan Vasilievich [III, 1462–1505] terminated it and brought the realm into the condition that you now witness. But Tsar Ivan [IV] was involved in countless wars, and was merciless and brutal by nature. He could not, therefore, evidence concern about the entire realm, as was necessary, nor did he introduce legislation indispensable for the long life of the realm and the general well-being of all of its inhabitants.

After the death of Tsar Ivan, his feebleminded son began to rule and there then followed the Time of Troubles, which witnessed the devouring of two tsars and their dynasties. Our father [Michael Feodorovich] inherited a realm that was weak, devastated, and virtually ruined. He tried in every way to rule so that it could again regain its former might. And, with God's grace, he ruled it so that under him the kingdom emerged more powerful than it was at any time in the past. As a result he left among you a good attitude toward him, while among foreign nations he acquired the reputation of an honest and merciful king. He was unable to set right certain laws that needed correction because of the enormous destruction within the kingdom.

God does not create everything all at once and does not grant all gifts to one individual. Instead, He distributes various favors to different individuals, so that everyone may have access to His goodness. This goodness of God, the Father of all favors, has given us peace, and has inspired goodwill and a desire to do what most of all would serve the glory of almighty God, our honor, and the good fortune of the Russian people and of all Slavic nations.

We wish above all else to repeal the monopoly on taverns and all other monopolies, which we find very burdensome to the people. We wish to grant to all ranks and classes of people appropriate privileges, so that all of them will be content with their condition and destiny.

We wish to reaffirm and expand privileges of the clergy. We wish to grant the *boyars* extensive rights and privileges, so they can enjoy them on their estates, and to bestow on them other distinctions, similar to those we encounter in other countries of Europe. Lesser nobles and soldiers will also receive appropriate privileges. Finally, free townsmen, craftsmen, and peasants will receive such of our favors that they, too, may be fully contented.

We have examined and investigated the legislation of various kingdoms—Greek, French, Spanish, German, and Polish—and those laws which we have considered to be good, appropriate, and necessary for our kingdom we wish to grant generously to you. However, before all of this can be accomplished, it is necessary to examine and analyze the essence of public wealth, or those items that contribute to the glory of God, and to the might, longevity, and honor of the nation. It is essential to introduce laws that will not only give us temporary satisfaction, but will also permanently strengthen the kingdom. Before we abolish monopolies and some other burdens, therefore, it is necessary that you tell us by a general consensus, what system you would like to adopt in order that our treasury receives the revenues necessary for the defense of the realm and other public expenditures.

Furthermore, before we repeal some of the oaths now taken by our officials, which involve the kissing of the cross (especially those pertaining to the increase of our treasury), and before we grant privileges to all classes, we request that all of you give us a new, just, and in all respects dignified oath on the cross, pledging that you will never under any circumstances accept a foreigner as your sovereign. This applies also in the event that our present dynasty fails to produce heirs and you are compelled to elect a sovereign freely. You should then elect as your tsar not a foreigner, but a person of Slavic race, in compliance with God's commandment.

On our part we, too, will take an oath binding our descendants not to marry their daughters to anyone except to rulers of Slavic nations who themselves are Slavs, or to their subject princes and *boyars*. Likewise, we will not take wives from any foreign nation, but only from the families of Slavic rulers and our own subjects—the daughters of princes, lords, and *boyars*.

43

The Tsar's address to the realm: laws against national discontent

NEEDS AND PRIVILEGES OF ALL CLASSES

Clergymen, priests, churchmen, monks, nuns, and all of religious rank will be freed from supervision by government and civil courts, and will dispense justice among themselves. They will also be freed from general public impositions and work, and all kinds of burdens. For, since they have been designated to serve God, they cannot be compelled to serve humans too. God speaks of this as follows: "Whoever touches you touches the apple of his eye" (Zechariah 2:8). Even during the time of the heathen Egyptians, Joseph purchased for the king the entire land, except that of the clergy. That is, priests owned their villages without performing any burdens or paying any taxes.

We consider the honor of our loyal servitors—princes, lords, *boyars,* and all nobles—to be our honor and dignity. The dignity of the *boyars* elevates the dignity of the king, because the better off are those he rules, the better and more dignified the ruler.

For this reason, we believe that it would be good and proper to grant specific rights to, and advance the honor of, our loyal servitors and nobles. Wherever lords have satisfactory freedoms, dignity, and advantages over the common people, their royal dignity is higher, and safer from the malignant gossip of foreigners and mad and dishonest attacks by the local common folk.

An example is provided by the French and Spanish nobles who have decent hereditary privileges and advantages. Thus neither the commoners nor the military there bring any dishonor to the kings. Among the Turks, on the other hand, where nobles enjoy no privileges, rulers are at the mercy of the whim of ordinary infantrymen, because whatever the janissaries wish, the ruler must do. Sultan Osman [II, in 1622] and Sultan Ibrahim [I, in 1648] were strangled by them recently, and they also strangled many nobles in front of the sultans, who pleaded with them for mercy. All of this happens as a matter of course.

Roman soldiers trifled with their emperors. They easily deposed or killed one and placed another on the throne. They literally played dice with them.

The foolishness of the common people, which has occurred here twice and about which you know,[1] the Germans have written about in their books. And this foolishness stemmed from the fact that the *boyars* possessed neither the strength nor firmness to bridle and control the common folk from mad actions. For that reason we wish to grant you, our servitors, proper privileges.

In their conquered territories, the Turks grant their own people more privileges than they do the old inhabitants. But here the opposite is true. And this is improper.

In distributing privileges we should not imitate the customs of any other nation. Many privileges, especially those enjoyed by the Poles and Germans, were secured by force, and are contrary to common sense. Privileges enjoyed by whole classes or separate individuals should be granted only to the extent that they benefit the entire society. And, conversely, if any privilege does not benefit the society, it should not be granted, and if it was granted earlier, it should be rescinded. Especially detrimental to the society are those privileges that undermine absolute monarchy.

THE PREROGATIVES OF SUPREME AUTHORITY

(1) No one is allowed in perpetuity to mint money on his own behalf, or that of the tsar, without royal permission.

(2) No one may have personal military units. Princes, lords, and *boyars* may have as many domestic servants as we will allow them.

(3) Princes alone may have one fortified town. No one else has the right to control a city and to surround it with a wall. However, we may allow some individuals to own and fortify a town in border areas but not on hereditary basis. Everyone is allowed to own a courtyard for his servants and to build his own court.

(4) No one is allowed to hold any of our departments or an official position on a hereditary basis. By our edict we may grant some departments and assignments for life.

(5) No town may on its own authority designate elders, adminis-

---

[1] Krizhanich refers here to the popular discontent of 1648 and 1662.

trators, and commanders. Our officials will appoint all town elders and judges.

(6) Without our edict no one is allowed to call any legislative assemblies or councils into session.

(7) Neither a prince nor a lord nor any other individual is allowed to sell his estates without first giving notice of it. No one is allowed to purchase hereditary estates, and other immovable properties in excess of what we or our officials may allow.

(8) Conclusion: no one is allowed to appropriate for himself any rights, or acquire property, privileges, power, and authority that might undermine the authority of our majesty.

(9) We and our successors will bind ourselves and take an inviolable oath that we will observe all the privileges we today grant and bestow upon you, our loyal subjects. However, if subsequently you or your descendants from any class exhibit disobedience—that is, if people, by hiding behind some privilege, will not obey and fulfill our orders—we and our heirs are not obligated to preserve the privilege which resulted in disobedience, and we shall neither grant nor issue any such right.

Simply and briefly put, the matter is this. The tsar is God's lieutenant and a living law. He is not subject to any laws except God's, and is above all human laws. The tsar should not, and may not, proclaim a law that would be above him, because God has elevated him above human laws. For that reason, too, all of these privileges will always remain in our power and in the power of our heirs so that we may amend or withdraw them whenever we wish, but not without just and appropriate causes. Consequently, do not think that these privileges have given you some authority or independence which we are powerless to withdraw. Know only that these privileges express for you our love, mercy, and reward, which will remain as long as our good will prevails. However, we and our heirs will bind ourselves by an oath not to violate, alter, or withdraw these privileges without just and appropriate cause.

Therefore, in the name of the Most Holy and Indivisible Trinity, God the Father, the Son, and the Holy Ghost, we by God's Grace [name], grant and bestow in perpetuity the following privileges, rights, and dignities on you, our loyal servitors and courtiers, and on your descendants.

First of all, we shall divide you into three groups and create among you three distinguished noble classes.

Nobles of the first class will be called princes. No one, however, should be called a prince if he does not have a fortified town or an *ostrog* under his authority. But no prince should have more than one town. Let there also be a limit on the number of princes. Twelve should be sufficient and no more.

Let the second class consist of those who are now called *boyars*. And let these two classes jointly be called distinguished *boyars* and lords.

Let the third class be called *plemiane* [kingsmen], rather than *deti boyarskie* [petty nobles].[2]

We shall designate princes by the granting of banners.

Next, we are freeing you from all servile obligations and are removing you from the list of our slaves. You, our loyal subjects, princes, *boyars,* and *plemiane,* will henceforth be known as our loyal servitors, courtiers, and kingsmen, and not slaves. And in perpetuity you will be free from all slavelike obligations, work, taxes, impositions, collections, cart service, agriculture, crafts, all other work performed by slaves, the lower classes, and townsmen, and from handicrafts. You will also be exempted from sentry service and from all burdensome military service in peacetime. No one, however, will be exempted from any service or work when armies are in the field or in towns under siege.

Nobles henceforth will not be called by their diminutive names— Borka, Volodka—but by their full names—Boris and Vladimir. Moreover, they should not be called by their patronymics, but by full noble family names: not Boris Ivanovich Morozov, but Boris Morozov. This has a much more distinguished, noble, and sonorous effect than patronymic reference, because all peasants and all the lower classes have fathers and may use patronymics, but they do not have noble or family names.

Henceforth let no one bow his forehead to the ground before anyone. Bowing is appropriate only to God and the holy icons, not to humans. If anyone should bow to the ground before any human or before our own majesty, he should be reprimanded for the first offense and be penalized for the second and third offenses.

Everywhere in Europe and among our neighbors (except the Persians and the Turks) nobles have certain honorary titles, both recorded and unrecorded, and it has come to our attention that you, our courtiers receive less respect because you are not using such titles. Therefore, to enhance your dignity with foreign nations, we hereby grant you such

---

[2] In the sixteenth and seventeenth centuries, the term *deti boyarskie* (singular *syn boyarskii*) was used to describe a large group of impoverished nobles. In Siberia these men played a prominent role as middle-ranking military commanders and civil administrators. For a discussion of the *deti boyarskie*, see Lantzeff, *Siberia*, 63–65.

honorary titles (recorded and unrecorded) as exist in practice, or may be considered honorable by other nations, with but one exception: they may not be foreign titles but our own Slavic terms, and, moreover, must adhere to our language and be used in conversation.

Everyone should refer to princes, *boyars,* and *plemiane* as "Your Grace" and not "Thy Grace" (referring to a single person), as is incorrectly done by the Poles and Croats. In addressing a prince one should say "Gracious prince," or "Gracious *gospodin*" [lord], or "*Gospodin* prince." Addressing a lord say simply: "Gracious *pan.*" When addressing a *boyar* simply use *pan* and his family name: for example, *Pan* Bunich, *Pan* Peranskii; or use his Christian name: *Pan* Boris, *Pan* Vladimir.[3] When an equal addresses his equal, a prince addressing a prince, he should say "*Pan* Peranskii," "*Pan* Vladimir," or "*Pan* Prince." In correspondence a prince should be addressed as follows: "Honorable *gospodin* Bogdan Voinovich, Prince Maglaiskii (that is, administrator of the town of Maglai), my gracious benefactor." A lord should be addressed as "Great Lord, *Pan* Vladimir Buzhinskii, my gracious lord." Should he have special distinctions (that is, if he should be our *okolnichii, chashnik, koniushii, ban,* colonel, or the like), he should be addressed as "The Gracious *Pan, okolnichii* Vladimir Buzhinskii." A *boyar* should be addressed as "The Noble *Pan* Mikula Stoianov." But if he should be our courtier, captain, or a person of similar distinction, he should be addressed as "The noble *Pan* captain (or courtier) Mikula Stoianov." Temporary titles should not be mentioned, that is, if someone is temporarily appointed to be a town administrator, one should not put it in a letter, except in official correspondence when this is required.

We are bestowing the title of *pan* on you because it is a Slavic term, while *szliachta* and *hetman* are German terms. *Syn boyarskii* and *voiskovoi golova* [military head] are Turkish terms. For that reason, we consider the term *pan* appropriate, and reject foreign terms and will use not *szliachta* but *boyar,* nobleman, or noble, and not *hetman* but *ban,* and not *syn boyarskii* but *boyar,* not *golova* but *voevoda.*[4]

---

[3] *Pan*: a Polish term for lord or master.

[4] *Okolnichii*: a high-ranking court official in seventeenth-century Russia whom the tsar often entrusted with military, civil, and diplomatic assignments; *chashnik*: a cupbearer; *koniushii*: master of the stables; *ban*: a Croatian term for a high-ranking military commander; *szliachta* (singular *szliachcic*): a Polish term for the nobility; *hetman*: chief military commander in Poland–Lithuania and among the Ukrainian Cossacks (the word apparently derives from the German *Hauptmann*); *zhupan*: a Serbo–Croatian term for civilian administrators of territories or towns; *voevoda*: an old Slavic term meaning military commander, which in seventeenth-century Russia signified an administrator appointed by the tsar, usually a *boyar*, holding military, civil, and judicial powers in a region.

Military titles should not be confused with those of civilian town officials. Therefore, we will call our town and *uezd* administrator not *voevoda* but *zhupan*. This will be explained in detail in another place.

Princes will be allowed to enter Moscow and other towns with four musicians and two heralds; lords with two musicians and one herald; *boyars* and courtiers with two musicians, without heralds: and military commanders in wartime with such a suite and such musicians as they are entitled to.

All nobles should forever be freed from knouting, whipping, and from disgraceful punishment. This includes the mutilation or severence of the nose, ears, or limbs. Their punishment should include imprisonment, expulsion from office (if the individual is an official), exile, or other punishment.

Should anyone be convicted and given the death penalty for minting of money, or for treason, or for any other serious crime, the case should be resolved as follows. If the crime is a direct affront to God or to our royal authority—that is, if heresy or treason has been committed, or an attempt made on our royal health or life, or if someone has tried to introduce alien rule, a marriage with foreigners, or in some way committed treason against us or against the country and the entire nation—then that criminal should accordingly be condemned to death, and his estate and all of his property should be confiscated and incorporated into our treasury. Before they are executed, such criminals, thieves, and bandits should be deprived of the rank—that is, they should be deprived of all their *boyar* rights and privileges. But should they be condemned to death for some other crime, their property should not be confiscated, but granted to their heirs.

The sovereign has the exclusive right, without resorting to the courts, to exile dangerous *boyars,* but they should be neither tortured nor executed nor have their property confiscated without due process of law.

No one should enslave a nobleman. Those who will do so will be punished severely. A prince will be allowed to hire the son of a lord as his temporary attendant, while a lord may hire the son of a *boyar.* However, peers may not be hired—that is, a prince cannot hire another prince as his temporary attendant, a lord another lord, or a *boyar* another *boyar.* And when any petty noble sells himself into slavery, he may regain full freedom from his master by appearing in the appropriate government office. He will, however, forfeit his title and will become a commoner.

Only *boyars* will be entitled to hold landed estates. Ordinary taxpayers will not be allowed to hold large estates. Necessary fields near town walls are an exception. We will designate such fields for each town. All other lands that they now hold they must sell.

Boyars must have preference and freedom in selecting their clothes to distinguish them from commoners, and lords to distinguish them from *boyars.* It is uncomely and improper that a commoner should have the same clothes as the master. For example, only princes will be allowed to wear sable hats made from black fox pelts an inch thick. And only lords and military commanders will be allowed to wear three white crane feathers.

To each of our princes and lords we grant special distinguished family heraldry or honorary insignia that will testify as to the bravery and stability of each family. Our noble servants should inscribe this coat of arms on their shields, and during parades or ambassadorial receptions their shield-bearers should carry them either in front of or behind them. Thus, a mounted shield-bearer must hold his master's bow and arrows and decorated shield. We will not grant crests to all *boyars,* only to those who earn them by brave deeds.

While our shoulders will never be free of the burden of governing the nation or our head from its prescribed concerns, nevertheless we shall grant some relief from work to our loyal servitors, you distinguished *boyars*—that is, princes and lords (who, more than anyone else help us to carry the heavy burden of our crown). We are thus freeing you from services and permanent attendance at court.

Any prince who has spent three years of continuous service to our royal person or who has served in the military is freed for life from service at court. As a result, he should not come to live in Moscow if we have not personally requested him to do so. Any lord who has spent six years in our service will also be freed. However, we grant this privilege and right not under oath but of our own goodwill. It will be valid until we or our descendants issue a new edict.

Those distinguished *boyars* who will be in Moscow in person serving at our court, need not perform their service continuously or all at once. They should alternate, each serving at a designated date and time.

Those princes, lords, and *boyars* who have served many years in the army, if they have become old or ill, will have the right to hire another person as a substitute for themselves in that service. Sons of all princes and lords, but not all sons of *boyars* and townsmen (the latter will include only those necessary and essential for the realm such as our officials will designate), will be allowed to study Greek and Latin in order for them to know national history, philosophy, and politics. Other, difficult and less noble disciplines, such as accounting, astronomy, land surveying, and medicine should be studied by sons of townsmen and of poor *boyars* in such numbers as necessary for the kingdom.

Every prince and lord will have the right to build and fortify for himself one town and maintain there or nearby his personal, fortified courtyard, or to own a town which the king may give him as a gift. Therein he will have the right to punish all criminals, except those guilty of undermining the tsar's majesty. Those he should dispatch to the appropriate royal department.

Nobles, eminent and otherwise, will not henceforth be required to undertake any ambassadorial assignment at their own expense, unless choosing to do so. No gifts (which the *boyars* bring the tsar) should develop into a custom or obligation. We will not accept from you any annual gifts that would be considered obligatory or customary. Only when anyone brings a gift without custom or obligation will we accept it, provided our will is the same.

Consequently, since we have such high regard for you and intermarry with you, you should see to it that your own honor and dignity are of long standing and that your family and noble title remain proper and permanent.

With the growth of the family, there takes place a division of property, impoverishment of descendants, and a diminution of dignity. In order to prevent this, we hereby decree the following throughout our entire tsardom: henceforth, till eternity, there shall be no division of our tsardom among our descendants. The eldest son will inherit the throne and his younger brothers will receive landed estates and princely titles. Our daughters will receive dowries in money.

For the same reason, on your own behalf, we also hereby decree the same policy for you, the princes and lords. Your hereditary as well as non-hereditary estates shall not be divided. Instead, the eldest son will assume a princely title and will receive all the hereditary estates and property of his father. He should give his sisters dowries in the amount he can afford. His younger brothers should be satisfied with *boyar* titles and service at our court until they are famous and become lords in their own right.

Let the same law apply to the sons and daughters of lords.

We measure and judge ourselves by our own standards and do not consider ourselves to have descended either from the divine or the angelic family, but from humans. We therefore do not scorn your class but enter into marriages and family ties with you, our subjects, as was done by Roman, Greek, Persian, Assyrian, and Jewish kings, and we wish you, too, not to scorn the class below you. Let no prince consider it dishonorable to intermarry with the family of a lord, or lord with that of a *boyar*, or *boyar* with a distinguished townsman's family.

Our own dignity and the dignity of our royal sons is in no way diminished by the fact that we were mothered by *boyar's* daughters. We therefore decree and firmly order that no one should ever consider a prince mothered by a *boyar's* daughter, or even the daughter of a townsman, to be less than a prince mothered by a princess. We decree that his mother's background shall not diminish a man's dignity, and that family dignity is transmitted not through the mother (contrary to German contentions), but through the father, as once the rulers of the world all believed and is today believed by the Persians, the Turks, and all Asian and Eastern nations. This, our decree, can bring you, princes and lords, immense benefit. Your second sons can marry daughters of rich townsmen, purchase hereditary estates, and become famous.

Out of the fatherly affection we entertain toward the entire nation, and also because of our concern that this tsardom should under no circumstances ever experience a division, we hereby decree, affirm, and order that the following rule be kept for ever: that no woman, even from our own royal family, be entitled to any right to inherit the tsardom or the throne. At the same time, our sisters and our daughters should not be viewed as if they did not exist at all.

We furthermore decree—and we will take an oath on it and will bind our heirs to it—that no foreigner or a heretic shall ever become a Russian ruler. And if, to our misfortune, one manages to gain the throne, let no one obey him. And should anyone swear allegiance to such a person, we (in accordance with the advice and decision of the Holy *sobor* [council] of our spiritual fathers) declare in advance that such oaths, swearings, and kissings of the cross are worthless and invalid, and that individuals are not bound to fulfill them, because they are illegal and were administered contrary to the national custom and national wellbeing. This is the same as if someone swore that he wanted to kill another person. Such an individual is not bound to adhere to his oath: on the contrary, he will commit a sin if he should stick to it and kill a person.

Should any of our descendants have a daughter and marry her to a foreigner, and should he induce you to take a new oath and to amend this oath, then you and your descendants should know that that oath is worthless. Unjust laws cannot replace just and generally accepted laws, and the king must not force people to take an unjust oath in contravention of the just oath they took before.

In addition, we hereby decree that our heirs take an oath that they will not invite foreign kings, princes, royal heirs, princely heirs, or lords to Russia, nor accommodate any who would like to come here of their own volition, except such as may seek refuge from some disaster; who should be treated as time dictates and after the fashion of other European kings.

Moreover, we decree that no foreigner shall be made tsar, prince, *ban,* lord, *okolnichii, voevoda, boyar,* courtier, or town administrator. Foreigners shall, moreover, have no right to own landed estates, a courtyard, a house in town, or any other immovable property. Poles, Czechs, Serbs, Bulgars, and Croats should not be considered foreigners. We also decree that no foreigner ever be allowed to receive citizenship among us, be considered a Russian, or be granted Russian rights and privileges.

Should there ever develop discord among us, let the following rule prevail: whoever invites foreign armies into the country, automatically forfeits his right to the throne, even though he should be the heir and the legal successor to it. Moreover, that person shall never regain his rights and shall always be deprived of and excluded from any consideration to the throne. This law, and some other important laws should be read annually in the *boyar* assembly and be reaffirmed by an oath taken in the cathedral.

In time of war with foreign enemies, we may hire foreign mercenaries. But in peacetime our heirs should not hire foreigners mercenaries or military commanders. After a war such soldiers and their officers should be required immediately to leave the realm for their homeland or go to other countries. And those foreign mercenaries who come to Russia during a civil war (except those who may be hired by the reigning king) should be executed. Some countries allow them to leave, but we hereby decree that they not be allowed to leave alive.

Merchants, craftsmen, and all townsmen, indeed whole towns, may receive from us, if they so desire, royal privileges, which we shall enumerate here. They should also send their delegates to us requesting greater or lesser rights and privileges according to the merit of each. Our first privilege will deal with the elimination of the tavern monopoly. Towns must, however, see to it that no harm comes to our treasury. For that reason, we will annually reserve one or two months of collecting revenue for ourselves. Should any town fail to pay its taxes, then our tavern monopoly will be re-established for the entire year as before.

Furthermore, we will repeal all monopolies on salt, fish, caviar, bread, honey, potash, hides, iron, and all other such monopolies [in towns]. This is so that no foreigner or a local inhabitant ever will be able to maintain any tax-collecting rights in our realm.

Moreover, no Scots, Englishmen, Swedes, Jews, Armenians, Gypsies, and Tartars outside of Russian control will be allowed to have their own inns, warehouses, special cellars, shops, officials, and commercial agents in our realm. Only Persians and Greeks will be allowed to come and trade in our country, but without the rights and privileges which foreigners now enjoy, which they had received from our predecessors to our great detriment and to the disgrace of our nation.

To our largest towns we shall grant the right of expulsion of unwelcome guests, so that they dare and are able and obliged to expel from their confines and from our country all merchants belonging to the above-mentioned nations. And if they will not expel them and it is revealed that a foreign merchant has purchased a home or a store in a town or has peacefully and openly lived there for a year, then that town will pay a large fine or will lose its privileges and freedoms.

Furthermore, towns that receive privileges will have their own elders, shop overseers, councilors, and supervisors of order appointed from among the townsmen. But the chief elder, secretary, and the judge should always be selected from among the *boyars*.

Judges should handle simple cases on their own authority. Criminal cases should be decided by a majority of votes, but a judge has the right to try and punish all criminals, bandits, and counterfeiters from among the commoners. All other criminals and *boyars* will be judged by our town administrators and judges whom we will appoint to those posts.

Our administrators will also appoint all town elders. But let townsmen designate their own shop overseers and judges.

Moreover, craftsmen should have their own associations and their own teachers. They should not be forced to labor without payment.

Everyone should be allowed to play the violin, to smoke, and to cut his beard and his hair as he wishes (but not in the Tartar style).

Foreign coins made from pure gold and pure silver should be accepted throughout the realm and should be used at all fairs in accordance with their proper price, corresponding to the value of gold and silver in Germany, Persia, and Turkey. They should be accepted and issued by the treasury at the prevailing price. Debased foreign coins should not be accepted. Swedish coins made from pure copper should be accepted, but at a lower price than copper.

We also decree that four kinds of coins of precise value and weight circulate throughout our tsardom in perpetuity. They must bear a royal image and emblem and a designation of the town where they were minted. Our coins must be made of gold, silver, copper, and a mixture of silver and copper. The pure gold coins should be called *zolotniki*—that is, gold rubles similar to the Dutch gold coins. Pure silver coins—that is, those minted from fourteen-carat silver—should be called *poltini* and *grivni*. Three *grivni* should equal one ruble, and one and a half *grivni* should equal a *poltina*.[5] A list giving the exchange value of these *grivni* should be posted in our offices and at trade fairs.

Silver should also be used to mint *shestiny*. Six of these will equal a

[5] See Table of Measures, p. ix.

ruble, three will equal one *poltina,* and two one *grivna.* The mixture should be uniform—half silver and half copper. The weight of the coin should be exact, so that sixty *dudki* contain as much silver and copper as one may purchase for a ruble at a marketplace. The mixture should also be used to mint *novtsy,* four of which will be equal to a *dudka* and 240 to a ruble.

The last denomination, minted exclusively from copper, should be called *broiaki.* Let these have the final and unchanging weight of one *zolotnik,* but let its value in the realm differ, depending on the price of copper—but everywhere be the same.[6]

We further decree that all of the laws and decisions about currency enumerated above, along with all of our other resolves concerning this matter, should be recorded and published for future reference—namely, what currency is allowed to circulate in our tsardom, what its weight and price are, and from what substance it is produced. All coins that are light in weight, that are debased, or illicit, should henceforth and for ever be declared invalid, be recalled, destroyed, and prohibited from circulation in our realm by an immutable law. No one should accept any currency that in some way would be contrary to the law.

And should anyone come to a town that enjoys privileges and in the name of the tsar offer and distribute such currency, such towns are authorized to execute such individuals. They should, however, be allowed to confess. Large privileged towns can afford, and indeed should have, public officials to weigh and to test the quality of coins.

Moreover, we make it known to all of our loyal subjects, and especially our towns, settlements, peasants, and all taxpaying people, that if you wish to receive from us our great favors and benefits accruing from the abolition of debased currency, taverns, monopolies, and foreign merchants, you must obediently and willingly execute all of your orders pertaining to taxes. In return we pledge that without dire need we will not raise them.

All people in settlements and all peasants—without exception—must pay taxes. This includes above all people in our settlements, state peasants, inhabitants of our royal villages, and peasants belonging to the church, to princes, lords and *boyars.* Should any town disobey us, it will be deprived of its privileges.

Furthermore, we decree and grant to our four loyal cities—Vladimir, Yaroslavl, Pskov, and Novgorod—the honor and obligation of minting

[6] In Serbo–Croatian, *novtsy* (singular *novats*) signifies "new money," while *broiaki* (singular *broj*) means "number."

our coins. Accordingly, Vladimir should annually mint gold, Yaroslavl silver, Pskov mixed silver and copper, and Novgorod copper coins. To enable these towns annually to mint a set number of coins at their expense and to deliver them to our treasury they are allowed to receive the raw material from our treasury. In addition, all towns that receive privileges, but especially those four cities, must have full authority against counterfeiters and be entitled to apprehend them throughout the tsardom and to prosecute them in accordance with their crime and punishment.

The favors which we have bestowed on our peasants and landholders have always been extensive. Everyone knows that in our tsardom peasants are better off than their counterparts in neighboring countries where *boyars'* servitors and warriors abuse peasants without punishment. There is no such practice among us. These old customary favors, which our well-to-do peasants, landholders, and villagers enjoy, we endorse for the future and hereby decree that no one should abuse village inhabitants in any way, or insult or burden them with public work or taxes without our edict.

Guardians of our treasury and all of our officials customarily take an oath by kissing the cross, and hence pledging they will always seek by every possible means to enhance our treasury. We now free them from this oath, and in the future will not require such an oath from them or from other individuals before they become government officials. We also repeal the rule that requires all our officials to appear in expensive, colorful clothes on official occasions. We hereby make it known that we will be more pleased by those who dress in modest clothes than those who wear pearls, gold, silk, or other foreign luxuries.

Those of our officials who have hitherto received low salaries from our treasury may expect to receive more because we intend to decrease the number of officials.

To strengthen this tsardom and to create unity among all its people, so that all of you and your children forever take the oath of allegiance and kiss the cross for us and for our descendants and lawful Russian sovereigns, we today decree that the wording of that oath be as follows:

> I, [name], acknowledge you the only sovereign and consider you prince, tsar, and sovereign under God, my ruler and ruler of all Russia and its people. I do not acknowledge anyone in Russia to be prince, or tsar, or sovereign, or administrator of Russian territory and of the Russian people (wholly or in part) under any name or whatever right, be it new or old, unless that right be granted to that individual by the will of God or by your mercy. Whomever you, sovereign, name prince or lord in Russia, I will call him so, but no one else.

Those who now hold princely titles, we hereby prohibit from using them. If they wish, we shall allow them to use the title "princelings" (*kniazhichi*). If there should be found among them such as possess sufficient property to be able to enjoy princely title with dignity, based on their dignity and loyal service, we will not deny them their titles, provided they will view them as having been received from us, and not as having been inherited from their ancestors. Will not those who become impoverished, or nonentities, and therefore cannot uphold their title with pride, but still nevertheless call themselves princes, disgrace those who can enjoy that title in dignity? To prevent such disgrace in the future, we decree that all old princes renounce and relinquish all of their princely rights, authority, and titles. We do not intend to disgrace them in any way. On the contrary, they, too, will participate in the general wellbeing, peace, tranquillity, and strength.

Anyone who was expelled from his patrimony by earlier grand princes or by the tsars, our ancestors, and was deprived of princely possessions and rights and considers himself offended, should know that we cannot take up such ancient matters because it is impossible to resolve them satisfactorily. For even if Prince Bogdan was illegally driven from his principality, no one knows whether that same Bogdan or his ancestors forcefully drove out someone else and seized his property. This is why we do not wish to pass judgment on and resolve ancient matters that did not occur in our lifetime.

We do not wish to offend anyone or to cause him any violence. What will it benefit a person to gain control of the world but in the process lose his soul? Therefore if there is anyone in our tsardom whom we or our father may have offended in some way, let him appear before us, and we will give him a satisfactory recompense. Ultimately, our concern is directed toward the general national wellbeing and the preservation of national unity.

To quiet our conscience it will be sufficient for us to observe *the contract accepted by the entire nation*. Our father of blessed memory did not deprive anyone of his patrimony. He accepted this realm on behalf of himself and his descendants for eternity in accordance with the free and concordant election and contract of the nation. We are the heirs to this election, and on this legal foundation we determine and reaffirm our rights, full royal authority, and dignity for the benefit of the entire nation, its wellbeing, and the immutable unity of the realm. We wish to preserve the unity and inviolability of this tsardom as we inherited it, and to maintain the honor of every social class. For that reason we will tolerate here no illegal princes or distinguished individuals to whom we ourselves have not granted that honor and authority.

The whole nation should know what the pillars and supports of this tsardom are and why it has hitherto been solid, glorious, and strong. Let all loyal subjects and zealots of the public weal know what they must protect, defend, and even die for.

The first fortress of our tsardom and of the nation has hitherto been the Orthodox faith that has prohibited and prevented heresies, and has strictly upheld beneficial laws and customs such as vespers, liturgy, celebration of mass, and fasting. This custom we approve, preserve, and strengthen for eternity. Also, neither we nor any of our successors should be allowed to disseminate, adhere to, or believe any heresy. Equally we desire and hereby decree that none of our subjects is allowed to believe any heresy, adhere to it, or introduce it in our country. Anyone found guilty will be executed without mercy.

The second national stronghold is the total *samovladstvo* or humble submission of subjects to their tsar. We will strengthen this system as follows. Should anyone in our tsardom try to hide behind some privileges and not listen to our orders or instructions or those of our heirs, he will lose all of his privileges and will be punished accordingly.

The third stronghold has been the inviolability of the tsardom and its protection from foreign domination.

The fourth fortress is the closure of frontiers. Our people like and benefit greatly from this wonderful law, which prohibits our subjects from traveling in foreign countries and does not allow all foreigners to come and inspect our land. This way we protect ourselves from many sins, vices, and bad customs. Moreover, we do not expose ourselves, as do the Poles, to the ridicule of all other nations, we do not lose any money, and we do not oppress our poor peasants beyond their capabilities. There are also other benefits that accrue from this law, which we hereby reaffirm for eternity.

Our fifth fortress is the preoccupation of all classes and the prohibition of idleness and unemployment. One should never allow a situation to develop in this realm where people live idly and contribute nothing to the public good. It is completely unjust and ungodly that those who do not help in creating national wealth by their work should consume the sweets and fruits of the land and control a large portion of the income of the nation. For that reason, we decree and order that no prince and no member of any class be freed from national public service and from the business associated with his class, such as service at the court or the *prikaz*, military or ambassadorial; or taxpayers from their burdens and work; or religious people from their prayers and church services.[7]

The sixth fortress should be this. The acts of every tsar—that is, laws, grants of rewards, and confiscation of hereditary and non-hereditary landed estates—be reviewed and evaluated upon his death by a national assembly, and that assembly should request the new tsar to correct those laws that appear to be contrary to the national good. This should be done before the new tsar takes the oath. After the royal oath, the nation should take the oath.

We will conclude with the words of Jesus Christ, the King of all kings, whose kingdom will endure forever. The Lord speaks of himself as follows: "I will not accept human evidence because my father has testified about me." He also said: "I will not accept human praise because my father has already glorified me."

---

[7] In sixteenth- and seventeenth-century Russia, *prikaz* (plural *prikazy*) designated a department of the central government. Between 1500 and 1700, there were more than sixty *prikazy*, each of which was set up or dissolved on the tsar's orders and was, as a rule, headed by a boyar, assisted by scribes and clerks. Officials of a *prikaz* were known as *prikashchiki*.

44

Xenophobia

[Jesus] the son of Sirach says: "Allow a foreigner to settle in your homeland and he will ruin you." We Slavs are constantly being deceived by foreign beauty, eloquence, cunning, and flattery. For that reason no nation should be as wary of foreigners as we. Other nations offer us some examples.

The Spartans or Lacedaemonians (a well-known Greek people) had the following law, instituted by their famous lawgiver Lycurgus: at a designated time (as well as whenever it was necessary) they dispatched trusted officials throughout the country to expel any foreigner they could find. And they punished or fined those natives who protected foreigners more severely than those who protected thieves or bandits. They called this famous law *xenilacis,* which in our language means *gostogonstvo* or the purging of the nation and the state of a useless weed.

To prevent foreigners from worming their way among them through marriage, the French introduced their well-known Salic Law, which deprives women of the right to the throne.

The Moors, an African people, came with their army to Spain, conquered many regions, and during a period of some 700 years had two or three kingdoms there. But the Spaniards eventually gained the upper hand and conquered the Moors. After they subdued them, they did not impose obligations, tribute, or personal taxes on them. They simply expelled all Moors. Several hundred thousand people were forced to leave Spain. Spain also had many Jews. King Ferdinand expelled them, like the Moors, with all of their belongings. Several hundred thousand left as a result. Since then the Spanish nation has expanded its state and gained for itself a glory that it never enjoyed before.

Some German states also expelled the Jews, while others would not allow them in. The Germans will not allow the Gypsies to live in their towns and villages. They also will not allow vagrants or lower-class foreigners to enter their towns. They will not grant any privileges to a newcomer (even if he is a German) until he has lived in a town for ten or even twenty years. They will not allow him to open a shop or a tavern, or to buy a home.

In Austria Luther's heresy spread everywhere, and there were many heretics. Emperor Ferdinand II ordered the heretics to sell their belongings. A multitude of people then left and took great wealth with them. This set many German towns against Ferdinand and started a civil war. But God helped Ferdinand to defend his state and he even strengthened it considerably.

The Egyptians are a sufficient example of what evil always comes from being kind to foreigners. They allowed Jacob and his folk, consisting of sixty-six males, to come in, and they also gave him some land to live on. Nothing could have been more just and appropriate than this welcome of foreigners. But in time the Egyptians paid dearly for this noble deed and cursed the earlier welcome to foreigners. The Israelites soon began to proliferate so fast and emerged so powerful that the Egyptians were forced to consider their expulsion. The pharaoh ordered the drowning of all Jewish boys. In consequence the Egyptians suffered God's punishment.

Our own realm, however, has an unsatisfactory record in these areas. We Slavs, for the reasons we have noted here on many occasions, must have a much firmer anti-foreign policy than other nations. We should let in as few foreigners as we can (and those only for urgent need) and send them away as soon as possible. It is best not to oppress one's own people, but to govern them thoughtfully and kindly and not waste huge sums of money on foreigners. It is a bad policy to take away bread from children and toss it to the dogs.

Many people do not know why foreigners are not sent back after our need for them is over, but are in fact compelled to remain. This does not happen for any serious reason but casually and arbitrarily. Four arguments might be put forward. First, that we thus cut down on hiring foreign soldiers and craftsmen. Second, that it enables us to hire them at lower salaries. Third, that they will be more loyal to us. Fourth, that they will not spread our secrets around the world. But actually none of these reasons is valid. If foreigners were allowed to return home, we would have more soldiers and craftsmen for every need and better ones than we now have. Besides, we could hire them for less. Foreigners are unanimous about this and doubtless it is true. As far as loyalty is concerned, no man will be truly loyal if he is compelled to serve by force. And we hide our secrets in vain from hired people, because foreign ambassadors and merchants, whom we cannot disregard, spread all of our secrets abroad.

The real cause of this detention is the tyrannical custom and foolish example set by Tsar Ivan. As a murderer and torturer of people, he could not keep servitors or slaves for any amount of money. And, since Russia then was even shorter of craftsmen than it is now, the tsar was compelled to capture them and hold them by force. Then this policy which was poorly conceived, quickly became a custom and a law, and is viewed as being beneficial for the state, although actually it is harmful. By saying this I do not imply that we should allow every foreigner who wants to leave to go without cause. Here we need careful discrimination. Good craftsmen should not be released until they teach our young people their crafts. Other foreigners, even those who would like to stay here, should be expelled.

In 1451 all foreigners, and especially those from Nuremberg were prohibited from having homes and stores in Poland. In Russia such a law can be implemented in the following manner. All towns and tax-paying people should pledge, by oath, always to pay the customary taxes and special levies to the great sovereign. In return for this pledge, the sovereign tsar would grant the towns the following four privileges. First, the right to punish thieves and brigands. Second, that the tsar will never mint debased coinage except in extreme emergency and not without the consent of principal cities. Third, that all monopolies be repealed and abrogated. Fourth, a law should expel and ban for ever all foreign merchants, and their commercial agents, permanent embassadors, or observers who are known as factors or consuls. They should not be allowed to have houses, stores, warehouses, or goods in Moscow or anywhere in Russia. Eternally true and obvious is the saying that if a nation becomes intermingled with another nation, it cannot preserve its strength, dignity, and authority. For that reason we will list here the various foreign individuals and foreign associations whom we should fear most of all.

(1) A king, prince, administrator, or the military commanders of land and naval forces should not be accepted or allowed to enter Russia.

(2) A foreign queen, princess, or noble lady should not be allowed in. Neither should we marry our royal princes or the daughters of our nobles to foreigners.

(3) Foreign royal heirs, princes, and other members of the nobility should not be allowed to come to our country, unless they are in dire need or have been driven out from their countries. Then we should accept them, but should send them back as soon as possible.

(4) No foreigner should be allowed to secure privileges of nobility or to

become a prince, lord, *boyar,* or high-ranking administrator of a town or county, or be appointed to any responsible office of the central govern⌐ ment.

(5) No foreigner should ever be granted citizenship. And should a tsar grant this then after the death of that tsar it should be declared void. The property of that foreigner should be confiscated and any native be entitled to expel him.

(6) No foreigner should be allowed to build a stone house, or to purchase one, or to rent or lease one for any period of time, be it long or short.

(7) Itinerant people, Scotsmen, Jews, Armenians, Gypsies should not be allowed to cross our frontiers for any reason. Also we should not let these people in when they accompany ambassadors. Exception to this are when Scotsmen come with the ambassador from England, Scottish merchants in Archangel, or when rich Armenian merchants accompany Persian ambassadors or Persian merchants. But do not let them in otherwise. And do not admit itinerant Armenians.

(8) Should any such itinerant foreigner wish to be baptized and become Russian Orthodox we should grant his wish but immediately after baptism we should send him away from our country to wherever he wants to live.

(9) The advocates of the devil's sciences should be punished and expelled. Astrologers and alchemists should be whipped, branded, and expelled. Magicians and sorcerers should be burned at the stake.

(10) Promoters of games and seducers should be beaten with sticks and expelled. These include dancing, fencing, and riding masters, those who put on comedies, set up fireworks displays, or charm snakes, and similar individuals.

(11) We already have commented on foreign merchants. They should not be allowed to come and live in the tsardom, except in designated frontier towns or at fairs. And there they should be allowed to live only for a designated period of time—two, three, or four weeks.

(12) We should not receive any ambassador without sufficient reason, and should send them back as soon as possible. We should likewise not send our own ambassadors anywhere without good reason.

(13) We should receive as many doctors, interpreters, portrait painters, musicians, and other craftsmen as we need. All of them should be

obligated to train our young people. And when our people master any craft, we should not accept any other foreign practitioner of that craft.

(14) Common foreign soldiers and foreign officers should be recruited only in wartime. After the conclusion of peace, they should be demobilized, as is the practice in other countries. And no one should be allowed to remain.

(15) In the name of the Lord, impoverished patriarchs, bishops, monks, and captives should be allowed to come and go freely.

(16) Should there come some deserters or traitors, time will dictate what to do with them.

It is clear that the problem of foreigners should receive proper attention. This is because foreigners are the sick components of the body politic. Natives receive small pay, on which they cannot live and for which they work for the sovereign day and night the whole year without rest. Foreigners receive enormous salaries, all of their work consists in useless sitting around and drinking, and they only appear on special occasions in their colorful uniforms. Our merchants are obligated to trade government goods for the sovereign in Archangel, while foreign merchants have been allowed to flood our country with their goods, to introduce monopolies, and to capture the best profits from local merchants in the Archangel trade. By right these profits belong to the great sovereign and then (if this is his wish) to local merchants.

No native Russian is allowed to produce liquor at home, even for his own use. But all foreigners, even those who have been disgraced and who are in exile, are allowed to manufacture it freely. Most disgraceful and unbearable is the fact that our Slavic nobles, military leaders, and officers are required to kowtow to such disgraced foreigners in order to be able to use their equipment to produce liquor for their personal needs. I have often heard Germans say, *"Whoever wants to eat free bread should go to Moscow."* Accordingly they feast and drink constantly, and whenever our people casually appear among them, the Germans call them dogs, pigs, and other animal names, and frequently even beat them.

Boris, you will say that we need the Germans to teach us military matters, but I will tell you that we do not need to learn anything at all about German cavalry tactics. In fact, we should unlearn them as quickly as we can. And if we have failed to master infantry tactics by now, we will never master them at all.

I know well that the Germans have no military secrets that the Russians could not master in war. Those Germans we have hired are kept in

Moscow for one purpose only: to display them at parades and the reception of ambassadors. They boast, brag, and argue that our system could not exist without them. And since they are more handsome than we are their looks bring them glory and praise. Our humble faces appear even more humble alongside theirs, and our roughness is exaggerated.

Boris: When Theseus built Athens, Romulus Rome, and Alexander Alexandria, these wise kings accepted all foreign guests and newcomers who wanted to build their houses in the newly built cities.

Khervoi: It is one thing to plan a city and another to rule a nation. To Athens came only its neighbors, people who spoke Greek; to Rome came only the Latins; and to Alexandria, the Egyptians and the Greeks, because Alexander built that city not in his homeland and not for the welfare of his nation but for his personal glory. If any ruler wished to build a new city in Russia, and if he were truly a zealous proponent of national welfare, he would not allow the Germans to live in the city.

The Germans usually boast that their people are steadfastly loyal and incapable of committing treason. This illustrious tsardom, like other nations, has learned enough about their so-called "loyalty." [Peter Feodorovich] Basmanov, the principal advisor and accomplice of False Dmitrii, was a German. [Michael Borisovich] Shein was the ill-fated military commander who, together with a German named Leslie (willingly or unwillingly, that I do not know) disgracefully lost Russian armies at Smolensk.[1] Also a German was the individual who promised the great sovereign to capture Riga and then deserted to Riga. It was also Germans who basely committed treason at Klushin, betrayed Tsar Vasilii [Shuiskii], and gave this kingdom over to be ravaged by its enemies. Similarly, German mercenaries, hired by Francis I, betrayed the king into the enemy's hands [at Pavia in 1525].

[1] Krizhanich is wrong on several counts here. Neither P.F. Basmanov (see ch. 25, n. 4) nor M.B. Shein (d. 1634) was German. The latter was a member of an old Muscovite *boyar* family who was executed for his loss of Smolensk to the Poles. Only Alexander Leslie, a Scottish adventurer in Russian military service, was a foreigner.

45

The preservation of government authority

Sometimes it is more difficult to preserve high authority within the realm than to expand it. It seems that everything in the world resembles the Moon—first it waxes and then it wanes. The most important task is therefore to preserve government authority as it is, and whenever it increases, to keep it from decreasing. In many ways the acquisition of authority depends on chance and on dissent among enemies—that is, on inherent human causes—while the preservation of things acquired depends on natural skill and a high level of intelligence. To acquire something, all that is usually needed is boldness; but to preserve the thing acquired requires not only courage and valor, but skill. In times of crisis, even the weakest individuals find strength. Peace and tranquility require good sense.

To demonstrate that it is more important to preserve what you have than to acquire something that belongs to somebody else, the Spartans punished only those who lost their shields in battle, not those who lost their swords.

It is not surprising, then, that those who have conquered other kingdoms have always been more glorified than those who have tried to preserve their own. In their affairs, the former deal with more novelty and are more constantly in public view. Military matters cause people to talk more than the art of peaceful preservation.

The activities of such Tartar rulers as Tamerlane and Batu; Otokar, king of the Czechs; Attila, king of the Huns; and similar kings, are not praised highly, because these warriors gained much, but were unable to consolidate their conquests by introducing wise and firm laws. Alexander the Great followed the same road and, as a result, his kingdom disintegrated shortly after his death and was never as famous as that of Rome.

Tsar Ivan [IV] also expanded the Russian state by annexing Kazan, Astrakhan, and Siberia. But I have been unable to recall any beneficial laws introduced by him to contribute to the happiness and the longevity of the realm. I only know that after his death, the realm was plunged into great troubles and misfortunes, from which it has thus far been unable to extricate itself. It will not escape this legacy until we establish good laws.

According to Aristotle: "The responsibility of the lawgiver (or the founder of a state) is to establish a city, to build its walls, and to teach his successors how it should be preserved for a long time, indeed, for ever." And the Roman historian [Lucius Annaeus] Florus says: "To preserve a state is much more difficult than to gain it. To conquer a country by force and then to preserve it requires justice." And justice means good laws.

One should not listen to those who say that since this tsardom has done well without wise laws until now, it can do without them in the future. One should answer that people can also manage to live without bread and salt, but their lives become miserable. It is possible for a tsardom to live with its own misfortunes and misery and be despised by all nations but it cannot be content without good laws.

Boris: What is meant by the saying: "Authority is preserved by the same means by which it is acquired?"

Khervoi: It means that a new ruler who is trying to tighten his authority by some clever means should not hurry or alter national laws unnecessarily if he wants to strengthen and preserve his authority. It does not apply to the problem of how to make an entire nation powerful without good laws. Some kings, such as Alexander the Great, Julius Caesar, Constantine the Great, and Charlemagne and others, were stern military men, famous heroes and founders of new kingdoms. God endowed them with many virtues. But their kingdoms did not last long, because discord and bloody feuds developed among their descendants, which resulted in a bitter death for the majority of them.

This happened because these heroes, worthy of all praise, did not introduce good laws to strengthen their kingdoms and, above all, a law governing the succession of their descendants; smooth succession is the foundation of national might, as we shall see in the next chapter.

Good laws that protect the entire nation are a great gift of God, but such laws are rare. This is because many nations did not at their inception have a wise leader who could introduce good laws. The Greek Athenians had Solon; the Spartans had Lycurgus as their lawgivers. And both of these cities were powerful and famous for several centuries because of good laws. The Romans received their wise laws from their king Numa, but even so they dispatched their ambassadors to the Athenians and adopted some laws from them. Thanks to all of these beneficial laws, Rome maintained her glory for about 700 years, until the imperial period.

The city of Venice has been able to maintain its glory because it has remained unaltered for more than 1,200 years, and no one has been able to conquer it. And why? Simply because the Venetians have borrowed what was best among others and introduced it into their own laws.

My distinguished tsar, you have the means to preserve this tsardom for your descendants for many centuries (provided peace lasts that long) and make it peaceful and free of civil strife. But to do so it is essential to examine the basic laws of these famous kingdoms and borrow those few that stand out among the rest. For example:

(1) Solon's law that states that no one should live in idleness and that every person should annually report to authorities what he is doing for his livelihood.

(2) The law against foreigners introduced, as noted earlier, by Lycurgus.

(3) Thrasybulus of Athens conceived the idea of amnesty, a very praiseworthy means of doing away with discontent.

(4) The French law that deprives women of the right to inherit the throne.

(5) The Venetian law that prohibits the division of estates among brothers.

(6) The Venetian law of electing a prince.

(7) The Chinese, and our own Russian, law that imposes the closure of frontiers.

(8) Our own law that exiles people, but provides them with some government subsidy and the right for even dangerous individuals to perform some service.

One should take as an example the activity and speeches of the famous heroes whom God has set up as an example for other kings. Just as some of God's saints have been glorified through their miracles and are called "miracleworkers," so, too, some kings with the help of God have accomplished great deeds and are revered as "heroes" and the founders of new kingdoms. Above all, we should affirm that all of these famous heroes and founders of great, powerful kingdoms acknowledged God.

46

Royal glory

Boris: Is it proper for the king to be ambitious?

Khervoi: He should be ambitious, but not haughty. He can attain that goal if he dedicates all of his actions and his glory to God and follows the steps of virtue towards genuine honor rather than vainglory.

Boris: How can a king attain genuine honor rather than vainglory?

Khervoi: If he works to make his people content. Also if he does not lose patience with human ingratitude and *does not terminate good works in behalf of his people* in spite of their ingratitude. He should try to see to it that his successors continue his works, while he personally should follow the example of the wise, generous, and pious kings of the past.

Boris: How should the king follow the examples of famous kings and heroes?

Khervoi: When they hear the name of Cyrus, Alexander, or other praiseworthy ancient kings, some people think only about their wars, battles, and conquests. A wise king must think differently. He should imitate those heroes not in their wars, but in their good laws and in good rule. Attila, Batu Khan, and Tamurlane were great warriors and they conquered and subdued many countries and peoples, yet in their achievements there is nothing worthy of imitation. In contrast Augustus, Trajan, Constantine, Theodosius, and several other Roman emperors did not annex a single new territory. Yet, by ruling peacefully, they acquired eternal glory for themselves and left behind a memory of their activities so worthy that all other kings should treat them as examples and imitate them.

Boris: Is it beneficial for the king to do something simply for the sake of temporary advantage?

Khervoi: Of course it is, provided that it promotes the permanent welfare of the country. For once the king expresses concern about not only the spiritual but also the material well-being of the nation, why shouldn't

L

he act in a way that will simultaneously have long-term as well as short-run benefits.

Boris: Why are some kings called "great" and "heroic"?

Khervoi: Because they accomplished great and praiseworthy deeds.

Boris: What are these praiseworthy deeds by which eternal glory is subsequently gained?

Khervoi: They are *those that benefit the largest number of people for the longest period of time*.

Boris: But what about military valor and the conquest of new lands?

Khervoi: They contribute nothing at all.

Boris: Then tell me which are royal deeds that are praiseworthy, and what constitutes royal obligation and duty.

Khervoi: The obligation of every king is to guarantee piety, justice, peace, and material abundance—in other words, faith, justice, peace, and availability of necessities at low prices. Every king should guarantee these four things to his people. It is for that reason that God has designated him king. To accomplish this, the king should call assemblies, promulgate laws, build new towns and fortify old ones, fight just wars, reform the language, and establish and spread throughout the kingdom industries and other enterprises that are beneficial to the public.

Boris: You say that the king should keep in mind those four things: piety, justice, peace, and material abundance. Why didn't you include military or warlike activity among royal obligations?

Khervoi: Because every king should concern himself with the peace and tranquility of his nation, and no one should fight unless he is forced into it. Some powerful kings have been designated by God to punish other kings and other cities. But this is an exception, and therefore not every king should wage war.

Concerning royal dignity and honor you are right. We Slavs must consider this problem because all other nations deceive us. For that reason, our Slavic rulers must keep the national honor in mind above all, and take appropriate steps to guard against foreign encroachment.

Boris: Are philosophy and knowledge useful for kings?

Khervoi: Not only are they useful, they are absolutely indispensable. Most of mankind lives without knowing anything about the most elementary things that all children should know; one could say that people live without the ABC's of life. Boris, if you were to ask all kings in the world what they considered to be royal obligations, obviously you would have found many who would not have been able to explain why God created kings and gave them authority over people. There are kings who think that God did not create them for the benefit of their kingdoms and peoples, but that kingdoms were created for the benefit of kings. There are kings who think that their responsibility centers only in ruling, ordering, and enjoying luxury, and not in expressing constant concern about the national well-being. There are kings who consider themselves to be infinite lords and not God's lieutenants, or administrators obliged to give God a detailed account of their rule. How can you expect good and beneficial rule from anyone who knows nothing about his obligations and responsibilities? If such rulers accomplish anything that is good, they do it out of necessity and not because of the purity of their hearts.

Thus far we have talked about haughty, arrogant, uncultivated kings— that is, those who do not know the true faith and are ignorant of God's commandments. Because of their blindness, vices, and ill manners, they commit errors. A knowledge of philosophy would doubtless save them. Boris, I will tell you this: knowledge of philosophy is indispensable to all kings, young and old, believers and unbelievers, good and bad. For God created philosophy (or knowledge derived from books) not for nothing, but to benefit people. And there is no one to whom it is more beneficial and useful than to kings. I am not talking about young, unbelieving, uncultivated kings, but about those who are wise, Orthodox, and virtuous.

Among the problems a king must face, many require daily attention. One frequently encounters problems that involve careful thought, analysis, research, and even anguish. The king and his advisors, who are preoccupied with other matters, cannot keep track of them all. They desperately need philosophical training to familiarize them with such matters. In books, examples may be found of similar problems in the past.

Kings and their advisors, princes, and lords are constantly surrounded by flatterers who offer poor advice and approve every stupid thing that the rulers conceive. There is absolutely no doubt that flatterers have led many kings into difficulties, disgrace, and even to their demise. It would be good, therefore, indeed indispensable, if every wise king had at his disposal one or two philosophers to serve as historians, chroniclers, and language experts who could tell him the truth. If they were afraid to tell the truth, at least they could draw his attention to books that were not afraid to do so.

Boris: Our sovereigns and the councillors of this tsardom, as well as of many other kingdoms in the world, acquire their wisdom on the basis of their own experience. Is this not therefore better than to learn it from books?

Khervoi: You are correct in saying that personal experience is the best advisor. But this wisdom has two shortcomings. First, it is acquired late in life, because experience bestows it on old people, not on young ones. Wisdom, secured through experience, does not benefit those who gain it, because by the time they acquire it, they have neither strength nor desire left. Conversely, wisdom acquired from books is available to young people. An example of this is Alexander the Great who at the age of eighteen commenced his heroic activity, and accomplished his conquests in a short time. And the surprising thing about his activities is not that he conquered so many towns, kings, and peoples, as the fact that he was able to hold them in fear and love and to control his own Macedonian warriors, who became tired of so many campaigns and wanted to desert their king. Alexander acquired this wisdom not from experience, but from Aristotle and from philosophy.

The second shortcoming is the fact that experience involves many mistakes and losses. Anyone who learns only by personal experience is often forced to make a mistake and suffer a loss. Hence the saying: "People learn by trial and error." But those who practice philosophy are spared this. Consequently, there is no one in the world in greater need of philosophy than the king. For kings cannot afford to learn by mistakes, because royal mistakes are ruinous and detrimental to nations.

Boris, now you see that book wisdom and philosophy are indispensable to all rulers. Unfortunately, to our sorrow, many kings and princes not only fail to invite philosophers to be their advisors, but frequently drive them away and even kill them. The Athenians exiled their lawgiver Solon. Alexander killed his chronicler Callisthenes because he wisely counseled him not to make himself a god. Jewish kings exiled and killed their prophets. The moral lesson is this: whoever tells the truth is despised everywhere.

Boris: Who among the heroes is the most worthy that our rulers should follow in example?

Khervoi: I will name three: Cyrus, Constantine, and Charlemagne. You can discover others from books. Cyrus I, the king of Persia, was one of the most praiseworthy heroes and kings in the world. God granted him great royal valor, special luck, good rule, and many famous triumphs. With the help of the prophet Daniel, He also compelled him to acknowledge the true God. Through Isaiah God said of him: "I say to Cyrus: You are my shepherd and the executor of all my orders." The Greek historian Xenophon wrote an entire book [*Anabasis*] about Cyrus's achievements.

Those rulers whom God has endowed with high dignities we should consider not simply our sovereigns but the instruments of God's mercy. That is, through them God has decided to help people to establish peace, justice, and moderation, and to punish impudent and haughty rulers.

To conclude, God created powerful kingdoms in order to use them as a means to compel tyrants and inhuman oppressors, as well as arrogant city states that live off the fat of the land, to moderation and to modesty, and also to protect the weak from powerful thieves and thus introduce modesty, justice, peace, and good laws. Boris, you should know that to suppress haughty tyrants and luxuriant towns, God created and designated not only those four kingdoms—the Assyrian, Persian, Greek, and Roman—but all the other kingdoms that exist in the world that are powerful, great, and famous. This is so that justice and legality may be preserved in the world by goodness and might.

Briefly, I will tell you about Constantine (as I promised earlier). This pious and praiseworthy emperor was a true, and not simply imaginary, Roman emperor because he ruled over the entire Roman empire. And he acquired the title "Great" not because of his military achievements or battles but through peaceful activity. The bishops bestowed this name on him because he fervently and truthfully respected God and was deeply concerned about piety. He called church councils into session, built churches, endeavored to resolve religious disputes, was humble before bishops, and did not wish to interfere in their courts.

However, I believe that not one king from the beginning of time offered his successors so many good and worthy deeds to imitate as did Charlemagne, emperor of the Germans and Rome. He fought successfully in many wars and conquered several kings and princes. He expelled the Saracens from France. After thirty years of warfare, he compelled the Saxons to accept Christianity. He freed Rome from the Lombards and restored the freedom of the pope. For these reasons, Charlemagne was one of the great heroes designated by God to establish justice and peace, as were David, Cyrus, Alexander, Julius, Augustus, Constantine, and Theodosius.

Such heroes should not only engage in wars, but must also be concerned about justice and piety. Charlemagne distinguished himself in both of these respects. He conducted fierce, long, and constant wars until his death. Yet he never forgot his peaceful obligations. He called several councils—in Rome, Frankfurt, and France. He founded three schools—in Bologna, Pavia, and Paris. In Germany he established many monasteries that maintained schools. He ordered the codification of the French laws. He gave instructions that old German songs and stories be put in order. In his old age, he began to study philosophy and astronomy. He ordered that during his meals someone read him the writings of St Augustine. He sang Lauds, led prayers, and ordered his princes to do likewise. Through his ambassadors, he reached an agreement with the Saracen rulers calling for better treatment of Christians. He ordered that German names be given to the winds and the months, which they had not had until then.

From all of this, it is evident that God endowed and adorned this emperor with high distinction, many virtues, and great success; for these reasons he was justly called Charles the Great.

47

Succession to the throne

Following the death of a king, frequently there are wars and other discord over the succession to the throne.[1] For this reason it is important to strengthen and to prolong the life of a kingdom, and to do this nothing is more important than the establishment of a firm rule of succession to the throne. We shall analyze this problem.

Boris: What is the best form of government? When a city is democratic, as Athens was and Venice is now? Or when a nation is governed by many princes as Russia once was and Germany is now? Or where a country is governed by a single king?

Khervoi: There is no need to discuss this question at any length. The issue is quite clear. Homer says, and all wise men agree, "It is very bad when there are many rulers, and therefore there should be only one."

Boris: If autocracy is a better form of government, then, Khervoi, tell me what is more reasonable: to elect an autocrat by popular vote, or to let the sons succeed their fathers?

Khervoi: Well, which do you think is better?

Boris: I think election is better than dynastic or hereditary authority.

Khervoi: On what evidence do you base your choice?

Boris: First, election is older than hereditary rule. After all, in early times people elected their kings.

Khervoi: It is not surprising that you should select the elective principle. When a royal dynasty expires, election is unavoidable; and in the old days, when elections were the custom, people grew experienced at choosing what was best for them. But at present the hereditary system is more common and more accepted.

Boris: Second, with elections it is possible to select the best and most suitable ruler, while under a hereditary system a designated individual, whether good or bad, must be accepted.

---

[1] In writing this chapter, Krizhanich relied on the work of J. Lipsius, *Monita et exempla politica* (Amsterdam, 1630), 98–112.

Khervoi: It is true that in theory people can elect the best person. But do they? Examine what actually happens, and you will not find such people anywhere. It happens rarely or rather, *never,* that elections are conducted without personal partisanship and ambition. The electors look for a man who is good not for the nation but for themselves. Often the matter is resolved by gifts and promises, sometimes by hostility.

Boris: The third reason is that under the electoral system a grown man is selected to be king, whereas under hereditary systems the authority sometimes falls into the hands of babes in arms, who cannot govern the country.

Khervoi: Boris, we acknowledge that under a hereditary system such failures do occur, but the electoral system has its own shortcomings. Whenever the throne is vacant the country is without a sovereign, and this causes more evil and damage than the infancy or foolishness of any sovereign. For whenever a rupture or interregnum in government occurs, the law is silenced, and willfulness and brute force take the upper hand.

The second great evil associated with elections is disagreement among the electors, which leads to discord, conspiracy, and war. Not one election has been free of military conflict. Just look at Poland, Germany, and Rome under both the ancient emperors and the popes, and you will see that frequently they had two or three emperors and two or three popes simultaneously—a situation that resulted in considerable bloodshed. This is in itself an adequate reason to reject elections.

Third, you say that the hereditary system sometimes leaves us with a young king incapable of governing the country. But, Boris, elections do not spare us this either. Just look at the Poles: once they crowned a king who was so dimwitted he could not even take an oath. The Hungarians crowned babies in their cradles.

Boris, you should also be aware of the fact that elections of kings are elections in name only. Actually the principle of succession prevails everywhere. Elected kings always find means to safeguard the kingdom for their children, sometimes even their daughters.

Boris: Yes, it would seem that elections are simply deceptions, empty words. Yet, Khervoi, I will give you a fourth reason in their favor. It is said that an elected king rules more mildly and humbly than a hereditary king, and moreover that he oppresses his subjects less than one who possesses full authority.

Khervoi: You suggest that his authority will be milder. But Boris, you might as well also say that there will be less order, less concern, and less attention, because there is no reason to give much concern to something that belongs neither to me nor my descendants. Also, such kings are always indebted to the lords who helped them to the throne, and besides to anyone who may either limit or remove their authority. Just look at Poland. The lords of an elected king are willful; justice suffers; force triumphs; and the king closes his eyes to their transgressions. Look as well at the German emperors, who without any reasonable cause took cities and whole territories away from the empire and distributed them to their children and relatives and even to foreigners. Sometimes they did this for money, sometimes from generosity, and sometimes to bribe the electors so that the latter would elect their sons to the throne. Under hereditary government, such abuses do not exist.

Boris: The fifth reason in favor of election is this. The system forces lords and *boyars* to behave properly—to be resourceful and brave—because they hope to become sovereigns themselves.

Khervoi: Such a notion deserves to be spat on. It is not worthy of discussion. Do you think princes will try to be good just because one of them is going to be elected—and not intentionally, but accidentally? If we look at any country, we will see elections of various kinds, and the frequent election of stupid rulers. Let Rome speak for its emperors, and the Germans for theirs.

Boris: To continue, there is a sixth reason. Aristotle is said to have preferred the electoral systems and favored the Carthaginians, who elected their king, over the Spartans, who transmitted their throne on a hereditary basis. And Christian nations like the Czechs, the Danes, and the Hungarians had elected kings until recent times, while the Poles have them even today.

Khervoi: Aristotle's opinion in this matter refutes nothing. Aristotle was a wise man, not a prophet, and even the wisest men make mistakes. It is not surprising that Aristotle, as a Greek, adhered to the Greek view. The Greeks at the time practiced democracy, and acknowledged neither hereditary nor elected kings. For that reason, Aristotle praised the kingdom most like their republican form of government. Moreover, examples of royal election among ancient and modern nations—the Carthaginians, the Poles, and others—are poor evidence, because the contrary custom so prevails that for every example of election there are a hundred examples of the hereditary principle.

Let us conclude this discourse by agreeing with Lipsius, who says that with a hereditary system a kingdom is governed better and expands more than under elected monarchs. There is no need to elaborate this first point because it is evident: simply look at the countries on both sides of the issue. Second, he says that wherever kingdoms have been famous and praiseworthy—the Persian, Macedonian, Egyptian, Chinese, and Jewish kingdoms, for instance—the throne was hereditary. Third, he notes that kingdoms in which the kings are elected by parliaments have never lasted long, nor will they ever do so. A king who is wiser and more daring than the rest will inevitably appear, and he will use rewards, money, cunning, and force to secure for his descendants the throne entrusted to him. The examples of Denmark and Bohemia show this, and the same may happen in Poland.

Boris: I now concur with you, and acknowledge that hereditary rule is better than elective. But what should be done when the king is young?

Khervoi: If his mother is alive, she should be allowed to rule for her son along with wise advisors. It would be a mistake to entrust the kingdom to the lords alone: if one of them becomes the guardian or protector of the young king, he is in a position to seize power or cause other trouble, rob the treasury, and appropriate public wealth; but if many of them become protectors, they will be unable to prevent conflicts and discord.

For example, Louis XIII left his throne and his son to the authority of his queen mother and designated Cardinal Mazarin, an Italian of humble origin, to be equal with her as viceroy and protector of his son. Louis hoped that a little-known foreign cleric would not bring any harm to the country. But this amiable guest soon began to purchase huge estates and to arrange marriages between his relatives and great French lords. Some princes felt it an insult to be under the authority of a greedy foreigner and began to press the queen to send him away. But he had a good number of strong supporters, and the upshot was the bitter civil war [known as the Fronde].

Charles of Sweden, who left his son and throne both to his queen and to four influential lords in 1660, did better. To make certain that the queen would not rule and promulgate laws alone, he stipulated that she do this jointly with the four advisors.

Where the queen is not available, the principal leader of the native church should be designated, i.e., here in Russia the patriarch, in Poland the archbishop. Should the king leave many children, or both sons and daughters then without doubt preference should always go to the males, not the females, and to the older brothers, not the younger. These natural laws should not be violated.

We will discuss this problem later. First, however, we will discuss the unity of the state, and internal peace. Many kings, carried away by love of their sons, have divided kingdoms among them, thereby committing a grave error. They violated their obligation, and sinned before God and the nation. They wanted to assure that their family be illustrious, that it rule for a long time, and that none of their sons be a subject. Instead of greatness and longevity, however, by involving them in bitter struggle and fratricide they brought about quick and pointless ruin.

There is no large country in the world that, once united, can be satisfactorily divided between two brothers. See how enormous the Roman state was, and still it was inadequate for three brothers. Constantine the Great divided the realm among his three sons: Constantius was to rule Constantinople and the East; Constantine [the younger] Spain, France, and Germany; and Constans was to rule Rome, Italy, and Illyria. But Constantine the younger was not satisfied with the division of the empire. Wanting to be the sole master over it, he declared war against Constantius and soon was himself killed. Later Constans was murdered by his military commander, Magnetius, who in turn committed suicide.

Our own Vladimir the Great also divided his authority among his twelve sons. What good did it do? Sviatopolk killed the blessed Boris and Gleb. Iaroslav defeated Sviatopolk, and drove him and his Polish allies out of Kiev. Sviatopolk returned with a Polish king, Boleslav, and drove Iaroslav to the Pechenegs. When Sviatopolk later attacked Iaroslav with the aid of the Pechenegs, he was defeated and fled to the Poles, where he died. Then Mstislav drove Iaroslav to Novgorod and so began a bloody feud between them. That such fratricidal struggles occurred in Russia was bad enough, but the worst thing was that the country was so divided, and the people so weakened, that it was easy for the Poles and the Lithuanians to capture Kiev, Lvov, and other territories, and for the Tartars to conquer the rest of the nation and keep it in cruel slavery for a very long time.

Those two cases, in Rome and in Russia, are sufficient to illustrate the point. Should anyone wish to search the ancient accounts, he would find an abundance of similar examples in Russia, Poland, and other kingdoms. All this indicates that the division of a kingdom is harmful, not only for subjects but for the rulers themselves.

Moreover, we are talking about conscience and royal obligation (as well as practical consequences). Kings should never forget that nations were not created for them, but they—by God—for nations. It is thus improper for kings to endanger the public weal for personal ends. Things that ancient kings created and achieved with great effort and bloodshed their successors have no right to dismantle and divide among their children. Therefore, only one of the royal heirs should be entitled to the autocratic throne, and the remaining brothers and sisters should be content with the status of subjects. If the king analyzes the situation properly, he will realize that for the glory and longevity of his line, it is far better that the rest of the family be subjects. When only one son rules, he carries on the glory of his father, preserving the realm in its totality.

Some kings, when they recognized the harm brought about by the division of authority, went to another extreme. They forgot not only natural love of their families, but also simple humanity, and introduced the custom of killing their own sons. They became their vicious murderers. Turkish sultans act in this manner, sparing one son and killing the rest. The Greek kings, who acted not much better, forced their relatives into monasteries, emasculated them, or blinded them, albeit only those they suspected of being especially dangerous. This diabolical craving for power forced brother to do such things to brother, father to son, and son to father.

The ancient Roman emperors, like the Greek ones, sometimes adopted their trusted friends as their brothers. Diocletian, for example, elevated Maximian on a par with himself, made him co-ruler, and gave him authority that equalled his own. Because they shared supreme power, both were called Caesars. Diocletian chose Galerius, while Maximian selected Constantius, the father of Constantine the Great. This custom should not be initiated, though, because it rarely leads to anything good, especially in kingdoms smaller than Rome. In governing a state, there are often problems on which two individuals cannot reach agreement.

The Germans have devised their own solution to this problem. They put the younger brothers of the ruler in a monastery, but only make them churchmen, not priests or deacons. Dressed in church attire and given one, two, or even three bishoprics, these so-called "bishops" receive church revenues and live quite well. They appoint a bishop's assistant to take care of church matters in their place, and though they cannot marry, they are involved in all sorts of worldly affairs—they wage wars for example. One can properly call them bishops in form, but not bishops of the Church. In fact when the brother—the ruler—dies childless, one of these bishops discards his priestly attire, assumes the authority and the crown, and gets married.

The Abyssinians keep all of their royal sons and relatives in a fortress, away from the people, so that they will not form conspiracies or cause trouble. This fortress, called Anga, is located on an inaccessible mountain and guarded by a powerful garrison. When their king dies, they enthrone the young heir who is most appropriate in the judgment of lords and overseers.

Boris: You disapprove of the division of authority, of the Turkish practice of suffocating potential rivals, of the Greek practice of blinding, emasculating, or tonsuring them, of Roman adoption, and of German so-called consecration. What *do* you approve of and advise? What system should be adopted if several imperial personages seek the throne?

Khervoi: Boris, I favor two things: *self-knowledge and good laws.* With the help of these two, every king can find a way to resolve the fate of his children. I do not speak about sons, brothers, and other individuals who would like to become heirs and seek the throne: it would be foolish to expect wise decisions from them, because the thirst for power is a temptation that ultimately blinds a person, that makes him as stupid as a domestic or wild animal. In fact, animals do not kill their own kind, but a human being thirsty for power is ready to kill his own brother, sister, mother, or father. To go on, I would turn to the old king who is sated with power—to one who no longer seeks it, but meditates on how to part with it. There is no need to divide the kingdom, to incarcerate his sons in a monastery, or to tonsure, emasculate, blind, or suffocate them. All of this is contrary to reason and God's commandments. What is necessary is to restrict them by good laws, so that instead of serving as a focus for rebellion they will be forced to remain within the bounds of reason and decency. A king who wishes to introduce good laws in this connection, however, must first truly know himself. He must realize that he is neither god nor angel but a human being, and that no royal dynasty ever starts with kings or lords; rather, all kingdoms begin with slaves, peasants, and other humble people.

The following laws and measures against the division of authority and power-seeking individuals should be introduced in our tsardom:

(1) There should be twelve princes in Russia entitled to sit on the throne.

(2) If the royal family should expire, one of those princes should be elected as the new tsar.

(3) Rules should be established governing the election, to which I will soon refer.

(4) The tsar should not marry a foreign woman; he should take as his wife the daughter of one of his princes, lords, or other Slavic rulers. (Tsars should also be on guard lest their wives influence their decisions. For whenever the tsar takes a second or a third wife who gives birth to a son, she will use every possible device to persuade the tsar to place her son on the throne and alienate him from the eldest son.)

(5) The tsar should not marry his daughters to foreigners; he should marry them to his princes or lords, and other Slavic rulers. (The ancient Roman and Byzantine emperors married their daughters to their nobles and their honor did not suffer.)

(6) Royal daughters should have no right to inherit the throne, except in the case of a young unmarried daughter when there are no male heirs.

(7) Under no circumstances should the tsardom be divided.

(8) The throne should always pass on to the eldest son or the closest or eldest member of the royal family (provided he is neither a heretic nor insane).

(9) Each of the remaining brothers should be allowed to rule only over one small town or fort.

(10) They should be called princes, but in the national assembly they should not have any place, voice, or right of free participation.

(11) They should not be entitled to have servants above a designated number established by law.

(12) Any attempt to seek an alliance with them, or for them to respond favorably to such an attempt, should be considered a criminal offense.

(13) The heir to the throne should be the first to take an oath to uphold the rights of the people.

(14) Then the subjects should take an oath that they will obey the tsar, and after him his legal heirs—tsars who will be legally crowned. And should someone seize the throne illegally by force or cunning, no one should obey him. And should someone take an oath of allegiance to him, that oath should be considered as coerced, inoperative, and non-binding, because it was given in violation of the public, national, legal, and earlier oath.

Boris: But what should be done in ambiguous cases?

Khervoi: Cases that are difficult to resolve are rare; there is no need to have any special concern about them. Besides, it is possible to establish a rule under which thirty or forty judges would decide the issue by secret ballot or lot. The rule should stipulate that during these proceedings, no one should resort to arms. Whoever starts a war should be deprived of all his rights and never allowed to exercise power. The oath of allegiance that people have taken to him should be invalidated, because it was contrary to national law.

Boris: And what do you think about the daughters of kings?

Khervoi: Europe abounds in sad examples of horrible bloodshed and ruinous foreign domination caused by female rights to the throne. French legislation is worthy of imitation: Russia will never escape foreign domination as long as our women are allowed to inherit the throne.

Boris: What should be done if the king dies without leaving an heir?

Khervoi: What else, except election?

Boris: But elections vary. What kind do you favor?

Khervoi: Elections may produce a great amount of evil and for that reason, too, a good law should be introduced. Boris, here is how elections differ among various nations.

(1) The Persians once decided that their high princes should assemble on horseback one morning in a public square, and the man whose horse neighed first would become king. The horse of Darius neighed first, so Darius became king.

(2) Among other fables, there is a Polish story: after the death of King Przemysl, it was decided to stage a horse jumping contest, and whoever was the first to reach the finishing line would become king. A certain Leszek, using cunning, bypassed everyone but was killed, so another man who reached the destination walking was made king and was known as Leszek II. (There was also a custom among the Serbs that a young man must win his bride in a horse race, and there is still a saying, "He whose horse is faster will win the maiden.")

(3) At one time the Czechs had no ruler, so they sought advice from Libuša, a famous prophetess. Libuša replied: "Go into the field and find a person who eats bread at an iron table and make that person your king." So they went and found a peasant named Přemyśl, who was eating at a resting trough. They took him with them and made him their king.

(4) The Arancanians, who live in the Indies, elect the strongest among them as their king. They use the heavy trunk of a tree to test for strength, and consider whoever is able to hold it on his back without tiring capable of bearing the heavy burden of government.

(5) During the era of the Republic, the Romans elected their consuls and administrators annually by popular vote; that is, the taxpaying commoners elected nobles to those positions. Moreover, nobles did not consider it dishonorable to bow, plead, and ask poor people for their votes in the street, and to pledge and promise to govern properly, just to be elected. This was known as "ambitia"—that is, seeking power.

(6) During the reign of the Roman emperors, appointment to the throne became the prerogative of soldiers, who often willfully killed emperors and chose new ones. Sometimes they put the throne up for sale, and sometimes for sport or as a joke. Whoever offered most became emperor. Emperor Claudius was the first to pay for the votes of his

soldiers; he promised and paid fifteen *sestertia,* or fifteen Roman rubles, to every soldier. Subsequently, this military selection of emperors resulted in astonishing spectacles and merciless clashes and bloodshed, so that before the reign of Constantine, or in the course of 300 years, more than thirty emperors perished violently.

(7) The Turkish court soldiers known as janissaries have not as yet attained such willfulness, because they have been unable thus far to appoint anyone not of royal blood as sultan. But there, too, gruesome lawlessness rules, because whenever they want to they murder the sultan and put the sultan's son or brother on the throne. And they do this with impunity.

(8) The Hungarians elected their king in Rákos, an exercise field near the capital city of Buda. All the nobles assembled there, and held a council in the open field under tents. The Poles adopted this custom, and added the provision that whenever they wished to conspire against their king, they would assemble in council at an agreed-upon place. That council they named "Rokosz," to imply that this was like an assembly at the real Rákos. The Hungarian kingdom perished as a result of these "rákoses," and the Polish kingdom is very close to its demise.

(9) When Martin of Aragon died, he left behind four powerful family administrators. Their quarrels about the succession almost resulted in a war, and they agreed to choose judges to determine who should be the next king, something that rarely happens in such disputes. Accordingly, they selected three men, who were distinguished by their piety and intelligence, from the three provinces of the kingdom. In the town of Caspa on a designated day, the judges (together with Pope Benedict) issued their decision that Ferdinand, the heir to the Spanish crown, should be king.

To ensure that the Italian kingdom remained under the authority of Germany, Emperor Otto III conceived the following scheme. He secured a promise from the Romans that they would elect his cousin Bruno as Pope Gregory V. Then Otto, together with Pope Gregory, appointed six Germans to be electors of the emperor of the Holy Roman Empire and verified this procedure by an eternally binding imperial and papal decree. Three archbishops, those of Mainz, Cologne, and Trier, and the secular princes of the Rhine, Saxony, and Brandenburg, received the right to elect the emperor, but the person they selected was not entitled to call himself emperor until the pope approved and crowned him. Some emperors, in fact, have not been crowned by the pope, and therefore do not enjoy the full imperial title: they are simply called "elected Roman emperors."

In German, the electors, or people who select the emperor, are called *Kurfürst*, from the word *Kur* (that is, concern) and *Fürst* (prince)—they are "concerned protectors of the throne." Emperor Rudolf I added a seventh elector, the king of Bohemia, in order that he might break a deadlock should they be unable to reach a decision.

The election of Roman bishops [i.e. popes) has since time immemorial been conducted at a local church council. Local rulers, and later German emperors, often took an active part in this selection. To serve as an example in preventing schisms, disturbances, and temptations, one of the popes—I do not know which—introduced a rule that future popes should be elected by cardinals locked up and under strict guard. That is, a few days after the death of a pope, all the cardinals present in Rome must assemble in one guarded place. Then the door of that place, which is known as the conclave, is walled up so that no one can enter or leave it, and guarded by a town supervisor with his men. The cardinals receive their meals through a revolving door which prevents anyone from being seen and through which no one can crawl. The supervision and protection of this building, and of the entire city, is entrusted to a specially appointed overseer and that responsibility is hereditary so that it will be executed well and the city will enjoy peace in such anxious and troubled times. At present this responsibility belongs to an ancient family of princes called Savelli.

The cardinals must be locked up, if need be, for a whole year or longer, until they elect a pope. It has been agreed that whoever receives two-thirds of the votes will become pope. Every morning after Mass, each cardinal writes one name on his paper ballot and places it on the altar. Then they tabulate the results, and if one of the cardinals receives two-thirds of the votes, they all immediately bow to him and declare him pope. This method was conceived in order to control the unrestrained human lust for power. And, with God's grace, for the past 220 years everything has moved along peacefully, and there have been no schisms within the church.

The Venetians also elect their prince. First, if I am not mistaken, they select a hundred electors from among them through an open vote. Second, these hundred electors elect three individuals through a secret ballot; that is, each elector writes down the names of three persons, the votes are tabulated, and the three who have the most votes become the candidates. Third, the names of the three candidates are written in big letters, and below each name they place a basket with a hole for balls. The baskets are placed in such a way that anything thrown into them can get there only through one large opening, and when someone throws a ball, no one knows for which name or into which basket he threw it through the opening. A secretary reads the list and calls the names of all Venetian nobles or wellborn people. They come and each throws one ball into any basket he wishes. The balls are soft buttons made of paper, so that their sound will not reveal where they are falling. Then they empty each basket and count the balls. Whoever receives a majority becomes their prince.

In other instances when they try to resolve what to do or not to do, each person receives two beans, one white and one black. If there are more white beans cast, the measure is passed; if more black, it fails.

Boris: Khervoi, in your judgment how can these various forms of election among other nations benefit us?

Khervoi: First, there is no doubt that horse jumping or neighing, bodily strength, promises, purchase, or tricks are silly means of determining supreme authority. Wherever matters are decided by the willfulness of soldiers (as is the case among the Turks) or via open assemblies, a vicious anarchy prevails, one that undermines the foundations of sound government.

Second, neither the pope nor any foreign ruler should be requested to arbitrate the disputed election of a ruler, because they will choose according to their own personal advantage. Nations should not be allowed to arbitrate either because they will be afraid of antagonizing one of the interested parties.

Third, the system under which only one city, Rome—actually one pope, as the head of that capital—is allowed to select and crown a foreign king or emperor to govern all of Italy is very unreliable.

Fourth, under such circumstances, great anarchy is bound to ensue. Emperor Otto, by appointing the electors, tried to make certain that Italy would never escape the control of the German people, but at the same time, he caused much trouble for his successors and the Germans. After they received authorization as electors, these princes were unwilling to obey the emperors. Instead, they began to order the emperors around and elect new emperors while old ones were still alive, and much disturbance and bloodshed was brought about.

Fifth, since time immemorial, Roman bishops have been elected by a Church council. Those who have violated this custom have attained nothing worthwhile.

Boris: Please would you explain the former problem at greater length?

Khervoi: The fact is, after the German kings secured the imperial throne by means of free election, they appointed German electors, thereby establised their control forever, and in the process deprived the Romans of the right of free election. Not satisfied with this, however, they began to seize the popes, incarcerate them, and overthrow them, and this led to no good. Indeed, all sorts of trouble resulted. For one thing, because the emperors were excommunicated by the popes, they suffered bitter deaths. Henry I had to flee from his own son and died from grief. Frederick I drowned. Philip was killed. Otto IV was defeated and died in despair. Frederick II was overthrown and also died in despair. Conrad was overthrown as well. For another, the popes overthrown by these emperors always returned to Rome and overthrew the emperors' antipopes. Similarly, during the reign of the pagan emperors, though more than thirty popes were tortured to death over a period of 300 years, the problem of succession was never interrupted. It was God's will that the appointment of antipopes never interfered with the progression of the true successors of St Peter.

But let us return to our principal discourse. On the basis of what has been said, I conclude that some of the most powerful and illustrious kingdoms were not meant to have a prolonged existence. In ancient times, it was republics such as Sparta, Athens, and ancient Rome under the Republic which were famous because of their benevolent laws. In autocratic empires or kingdoms, however, good laws conducive to the longevity of the realm, to national tranquillity, and to contentment are rarely found. For example, in ancient Athens I see the amnesty sponsored by Thrasybulus; in Sparta, the chauvinism inspired by Lycurgus; in Venice, the three-tier voting system; in France, the Salic law; and in Rome, secret elections. Nor is there any reason, in my view, to praise the seven German electors! Thus, Boris, you can see that virtually nowhere in the world have even the greatest kingdoms developed inviolate laws. If there are such laws, they appear only after much suffering, experience, and wise council.

Boris: In other words, Khervoi, kings are concerned with the succession and seldom think about anything else. They do not consider that their dynasties may come to an end. Yet they can and should recall the experience of other kings, and realize that Alexander, Julius, and Augustus did not have any successors—moreover, that the dynasties of Cyrus, Constantine, and Charlemagne, as well as of many other rulers, were also terminated early. Some kings believe their dynasties will be eternal; other feel it is sufficient that they have designated successors, leave the concern to them, and pay no further attention to the problem.

Khervoi: In my view, the best and the most promising system is the one used by the Venetians, who vote openly, with ballots and little balls, and who have established who is entitled to elect and who can be elected. No one has the right of election except Venetian authorities and nobles, and no one can be elected except the authorities, or those nobles who hold the highest positions on the council. I believe that it would be beneficial and salutary for this tsardom to follow that example. Should the tsar's family die out, elections to the vacant throne should be conducted as follows:

(1) No one should be elected or proclaimed tsar except our own Russian princes.

(2) After the death of the tsar, all military forces should be placed under the command of the patriarch—or of some other high prelate—who will then appoint an assembly and designate the date when bishops, abbots, princes, lords and *boyars* will assemble.

(3) On the designated date, bishops, abbots, princes, and lords (but not *boyars*) should assemble in the capital. Everyone should write down the names of three princes, and submit his choices to the patriarch and the bishops sitting at the table. They should then read the names on the master list, which should be passed around. The three names that receive the most votes should be selected.

(4) These three names should be posted on three baskets, as explained before. Then all the *boyars* should be summoned into the court to cast their ballots. Whoever receives the most of these ballots would become the tsar.

Appendix

Number of class members in the Boyar Duma and composition of political power

Year	Aristocrats Boyar & Okol'nichii	Servitors Dvorianin & D'iak	Aristocratic political power (percentage)	Servitors political power (percentage)
1613	27	2	93	07
1614	31	4	89	11
1615	30	4	88	12
1616	35	4	90	10
1617	33	3	92	08
1618	33	4	89	11
1619	30	4	88	12
1620	32	4	89	11
1621	33	3	92	08
1622	32	3	91	09
1623	32	4	89	11
1624	33	4	89	11
1625	33	4	89	11
1626	31	4	89	11
1627	31	5	86	14
1628	30	5	86	14
1629	26	5	84	16
1630	23	5	82	18
1631	23	5	82	18
1632	23	5	82	18
1633	23	6	79	21
1634	23	6	79	21
1635	25	6	81	19
1636	28	6	82	18
1637	29	6	83	17
1638	29	6	83	17
1639	30	3	91	09
1640	29	3	91	09
1641	29	3	91	09
1642	30	4	88	12
1643	27	3	90	10
1644	25	5	83	17
1645	22	6	79	21

Year	Aristocrats Boyar & Okol'nichii	Servitors Dvorianin & D'iak	Aristocratic political power (percentage)	Servitors political power (percentage)
1646	33	6	85	15
1647	38	7	84	16
1648	43	8	84	16
1649	45	7	87	13
1650	49	8	86	14
1651	50	8	86	14
1652	50	10	83	17
1653	52	10	84	16
1654	56	9	86	14
1655	54	9	86	14
1656	58	9	87	13
1657	60	9	87	13
1658	60	8	88	12
1659	62	9	87	13
1660	60	11	85	15
1661	59	11	84	16
1662	58	12	83	17
1663	54	13	81	19
1664	53	13	80	20
1665	52	16	76	24
1666	52	17	75	25
1667	51	17	75	25
1668	47	20	70	30
1669	45	22	67	33
1670	42	23	65	35
1671	41	28	59	41
1672	41	30	58	42
1673	42	32	57	43
1674	39	33	54	46
1675	40	30	57	43
1676	36	30	55	45
1677	55	32	63	37
1678	68	25	73	27
1679	68	27	72	28
1680	67	25	73	27
1681	70	29	71	29
1682	74	33	69	31
1683	94	37	72	28
1684	97	43	69	31
1685	97	44	69	31
1686	98	47	68	32
1687	97	47	67	33
1688	93	44	68	32
1689	98	47	68	32
1690	106	47	69	31

Source: Adapted and calculated from Robert O. Crummey, Aristocrats and Servitors: The Boyar Elite in Russia, 1613–1689 (Princeton, 1983), Appendix A, 175–7. The figures for 1613 refer to the time of the coronation of Mikhail Romanov, June 11; thereafter the figures are for January 1 of each year.

Selected bibliography

For convenience and clarity, this bibliography comprises the following categories: (I) principal published writings of Krizhanich; (II) works cited by Krizhanich as relevant to his mission to Moscow and to the writing of the *Politika*; (III) principal periodical and secondary literature—including unpublished monographs and dissertations—on Krizhanich's life and work; (IV) papers prepared for the symposium commemorating the 300th anniversary of Krizhanich's death, Zagreb, 1983; and (V) works cited in introductory analysis.

To the best of our knowledge, included here are the most important of the surviving writings of Iurii Krizhanich that have been published and the basic studies pertaining to his life and work. Individual letters or statements by Krizhanich and brief comments on, or reviews of, his writings have been omitted. Readers interested in such material, and in surviving but unpublished, lost, or undiscovered writings of Krizhanich, may wish to consult Thomas Eekman and Anté Kadić (eds) *Juraj Križanić (1618–1683): Russophile and Ecumenic Visionary* (The Hague, 1976): 329–51, hereafter cited as "Eekman and Kadić." Readers of Croatian may also wish to refer to A.L. Goldberg, "Bibliografija o Jurju Križaniću," *Historijski zbornik* 21–2 (1968–69): 513–28; and Ivan Golub and Jaroslav Šidak, "Bibliografija o Jurju Križaniću," *Život i djelo Jurja Križanića* (Zagreb, 1974): 259–77. For a comprehensive catalogue of the writings by, and on, Krizhanich—listing 562 items—the interested reader may wish to consult Kornelija Pejčinović, *Život i djelo Jurja Križanića* (Zagreb, 1983). See also the extensive bibliography in Eekman and Kadić.

I PRINCIPAL PUBLISHED WRITINGS OF IURII KRIZHANICH

"Beseda k. Cherkasom" [1659]. Published under the title "Beseda ko Czirkasom wo osobi Czirkasa upisana," edited by V.N. Shchepkin and V.N. Kolosov, in *Sobranie sochinenii* (Moscow, 1891). Also published with an introduction by P.A. Kulish under the title "Malorusskie kazaki mezhdu Rossiei i Polshei v 1659 g. po vzgliadu na nikh serba Iu. Krizhanicha," *Chteniia v Obshchestve istorii i drevnostei rossiiskikh* 98 (1876): 109–24; and under the title "Jurii

Krizhanich v Rossii. Iz dukhovnoi zhizni moskovskogo gosudarstva v XVII v.," edited by S.A. Belokurov, *ibid.* 206 (1903): 28–32.

"De providentia Dei" [1666–1667]. Edited by P.A. Bezsonov and published in an abridged form under the title *O promysle* (Moscow, 1860).

Gramatichno izkazanie ob russkom jeziku [1665]. Edited by O.M. Bodianskii (Moscow, 1859). Originally published in *Chteniia v Obshchestve istorii i drevnostei Rossiiskikh* 23 (1848): 1–120, and reprinted in *ibid.* 30 (1859): 121–256.

"Historia de Sibiria" [1680]. Translated and edited by G. Spasskii, in *Sibirskii vestnik,* 1822, Nos. 17–18: 1–92. Reprinted in *Sibir v XVII veke,* edited by A.A. Titov (Moscow, 1890): 115–216, and in *Sibir v izvestiiakh inostrannykh puteshestvennikov i pisatelei,* edited by M.P. Alekseev (Irkutsk, 1941): 552–68.

"Memorandum to Francesco Ingoli, Secretary of the Congregatio de Propaganda Fide, Rome" [1641]. Published under the title "Zapiska Krizhanicha 1641 g. Iurii Krizhanich v Rossii. Iz dukhovnoi zhizni moskovskogo gosudarstva v XVII v. (Prilozheniia)," edited by S.A. Belokurov, in *Chteniia v Obshchestve istorii i drevnostei Rossiiskikh* 206 (1903): 87–126. Reprinted with revisions under the title "Križanić's Memorandum" (1641) by Ante Kadić in *Jahrbücher für Geschichte Osteuropas* 3 (1964): 331–49, and in the same author's *From Croatian Renaissance to Yugoslav Socialism* (The Hague, 1969): 74–92.

"Naratio de hodierno statu schismatis in Moscovia [1647]." Reproduced by S.A. Belokurov in his 'Iurii Krizhanich v Rossii: Iz dukhovnoi zhizni moskovskogo gosudarstva v XVII v. (Prilozheniia)' in *Chteniia v Obshchestve istorii i drevnostei Rossiiskikh* 206 (1903): 237–44.

"Objasnenje vivodno o pismé slovenskom [1660–61]." Reproduced in *Zhurnal Ministerstva Narodnogo Prosveshcheniia* 12 (1888): 179–207; in Iu. Krizhanich, *Sobranie sochinenii,* edited by V.N. Kolosov (Moscow, 1891); and in *Sabrana djela Jurja Križanića,* Kniga I, edited by Josip Hamm (Zagreb, 1983).

"Ob svetom kreshcheniu [1670–73]" in Iurii Krizhanich, *Sobranie sochinenii,* 391, edited by A. Bashkirov (Moscow, 1892).

"Opisania izo Lvova do Moskvy" in "Iurii Krizhanich v Rossii: Iz dukhovnoi zhizni moskovskogo gosudarstva v XVII v. (Prilozheniia)" in *Chteniia v Obshchestve istorii i drevnostei Rossiiskikh* 206 (1903): 33–8. This work also appeared under the title "Putno opisanie ot Lewowa do Moskwi" in Iurii Krizhanich, *Sobranie sochinenii,* edited by V.N. Shchepkin and V.N. Kolosov (Moscow, 1891).

[Politika.] *Ekonomicheskie i politicheskie vzgliady Iuriia Krizhanicha. (Fragmenty iz "Politiki"),* edited by V.I. Picheta (St Petersburg, 1913).

Politika ili razgovori o vladatelstvu. (Fragmenti), translated and edited by M. Malinar; Introduction by V. Bogdanov (Zagreb, 1947).

[Politika.] "Iz rukopisnogo nasledstva Iu. Krizhanicha," edited by L.M. Mordukhovich, in *Istoricheskii Arkhiv* 1 (1958): 154–89.

Politika. Prepared for publication by V.V. Zelenin; translation and commentaries by A.L. Goldberg; edited by M.N. Tikhomirov (Moscow, 1965).

[Politika.] "Russkoe gosudarstvo v polovine XVII v. Rukopis vremen tsaria Alekseia Mikhailovicha." Abridged and edited by P.A. Bezsonov and published in *Russkaia Beseda* 1–6 (1859). This work was published in book form (2 vols) under the same title in 1860.

"Privetstvo Tsariu Feodoru Alekseevichu," edited by I. Dobrotvorskii, *Uchenye Zapiski Kazanskogo Universiteta* 1 (1865): 1–21.

Sobranie sochinenii, edited by A. Bashkirov (Moscow, 1892): contains Krizhanich's "Oblichenje na Solovecheskuiu chelobitnu" and "Ob svetom kreshshcheniiu."

Sobranie sochinenii, edited by M. Sokolov (Moscow, 1891). This volume contains Krizhanich's "Tolkovanie istoricheskikh prorochestv."

Sobranie sochinenii, edited by V.N. Shchepkin and V.N. Kolosov (Moscow, 1891). This volume contains the following works by Krizhanich: (1) "Putno opisanie ot Lewowa do Moskwi"; (2) "Besida ko Czirkasom wo osobi Czirkasa upisana"; (3) "Usmotrenie o Carskom Weliczestwu"; and (4) "Objasnenje vivodno o pisme slovenskom."

II WORKS CITED BY KRIZHANICH AS RELEVANT TO HIS MISSION TO MOSCOW AND TO THE WRITING OF HIS *POLITIKA*

Abelin, J. [also known as J. Gotofredus], *Archontologia cosmica* (Frankfurt, 1628).

Baronius, C., *Annales ecclesiastici,* Libri XII (Rome, 1588–1600).

Bellarmino, R., *De arte bene moriendi* (Cologne, 1626).

Biondo, Flavio, *Historiarum romanorum decades tres . . .* (Venice, 1483).

Bonfini, Antonio, *Rerum Ungaricarum decades quatuor . . .* (Basel, 1568).

Chyträus, David, *Vandalia* (Rostock, 1589).

Cnapius, G., *Thesaurus polono-latino-graecius* (Cracow, 1643).

Commines, Philip de, *De rebus gestis a Ludovico IX et Carolo VIII* (Frankfurt, 1594).

Cromer, M. *De origine et rebus gestis polonorum* (Basel, 1555).

Faust de Aschaffenburg, M., *Consilia pro aerario civili, ecclesiastico et militari* (Frankfurt, 1641).

Giovio, Paolo, *Libellus de legatione Basili magni . . . ad Clementem VII* (Rome, 1525).

Hammelmann, Herman, *Oldenburgisches Chronicon* (Oldenburg, 1599).

Heidenstein, Reingold, *De bella Muscovitico commentariorum,* Book 6 (Cracow, 1581).

Henning, Solomon, *Lifflandische-Churländische Chronica, was sich von 1554–1590 in den langwirigen Moscowitischer und andern Kriegen . . . zugetragen* (Rostock, 1590).

Herberstein, Sigismund von, *Rerum Moscoviticarum Commentarii* (Vienna, 1549).

Klonowicz, Szymon, *Roxolania* (Cracow, 1584).

Lipsius, J., *Monita et exempla politica* (Amsterdam, 1630).

Muntius, H., *De Germanorum primi origine . . .* (Basel, 1539).

Odeborn, Paul, *Johannis Basilidis, magni Moschoviae ducis vita* (Wittenberg, 1585).

Olearius, Adam, *Vermehrte Newe Beschreibung der Muscowitischen . . . Reise* (Schleswig, 1656).

Paruta, Paolo, *Discorsi politici* (Venice, 1599).

——*Historia Venetiana* (Venice, 1605).

Pernisteri, Philippi, *Relatio de Magno Moscoviae Principe* (Frankfurt, 1579).

Petrejus, Peter, *Historien und Bericht von dem grossfürstenthumb Muschkov* (Leipzig, 1620).

Piasecki, Pawel, *Chronica gestorum in Europa singularium* (Cracow, 1648).

Possevino, Antonio, *Moscovia* (Vilna, 1586).

Rufus, Q. Curtius, *De rebus gesti Alexandri Magni* (Amsterdam, 1648).

Starowolski, Szymon, *Polonia, nunc denuo recognita et aucta* (Cologne, 1632).

——*Reformacya obyczajow polskich* (Cracow, 1649).

In addition to these writings, Krizhanich frequently referred to the Bible and to classical works by such authorities as Aristotle, Cicero, the Byzantine emperor Constantine Porphyrogenitus, Machiavelli, Livy, Plato, Plutarch, Polybius, St Augustine, Thomas Aquinas, Tacitus, Vergil, and Xenophon.

III   WRITINGS ON KRIZHANICH: PRINCIPAL PERIODICAL
AND SECONDARY LITERATURE—INCLUDING UNPUBLISHED
MONOGRAPHS AND DISSERTATIONS—ON KRIZHANICH'S
LIFE AND WORK

Alekseev, M.P., "Iu. Krizhanich i folklor moskovskoi inozemnoi slobody" in *Trudy otdeleniia drevne-russkoi literatury Akademii nauk SSSR* 24 (1969): 299–305.

Alpatov, M.A., "Istoricheskaia kontseptsiia Iu. Krizhanicha," *Sovetskoe slavianovedenie* 3 (1966): 31–44.

Badalić, Josip, "Gospodarsko-politički pogledi Jurja Križanića," *Politička Misao* 9:1 (1972): 9–21. This article was republished in *Život i djelo Jurja Križanića: Zbornik Radova* (Zagreb, 1974): 152–69.

——"Juraj Križanić kao pjesnik (1618–83)," *Slavia* 39:2 (1970): 198–217.

——"Juraj Križanić—mejduslavenski prosvetitelj," *Rusko-hrvatske književne studije* (Zagreb, 1971): 51–126.

——"J. Križanić-pjesnik Ilirije," *Radovi Slavenskog instituta u Zagrebu* 2 (1958): 5–23.

——"J. Križanić—preteča I. Pososhkova," *Radovi zavoda za slovensku filologiju* 5 (1963): 5–24.

——"J. Križanić i Slovenci," *Slavistična revija* 2 (1969): 9–15.

Bakhrushin, S.V., "Iu. Krizhanich," *Istoricheskii Zhurnal* 1–2 (1942): 145–51.

Baletić, Zvonimir, "Politička Ekonomija Križanićeve 'Politike'," *Život i djelo Jurja Križanića: Zbornik Radova* (Zagreb, 1974): 170–203.

Baron, Samuel H., "Križanić and Olearius," in Eekman and Kadić: 183–208.

Beilis, I.M., "Krizhanich kak merkantilist," *Nauchnye zapiski Kharkovskogo instituta sovetskoi torgovli* 2 (1941): 15–26.

Belokurov, S.A., Iu. *Krizhanich v Rossii. Iz dukhovnoi zhizni moskovskogo obshchestva XVII v* (Moscow, 1902). Published under the same title in *Chteniia v Obshchestve istorii i drevnostei Rossiskikh* 205 (1903): 1–210, and appendixes in 206 (1903): 1–306.

Berezhkov, M.N., "Plan zavoevaniia Kryma, sostavlennyi v tsarstvovanie gosudaria Alekseia Mikhailovicha Iu. Krizhanichem," *Zhurnal Ministerstva Narodnogo Prosveshcheniia* 10 (1891): 483–517 and no. 11: 65–119.

Bessonow, P., "Über eine Handschrift aus der Zeit des Zaaren Alexei Michailowitsch," *Russische Fragmente,* edited by F. Bodenstedt (Leipzig, 1862): 2: 243–305.

Bezsonov, P.A., "Katolicheskii sviashchennik serb (khorvat) Iu. Krizhanich, revnitel vossoedineniia tserkvei i vsego slavianstva v XVII v," *Pravoslavnoe obozrenie* vol. 1 (1870): 129–59, 339–93, and vol. 2: 1–79 and 1–86.

Bilbasov, V.A., "Iu. Krizhanich," *Istoricheskie monografii* 2 (St Petersburg, 1901): 77–105.

———"Iurii Krizhanich: Novye dannye iz rimskogo arkhiva," *Russkaia Starina* 12 (1892): 445–68.

Bogdanović, D., "J. Križanić," *Pregled književnosti hrvatske i srpske* 2 (Zagreb, 1932): 428–36.

Bozičević, J., "Juraj Križanić: Seventeenth Century Pan-Slav Visionary" (Ph.D. dissertation, Georgetown University, Washington, DC, 1968).

Brkić, L., "J. Križanić in Russian, Croatian and Serbian Scholarship, 1859–1965" (Ph.D. dissertation, University of Wisconsin, Madison, 1969).

Brückner, Alexander, "Ein Finanzpolitiker in Russland im XVII Jahrhundert," *Russische Revue* 1 (1891): 292–333.

———"Ein Kleiderreformproject von Peter dem Grossen," *Russische Revue* 2 (1873): 426–44.

———"Iu. Krizhanich," *Russkii vestnik* 6 (1887): 575–619 and no. 7: 9–51.

———"Iu. Krizhanich o vostochnom voprose," *Drevniaia i novaia Rossiia* 12: 385–95 (St Petersburg, 1876).

———"O sochineniiakh Iu. Krizhanicha," *Russkii vestnik* 6 (1889): 3–29.

Bryner, C., "The Political Philosophy of J. Križanić," *New Scholasticism* 2 (1939): 133–68.

Daničić, Gj., "Gramatika G. Križanića," *Rad Jugoslavenske Akademije Znanosti i Umjetnosti* 16 (1871): 159–98.

Datsiuk, B.D., Iu. *Krizhanich* (Moscow, 1946).

———Iu. *Krizhanich—pobornik svobody i edinstva slavianskikh narodov* (Moscow, 1945).

Deželić, S., "J. Križanić, naš markantni ekonomsko-politički pisać XVII," *Jugoslavenska narodna privreda* 3 (1933): 23–4 and no. 4: 28–30.

Dolobko, M.G., "Iu Krizhanich o russkom iazyke," *Sovetskoe iazykoznanie* 3 (1937): 3–41.

Du Feu, V.M., "Common Slavonic Syntex and Križanić's Grammar," in Eekman and Kadić: 287–302.

Eekman, Thomas, "Grammaticheskii i leksicheskii sostav iazyka Iu. Križanića," *Dutch Contributions to the V International Congress of Slavicists* (The Hague, 1963): 43–77.

——"J. Križanić et ses idées sur l'orthographie des alphabets latin et cyrillique," *Slovo* 17 (1967): 60–94.

——"J. Križanić o Polsce," *Literatura, komparatystyka, folklor* (Warsaw, 1968): 177–97.

——*Slavische dromen. De figur van J. Križanić* ('s-Gravenhage, 1962).

——"Vatroslav Jagić on Križanić," Eekman and Kadić, 302–26.

——and Anté Kadić, eds. *Juraj Križanić (1618–1683) Russophile and Ecumenic Visionary: A Symposium* (The Hague, 1976).

Epifanov, P.P., "Proiski Vatikana v Rossii i Iu. Krizhanich," *Voprosy Istorii* 10 (1953): 18–36.

Fermendžin, E., "Prinos za životopis Gj. Križanića, svećenika i kanonika zagrebačke biskupije," *Starina* 18 (1886): 210–30.

Frančić, Miroslav, "Dzieje badań nad życiem i tworczością J. Kryžanića," *Pamietnik słowiański* 19 (1969): 3–25.

——"Juraj Križanić—życie i dzielo." *Sprawozdania z prac naukowych Polskej Akademji Nauk* 1 (1969): 1–13.

——*Juraj Križanić: ideolog absolutyzmu* (Warsaw-Cracow, 1974).

Georgievskii, A.P., "Iu. Krizhanich i sovremennaia deistvitelnost," *Vestnik obrazovaniia i vospitaniia* 9(1914): 727–36.

Ginzburg, M.S., "Slavianstvo i Rossiia v mirovozzrenii Iuriia Krizhanicha" *American Contributions to the IV International Congress of Slavicists* (The Hague, 1958): 103–6.

Goldberg, A.L., "Bibliografija o Jurju Križaniću," *Historijski Zbornik* 21–22 (1968–69): 513–28.

——"Ideia slavianskogo edinstva v sochineniiakh Iu. Krizhanicha," *Trudy otdeleniia drevnerusskoi literatury Akademii Nauk SSSR* 13 (1963): 373–90.

——"Istoricheskaia nauka o Iu. Krizhaniche," *Uchenye zapiski Leningradskogo gosudarstvennogo universiteta* 117 (1949): 84–119.

——"J. Križanić und Adam Olearius (Aus der literarischen Polemik des 17 Jahrhunderts)," *Veröffentlichungen des Instituts für Slawistik der Deutschen Akademie der Wissenschaften* no. 28, part II (1967): 94–113 and 390–4.

——"Juraj Križanić i Rusija," *Historijski zbornik* 21–2 (1968–69): 259–81.

——"Juraj Križanić in Russian Historiography," in Eekman and Kadić: 51–69.

——"Iu. Krizhanich o russkom obshchestve serediny XVII v," *Istoriia SSSR* 6 (1960): 71–84.

——"J. Križanić u russkoj historigrafiji," *Historijski zbornik* 19–20 (1966–67): 129–40.

——"Iu. Krizhanich i Sh. Starovolskii," *Slavia* 1 (1965): 28–40.

——"Rabota Iu. Krizhanicha nad russkoi letopisiu," *Trudy otdeleniia drevnerusskoi literatury Akademii Nauk SSSR* 14 (1958): 349–54.

——"Sochineniia Iu. Krizhanicha i ikh istochniki," *Vestnik istorii mirovoi kultury* 6 (1960): 117–30.

——"Sochineniia Iu. Krizhanicha i russkaia deistvitelnost XVII v" (Ph.D. dissertation, University of Leningrad, 1950).

Golub, Ivan, *Juraj Križanić: Glazbeni teoretik 17. stoljeca* (Zagreb, 1981).

——*Slavenstvo Jurja Križanića* (Zagreb, 1983).

——"Biografska pozadina Križaniževih djela," *Život i djelo Jurja Križanića* (Zagreb, 1974): 35–104.

——"Contributions à l'histoire des relations de Križanić avec ses contemporains (1651–1658)," in Eekman and Kadić: 91–146.

——"Juraj Križanić i pitanje prava Slovenaća na svetojeronimske ustanove u Rimu," *Historijski zbornik* 21–2 (1968–69): 213–58.

——"Juraj Križanić's 'Asserta Musicalia' in Caramuel's Newly Discovered Autograph of 'Musica'," *International Review of the Aesthetics and Sociology of Music,* IX, no. 2 (Zagreb, 1978): 219–78.

——"Juraj Križanić u Carigradu," *Historijski Zbornik* 29–30 (1976–77): 193–202.

——"Križanić théologien—sa conception ecclésiologique des événements et de l'histoire," in Eekman and Kadić: 165–82.

——"Križanićevo teolosko poimanje zbivanja," *Život i djelo Jurja Križanića* (Zagreb, 1974): 105–29.

——"Nova grada o Jurju Križaniću iz rimskikh arhiva (1653–57)," *Starine JAZU,* Kn. 57 (Zagreb, 1978): 111–210.

——"O sačuvanim primjercima Križanićevih 'Asserta musicalia'," *Arti Musices (Muzikološki zbornik)* 2 (1971): 31–41.

——"Otkriven autograph Križanićevog djela 'Bibliotheca Schismaticorum Universa'," *Kolo* 9 (1971): 1057–8.

——"Pojam filozofije u J. Križanića," *Bogoslovska smotra* 3–4 (1967): 469–75.

——"Tri jezična spomenika iz Križanićeva rodnog kraja (1656–72)," *Grada za provijest književnosti hrvatske JAZU,* Kn. 32 (Zagreb, 1978): 123–64.

——"De mente ecclesiologica Georgii Križanić" (unpublished dissertation, Pontificia Universitas Grigoriana, Rome, 1963).

——and J. Šidak, "Bibliografija o Jurju Križaniću," *Život i djelo Jurja Križanića* (Zagreb, 1974): 259–77.

Hamm, J., "Križanić and his Accent" in Eekman and Kadić: 263–86.

——"Prosodijski sistem Križanićeva govora," *Politička Misao* 9:1 (1972): 39–58; and *Život i djelo Jurja Križanića* (Zagreb, 1974): 212–38.

Heaney, M., "Križanić's Grammar: The Theory of Gramatichno izkazanie and the Practice of Politika" *Oxford Slavonic Papers,* n.s. 4 (1971): 105–24.

Hraste, M., "Prinosi poznavanju hrvatsko-srpskog jezika J. Križanića," *Radovi zavoda za slovensku filologiju* 5 (1963): 25–34.

Jagić, V., *Život i rad J. Križanića* (Zagreb, 1917).

Kadić, Anté, "Križanić's Formative Years," in *American Contributions to the V International Congress of Slavicists* (The Hague, 1963): 167–200.

——"Križanić's Memorandum," *Jahrbücher für Geschichte Osteuropas* 3 (1964): 331–49.

——"Križanić and Possevino—Missionaries to Muscovy," in Eekman and Kadić: 73–90.

——"Križanić and his Predecessors—the Slavic Idea among the Croatian Baroque Writers," in Eekman and Kadić: 147–64.

Kliuchevskii, V.O., "Iurii Krizhanich," in *Kurs russkoi istorii* 3 (Moscow, 1908): 316–29.

Kolosov, V.N., "O vnov otkrytom sochinenii Iu. Krizhanicha," *Zhurnal Ministerstva Narodnogo Prosveshcheniia* 12 (1888): 179–207.

Kostomarov, N.I., "Iurii Krizhanich," in *Russkaia istoriia v zhizneoposaniiakh ee glavneishikh deiatelei* 5 (St Petersburg, 1874): 429–58.

Krempler, P., "J. Križanić," *Vienac* 40 (1873): 633–7 and 41: 651–5.

Krleža, M., "O patru dominikancu J. Križaniću," *Knjizevnik* 1:2 (1929): 1–13.

——"Pogovor za dvije drame o Areteju i o J. Križaniću," *Forum* 5 (1962): 663–715.

Kukulević-Sakcinski, I., "Juraj Križanić Nebljuški, hrvatsko-ruski pisac," *Arkiv za povjesnicu jugoslavensku* 10 (1869): 202–66.

Kurmacheva, M.D. and V.G. Shestobytova, "Obsuzhdenie voprosa o deiatelnosti Iu. Krizhanicha," *Voprosy istorii* 2 (1957): 202–7.

Kvapil, M., "Jurij Križanić," *Slavia* 4 (1957): 540–51.

Lah, I., "J. Križanić," *Njiva* 4/6 (1922): 99–108.

Lavrin, J., "Y. Križanich," *Russian Review* 4 (1966): 369–82.

Leger, L., "[Juraj Križanić]," *Le Monde Slave*, 308–17 (1873).

——"Un precurseur du panslavisme au XVII siècle," *Nouvelles études slaves* (1880): 1–47.

Liatskii, E., "Po povodu novoi knigi o Križaniće," *Sveslavenský zbornik* (1930): 207–13.

Lisiutin, V.I., "Ekonomicheskie vozzrenia Iu. Krizhanicha" (Ph.D. dissertation, University of Moscow, 1948).

Maretić, T., "G. Križanić, hrvatsko-ruski pisac XVII v," *Vienac* 10 (1877): 155–58 and 11: 170–74.

Markevich, A.I., *Iu. Krizhanich i ego literaturnaia deiatelnost* (Warsaw, 1876).

Miliukov, P.N., "[Jurii Krizhanich]," in his *Ocherki po istorii russkoi kultury* 3 [Jubilee edition] (Paris, 1930): 135–56.

Mirzoev, V.G., "Iu. Krizhanich," in his *Istoriografiia Sibiri* (Moscow, 1970): 38–45.

Moguš, M., "J. Križanić kao jezikoslovac," *Kolo,* 10 (1968): 356–62.

——"Križanićevi naglasci," *Život i djelo Jurja Križanića* (Zagreb, 1974): 239–46.

Mordukhovich, L.M., "Antifeodalna kontseptsiia Iu. Krizhanicha,,, *Kratkie soobshcheniia instituta slavianovedeniia* 26 (1958): 25–46.

——"Filosofskie i sotsiologicheskie vzgliady Iu. Krizhanicha," *Kratkie soobshcheniia instituta slavianovedeniia* 36 (1963): 61–84.

——"Iu. Krizhanich o dengakh i kredite," *Sovetskie finansy* 2 (1945): 28–34.

——"Juraj Križanić, W. Petty and Ivan Pososkov," in Eekman and Kadić: 223–44.

——"Jurii Krizhanich o 'rabstve'," *Drevnerusskie literaturnye pamiatniki* XXXIII (1979): 142–55.

——"Politicheskie vzgliady Iu. Krizhanicha," *Pravovedenie. Izvestiia vysshykh uchebnykh zavedenii* 1 (1962): 111–22.

——"Sotsialno-ekomicheskie vzgliady Iu. Krizhanicha" (Ph.D. dissertation, Moscow University, 1962).

Nedelković, D., "Filosof J. Križanić: Povodom 350-godisnice njegova rodjenja," *Letopis Matice srpske* 401: 1 (1968): 43–58.

O'Brien, C. Bickford, "Early Political Consciousness in Muscovy: The Views of Juraj Križanić and Afanasij Ordin-Nashchokin," Eekman and Kadić: 209–22.

Palmieri, A., "Un' opera polemica di Massimo il Greco tradotta in latino da Giorgi Krijanitch," *Bassarione,* 3rd ser. no. 119: 54–79 and nos. 121–2: 379–84.

——and G. Coressi, "De processione Spiritu Sancti dialogus in latinum a G. Križanić conversus," *Acta Academiae Velehradensis* 8: 1 (1912): 41–58.

Parry, Albert, "Juraj Križanić's Views on Siberia and China of the Seventeenth Century," in Eekman and Kadić: 245–62.

Pavić, Radovan, "Neki političko-geografski i geopolitički aspekti u djelima Jurja Križanića," *Politička Misao* 9:1 (1972): 22–38; also in *Život i djelo Jurja Križanića* (Zagreb, 1974): 130–51.

Pavić, Radovan (ed.), *Život i rad Jurja Križanića. Zbornik radova* (Zagreb, 1974).

Pejić, Lazar, "Juraj Križanić," *Jugoslovenski Merkantilisti* (Smederevo, 1979): 71–89.

Perwolf, I., "Iurii Krizhanich, khorvat slavist i panslavist," *Slaviane, ikh vzaimnye otnosheniia i sviazi* 2 (1888): 309–51.

——"J. Križanić patriarcha slavistiky," *Slovansky sbornik* 5 (1886): 1–4.

Petrov, K.V., "Iu. Krizhanich. Zhizn, deiatelnost i politiko-sotsialnye vzgliady" (St Petersburg, 1911): Manuscript in the Leningrad University Library.

Petrovich, M.B., "J. Križanić: A Precursor of Panslavism," *American Slavic and East European Review* 18–19 (1947): 75–92.

Peunova, M.N., "Iurii Krizhanich," *Istoriia filosofii v SSSR* 1 (Moscow, 1968): 269–75.

Picheta, V.I., "Iu. Krizhanich i ego otnoshenie k Russkomu gosudarstvu," *Slavianskii sbornik* (Moscow, 1947): 202–40.

——"Politiko-ekonomicheskie vzgliady Iu. Krizhanicha v sviazi s sostoianiem Moskovskogo gosudarstva vo vtoroi polovine XVII v," *Letopis Ekaterinoslavskoi uchenoi arkhivnoi komissii* 1 (1905): 47–68.

——"Zapiska Iu. Krizhanicha o Malorossii," *ibid.,* 1 (1904): 1–17.

Pierling, P., "Un panslaviste missionaire," in his *La Russie et le Saint Siège* (Paris, 1907) chapter 4: 1–39.

——"Un protagoniste du panslavisme au XVIIe siècle," *Revue des questions historiques* 1 (1896): 186–200.

Plekhanov, G.V., "Pervye zapadniki i prosvetiteli. 4. Krizhanich," in his *Istoriia russkoi obshchestvennoi mysli* 1 (Moscow, 1914): 286–304.

Popruzhenko, M.G., "Neskolko zamechanii o sochineniiakh Iu. Krizhanicha," *Izvestiia otdeleniia iazyka i slovesnosti Akademii nauk* 2:2 (1897): 302–19.

Požanin, Ante, "Pojam mudrosti i filosofiji Jurja Križanića," *Život i djelo Jurja Križanća* 7–14 (Zagreb, 1974); and in *Politička Misao* 9:1 (1972): 3–8.

Pushkarev, L.N., "Ob otsenke deiatelnosti Iu. Krizhanicha," *Voprosy istorii* 1 (1957): 77–86.

——*Iurii Krizhanich. Ocherk zhizni i tvorchestra* (Moscow, 1984).

Pypin, A.N., "Obzor russkikh izuchenii slavianstva," *Vestnik Evropy* 1 (1889): 606–25.

Radić, S., "Nejdokonalejši představitel slovanské myšlenky," *Slovanský Přehled* 4 (1902): 21–8, 119–24, 172–5.

Radojčić, N., "Jurko Križanić Srbljanin," *Društveni život* 1 (1920): 46–54.

Ravlić, J., "J. Križanić," *Forum* 7–7 (1970): 73–91.

Rendulić, Nedjeljko, "Juraj Križanić—Jedan od preteča teorija lokacije," *Život i djelo Jurja Križanića* (Zagreb, 1974): 204–11.

Roganovich, I., *Iu. Krizhanich i ego filosofiia natsionalizma* (Kazan, 1899).

Scolardi, P.G., *Au service de Rome et de Moscou au XVIIe siècle. Krijanich messager de l'unité des chrétiens et père du panslavisme* (Paris, 1947).

Severnyi, N.E., "Otchet o zaniatiiakh pri stolichnykh bibliotekakh i arkhivakh v vakatsionnoe vremiia," *Chteniia v obshchestve istorii i drevnostei rossiiskikh* 61 (1867): 123–54.

Shakhmatov, A.A., "Iurii Krizhanich o serbsko-khorvatskom udarenii," *Russkii filologicheskii vestnik* 4 (1894): 250–60; 1–2 (1895): 298–327; 3 (1895): 87–124; 4 (1895): 204–22.

Shmurlo, E.F., "Iu. Krizhanich. Otchet uchenogo korrespondenta v Rime," *Rossiia i Italiia* 3 (St Petersburg, 1911): 52–114.

——"From Križanić to the Slavophiles," *The Slavonic and East European Review* 17 (1927): 321–35.

Šidak, Jaroslav, "Hrvatsko družstvo u Križanićevo doba," *Život o djelo Jurja Križanića* (Zagreb, 1974): 15–34.

——"Juraj Križanić als Problem der kroatischen und serbischen Literatur," in Eekman and Kadić: 3–49.

——"Problem Jurja Križanića u hrvatskoi i srpskoi literaturi," *Historijski zbornik* 23–24 (1970–71): 147–78.

——Počeci političke misli u Hrvata—J. Križanić i P. Ritter Vitezović," *Naše teme* 16 (1972): 1118–35.

——"Slavenska ideja u hrvatskom misaonom rezvitku. J. Križanić i P. Ritter Vitezović," *Historija naroda Jugoslavie* 2 (Belgrade, 1959): 1007–15, 1116–17.

Skerović, N.P., *Juro Križanić. Njegov život, rad i ideje* (Belgrade, 1936).

Smirnov, S.K., "Serbskogo popa Iu. Krizhanicha oproverzhenie Solovetskoi chelobitnoi," *Tvoreniia sviatykh ottsev* 4 (Appendix) (1860): 503–85.

Solovev, S.M., "Iurii Krizhanich," in *Istoriia Rossii s drevneishikh vremen* 13 (Moscow, 1863): 194–205.

Špralja, Izak, "Neki muzikoloski aspekti u Jurja Križanića," *Život i djelo Jurja Križanića* (Zagreb, 1974): 247–58.

Stremooukhoff, N.N., "Križanić, Ph. de Commynes et sa théorie de la royauté française," *Annales de l'Institut français de Zagreb* 14–15 (1940): 125–38.

Sviatlovskii, V., "Iurii Krizhanich," in *Istoriia ekonomicheskikh idei v Rossii* 1 (Moscow, 1920): 44–53.

Vais, J., "Třistaleté jubileum panslavisty missionaře J. Križaniće," *Časopis katolického duchovenstva* 59 (1918): 309–33.

Valdenberg, V.E., *Gosudarstvennye idei Krizhanicha* (St Petersburg, 1912).

——"Pososhkov i Križanić v ikh obshchestvenno-ekonomicheskikh vozzreniiakh," *Slavia* 5 (1927): 745–62.

——"Znakomstvo Krizhanicha s grekami," *Byzantinoslavica* 7 (1938): 1–24.

Van Son, H., *Autour de Križanić, étude historique et linguistique* (Paris, 1934).

Vidaković, A., "'Asserta musicalia' (1656) J. Križanića i njegovi ostali radovi s područja glazbe," *Rad Jugoslavenskej Akademiji Znanosti i Umjetnosti* 337 (1965): 41–160.

Vodovozov, V.I., "Patriarkh Nikon i Krizhanich," *Narodnaia shkola* 12 (Appendix) (1878): 1–12.

Vondrak, V., "Slovanska myšlenka u Križaniče a jeho soud o Slovanech voûbec," Masarykova Universita v Brne, *Inaugurace rektorů* (Brno, 1922): 103–18.

Von Frank, A., "J. Križanić: Ein katholischer Missionär des 17 Jahrhunderts in Russland" (Leipzig, 1923). Typescript.

Vujić, M., *Križanićeva "Politika." Ekonomsko-politična studija* (Belgrade, 1895).

Weingart, M., "Jiři Križanič, prvni programovy hlasatel slovenské vzájemnosti" *Slovanska vzájemnost* (Bratislava, 1926): 123–36.

Wierzbicki, J., "Miroslav Krleža—Juraj Križanić," *Pemiętnik slowianski* 1 (1969): 27–42.

Wilinski, W., "Jerzy Krzyzanicz a Polska," *Przegląd Powszechny* 184:550 (1929): 61–86.

Winter, E., "Jurij Križanić," *Russland und das Papsttum* 1 (Berlin, 1960): 333–56.

——"Križanić," *Zeitschrift für Slawistik* 4 (1959): 625–44.

Zelenin, V.V., "Iurii Krizhanich v kontekste svoego vremeni," *Istoriia, kultura, etnografiia i folklor slavianskikh narodov* (Moscow, 1983): 76–86.

Zelenka, I., "J. Križanić, missionario o panslavista" (Ph.D. dissertation, University of Rome, 1966).

IV PAPERS PREPARED FOR A SPECIAL INTERNATIONAL
SYMPOSIUM COMMEMORATING THE 300th ANNIVERSARY
OF KRIŽANIĆ'S DEATH, YUGOSLAV ACADEMY OF
SCIENCE AND ARTS, ZAGREB, SEPTEMBER 1–4, 1983

Baron, Samuel H. "Was Križanić a Mercantilist?"

Blagojevic, Obren, "Križanićeva ekonomska misao u djelu Mihaila Vujića."

Bozicevic, Joseph, "Juraj Križanić: Visions of Cultural, Economic, and Political Reciprocity Among Slavs."

Bratulic, Josip, "Jagićev Križanić."

Bushkotovitch, Paul, "Juraj Križanić i ruskoe staroverstvo."

Dartel, van Geert, "Nicolaas Witsen i Jurai Križanić."

Frančic, Miroslaw, "Juraj Križanić—ideologue de l'absolutisme."

Hamm, Josip, "Juraj Križanić i slavistici danas."

Kokade, Mijo, "Križanićevo školovanje kod isusovaća u Grazu."

Letiche, John M. and Basil Dmytryshyn, "Economic Ideas of Juraj Križanić's *Politika*: Their Historic and Contemporary Relevance."

Lukanović, Ilija, "Bečki Collegium Croaticum u Križanićevo doba."

Metzler, Josef, "Die Sacra Congregatio de Propaganda Fide zur Zeit Juraj Križanić."

Mohorovičić, Andre, "Pojava Jurja Križanića u kontekstu evropskikh kulturnih zbivanja."

Partridge, Monica, "Križanić and England."

Pejić, Lazar, "Križanićev odnos prema problemima ruskog drustva u XVII veku, reformama Petra Velikog i radu I.T. Posoškova."

Puskarev, Lev N. "Juraj Križanić v Tobolske."

Senyk, Sophia. "Juraj Križanić and Ukraine."

Stipetić, Vladimir, "Korijeni drustveno-ekonomskih pogleda Jurja Križanića."

V WORKS CITED IN INTRODUCTORY ANALYSIS

Adelung, Friedrich v., *Kritisch-Literärische Übersicht der Reisenden bis 1700 in Russland,* vol. 2 (St Petersburg, 1846).

Amburger, Erik, *Die Familie Marselis* (Giessen, 1957).

Aquinas, Thomas, *The Summa Theologica,* vol. 2, edited by Robert M. Hutchins (Chicago, 1952).

Arrow, Kenneth, *Social Choice and Individual Values* (New Haven, 1951, 2nd edn 1963).

Attman, Artur, "The Russian Market in World Trade, 1500–1860," *Scandanavian Economic History Review* 29, no. 3 (1981).

Avvakum, *The Life of the Archpriest Avvakum,* translated by Jane Harrison and Hope Mirrlees (Hamden, 1963).

Baddeley, John F., *Russia, Mongolia, China,* vol. 2 (London, 1919).

Bakhrushin, S.V., *Ocherki po istorii kolonizatsii Sibiri v XVI i XVII vekakh* (Moscow, 1927).

Baron, Samuel H., *The Travels of Olearius in Seventeenth Century Russia* (Stanford, 1967).

——"Who Were the Gosti?" *California Slavic Studies* 7 (1973).

——"Križanić and Olearius," in Eekman and Kadić: 183–208.

Bazilevich, K.V., "Kollektivnye chelobitiia torgovykh liudei i borba za russkii rynok v pervoi polovine XVII veka," *Izvestiia Akademii Nauk SSSR. Otdelenie obshchestvennykh nauk,* no. 2 (1932).

Belokurov, S.A., "Iurii Krizhanich v Rossii," *Prilozheniia, in Chteniia v imperator-skom obshchestvie istorii i drevnostei rossiiskikh* vol. 206, book 3 (1903).

Bezsonov, P.A., "Russkoe gosudarstvo v polovine XVII veka. Rukopis vremen tsaria Alekseia Mikhailovicha," in *Russkaia Beseda* (1859). Same material published with same title in two volumes (Moscow, 1859–60).

Billington, James H., *The Icon and the Axe: An Interpretive History of Russian Culture* (New York, 1966).

Blum, Jerome, *Lord and Peasant in Russia: From the Ninth to the Nineteenth Century* (Princeton, 1961).

Brückner, A.G., "Iu. Krizhanich," *Russkii vestnik,* July 1887.

Brückner, Alexander, "Ein Finanzpolitiker in Russland im XVII Jahrhundert," *Russische Revue* 1 (1891).

Bushkovitch, Paul, *The Merchants of Moscow, 1580–1650* (New York, 1980).

Chandaman, C.D., *The English Public Revenue, 1660–1688* (Oxford, 1977).

Cherniavsky, Michael, "The Old Believers and the New Religion," *Slavic Review* 25 (1966).

Conybear, F.C., *Russian Dissenters* (Cambridge, 1921).

Crummey, Robert O., *The Old Believers in the World of Anti-Christ* (Madison, 1970).

——*Aristocrats and Servitors* (Princeton, 1983).

Danilov, N.N., "Vasilij Vasilević Golicyn (1682–1714)," *Jahrbücher für Geschichte Osteuropas,* vol. 2 (1937).

Dempsey, B.W., *Interest and Usury* (Washington, D.C., 1943).

Diakonov, M., *Ocherki obshchestvennogo i gosudarstvennogo stroia drevnei Rusi,* 2nd edn (St Petersburg, 1908).

Dictionary of Russian Historical Terms from the Eleventh Century to 1917, compiled by Sergei G. Pushkarev, and edited by George Vernadsky and Ralph T. Fisher, Jr. (New Haven, 1970).

Dmytryshyn, Basil, "Russian Expansion to the Pacific, 1580–1700: A Historio-graphical Review." *Slavic Studies* 25 (Hokkaido University, 1980).

Duncan, Douglas, *Great Treasures of the Kremlin* (New York, 1979).

Eekman, Thomas, and Kadić, Ante, eds, *Juraj Križanić (1618–1683) Russophile and Ecumenic Visionary: A Symposium* (The Hague, 1976).

Eekman, Thomas, "Vatroslav Jagic on Križanić," Eekman and Kadić: 302–26.

Fisher, Raymond H., *The Russian Fur Trade, 1550–1700* (Berkeley, 1943).

Fuhrmann, Joseph T., *The Origins of Capitalism in Russia* (Chicago, 1972).

Galaktionov, I., *Rannaia perepiska A.L. Ordina-Nashchokina* (Saratov, 1968).

Goldberg, Aleksandr L., "Juraj Križanić in Russian Historiography," translated by Leslie Bailey, in Eekman and Kadić: 51–69.

Golikov, I.I., ed., *Pisma: i bumagi Imperatora Petra Velikogo,* 16 vols (Moscow, 1887–1979).

——*Deianiia Petra Velikogo,* 15 vols (Moscow, 1838).

Golub, Ivan, "Contributions a l'histoire des relations de Križanić avec ses contemporains (1651–58)," in Eekman and Kadić: 91–146.

——Križanić theologien—sa conception ecclésiologique des événements et de l'histoire," in Eekman and Kadić: 165–82.

——"Biografska Pozadina Križanićevih Djela." In *Život i djelo Jurja Križanića: Zbornik Radova* (Zagreb, 1974).

Hakluyt, Richard, *Principal Navigations, Voyages, Traffiques, and Discoveries of the English Nation* (Glasgow, 1903).

Hellie, Richard, *Enserfment and Military Change in Muscovy* (Chicago, 1971).

——"Recent Soviet Historiography on Medieval and Early Modern Russian Slavery," *Russian Review* (January 1976).

——*Slavery in Russia, 1450–1725* (Chicago, 1982).

Herberstein, Sigismund von, *Rerum Moscoviticarum Commentarii* (Vienna, 1549).

——*Notes upon Russia*, translated by R.H. Major, 2 vols (1851; reprinted, New York, 1963).

Hittle, J. Michael, *The City: State and Townsmen in Russia, 1600–1800* (Cambridge, Mass., 1979).

Hobbes, Thomas, *De Cive* (Amsterdam, 1647).

——*Leviathan* [1651] (Chicago, 1952).

Hull, Charles Henry, *Economic Writings of Sir William Petty* (Cambridge, 1899).

Ikonnikov, V.S., "Blizhnii boiarin Afanasii Lavrentevich Ordyn-Nashchokin," *Russkaia Starina*, XL (1883).

Jagić, V., "Zur Biographie G. Križanić's." *Archiv für slavische Philologie*, VI (1882).

Kadić, Ante, "Križanić's Formative Years as a Pan-Slavist," *American Contributions to the Vth International Congress of Slavists* (The Hague, 1963).

——"Križanić's Memorandum" in *Jahrbücher für Geschichte Osteuropas*, vol. 12, no. 3 (October 1964).

——*From Croatian Renaissance to Yugoslav Socialism* (The Hague, 1969).

——"Križanić and Possevino—Missionaries to Muscovy" in Eekman and Kadić: 73–90.

Kaganovich, Abraam F., *Arts of Russia: Seventeenth and Eighteenth Centuries*, translated by James Hogarth (New York, 1968).

Keep, J.L., "The Regime of Filaret, 1619–1633," *Slavonic and East European Review* 38 (London, June 1960).

Khromov, P.A., *Ekonomicheskoe razvitie Rossii* (Moscow, 1967).

Kirchner, Walther, *Commercial Relations Between Russia and Europe 1400–1800: Collected Essays* (Bloomington, 1966).

Kliuchevskii, V.O., *Boyarskaia duma drevnei Rusi*, 4th edn (Moscow, 1909).

——"Zapadnoe vliianie i tserkovnyi raskol v Rossii XVII v," *Ocherki i rechi* (Petrograd, 1918).

——*Istoriia soslovii v Rossii*, 3rd edn (Petrograd, 1918).

——*Kurs russkoi istorii* (Moscow, 1957).

——*A Course in Russian History: The Seventeenth Century*, translated by Natalie Duddington (Chicago, 1968).

Kostomarov, N.I., "Ocherki torgovli Moskovskogo gosudarstva v XVI i XVII stoletiiakh," in *Sobranie Sochinenii*, vol. 8 (St Petersburg, 1905; reprinted The Hague, 1968).

Lantzeff, George V., *Siberia in the Seventeenth Century* (Berkeley, 1943).

Letiche, John M., ed. and trans., *A History of Russian Economic Thought: Ninth through Eighteenth Centuries* (Berkeley, 1964), with collaboration of Basil Dmytryshyn and Richard A. Pierce.

———"The History of Economic Thought in the International Encyclopedia of the Social Sciences," *The Journal of Economic Literature*, Vol. VII, No. 2 (June, 1969).

Lukianov, P.M., *Istoriia khimicheskikh promyslov i khimicheskoi promyshlennosti Rossii do kontsa XIX veka*, vol. 2

Luppov, S.P., *Kniga v Rossii v XVII veke* (Leningrad, 1970).

Lyashchenko, Peter I., *History of the National Economy of Russia*, translated by L.M. Herman (New York, 1949).

Malynes, Gerald, *The Center of the Circle of Commerce* [1623] (New York, 1973).

Marshall, Alfred, *Principles of Economics*, 8th edn (London, 1938).

Massie, Robert A., "The Great Schism," in *Peter the Great: His Life and World* (New York, 1981).

Misselden, Edward, *The circle of commerce, or the ballance of trade* [1623] (New York, 1968).

Morduxović, L.M., "Juraj Križanić, W. Petty and Ivan Pososkov: a comparative outline of their economic views" in Eekman and Kadić: 223–44.

Mun, Thomas, *England's treasure by farraign trade* [1st edn 1664] (New York, 1903).

Nasonov, A.N., et al., eds, *Ocherki istorii SSSR. Period feodalizma. Konetz XV v – Nachalo XVII v.* (Moscow, 1955).

Noonan, John T., Jr., *Scholastic Analysis of Usury* (Cambridge, 1957).

Novoselskii, A.A., and Ustiugov, N.V., eds, *Ocherki istorii SSSR: Period feodalizma XVII v.* (Moscow, 1955).

O'Brien, C.B., "Early Political Consciousness in Muscovy: The Views of Juraj Križanić and Afanasij Ordin-Naščokin," in Eekman and Kadić: 209–22.

Ogorodnikov, V.I., *Ocherki istorii Sibiri do nachala XIX st.* (Vladivostok, 1924).

Olearius, Adam, *Vermehrte Newe Beschreibung Der Muscowitischen und Persischen Reyse* (Schleswig, 1656; reprinted Tubingen, 1971).

Pach, Pál, "The Role of East-Central Europe in International Trade," *Etudes Historiques* (Budapest, 1970).

Palmer, William, "The Replies of the Humble Nicon" in *The Patriarch and the Tsar* (London, 1871).

Parry, Albert, "Juraj Križanić's Views on Siberia and China of the Seventeenth Century" in Eekman and Kadić: 245–62.

Pascal, Pierre, *Avvakum et les débuts du raskol* (The Hague, 1963).

Paul of Aleppo, *The Travels of Macarius: Extracts from the Diary of the Travels of Macarius, Patriarch of Antioch. Written by the son of Macarius, Paul, Archdeacon of Aleppo, 1652–1660*, translated by F.C. Balfour (London, 1936).

Petrikeev, D.I., *Krupnoe krepostnoe khoziaistvo XVII v.* (Leningrad, 1967).

Platonov, S.F., *The Time of Troubles*, translated by J.T. Alexander (Lawrence, 1970).

Possevino, Antonio, *Commentarii de rebus Moscoviticus* (Vilna, 1586).

Posthumus, N.W., *Inquiry into the History of Prices in Holland* (Leiden, 1946–64).

Rabinovich, G.S., *Gorod soli: Staraia Russa kontse XVI-seredine XVII vv.* (Leningrad, 1973).

Riasanovsky, Nicholas V., *A History of Russia* (Oxford, 1984).

Scheltema, Jacobus, *Rusland en de Nederlanden,* vols. 2 and 3 (Amsterdam, 1818).

Schultz, Theodore W., *Transforming Traditional Agriculture* (New Haven, 1964).

——*Investing in People* (Berkeley, 1980).

Schumpeter, Joseph A., *History of Economic Analysis* (Cambridge, 1963).

Sen, Amartya, *Choice, Measurement and Welfare* (Oxford, 1982).

Shunkov, V.I., *Ocherki po istorii kolonizatsii Sibiri v XVII – nachale XVIII v* (Moscow, 1946).

——ed., *Istoriia Sibiri,* 5 vols (Leningrad, 1968).

Šidak, Jaroslav, "Juraj Križanić als Problem der kroatischen und der serbischen Literatur" in Eekman and Kadić: 3–49.

Smith, R.E.F., *Peasant Farming in Muscovy* (Cambridge, 1977).

Spada, Virgilio, "Discorso di Monete" [1647]. Manuscript, no. 12,489, available in the Department of Manuscripts, British Library, London.

Stigler, George J., "The Process and Progress of Economics," Nobel Memorial Lecture, 1982, *Journal of Political Economy* 91, no. 4 (August 1983).

Tikhonov, Iu. A., *Pomeshchi'e krest'iane v Rossii* (Moscow, 1974).

Titov, A.A., ed., *Sibir v XVII veke. Sbornik starinnykh russkikh statei o Sibiri i prilezhashchikh k nei zemliakh* (Moscow, 1890).

Tyzhnov, I., "Obzor inostrannykh izvestii o Sibiri s 2-i poloviny XVI [XVII]," in *Sibirskii Sbornik,* appendix to *Vostochnoe Obozrenie,* edited by N.M. Iadrintsev (St Petersburg, 1887).

Uroff, Benjamin P., "Grigorii Karpovich, Kotoshikhin on Russia in the Reign of Alexis Mikhailovich." Ph.D. dissertation, Columbia University, 1970.

Vernadsky, George, *The Tsardom of Moscow, 1547–1682,* vol. 2, parts 1 and 2 (New Haven, 1969).

Viner, Jacob, "Power versus Plenty as Objectives of Foreign Policy in the Seventeenth and Eighteenth Centuries," *World Politics* 1 (1948).

——*Studies in the Theory of International Trade* (New York, 1966).

——*The Role of Providence in the Social Order* (Philadelphia, 1972).

Vladimirskii-Budanov, M.F., *Obzor istorii russkogo prava,* 6th edn (St Petersburg—Kiev, 1909).

Vujić, Mikh. V., *Križanićeva "Politika": Ekonomsko-politična studija* (Belgrad, 1895).

Witsen, Nikolaas Corneliszoon, *Noord en oost Tartaryen* [1785] 2 vols (Amsterdam, 1692).

——*Moscovische Reyse, 1664–1665,* vol. 68, part 3 (The Hague, 1966).

Index

agriculture: as source of wealth, 41; books on, 42; buildings in, 45–6; development of, xlv, xliv–xlvii, xlix–l, lix, lxvii, lxxi–lxxii; equipment of, 46–7; in Germany, 45, 47; in Siberia, 45–6; productivity of, xlv–xlvi; products of, 41–3; survey of, 44–5; village officials' role in, 46

Aldrovandi, Ulysses, 42

Alexander the Great, 88, 235

Alexei Alexeevich, lxxiii

Alexei Mikhailovich, Tsar, xiv, xxi, xxii, xxiii, xxiv, xxxiii, xxxviii, xlii, lii, lxix, lxxv, 86, 88, 134–5, 169

Altyn, 30

appearance: Slavic, 98; non-Slavic, 98–9

Aquinas, St Thomas, 138

Archangel, xviii, xxxvi, lvii, lviii, lx, 20

Archbishop Semeon, xiv

archers, 63

Arctic Ocean, 21

Aristotle, 88, 185, 245

Armenians, 29

Aschaffenburg, Maxim Faust, 3

Astrakhan, lvi, lvii, lviii, 15–16, 20

Augsburg, 37

authority: Biblical views of, 172–4; mistaken view of, 187, 191; rights and prerogatives of,

172–3, 213–14; royal, 172, 183–6; ways to preserve, 234–6

autocracy: abuse of power, 52; defended, 168–71; defined, xl; ideal form of government, 206; in Europe, 167; pillars of, 226–7; a positive force in Russia, 114, 161–2

Avvakum, Archpriest, xxiii, xxiv

Azov, 16

Balorussia: identified, 24; possibilities of trade with, 22

Bashkirs, 43, 44, 59, 195

Bashmakov, D. M., lxxiii

Basmanov, Peter F., 134, 233

Bathory, Stefan, 65, 133, 145

Bezsonov, P. A., lxxiv

Bible: quoted, 5, 6, 9, 58, 89, 95, 132, 137, 168, 171, 172, 173, 174, 181–2, 184, 185, 187, 188, 189, 190, 193, 212

Bielewski, A. G., lxxiv

Bokhara (Bokharans): possibility of Russian trade with, 15–16, 22, 37, 55

books: on agriculture, 42; Krizhanich's use of for *Politika,* 3; on Russia, 120

Boreel, I., xv

Boyar Duma, xix, xl–xli, xlii, lxii–lxv, 10, 194

boyars, defined, 10; dwellings of, 118; power of, xli, xliii, lxiii–lxv;

275